A TREATISE ON NORTHER

Brendan O'Leary is the Lauder Professor of Political Science at the University of Pennsylvania and World Leading Researcher Visiting Professor of Political Science at Queen's University Belfast.

Praise for *A Treatise On Northern Ireland*

"The most prolific, perceptive and powerfully analytical writer on the north in the last 35 years, Brendan O'Leary, has just produced his magnum opus. At three volumes, *A Treatise on Northern Ireland*, is a rigorous analysis of politics and society here since the sixteenth century. It's an encyclopaedic work of unrivalled detail and scope. It will become the standard reference for anyone interested in the north. It should be required reading for any British politician in the present circumstances, but certainly for any proconsul."

Brian Feeney, *Irish News*

"The detailed coverage is astonishing, the range immense. The book exemplifies best practice in social science and history, combining both disciplines, asking analytic questions of the historical record and widening the remit of social science."

Professor John A Hall, *Dublin Review of Books*

"O'Leary colors his work throughout with lively writing, moving past equivocation and pulling no punches in his assessments of participants or previous scholarship. He sees the disputatious state of Northern Ireland as the result of attempts to instill an Irish or British national identity among its residents.... Although the cumulative length of this work might be daunting, the author has thoughtfully structured his books and chapters in a way that is accessible to both non-experts and specialists. Whatever the audience, this is a work of canonical importance for understanding Northern Ireland."

M. J. O'Brien, *CHOICE*

A Treatise on Northern Ireland

Volume 2: Control

The Second Protestant Ascendancy and the Irish State

BRENDAN O'LEARY

OXFORD

UNIVERSITY PRESS

OXFORD
UNIVERSITY PRESS

Great Clarendon Street, Oxford, OX2 6DP,
United Kingdom

Oxford University Press is a department of the University of Oxford.
It furthers the University's objective of excellence in research, scholarship,
and education by publishing worldwide. Oxford is a registered trade mark of
Oxford University Press in the UK and in certain other countries

First published 2019
First published in paperback 2020

Published in the United States of America by Oxford University Press
198 Madison Avenue, New York, NY 10016, United States of America

British Library Cataloguing in Publication Data
Data available

Library of Congress Cataloging in Publication Data
Data available

ISBN 978-0-19-883057-3 (Hbk.)
ISBN 978-0-19-887072-2 (Pbk.)

To the memories of my late mentors Liam Agnew, Alan Beattie, Walker Connor, Patricia Crone, Ernest Gellner, George W Jones, Tom Nossiter, and John. H. Whyte.

Preface

The second volume of three faces presentational difficulties. Is it the decorative filling, or does it have standing in its own right? The author insists that this case answers the latter question. What follows is an account of the rise and fall of a distinct control system in Northern Ireland between 1920 and 1972, set against the background of the trajectory of an increasingly independent Ireland, and a seemingly increasingly detached Great Britain. At the end of the experiment both the London and Dublin governments return to the story. A London-run army of counterinsurgents, accompanied by intelligence agents, is also deployed, initially as peacekeepers.

What happened in this half-century, it will be shown, cannot be explained without observing the effects of British and Irish state- and nation-building upon the peoples of Northern Ireland. This volume also has distinct standing because the control system, improvised amid the unfolding of the Irish revolution, marked a novel development in the annals of colonialism in Ireland. It was an outgrowth of colonialism, testament to the power of the settlers' descendants both in the north-east of Ulster and in the emergent British democracy to resist the restoration of Irish autonomy under Irish auspices. But it was also an innovation. For the first time, because of a carefully executed and manipulatively preserved partition, a distinct political system in Ireland would be controlled by a Protestant demographic and electoral majority. The leaders of the Ulster Unionist Party, exploiting a mini-model of the Westminster mothership that they had initially shunned, would improvise a control system that organized the settlers' descendants under a pan-Protestant alliance, and which disorganized cultural Catholics, Northern nationalists, and Irish republicans. All that they would do, including building a parliament at Stormont that would grace a country with twentyfold more citizens, would be done in the name of democracy, and the rights of the majority.

The elements of control systems are elaborated in the opening conceptual conspectus that delineates the political science that disciplines the rest of the volume. How and why Ulster Unionist leaders established a control system is set out in subsequent historical chapters, exploiting recent and past scholarship, while the concluding chapters explain its collapse, making similar usage of cumulative scholarship, governmental reports, archives, and interviews. In between, and certainly no filler in the sandwich, is a globally decisive moment: the Second World War and its repercussions.

Northern Ireland survived its first potential extinction just after sovereign Ireland was completing its political decolonization between 1937 and 1939. Ireland's neutrality during the United Nations war against the Axis powers, had demonstrated its newfound sovereignty, and cost Irish nationalism dear, especially in Northern Ireland. But it did set Ireland on the path to better economic development. The Second World War, especially its timing and its consequences, saved the recently established Belfast regime from bankruptcy, though it was not as close to forced reunification as many subsequently thought. After 1943 Basil Brooke would refurbish James Craig's control system, but he had to admit a trojan horse, the British welfare state. A generation later its alumni, healthier, better educated, and more self-confident than their parents, would unleash a civil-rights movement, observed on black and white TV screens, imitating another civil-rights movement unfolding in the USA. Most of the marchers did not intend to bring the house down. It was those who refused their claims that brought the walls down, and precipitated the implosion that followed. The story of the collapse of this control system explains the immediate causes of the violence that would continue over a quarter of a century.

In writing to an American correspondent in 1885, Friedrich Engels warned that the second volume of Marx's *Capital* would cause disappointment because it was purely scientific, and lacked much suitable material for agitation.[1] If this volume occasions disappointment, I suspect that will not be because it will be deemed purely scientific, or because it lacks material for agitators.

---

[1] Friedrich Engels to Sorge, 1885, cited in Howard and King (1989: 8).

Contents: Volume 2

Contents for All Three Volumes

VOLUME 1: COLONIALISM
THE SHACKLES OF THE STATE
AND HEREDITARY ANIMOSITIES

VOLUME 2: CONTROL
THE SECOND PROTESTANT ASCENDANCY
AND THE IRISH STATE

VOLUME 3: CONSOCIATION AND CONFEDERATION

FROM ANTAGONISM TO ACCOMMODATION?

List of Figures

List of Maps

List of Tables

List of Boxes

Abbreviations and Glossary

ACRI	American Committee for Relief in Ireland
AIA	Anglo-Irish Agreement, treaty between the governments of Ireland and the United Kingdom made in 1985
ANC	African National Congress
AOH	Ancient Order of Hibernians: Irish nationalist and religious organization, especially strong in the USA, previously strong in Belfast, but not since the 1930s
APNI	Alliance Party of Northern Ireland, originally supported power-sharing devolved government within the Union as well as an Irish dimension, now neutral on the Union; it explicitly claims Catholic, Protestant, and other support
ASU	active service unit of the IRA, small specialist cell
assimilation	here a government policy aimed at making people publicly and privately culturally alike—either through *acculturation*, in which the subordinate conform to the culture of the dominant, or through *fusion*, in which two or more culturally different groups merge into a shared culture
attainder	act of taking the estate of an outlaw, or depriving a convicted criminal of rights to inherit or transmit land
AV	alternative vote, a preferential voting system in which the winning candidate obtains a majority of all ballots, either after the counting of all first-preference votes, or after the elimination of lower-placed candidates and the transfer of any lower-order preferences expressed by those who had voted for them
BA	Belfast Agreement, the name unionists give to the Agreement reached on April 10, 1998
BIA	British Irish Association
BIC	British–Irish Council
B–IIGC	British–Irish Intergovernmental Conference
B Specials	armed reserve constables of the RUC, disbanded 1970
BREXIT	the misleading acronym to describe "Britain's" prospective departure from the EU; see UKEXIT
BRIC	Brazil, Russia, India, and China
Bunreacht na hÉireann	(Irish) Constitution of Ireland (1937, as amended)
CAIN	Conflict Archive on the Internet
CCAR	Chief Constable's Annual Report
CDRNI	Campaign for Democratic Rights in Northern Ireland
CEC	Campaign for Equal Citizenship
CDU	Campaign for Democracy in Ulster
C-IRA	Continuity IRA

CnP	Clann na Poblachta, party formed by Sean McBride in the belief that FF had ceased to be a proper republican party
cess	originally any local tax, but in Ireland also the levying of soldiers and provisions, or the billeting of soldiers
CLRNI	Campaign for Labour Representation in Northern Ireland.
condominium	political entity over which two or more states share sovereignty
confederation	states unified by treaty for certain public functions, but that retain their sovereignty, international identity, and usually rights of secession and veto
consociation	political system used to share governmental power proportionally between divided peoples—in the executive, the legislature, and public employment, including security forces; each community enjoys cultural autonomy, and public expenditure may be allocated on a proportional basis; in strong consociations the organized communities enjoy veto rights over major legislation
Continuity IRA	breakaway organization from the IRA
covenanters	Scottish Presbyterians who wanted the Scottish system of church government applied throughout Scotland, England, and Ireland; in 1643 a treaty with the English parliament appeared to give them what they wanted (The Solemn League and Covenant)
CRC	Community Relations Council
CRF	Catholic Reaction Force—see INLA
CSJ	Campaign for Social Justice, founded in 1960s; became part of NICRA
Cumann na mBan	(Irish) Irish women's republican organization
Cumann na nGaedhael	(Irish) pro-treaty party formed from Sinn Féin, which led governments of the Irish Free State from 1922 until 1932; later dissolved into Fine Gael; sometimes spelled Cumman na nGaedheal
DAAD	Direct Action Against Drugs (IRA front)
Dáil Éireann	(Irish) "trans. Assembly of Ireland," the official name for the lower house of the Irish parliament (Oireachtas)
devolution	act of creating a subcentral government with executive and legislative powers inside a state; the institutions are constituted by a delegated (and revocable) act of the political center
DEA	Department of External Affairs of the IFS, later the DFA of Ireland
DFA	Department of Foreign Affairs (Ireland), today the Department of Foreign Affairs and Trade
DFM	Deputy First Minister
DL	Democratic Left, a party formed in 1992 from a split in the Workers' Party, now absorbed by the Irish Labour Party–some say it was a takeover
dominions	originally the partly self-governing (white) settlement colonies of the British Empire; evolved in the 1920s into sovereign states of the British Commonwealth of Nations
DPPB	District Policing Partnership Boards

DRs	Dissident Republicans, expression and abbreviation used by the PSNI and MI5 to refer to post-IRA republican organizations that remain actively engaged in what they define as armed struggle
DUP	Democratic Unionist Party
EC	European Commission
ECB	European Central Bank
ECNI	Equality Commission for Northern Ireland
EEA	European Economic Area
EEC	European Economic Community
EFTA	European Free Trade Agreement
EMU	Education for Mutual Understanding, program for schools in Northern Ireland
EOC	Equal Opportunities Commission
EPA	Emergency Provisions Act: emergency anti-terrorist legislation applied in Northern Ireland
EPS	executive power-sharing
ethnonym	the name of an ethnic group
EU	European Union
FDI	foreign direct investment
FEA	Fair Employment Agency
FEC	Fair Employment Commission
federation	sovereign state in which executive and legislative powers are shared and divided between federal & regional governments, and intergovernmental relations are constitutionally regulated; see discussion of "federacy" at Vol 3. Ch. 5, pp. 202–4
Fenians	American sister-organizational name of the Irish Republican Brotherhood (1858–1923)
FET	Fair Employment Tribunal
Fianna Fáil	(Irish [lit. "Soldiers of Destiny"]), also known as the Republican Party; formed by Eamon de Valera in a breakaway from Sinn Féin; mobilized the defeated side in the Irish civil war and became the dominant party in independent Ireland until 2011
fine	Irish for "clan elite," the leadership of a clan and its leading families
Fine Gael	(Irish [lit. "Tribe of Gaels"]); formed from the merger of Cumann na nGaedhael, the pro-treaty party of independent Ireland, the Centre party, and the "Blueshirts;" usually the second most powerful political party in independent Ireland
FM	First Minister
FOI	Friends of Ireland
GAA	Gaelic Athletic Association (Irish, Cumann Lúthchleas Gael)
Garda Síochána	Full title: Garda Síochána na hÉireann—i.e., Guardians of the Peace of Ireland, the name of the Irish police force, also known as "the Guards"
GFA	Good Friday Agreement, the name most Irish nationalists give to the Agreement of April 10, 1998

GFA–BA	Good Friday Agreement–Belfast Agreement
GPI	Global Peace Index
HCNM	High Commissioner on National Minorities (of the Organization for Security and Cooperation in Europe)
hegemonic control	a system of ethnic domination, in which the power-holders make revolt by the controlled ethnic group(s) unworkable
HET	Historical Enquiries Team (of the PSNI)
HIU	(proposed) Historical Investigations Unit, suggested in the Haass–O'Sullivan proposals
HMSU	Headquarters Mobile Support Unit
IAPL	Irish Anti-Partition League
ICIR	(proposed) Independent Commission for Information Retrieval, suggested in the Haass–O'Sullivan proposals
IEP	Institute for Economics and Peace
IFS	Irish Free State, known as Saorstát Éireann in Irish
IGC	Intergovernmental Conference
IICD	Independent International Commission on Decommissioning
IIP	Irish Independence Party, formed in 1977 because it regarded the SDLP as insufficiently nationalist; dissolved before 1989
IIP	Irish Information Partnership
ILP	Irish Labour Party
IMC	Independent Monitoring Commission
IMDWCC	IMD World Competitiveness Center
IMF	International Monetary Fund
INLA	Irish National Liberation Army: Marxist rival to the IRA in Northern Ireland, formed from ex-Official IRA cadres and others in late 1974; sometimes operated under the names Catholic Reaction Force (CRF) and People's Republican Army (PRA)
integration	A policy of unifying a territory or culture under one set of public norms. Unlike assimilation, integration does not require the homogenization of "private" cultural differences (see O'Leary and McGarry 2012). British integrationists argue that Northern Ireland should be fully integrated into the UK's administrative system (England's, Scotland's, or Wales's?), into its party-political system, and that educational integration (socializing Protestants and Catholics within the same institutions) should be an imperative of social policy. Irish integrationists suggest, by contrast, that Northern Ireland should be administratively and electorally integrated into the Irish Republic. Integration is the policy advocated by supporters of a shared future: into exactly what people are to be integrated remains disputed
IPLO	Irish People's Liberation Organization, breakaway from the INLA, founded in late 1986, forcibly disbanded by the IRA in 1992
IPP	Irish Parliamentary Party, sought home rule for Ireland, 1882–1921: in the North its adherents formed the Nationalist Party after 1921; in the South most eventually joined Cumann na nGaedhael, or later Fine Gael

IRA	Irish Republican Army; Óglaigh na hÉireann (Volunteers of Ireland) is its Irish name; see OIRA and PIRA; PIRA recognized as IRA by most after 1972
IRB	Irish Republican Brotherhood, also known as the Fenians, also known as the Irish Revolutionary Brotherhood
IRG	(proposed) Implementation and Reconciliation Group, suggested in the Haass–O'Sullivan proposals
IRSP	Irish Republican Socialist Party, political wing of the INLA
ITGWU	Irish Transport and General Workers' Union
IUA	Irish Union Association
IV	Irish Volunteers
Jacobins	the most militant republicans in the French Revolution
Jacobites	those who continued to recognize the House of Stuart as the legitimate dynasty in England, Scotland, and Wales after 1688
joint authority	the sharing of sovereign governmental authority over a territory by two or more states (also known as a condominium)
JRRT	Joseph Rowntree Reform Trust
KKK	Ku Klux Klan
LAW	Loyalist Association of Workers
LRDG	Loyalist Retaliation and Defence Groups (name used by the UDA)
LVF	Loyalist Volunteer Force, breakaway from the UVF, founded in 1996
majority rule	simple "majority," "plurality rule," or "winner-takes all" is a decision-making norm used in many democracies, especially in electoral, constitutional, government-formation, and policymaking systems. It usually means rule by those with the most votes, rather than absolute majority rule. It is less pleasantly described as the norm of the "minimum winning coalition" or as the "tyranny of the majority."
majoritarianism	the conviction that a simple majority (50 percent plus one) should prevail in democratic decision-making, and a belief that rejects co-decision-making rights for minorities or qualified majority decision-making
marches	territories near boundaries or frontiers, often disputed, especially around the English Pale
MI5	the UK's domestic counter-intelligence and security agency
MLA	Member of the Legislative Assembly (of Northern Ireland)
MNC	multinational corporation
MPA	multiparty agreement
nationalizing state	a state that seeks to homogenize its citizens into one national identity; an expression owed to Rogers Brubaker (1996), it amounts to "coercive assimilation"
NATO	North Atlantic Treaty Organization
NCU	National Council for Unity
NDP	National Democratic Party
NI21	Twenty-first-century Northern Ireland, brief-lived political party
NICRA	Northern Ireland Civil Rights Association, formed to protest against discrimination by the Northern Ireland government and parliament
NIHRC	Northern Ireland Human Rights Commission

NILP	Northern Ireland Labour Party
NIO	Northern Ireland Office
NLN	National League of the North
NORAID	Northern Aid Committee
NPF	National Popular Front
NSMC	North–South Ministerial Council
NU	National Unity
NUI	National University of Ireland
NUPRG	New Ulster Political Research Group
OFMDFM	Office of the First Minister and the Deputy First Minister
OIRA	(Official) IRA, now disbanded
ONH	abbreviation for *Óglaigh na hÉireann* (Volunteers of Ireland), name for the IRA in Irish; it was the name of the organization founded to defend home rule in arms; it is the official name of the Army of Ireland in Irish; it was used throughout the years 1970–2005 by the Provisional IRA; the name is now claimed by a small "dissident" republican organization
OO	Orange Order, anti-Catholic and pan-Protestant organization, founded in 1795, often banned in the 19th century, integrally linked to the UUP until it decided to sunder its formal links in 2005
OASA	Offences Against the State Act, Irish counterinsurgency and emergency legislation
OSCE	Organization for Security and Cooperation in Europe
OSF	Official Sinn Féin, political faction that supported the OIRA, later became SFWP (Sinn Féin—The Workers' Party), before becoming simply The Workers' Party, often known colloquially as "the Stickies"
OUP	Official Unionist Party (see UUP)
PACE	Protestant and Catholic Encounter
PAF	Protestant Action Force, name used by the UVF
PAG	Protestant Action Group, name used by the UDA
PANI	Police Authority for Northern Ireland
partition	here, the division of a national homeland along a novel or fresh border
PBPA	People Before Profit Alliance
PCB	Police Complaints Board
PD	People's Democracy
PDs	Progressive Democrats, "New Right" liberal party formed in the Republic, 1985–2009
PIRA	(Provisional) IRA, later recognized by most as the IRA, now disbanded, sometimes operated under the names of DAAD and RAF (Republican Action Force), often known colloquially as "the Provos"
PLA	see INLA
PLO	Palestine Liberation Organization
PO	Prison Officer
power-sharing	see consocation, federation, and confederation

PR	proportional representation
PRONI	Public Records Office Northern Ireland
PSF	Provisional Sinn Féin
PSI	Policy Studies Institute (London)
PSNI	Police Service of Northern Ireland
PTA	Prevention of Terrorism Act
PUP	Progressive Unionist Party, political wing of the UVF
QUB	Queen's University Belfast
R&D	research and development
Republican	an advocate of a unified Ireland in a republic free of the British Crown; an advocate of the thesis that there should be one Irish nation—composed of its diverse multiple components—in which all share a common citizenship
Republican Clubs	see OIRA
RHC	Red Hand Commandos, name used by the UVF
RHD	Red Hand Defenders, name used by the LVF and the UDA after 1998
RHI	Renewable Heating Initiative
RIC	Royal Irish Constabulary
RIR	Royal Irish Regiment (regiment of the British Army created from the merger of the UDR with the Royal Irish Rangers)
R-IRA	Real IRA, breakaway from the IRA in 1997, which does not recognize either Ireland's or Northern Ireland's legitimacy
RLP	Republican Labour Party
RSF	Republican Sinn Féin, breakaway from Sinn Féin in 1986, which does not recognize either Ireland's or Northern Ireland's legitimacy
RTÉ	Raidió Teilifís Éireann (Ireland's public broadcaster, of both radio and television)
RUC	Royal Ulster Constabulary
SE	Saor Éire, left-wing republican grouping of the 1930s, revived briefly in 1969–71
Saorstát Éireann	(Irish) Irish Free State, name of dominion status for Ireland agreed in the Anglo-Irish Treaty and named as such in the first Constitution of Ireland established under that Treaty
SAA	Saint Andrews Agreement, reached in Scotland in October 2006 between the Governments of Ireland and the United Kingdom of Great Britain and Northern Ireland, and tacitly agreed by Northern Ireland's major political parties. Key elements included a change in the method of electing the First and Deputy First Ministers, the full acceptance of the Police Service of Northern Ireland by Sinn Féin, the restoration of the Northern Ireland Assembly and a promise to abolish its Suspension Act by the British government, and a commitment by the DUP to power-sharing with republicans and nationalists in the Northern Ireland Executive. The plan envisaged the devolution of policing and justice powers within two years of the restoration of the executive

SACHR	Standing Advisory Commission on Human Rights
SDLP	Social Democratic and Labour Party of Northern Ireland, party formed in 1970 from the merger of civil-rights activists, labor activists, and former members of the Nationalist Party and the National Democratic Party
SF	Sinn Féin (Irish; lit. "Ourselves"). Irish Republican political party, though originally formed in 1905 by Arthur Griffith and others to advocate a common monarchy presiding over independent British and Irish parliaments (modeled on the dual monarchy of Austro-Hungary). Radicalized as a republican (anti-monarchical) party in 1917, and after. It split during the making of the 1921 Treaty and the Irish civil war; and later after the formation of Fianna Fáil; it split again into Provisional and Official Sinn Féin in 1969–70; later, Provisional Sinn Féin's claim to the title Sinn Féin was uncontested. The party is organized in Northern Ireland and Ireland
sheriff	royal official within a shire (or county)
SHA	Stormont House Agreement (2014)
Stormont	the site of the Northern Ireland Parliament in a suburb of Belfast from 1932 to 1972, of the Northern Ireland Assembly of 1973–4 and 1982–6, and of the Northern Ireland Assembly since 1998
STV	single transferable vote, a preferential and proportional candidate-based voting system, in which more than one candidate is elected in a district, and in which the winners normally have to achieve a quota
Tánaiste	(Irish) literally successor to the chief, whence the title of Ireland's Deputy Prime Minister
Taoiseach	(Irish) Chief, whence the title of the prime minister in Ireland's constitution of 1937
TCD	Trinity College, Dublin University
TD	Teachta Dála (Irish), deputy elected to Dáil Éireann, equivalent to MP in the UK or Member of Congress in the USA
TRNC	Turkish Republic of Northern Cyprus (so-called)
TUV	Traditional Unionist Voice, a party formed by James Allister that broke from the DUP after the DUP formed a government with Sinn Féin 2007
UCC	University College Cork
UCD	University College Dublin
UCG	University College Galway
UDF	Ulster Defence Force
UFF	Ulster Freedom Fighters
Ulster Clubs	Loyalist organization formed in response to the AIA of 1985
UCDC	Ulster Constitution Defence Committee (see also UPV)
UDA	Ulster Defence Association, largest loyalist paramilitary organization
UDI	unilateral declaration of independence
UDP	Ulster Democratic Party, political party of the UDA
UDR	Ulster Defence Regiment, formed in 1970, dissolved into the RIR in 1992

UFF	Ulster Freedom Fighters, killing component of the UDA
UIL	United Irish League
UKIP	United Kingdom Independence Party
UK	United Kingdom of Great Britain and Northern Ireland
UKEXIT	the correct acronym to describe proposals to take the entirety of the UK out of the EU
UKEXITINO	a UK Exit In Name Only from the EU, otherwise known as a "soft BREXIT"
UKUP	United Kingdom Unionist Party, formed by Robert McCartney
ULDP	Ulster Loyalist Democratic Party
UMS	Ulster Marketing Services
unitary state	sovereign state in which sovereignty is monopolized at the political center; subcentral governments enjoy no autonomous sovereignty—all decentralization is a revocable act of delegation by the center
union state	state that recognizes at least some of the composite entities of which it was formed, in either their territories, their legal systems, or their cultures
Unionist	an advocate of the maintenance of the Union between Great Britain and Northern Ireland (previously between Great Britain and Ireland), and of the maintenance of the Union of Great Britain (between Scotland and England [and Wales])
UPNI	Unionist Party of Northern Ireland
UPV	Ulster Protestant Volunteers, loyalist militia formed in the 1960s
USC	Ulster Special Constabulary, also known as the B Specials, replaced by the UDR
UUC	Ulster Unionist Council
UULCC	United Ulster Loyalist Central Coordinating Committee
UUP	Ulster Unionist Party, known for a time as the Official Unionist Party (OUP)
UUUC	United Ulster Unionist Council, temporary coalition of the UUP, DUP, and VUP that fought to end the Sunningdale agreement of 1973
UVF	Ulster Volunteer Force, loyalist paramilitary organization
UWC	Ulster Workers' Council
VUP	Vanguard Unionist Party, hardline loyalist political party formed and led by William Craig in the 1970s
WC	(Northern Ireland) Women's Coalition, aka NIWC
Westminster model	a "majoritarian" political system, characterized by the concentration of executive power in one-party and bare-majority governments, the fusion of executive and legislative powers under cabinet dominance, and the plurality-rule (winner-takes-all) election system in single-member districts/constituencies
WP	Workers' Party, Marxist-Leninist party formed from Sinn Féin, the Workers' Party; previously OSF
WTO	World Trade Organization

Terminology

Charges of ethnic or sectarian bias accompany writing on Northern Ireland because terminology raises complex questions about objectivity. The following pedantry is therefore required. "Northern Ireland" is here the formal political unit, not the "Six Counties" or "Ulster," as republicans and loyalists respectively prefer. Ulster refers here to "historic Ulster"—that is, the province of nine northern counties of pre-1920 Ireland, and Northern Ireland to a "region" of the United Kingdom, not a province or *the* Province (though unionists often use the latter terms). Historic Ulster was a province of pre-1920 Ireland; it was partitioned in 1920, and remains a unified province in all-Ireland sports (for example, in rugby union, Gaelic football, and hurling), music and dance. Northern Ireland, however, is not legally a province of either Ireland or Great Britain. Northern Ireland is in Union with Great Britain but it is not part of Great Britain, which refers to England (incorporating Wales) and Scotland, the polity from which the colonies that became the United States of America liberated themselves. The "North of Ireland" is mostly employed by nationalists, and is not used here as a synonym for Northern Ireland, though the expression "the North," is used, because, along with "the South," it was jointly agreed in the text of the 1998 Agreement. Since that Agreement has nationalist, republican, unionist, and loyalist champions, and because this book culminates in an account of the making, potential stabilization—and potential disruptions—of this Agreement, "North" and "South" are used for the two entities, mostly after 1995.

Other lax usages, with no justifications in formal agreements or treaties, are out of order. The entity loosely called "the South" is a state; the other, loosely called "the North," is not; and it never has been. Two nations have come to exist in Ireland, one Irish, the other British, but the island does not consist of two states named Ireland and Northern Ireland. The two states that share the island are Ireland and the United Kingdom of Great Britain and Northern Ireland. Northern Ireland has never been a state, though distinguished people have suggested otherwise in their book titles.[1] Northern Ireland may become a "federacy," based on a distinctive federal relationship with Great Britain, but UKEXIT may put paid to that prospect.[2] Occasional reference may be made to two polities (or political systems) on the island after 1920, but this usage does not imply that Northern Ireland is or has been a state, because the Northern Ireland polity was, and remains—for now—part of the United Kingdom.

---

[1] See, e.g., Conor Cruise O'Brien (1974); Bew et al. (1996: 21 ff.); David Fitzpatrick (1998). These authors obtained Ph.Ds in history, but this matter is not disciplinary; it is simply mistaken usage. Northern Ireland has never been a state according to any standard definition; see, e.g., the work of Nicholas Mansergh (1936: 16, 108, 149), who emphasized that Northern Ireland was not sovereign, had no constituent power, was a devolved rather than a federative entity, and was (when he wrote) wholly subject to having its status altered by the Westminster parliament. The Stormont regime had attributes fairly described as those of a "quasi-state," but a quasi-state, no matter how quasi, is not a state. In this respect I agree with Brendan Clifford (2011).

[2] See Stepan et al. (2011); see also Vol. 3, Ch. 5, pp. 202–04.

"The British mainland" is not a synonym for Great Britain. Ideologically charged, the expression erroneously implies that Northern Ireland is geographically British, which a map inspection and its record of conflict put in immediate doubt. Great Britain encompasses islands off the coasts of Scotland and England, but no part of the island of Ireland.[3] "The British mainland" refers to the contiguous land mass of Scotland, England, and Wales, in contradistinction, for instance, to the Scilly Isles, Anglesey, and the Hebrides, to name genuinely British (though also Celtic) isles. The "Union" is between Great Britain and Northern Ireland; the previous relevant Union was between Great Britain and Ireland; the Union of Great Britain that preceded these unions runs in parallel with them: it is the Union of Scotland and England (in which Wales was presumed incorporated).

"Ireland" was one island-wide administrative unit when coerced (and bought) into Union in 1801, and remained so before it was unilaterally partitioned by the United Kingdom Parliament in the Government of Ireland Act of 1920. "Independent Ireland" or "the Republic of Ireland" refers to the state that occupies the space that the UK briefly tried to name "Southern Ireland," a policy rejected by Irish nationalist votes, and overturned in a guerrilla war and a diplomatic settlement in 1921, which recognized the Irish Free State, but which in UK law required the latter's formation through the parliament of Southern Ireland. These volumes by contrast, respect Article 4 of the Constitution of Ireland (1937), which established the name of the state as Ireland in the English language, and as Éire in the Irish language. This naming was recognized by the United Kingdom of Great Britain and Northern Ireland in 1999, in the treaty giving effect to the Agreement of 1998. The Government of the United Kingdom of Great Britain and Northern Ireland, to give it its official title, formally recognized the Government of Ireland by its official name in 1999, just as the Government of Ireland fully recognized the full name of the United Kingdom as a result of the referendum result of 1998. Since the two governments, and popular majorities in both jurisdictions on the island of Ireland, North and South, have officially recognized one another's official titles, these are followed here. The ugly abbreviations GUKGBNI and GOI are avoided.

Ireland and Northern Ireland officially are no longer contested titles, but are geographically inexact. Donegal, the most northerly part of the island of Ireland, is not in Northern Ireland; political *Northern* Ireland, geographically speaking, is *North and North-East* Ireland; whereas the political "South" references "*North-West, West, Central and South.*"

Using the expression "the twenty-six counties" rejects Ireland's legitimacy, just as the "six counties" rejects that of Northern Ireland. Such usages fetishize county jurisdictions, introduced by the English conquerors. The author is a citizen of Ireland (as well as of the USA), recognizes its legitimacy, and therefore references the twenty-six counties and the six counties only when considering the moment of partition (of which he plainly does not approve).

"Ireland" here therefore refers to the entire geographical entity, including its surrounding islands—for example, Rathlin or the Blaskets—*or* to the unit of

---

[3] Brittany had been "Little Britain," in contrast with "Great Britain," before the latter became the name of the unified kingdoms of Scotland and England (Hay 1955–6: 55–66).

administration before 1920 *or* to the government and territory of the Irish Free State, Éire, and the Republic of Ireland, the latter three of which have so far been coextensive. Sometimes sovereign Ireland is used for clarity to describe the state.

Terminological exactitude imposes further norms. "The Isles" here refers to Great Britain and Ireland, and their respective territorial waters and islands. "The *British* Isles" is a tendentious expression.[4] Ireland is an island behind an island, but it is not part of the much smaller isles that surround Great Britain (or Britain). The Romans knew better, and distinguished Hibernia from Britannia, but, alas, love of Latin has melted like the snows of yesteryear. The expression the "British archipelago" is avoided, because not all the archipelago is British, and the adjective "archipelagic," a term encouraged by a bright historian of ideas from New Zealand, would occasion pain for readers.[5] For the same reason I avoid "Atlantic archipelago." Try saying "archipelagic" with any variety of an Ulster accent; "consociational" is much easier.

Capital-letter designations reference formal political membership of an organization; lower-case designations refer to political disposition or doctrine. Thus "Nationalist" refers to the Nationalist party, whereas "nationalist" refers to an Irish nationalist who may not have been a member of the Nationalist party. Most unionists are British nationalists, but to avoid confusion and unnecessary debate they are called unionists, and labeled Irish, Ulster, or British unionists, as required. Irish unionists wanted all of Ireland to remain within the Union with Great Britain; Ulster unionists focused on keeping Ulster within the Union, and settled for Northern Ireland, which they renamed as Ulster without the consent of their opponents; while British unionists once wanted to keep Ireland or Ulster in Union, and now simply want to keep Northern Ireland in the Union—and Scotland, Wales, and England. "Unionist" with a capital U refers to one of the parties that bears this name, whereas a "unionist" refers to those who wish to preserve the Union.

"Republicans" are Irish nationalists who advocate a secular, united, and independent island of Ireland, free of the Crown and Government and Parliament of Great Britain. Not all Irish republicans are pacifists; but only some have been militarist, and none are monarchists. There are patriots of the state of Ireland who have no wish to see Irish reunification who also describe themselves as republicans, but others rarely describe them as such.

"Loyalists" are loyal to the British Crown. Typically, they are "ultras"—that is, more loyal to the loyalist community than toward the relevant Majesty's Government. There were Irish and there are Ulster loyalists—they often call Northern Ireland Ulster.

Catholic and Protestant are not synonyms for nationalist and unionist, though there has been and there remains a very significant correlation between religion of origin and political belief.

---

[4] This is to follow Norman Davies (1999), whose excellent book has a few mistakes, not surprisingly given its ambitious scope—e.g., it implies that the pro-treaty party was defeated in the Irish civil war (p. 905).

[5] See, e.g., J. G. A. Pocock (2005).

Lengthy "stroking" expressions are avoided: Catholic/nationalist/republican or Protestant/unionist/loyalist are inelegant mouthfuls, and will not be met again in this book.

The expression Derry/Londonderry for the disputed second city of Northern Ireland has some merits. Ordering the slashed term by the alphabet makes sense, and I have sometimes used it in other work. Here, however, I have reconsidered.[6] "Legenderry" is inappropriate. "Stroke city" might once have been just, to reflect the contested name and the high rate of heart disease encouraged by smoking, the local cooking, and the alcohol used to absorb it: "Ulster fries" continue to keep statins in business. Yet the city's cuisine and drinks, as with much else, are improving. The sober resolution to the naming questions that surround the second largest city in Northern Ireland follows: the county is Londonderry, even though some locals refer to it as Derry; the urban area of over 100,000 people on both banks of the Foyle, and governed by the City Council, is Derry or Derry city; and the interior of the old walled city, and the walls, is Londonderry. The rationale for this proposed trifold usage is that the county was defined by the English settlers, and did not replace any previous singular Irish territorial unit covering exactly the same space. The (now inner) walled city was new when it was created, and it was created as Londonderry, on a then largely ruined site—though there is evidence that the vicinity has been inhabited for over 6,000 years.[7] The name was an ethnic fusion of two place names from two languages, the English "London" and the Irish "Derry" (*Doire*). Sadly, the fusion did not represent tolerant binational sentiments. The "Arms of Londonderry" indicate that the fortress was created by the City of London. The built-up urban area was legally administered by Londonderry City Council (or Corporation) for much if its recent history, but since 1984 the City Council has officially called itself Derry. This change, put through by the then SDLP-led council, reflects the original Irish name, *Doire* (oak-grove). The pre-colonial settlement, which had existed before the London companies built their fort, had been *Doire Chalgach*, later *Doire Cholum Chille* (Colum Cille's oakwood), named after St Colmcille (Columba in Latin). When conversing, local residents call the entire city Derry, whether Catholics or Protestants or neither, but Protestants generally dislike the change to the name of the City Council. The subject remains, to my knowledge, under peaceful litigation, evidence of the lasting power of colonial (and anti-colonial) mentalities. My usages, intended to be accommodative, will offend those who wish to be offended.[8]

Throughout the text the term "paramilitaries" is generally used rather than "terrorists." The former expression is more precise. Paramilitaries are unofficial armed bodies, "militias." Terrorism, the deliberate killing of civilians for political purposes, has been practiced by governments and government-supporters as well as by insurgents in British and Irish history, as it has elsewhere. The term "terrorist" and its cognates are now used almost exclusively in mass media to refer to insurgents. But, when "terrorist" or its cognates are used here, it is usually

---

[6] Influenced in part by the arguments of Curl (1986, 2000).

[7] See *History Ireland*, 21/ 3 (May–June 2013), p. 6, col. 1.

[8] The first newspaper of the maiden city was *London-Derry Journal*, but routinely referred to by its editor as the *Derry Journal* in the late 1700s. Playing mild havoc with my resolution, on 1 April 2015 the City of Derry and Strabane districts were merged to create the Derry City and Strabane local government district.

because the views of the official authorities are being reported, or those of political parties opposed to particular uses of violence. These terms, however, are also used when it is plain that organizations, official or unofficial, have deliberately targeted violence against civilian non-combatants. That reflects my belief that the term terrorism should properly be confined to the tactic of those who *deliberately* kill non-combatants—as loyalists frequently did, and as republicans, soldiers, and police officers sometimes did in late-twentieth-century Northern Ireland. There is, however, no consensus on this subject.[9] The data reviewed in Volume 1, Chapter 1, show that loyalist paramilitaries killed more civilians deliberately—as a proportion of the total number of killings for which they were responsible after 1966—than either republicans or the UK's security forces. On the preceding definitions, they were therefore proportionally the most terroristic of the organizations in the recent conflict. This logical conclusion is not, however, one that loyalists or unionists are likely to embrace, and, upon absorbing these syllogisms, some loyalists (and unionists) may be inclined to cease reading any further.

The use of the term "paramilitaries" instead of "terrorists" does not indicate, and should not be construed to mean, any tacit support for any paramilitary organization in the Isles, past or present; it is, simply, a more accurate and helpful description than the available alternatives. The usage may be misunderstood by specialists on Latin America, who describe paramilitaries as right wing and pro-regime, and guerrillas as left wing and insurgent. Paramilitaries in Northern Ireland were unauthorized and unlawful combatants; loyalists were pro-regime and pro-state, and sometimes cooperated with government intelligence agencies and the police, but their members were not invariably right wing; republicans were anti-regime, and insurgent, and, though generally left wing, they were not always so, and not all of their violent or forceful actions took the form of guerrilla warfare. Experts in the ways of Northern Ireland may now think they know all of what is to follow, but they are invited, along with others who claim no such expertise, to read on.

[9] See O'Leary and Tirman (2007).

2.1

Conceptual Conspectus

Control

Groups intent on "institutionalized dominance"... will always use three methods of conflict management: (1) proscribe or closely control the political expression of collective interest among dominated groups, (2) prohibit entry by members of dominated groups into the dominant community, and (3) provide monopoly or preferential access for members of the dominant group to political participation, advanced education, economic opportunities, and symbols of status, such as official language, the flag, national heroes, and holidays, which reinforce the political, economic and psychic control of the dominant group.

Milton J. Esman, 1973[1]

The system metaphor... helps avoid the suggestion of comprehensive conspiracy by permitting analysis of how specific polices, because of the structural and institutional contexts within which they are adopted, tend to have *unanticipated* consequences which also reinforce one or another component of control.

Ian S. Lustick, 1980[2]

MODELS OF RULE AND ROLE MODELS

Greek philosophers taught that the first question of politics was who should rule? Aristotle answered that three good governments act in the interests of all—monarchy, aristocracy, and democracy—and are matched by three bad governments—tyranny, oligarchy, mob rule—in which the rulers govern solely in their own interests and thereby generate strife. Optimal government, he suggested, synthesized the three good types. A later Greek, Polybius, thereby explained the rise of the Roman Republic: its consuls, senate, and people's assemblies respectively displayed the three good governmental forms. This thinking, recovered and developed by Montesquieu, was resurrected in modern republican constitutional doctrine.[3] "Mixed government," monarchy in the executive, aristocracy in the senate, and democracy in the legislature, provided the recipe for

---

[1] Esman (1973: 56).   [2] Lustick (1980: 78–9).
[3] Aristotle (1962); Polybius (1979); Montesquieu (1989/1748).

a good constitution; not, however, because rulers would act in the interests of all, but rather because each institution, with its separate powers and functions, would check and balance the other, and thereby prevent bad government—tyranny, oligarchy, or mob rule. The American republic's constitution, as remade in Philadelphia in 1787, advertised this thinking. Its text and practices separated powers, and in more numerous ways than this summary allows. It was soon notorious, however, that mixed government was not always functional. Not just because divided government may lead to gridlock, but also because when the executive, legislature, and judiciary are controlled by the same party—or racial, ethnic group, or class—then checking and balancing radically diminish, especially from the perspective of minorities.

Key makers of the Philadelphia constitution thought they were formalizing the best of the British model of government, but today that model is no longer seen through the rose-tinted spectacles of Montesquieu or his American disciples. Rather, the virtue of the (British-style) parliamentary model is supposed to be that it creates "responsible government," which fuses rather than separates executive and legislative power. The cabinet, led by a prime minister, is supported by the popular chamber, which can bring down either individual ministers, or the whole cabinet, in a vote of no-confidence. The system identifies the government and the opposition for the citizenry, who can hold the government accountable at general elections—and replace it with the opposition. Notoriously, however, this model too may be dysfunctional; notably when the winning party, which controls parliament, and regularly dominates all key institutions, uses that power to entrench itself—often with significantly less than a majority of the votes.[4] In newly emergent democracies or states, constitutional debate often revolves around the merits of these rival American and British models—that is, choosing divided (presidential) or fused (parliamentary) models of executive and legislative power. Occasionally a minority voice advocates French-style variants, which synthesize presidentialism and parliamentarism by, in effect, allowing institutional alternation between these systems, or parliamentary hybrids such as the German constructive vote of confidence.[a] These four powerful exemplars—the USA, the UK, France, and Germany—typically exhaust the accumulated lay wisdom of the West on executive and legislative design.

More complex debates occur about the judiciary. Should there be a supreme court empowered to strike down legislation or executive action, especially that which violates the separation of powers, a specialized constitutional court, or a high court confined to safeguarding the rule of law and advertising when the government is acting unconstitutionally—but without the power to veto or nullify the will of the people's representatives?[5] Should the judiciary be an autonomous profession with the right to determine its own bench and docket, or should the highest court(s) be appointed by the executive and/or legislature? Should the judiciary specifically protect a bill of rights from encroachment by the executive or the legislature? What if judiciaries are simply the paint on the mask of majority tyrannies?

[4] Patrick Dunleavy (1991) emphasizes the manipulative "preference-shaping" opportunities that are exploitable under this model of government.
[5] Horowitz (2006).

These very important questions about executive, legislative, and judicial institutions are often believed to be what matters most in institutional design. But, what if the Greek philosophers were wrong? What if the first question of government is not who should rule, but instead over what place and people should rule be exercised? After all, what people(s) are represented in government is partly determined by the place the government rules. And what if neither responsible government nor the division of powers nor autonomous judiciaries suffice to prevent an ethnic tyranny? These questions address the case in hand.

Ulster Unionists were allowed to pick the territorial extent of Northern Ireland (six not nine counties). As Ronald McNeill, a leading Conservative and Unionist, put it: "The Act of 1920 . . . was the fulfilment of the Craigavon resolution—to take over the government 'of those districts which they could control.'"[6] Initially, however, the Ulster Unionist Party (UUP) did not pick the institutions through which it would rule. It was, however, allowed to adapt the institutions created in the Government of Ireland Act to suit its preferences—to increase control. In the making of the new polity for the six counties, no debates took place over parliamentary or presidential systems, either among the future Northern Irish, or within the cabinet committee that drafted the Better Government of Ireland Bill. A miniature Westminster model was adopted, not because that was the thought-through cultural and institutional preference of Ulster Unionists, but rather through British institutional habit and, more importantly, because the Government of Ireland Act envisaged granting home rule to two parts of Ireland. The "design" of Northern Ireland's institutions was not customized. Rather, it was the byproduct of (reluctant and ultimately abortive) concessions to what had been envisaged as Southern Ireland.

From 1921 until 1972 Northern Ireland would be governed under *two* Westminster models. The full powers of the Crown, Commons, and Lords continued to be held in London, while a parallel and subordinate devolved system, the Crown's Governor-General, Commons, and Senate of Northern Ireland, operated in Belfast. These two executives, two bicameral legislatures, supported by two judiciaries, had distinct and overlapping powers. Northern Ireland had no "state's rights." Any actions of its government could be overridden by the Westminster parliament, which in Article 75 of the Government of Ireland Act retained its undiminished sovereignty, and the Belfast government could be suspended or abolished by the Westminster parliament.[7] The 1920 Act explicitly and implicitly specified a functional and spatial separation of powers, but the system was not formally federal. Executive and legislative powers were fused in Belfast, but, unlike the mothership in London, Belfast would never experience alternation in power, or indeed much meaningful competition for power between the government and opposition. The same party, the UUP, was returned to executive office for fifty years (1921–72). It won every election. No opposition ever became the governing party. No other party joined the UUP in a coalition. No fear of electoral

---

[6] McNeill (1922: 280; see also 51, 93).

[7] It read: "Notwithstanding the establishment of the Parliaments of Southern and Northern Ireland, or the Parliament of Ireland, or anything contained in this Act, the supreme authority of the Parliament of the United Kingdom shall remain unaffected and undiminished over all persons, matters, and things in Ireland and every part thereof."

accountability, no concern about voter retribution, and no effective judicial protection of minority rights, prevented the UUP from running a dominant-party system that organized the local majority and disorganized the nationalist minority (and other minorities). The UUP monopolized the devolved government so long as London chose not to intervene or engage in critical surveillance. London officials, elected and unelected, sometimes claimed that they had no powers to intervene, thereby acting as though Northern Ireland was a dominion rather than a devolved government. It was a convenient conviction, but a fiction.[b]

THE PLACE OF THE DEMOS, AND THE DEMOS'S PLACE

That the citizen body should rule is a mandatory norm in most modern states. Even dictators and dictatorial parties rule in the name of the people, as its guardian or vanguard. Absolutist monarchies and neo-traditional theocracies are rare: ISIS's attempt to establish a caliphate will fail. But if ruling in the name of the people, and its subset, the demos of adult citizens, is the norm, what is to be done when there are rivalrous definitions of the people, or, put otherwise, multiple peoples or nations?

Early liberal, republican, and democratic thought rarely addressed strife related to nationality or ethnicity. In liberal and republican thought, the rights of property, independent persons, commerce and civil society, justice, liberty, freedom of conscience, and virtue were the animating themes, not the rights of nations, ethnicities, or linguistic groups.[8] Liberals and republicans typically presumed a demos, and debated whether its scope should be widened, or how government should be organized within it. Republican and liberal philosophies provided few express clues as to who should comprise the people from whom the demos should be composed. Implicitly the answer was simply provided by history, "exogenously given" in contemporary jargon. Three provisional answers can be detected in these traditions, however: the civic state, the nation-state, and the global-state. The (civic) statist asserts that the demos should comprise all adults permanently, lawfully, and legitimately resident within the state's political borders. Much rests on what is meant by permanent, lawful, and legitimate, and the answer takes for granted the rectitude of the state's borders, at issue in Northern Ireland's formation.[9] The (ethnic) nationalist would admit to the demos all adults who belong to the nation and its homeland, by birth, adoptive membership, or (sometimes) choice, an approach that immediately puts in doubt the validity of borders when the residencies of the national demos and the national territory are not congruent, or when rival nations contest sovereignty over the same place. The cosmopolitan answer, by contrast, proposes all of adult humanity as the demos. It is a nice response, but useless until there is a world government.

---

[8] See the works of Pocock (1980, 1982, 1985, 1987, 1989a, b, 1999, 2003, 2005, 2009; Pocock et al. 1993).

[9] Northern Ireland developed a cottage industry of "civic unionists" after the Anglo-Irish Agreement of 1985. The fluent writings of Aughey (1989) and Porter (1996) are exemplary, persuasive when they suggest that Ulster Unionists should be civic statists, but unconvincing in even hinting that civic unionism was the historically authentic Unionism.

These three answers reflect egalitarian ideals, and seem to fit with democratic thought, by prescribing or assuming one demos per unit of government (and one supreme unit of government per demos). The nation-state has been the most potent of the three answers.[10] Few states, however, are homogeneous nation-states. Equally no states are purely civic: most children inherit their citizenship rights through "blood ties." The global state is yet to be. The three answers are problematic in different ways. The (mono-) nation-state is a recipe for strife in the presence of multiple peoples, unless the minority develops "a finely tuned sensitivity to the majority's sensibilities, and [is] eternally alive to the invisible boundaries that dare not be crossed in the area of majority–minority relations."[11] The nation-state must accommodate its minorities—somehow. The civic state appears utopian, except when it is a nation-state in poor disguise—either collective identities have to be wished away, or the dominant people's identities and values are in fact what are promoted and expressed: the cultural neutrality of the state is a pipe dream. The global state, by contrast, seems unreal, the goal of utopians, fantasists, and theocratic fanatics, or disillusioned pragmatists.[12]

The three answers share a self-evident universalism. The champions of the civic state and the nation-state differ over who should be in the demos, but agree with the cosmopolite that citizenship should be an equal bundle of benefits and burdens, applied impartially to all entitled to be in the demos, and that all persons should have full and equal membership of a demos—somewhere. The principle is to each person a people, and to each people its polity: one people one state, one people one nation-state, or one humanity one cosmopolis. There have, however, always been multi-people polities, which are not universalist. The constitutions of some multinational confederations, multiethnic federations, and consociations recognize multiple constituent or founding peoples. These systems are not generally advocated in preference to the nation-state—or the civic state, or cosmopolis—because their exponents are more skilled and nuanced in philosophical reflection.[13] Rather multinational confederations, multiethnic federations, and consociations emerge from dialogue, bargaining, and conflict among the representatives of plural peoples. They are justified because the contending parties accept that the most feasible alternatives are either protracted war to the finish, a nation-state with effective minority rights, or a system of control, the subject of this second volume of this work.

Deciding who should comprise the demos cannot be authoritatively answered within liberal or republican doctrine, or indeed within democratic theory.[14] This conundrum is known as "The Problem of the Unit." In practice, it is decided

---

[10] See Kedourie (1960)—see my commentary in Brendan O'Leary (2002)—and Gellner (1983)—see my commentary in Brendan O'Leary (1997).

[11] Advice given in the *Jerusalem Post* to Arab mayors seeking a binational state, cited in Lustick (1980: 65).

[12] For a review, see Mazower (2012).

[13] Such claims could be advanced on behalf of some distinguished Canadian and Belgian philosophers, e.g., Charles Taylor (1993); Tully (1995); van Parijs (2011).

[14] "Whether the scope and domain of majority rule are appropriate in a particular unit depends on assumptions that the majority principle itself can do nothing to justify. The justification for the [political] unit lies beyond the reach of the majority principle and, for that matter, mostly beyond the reach of democratic theory itself" (Dahl 1989: 193–204).

through some conjunction of coercion, contention, consensus, contingency, and acquiescence. The demos of Northern Ireland was decided by the London government in 1920, *and* reinforced by the failure of the boundary commission in 1925, which left that demos's place unchanged. London initially granted Belfast no formal exclusive rights over citizenship, but eventually delegated de facto or de jure decisions over the franchise, electoral laws, and key citizenship rights. No popular ratification of either the place or the demos of Northern Ireland ever took place—not at the level of counties, constituencies, wards, or the entire place—until 1998. By then, however, most of the adults alive in 1920 were dead.

The leaders of the UUP established control, not as part of a grand plan, or through a superbly organized conspiracy, but incrementally, through numerous tactical and strategic choices, with ratchet effects.[15] Numerous actions and inactions in Great Britain, and in independent Ireland, served to lock in the distinct pattern of control pioneered by unionists. The leadership of the UUP, and its rank-and-file cadres, succeeded in creating and maintaining a political system that looked as if it had been entirely designed to organize the new majority and to disorganize the new minority, but in fact the social structure and institutions bequeathed to Northern Ireland were adapted to serve these control functions.

CONTROL SYSTEMS

The language of "control systems" is owed to Ian S. Lustick, who synthesized and advanced a literature developed by numerous social scientists investigating the racially polarized islands of the Caribbean, the white settler states of colonial Africa, and, more generally, plural or deeply divided colonial and postcolonial societies.[16] To simplify Lustick's work, and that of his predecessors, it is possible to argue that all control systems—colonial, postcolonial, internally colonial, and non-colonial—share two traits that distinguish them from those polities in which there are inequalities in advantages between the average members of groups (that is, all other polities). Control systems firstly organize the dominant people and disorganize subordinate others though direct and indirect exclusion. Secondly, whatever their genesis, control systems are particularist in their modes of incorporation of peoples. Differently put, control systems generate group-ranked tiers of citizenship rights, either formally or informally—that is, groups are hierarchically differentiated by deliberate political, economic, and cultural practices even when formal constitutional or statute law says otherwise (see Table 2.1.1).

In a control system, the demos may be overtly defined in law as a privileged or chosen people, and by reference to an Other, or others, who are not part of *the* people but who may legitimately be subjected to the rule of the people. These others are not entitled to separate nationhood—at least not here, in this place, and

---

[15] Lindblom (1959) provides the pioneering discussion of incrementalism.

[16] See, e.g., M. G. Smith (1965); Kuper and Smith (1969); Van den Berghe (1969); Esman (1973); Rabushka and Shepsle (2009/1972).

Table 2.1.1. Modes of ethnic management and incorporation

Mode of incorporation of groups and individuals	Dominant mode of ethnic management	
	Exclusionary orders (Control systems)	Inclusionary polities
Individuals as equal citizens	*Citizens versus non-citizens (aliens, metics, and guest-workers)*	Republican liberal democracy Unitary civic state (aliens, metics, and migrants as candidate-citizens)
Collective incorporation of groups as equals	*Coalition of dominant groups versus excluded groups*	Corporate consociations Multinational federations (migrants as candidate-citizens and candidates for adoption into communities or nations)
Collective and individual equal citizenship incorporation	*Coalition of dominant groups versus partially co-opted excluded groups*	Liberal consociations Multi-ethnic, multi-lingual & multi-religious federations or union states (migrants as candidate-citizens and candidates for adoption into communities or nations OR free to form their own communities or not)
Collective ranked incorporation of groups through overt hierarchical control in which the lowest tier(s) lack any citizenship rights	*Slavery Colonial rule (direct and indirect) Caste hierarchy Feudalism Traditional monarchies and aristocracies versus subject people(s)*	n.a.
Collective ranked incorporation of groups and some individuals through a combination of hierarchical control and some assigned legal rights to those in the lowest tier(s)	*Herrenvolk democracy Staatsvolk democracy Majoritarian democracy (migrants' rights are carefully controlled to avoid changing power relations between groups)*	n.a.

not now. Colonial rule, the best-known specimen of a control system, has already been discussed in Volume 1, so no detailed recital of its forms is needed here.[17] Colonial rule is, however, always particularist *par excellence*. In 1957 the Tunisian-born Albert Memmi, child of a father of Jewish–Italian descent and a mother of Jewish–Berber descent, wrote *The Colonizer and the Colonized*.[c] His arguments were overly "binarist," and overstated, as he later recognized, but his portrait of the mentality of the colonizer remains unsurpassed. The colonizer is a usurper who asserts his superiority, and who denigrates the culture, mores, and institutions of the colonized, hoping thereby to convert his usurpation into a justification of his civilizing mission. The edition of this book by Liam O'Dowd suggests that

---

[17] See Vol. 1, esp. Ch. 2.

The Colonizer and the Colonized "serves to challenge the collective amnesia which would consign the colonial legacy to a past which no longer informs the present."[18] Memmi argued that settlers fear, not without reason, becoming a minority within a native regime. They are consumed with anxiety that their subordination by a democratic majority, or after a revolution, would precede their subsequent extirpation, or extinction. Settlers are not, they invariably say, a mere minority. They are, rather, a superior people, a civilized people, a chosen people; certainly they are "no petty people"—the phrase W. B. Yeats declaimed in the Senate of the Irish Free State in defense of his people, Irish Protestants. When colonial settlers embrace nationalist ideas, they are often those of the imperial motherland, and, almost invariably, rivalrous to those of the natives (unless the latter are conveniently dead or long dispatched, in which case their identity may be taken).

Particularists rank peoples unequally *in their place*. This is palpably obvious in racist empires, or in polities that enslave or enserf others, or where outcastes are created on the basis of (alleged) ascriptive characteristics. It is less obvious when a group presides over a hierarchy while denying it—and indeed when it criminalizes claims to the contrary, as in contemporary Rwanda. Particularists can be global racists who insist on a racial hierarchy of merit among all peoples, but their racism may be confined to their own polity: we, they assert, simply have the right to run our own place. In either case they may adopt a "Herrenvolk" democracy, in which the master-people is alone entitled to full democratic citizenship.[19] For the racist, purity and impurity determine political inclusion and exclusion, and taboos of pollution are usually promoted to prevent mixing, exogamy, and subsequent fusion. Racism, of course, need not rest on variations in typical skin color; it may be exhibited among stocks of people who look quite similar to outsiders—for example, by the English toward the Irish, or by the Tutsi toward the Hutus, or vice versa.

The elect, chosen, special, or civilized people, nation, or community may be a fraction of the population of the relevant polity, sometimes less than a half, sometimes as low as a tenth.[20] Such peoples do not believe, however, that their right to rule is subject to numerical count, unless that is convenient. Particularist doctrines and practices are common among "chosen" or "elect" peoples. Any recital of such peoples would include a majority of Afrikaners in South Africa before de Klerk's political initiative;[21] most white Rhodesians who established a racially defined citizenry under Ian Smith before being forced to negotiate Zimbabwe with the forces of ZANU and ZAPU led by Robert Mugabe and Joshua Nkomo respectively;[22] most Israeli settlers in the West Bank and Gaza after 1967;[23] most white Americans in the Deep South of the USA after the failure of Reconstruction;[24] the descendants of African American settlers in Liberia (until 1980);[25] and the pan-Arabist Ba'athism once espoused by Sunni Arabs in Iraq and Alawite Arabs in Syria.[26]

---

[18] O'Dowd (1990: 30).

[19] The phrase is Pierre van den Berghe's—see, e.g., Van den Berghe (1969); it is also deployed in the opening passages of J. J. Lee's study (1989) of modern Ireland.

[20] For a comparative study that includes the case at hand, see Akenson (1992); on the general theme of chosen peoples, see Anthony D. Smith (1992).

[21] Adam (1971).   [22] Palley (1966).

[23] Some insist that the entire Israeli polity, including in its conception before 1948, and its demarcation between 1948 and 1967, is founded in ethnic particularism.

[24] Foner (2005).   [25] Ali and Matthews (1999).   [26] Baram (1991); van Dam (2011).

But is it appropriate, fair, let alone sound social science to compare twentieth-century Ulster Unionists with such particularists? Surely this is to engage in denigration through comparative insinuation? The opening answer has to be that Ulster Unionists have often made such comparisons themselves:[27] Rhodesian, old South African, and Israeli emblems and flags have been flown alongside the red hand of Ulster in loyalist Belfast. Historians who are not Irish nationalists have also made such comparisons.[28] The answer here is that Ulster Unionists built a particularist regime that would not, because it claimed it could not, incorporate the disloyal Irish nationalist and Catholic population as fully equal citizens, *because they were disloyal.*[d] Partnership in a binational (or bi-religious) subpolity, or co-nationality in an Ulster nation, was never proposed by Ulster unionists, let alone attempted before 1972. Unlike several of the settler–colonial peoples just cited, however, Ulster Unionists built their system of control without an overtly national, ethnic, religious, or linguistic exclusionary franchise. They could do so because they had selected the space that they could control, and they kept (and modified) the restricted local government franchise they had inherited from the Union government.

What makes Northern Ireland from 1921 until 1972 of comparative interest is that particularist control was established within the formal apparatus of liberal democracy. In these respects it bore some resemblance to Israel inside its 1967 borders, but unlike Israel it was not sovereign, had no project of gathering in its "exiles," or of creating fresh settlements; it also had no army of its own, and no early socialist ethos in the governing party. Northern Ireland's institutions also displayed some of the hallmarks of a *StaatsVolk* democracy in which "the people" who name and control the state are dominant even if others have citizenship rights. Ulster Unionists were not a formal *StaatsVolk* because they did not possess sovereign statehood—and feared to seek it. They were British folk in the province of Ulster, as they put it. Northern Ireland certainly exhibited the "dominant majority configuration," sketched in Alvin Rabushka's and Ken Shepsle's *Plural Societies: A Theory of Democratic Instability*:[29] here, the symbols of democracy exist, but the substance atrophies at the hands of a machinating majority, an entrenched cultural, demographic, and electoral majority.

While not all control systems are colonial—that is, set up by settlers over natives, or by metropolitans and settlers over natives—they usually display colonial traits. Three cases from south Asia, central Asia, and south-eastern Europe illustrate the point—namely, Sri Lanka, the Kyrgyz Republic, and the former Serbian Republic of Yugoslavia. In postcolonial Ceylon, Sinhalese politicians built a control system over Tamils—imposing a Sinhala-only language policy and renaming the state Sri Lanka with strongly Buddhist connotations. It broke down under the assaults of the Liberation Tigers of Tamil Eelam, ruthless ethnic and Marxist-Leninist revolutionaries. The Tigers were no pillars of human rights,

---

[27] An Ulster Presbyterian clergyman devoted a chapter of his portrait of Ulster Protestants to a comparison with Afrikaners, emphasizing Calvinist pre-destinationism, a chosen race, social and educational segregation, a siege mentality, and an anachronistic theology and politics (Crawford 1987: 106–17).

[28] Most notably Akenson (1992).   [29] Rabushka and Shepsle (2009/1972).

but would not have emerged, however, without the provocations generated by Sinhalese efforts to impose control—and the crushing defeat of the Tigers has not definitively resolved the conflict. Sinhalese still refuse major territorial autonomy concessions to the Tamils as a nationality, and, though Tamils and Sinhalese have cohabited for over a millennium, each community has many convinced that its people is the truly indigenous, and that the other comprises intrusive settlers.

In the debris left by the Soviet Union, Kyrgyz dominate and discriminate against Uzbeks, who mostly live in the south and southwest of what was known as Kyrgyzstan. Both peoples were territorially incorporated into the new republic in decisions made by Soviet commissars in the 1920s. Both are natives to the lands in which they reside—as far as anyone can reliably tell, though Kyrgyz were more nomadic than Uzbeks. The Kyrgyz fear loss of national majority status because they experienced that fate in Soviet times (when large numbers of Russians and Russian-speakers settled in the republic, and reduced Kyrgyz to the plurality group). They have renamed the state the Kyrgyz Republic, emphasizing their control as a titular nationality. Today they fear the demographically diminished Russians much less, but in direct and displaced aggression fear Uzbeks, whom they portray as the fifth column of neighboring Uzbekistan, and suspect of wishing to restructure their territory.[30] Urban pogroms have been incited against Uzbeks in post-Soviet times—not against Russians—partly because Uzbeks are seen as a long-run demographic threat.

In the post-Ottoman and post-communist Balkans, Serbs attempted to establish, re-establish, and keep collective control in Kosovo (or Kosova, as Albanians know it). Exclusivist Serbian nationalism had simmered in this site since the nineteenth century, and Serb settlers intermittently colonized and displaced Albanians. But under communist rule Kosovo was supposed to enjoy the benefits of autonomy. Serb politicians overturned this status, however, shortly after the death of Marshall Tito. It proved to be the opening moment in the break-up of Yugoslavia. They did so partly because Serbs had become radically outnumbered after fast-paced demographic growth among Kosovar Albanians. Serb control projects in Kosova were eventually defeated, but only after great-power intervention.[31]

These three tightly summarized examples suggest that control systems need not be directly colonial—that is, involve the rule of present-day or recent settlers over natives, or of metropolitans and settlers over natives, but they can quickly develop colonial traits. The rulers and the ruled may be equally indigenous, long settled in the relevant territory (as with Tamils and Sinhalese, though their respective myths say otherwise), or both may be equally recent or long-ago migrants to the relevant space (as scholars believe of Kyrgyz and Uzbeks). But the examples also suggest what political discourses to expect in contested control systems. Controllers will not always speak and justify themselves exactly like Memmi's colonizers, but they will usually insist that they are special or civilized, at least by contrast with those whom they are obliged to control. Those subjected to control and intent on resisting it, by contrast, will invoke the arguments and language of anti-colonial self-determination.

---

[30] For a useful discussion of direct, displaced, and cumulative ethnic aggression, see Horowitz (1973).
[31] For comparisons between Serb and Israeli patterns of control, see Ron (2003).

A major difference among control systems is whether the dominant group controls a sovereign state—either an independent state or a federal region with sovereign state's rights. In 1966 Tutsi soldiers and politicians established a sovereign control system in Burundi, shortly after Belgian decolonization, deposing the traditional monarchy, whose apologists had defended it as an impartial arbiter of differences between Hutu and Tutsi.[32] The Tutsi were a distinct minority, which is why its chauvinists rejected universal suffrage and developed a one-party regime. An example of regional control is provided by the defeated slaveholding states of the American Confederacy, which initially appeared headed toward racial equality after the Union victory in the civil war. But Southern whites successfully resisted "radical reconstruction,"[33] and went on to organize a system of overt control over African Americans, which lasted from the 1880s until the mid-1960s. These southern states were, however, partly constrained by the federal laws and norms of the United States. They therefore carefully developed laws and norms to exclude and discourage ex-slaves, and their descendants, from exercising their nominal full citizenship rights, including the right to vote, and relied on states' rights to minimize federal scrutiny of their conduct (largely perfunctory until the 1940s). Over time they developed a one-party dominant system throughout the South under the aegis of the Democratic Party. Northern Ireland resembled these southern states in some respects, but it was not overtly racist, had no formal federal state rights, and it kept full parliamentary forms, including universal suffrage for elections to the Belfast parliament. Had a nine-county Northern Ireland been created in 1920, perhaps there would have been an organized push to dispense with such niceties.

HEGEMONIC AND CONTESTED CONTROL

The concept of a control system was developed by Lustick to account for the surprising political quiescence of the Arabs of Israel inside Israel's 1967 borders. His book addressed the period from 1948 until 1980 (his Ph.D. thesis was submitted in 1976). His argument was that a control system—through a multilevel process of segmentation, dependence, and cooption—can preserve political stability, despite deep divisions that threaten potential violent revolt. Later, John McGarry and I suggested that control regimes can be especially stable if they exemplify "hegemonic control," but, since this notion was developed before "the hegemonic analysis" subsequently published by Lustick in *Unsettled States, Disputed Lands: Britain and Ireland, France and Algeria, Israel and the West Bank-Gaza* (1993), let me explain this thicket of words.

"Control" once meant to check, test, or verify from evidence, and the word derives from (medieval) Latin (*contra* (against) + *rotulus* (roll)). This meaning survives in the practice of audit, but, outside of financial management, control now means to exercise restraining or directing influence over a subject or target— that is, to dominate it, or, in softer usages, to regulate, or to steer a subject.

---

[32] See Lemarchand (1970).   [33] Foner (2005).

The ancient Greek word "hegemon," by contrast, originally described the leader of a military alliance, but in most current usage "hegemonic" denotes exercising preponderant influence or authority—that is, domination. This excursus therefore suggests that "hegemonic control" is a pleonasm—that is, it seems to mean "dominating domination," a specimen of academic jargon-ridden wordiness. That understandable reading should be resisted, however. Hegemonic control, as defined here, and consistent with Lustick's earlier work, exists whenever a particularist conception of the people is successfully institutionalized to support the domination of executive, legislative, and judicial power by one people, and directly or indirectly excludes at least one other people from equal or proportionate access to those powers. The exclusion is not of a social class, but rather of a people or other peoples per se. Under hegemonic control, political leadership is usually in the hands of a party (or coalition of parties) that overtly represent the particularist people.[e] Rival conceptions of the nation are disorganized, and potential antagonists among the excluded people(s) are managed into quiescence. Potential reformers within the ranks of the dominant people are successfully stigmatized as traitors.

Hegemonic control is coercive—enforced by soldiers, police, judges, prisons, and repressive laws—but it is not just overtly coercive. When it works effectively, coercion is not always visible. It may rely upon, or actively increase, the fragmentation of the controlled. It may be co-optive, both to overcome divisions among the hegemonic people, and to prevent solidarity among the dominated people(s). When fully operative, hegemonic control makes unworkable an ethnic or nationalist challenge to the prevailing order from among the subordinated people(s). When there are revolts, rebellions, and sustained major protests, control ceases to be hegemonic; control is then being contested. The symptoms of contested control will include pogroms, deadly ethnic riots, and overt normative challenges to the right of the dominant people to monopolize rule. In short, sustained normative and violent expressions of dissent signal crises in control systems.

Differently put, hegemonic control unifies the loyal people, disorganizes the disloyal, and renders revolution, rebellion, or protest futile, or at least exceptionally costly. In Northern Ireland, Ulster Protestants were the loyal people, and the UUP successfully presented itself as this people's party. It unified the loyal, both across social classes and across the diverse Protestant sects. In office, it manifestly and privately sought to disorganize disloyal Irish nationalists, not just republicans. Intermittently, it co-opted or outflanked Protestant socialists who considered class alliances with Catholic workers, and frequently demonized as traitors those socialists who sought to create separate labor parties. The UUP government infrequently co-opted Catholics, but not into the party, however, and only as long as they were loyal to the Union—so there were *some* Catholic justices, civil servants, public-sector professionals, and police (particularly in Catholic villages). Too much incorporation of Catholics, however, would have destabilized the UUP's cross-class and cross-sect alliance among Protestants. Political vigilantes in and outside of the Orange Order regularly emerged to set very tight limits to permissible incorporation.

The possibility of hegemonic control seems less feasible in democracies than in empires, extractive colonies, conquered and occupied territories, or in one-party authoritarian regimes. After all, democracies permit and facilitate collective self-organization and mobilization, including ethnic organization, at least when ethnic interest groups and parties are not constitutionally banned or outlawed.[34] In principle, liberal democracies make opposition and contests for governmental power thinkable and workable, but Northern Ireland's first fifty years demonstrate that hegemonic control is fully feasible in liberal democracies. It can persist when one community (or perhaps coalition of communities) is mobilized in a sustained manner to dominate another through its political, economic, and ideological resources *despite* universal suffrage and parliamentary conditions.

Hegemonic control does not require colossal collective brain washing, as is sometimes implied in Marxist, especially Gramscian, discussions of hegemonic analysis.[35] What matters is the arranging of institutions and incentives to keep *the* people unified, and to keep their opponents in other people(s) disorganized. Potentially subversive opponents must be kept politically demoralized. Hegemonic control, as defined here, does not require that the controlled accept or internalize the regime's "newspeak." It is not totalitarian.[36] Majority-rule democracy and hegemonic control are compatible when the particularist people's dominant party is effectively able to manage citizenship, institutions, and territory to perpetuate its dominance, and to prevent class or programmatic alliances that might disrupt the unity of the titular nationality.[37]

The thesis advanced here is that hegemonic control was established between 1920 and 1925 by the UUP, and, aside from a few exceptional moments, exercised successfully until 1966. After 1925 opportunities for effective opposition, dissent, disobedience, or usurpation of power were minimal. The major possibilities of disruption came from the outside, from independent Ireland or from Great Britain, from geopolitics, or the world economy. Eventually, when external forces of disruption combined with major endogenous changes, hegemonic control would be contested, and would shatter. But at no juncture did Northern nationalists or Irish Catholics in the North internalize the UUP's rhetoric, or become significantly British by cultural designation.[38] When the civil-rights movement learned to exploit the claim to be British citizens entitled to British rights, the regime's days were numbered.

What follows surveys the genesis, structure, and maintenance of hegemonic control in Northern Ireland, and its eventual breakdown. Insurrection by nationalists was never rendered literally unthinkable—the IRA made insurrectionary

---

[34] See, in particular, the work of Bogaards (2008) on the regulation of parties.

[35] Abercrombie et al. (1980) provide an astringent evaluation, as does Parkin (1979). Hegemonic analysis in Lustick's hands shifted from analyzing relationships between classes to those between national, ethnic, and religious groups—a move that many do not accept; see the comments in Brendan O'Leary (2001). For a sharp review of the contradictions in Gramsci's original thinking, see Anderson (1976), revised and updated in Anderson (2017).

[36] This was the key analytical error in the otherwise perceptive analyses of Ultach (1940, 1943)—the pseudonym of J. J. Campbell, who later co-authored the report of the Cameron Commission. Ultach means "Ulsterman."

[37] To repeat, typical Gramscian hegemonic analysis applies to interclass relations. Such approaches are especially useful in examining intra-Unionist class relations—e.g., the subsequent partial success of unionist writers and politicians in persuading loyalist workers that only disloyal or feckless Catholics suffered during the Famine (as Kerby Miller has observed in correspondence).

[38] Todd (1990).

efforts—but it was unworkable from the mid-1920s until the late 1960s; and Northern nationalists failed to build any truly organized political party or counter-movement, as opposed to intermittent ad hoc alliances (Chapter 2.2). How Irish state-building reinforced the UUP's hegemonic control is explained in Chapter 2.3. The repercussions of the Second World War set in train the events that led to the collapse in the control system during the premierships of Terence O'Neill, James Chichester-Clarke, and Brian Faulkner (Chapters 2.4 and 2.5). But before the establishment, maintenance, and collapse of control in the North is traced, an inventory of the components of control, as suggested in the early work of Ian S. Lustick, merits review.

COMPONENTS OF CONTROL

A *system* of control has three components, according to Lustick: *segmentation*, the isolation *and* fragmentation of the controlled group; *dependence*, the economic underdevelopment and comparative social and political vulnerability of the controlled group; and *co-option*, the incorporation (and division) of elites, notables, or leaders in ways illustrated in Table 2.1.1, which weaken the controlled group's cohesion and prospects of collective action. Focusing on the Arabs of Israel (1948–76), Lustick explored how each of these components emerged from strategic and tactical choices by Jewish political leaders who exploited *structural* features and possibilities (geographic, social structural, and historical legacies) that made Arabs vulnerable to control; developed *institutional* arrangements (the normal operating procedures of political, economic, and social organizations) that indirectly consolidated that control; and pursued *programmatic* policies that deliberately sought to control the minority. What makes control "systemic" in Lustick's view is that these components are synergistic. Their interactions maintain an overall dynamic stability that serves to keep the subordinate group quiescent, even though only the programmatic policies are deliberately intended.

Lustick's framework developed for Israel is transferrable to Northern Ireland from 1920 until 1972, even though the trajectories, morphologies, and geopolitics of the two cases are different. Again, Israel became a sovereign and independent state in 1948, whereas Northern Ireland has never had this status. Structurally, however, Northern nationalists and Catholics were vulnerable to control. They were not sufficiently spatially concentrated to create a strong territorial base for secessionist organization within the North. The possible exceptions were in comparatively sparsely populated border regions; in west Belfast, whose denizens were geographically isolated from their co-ethnics, and surrounded until the 1980s by districts with strong Protestant demographic majorities; and in Newry and Derry, which bordered the republic. The latter towns became the locus of programmatic control policies, and for that reason the epicenter of the civil-rights movement.[39] Northern nationalists and Catholics were not uniformly spatially dispersed— for example, at the level of the electoral ward. Had that been so, that would

[39] Ó Dochartaigh (1997).

have created opportunities for tactical electoral alliances *if* unionists had been significantly divided politically—one-third of the electorate, counterfactually, had abstract possibilities of becoming pivotal voters at ward level. Northern nationalists were also politically vulnerable. Though Northern Catholics were religiously homogeneous—unlike Northern Protestants—they entered the new polity politically divided. There were supporters of both the IPP and Sinn Féin, with the former stronger and the latter weaker in Ulster than in the rest of Ireland. Subsequently, Sinn Féin and IRA supporters subdivided into pro- and anti-treaty factions, mirroring the divisions of the Irish civil war. These divisions partly coincided with two others among Northern nationalists—namely, dispositions toward partition and repartition, and a rural–urban cleavage. Catholics in west Ulster, especially in Fermanagh and Tyrone, but also in border regions and border towns, had strongly opposed partitionist compromises before 1920. Subsequently, they entertained strong hopes that the boundary commission would deliver them to the Free State. By contrast, Catholics in Belfast and East Ulster could not realistically entertain such prospects. Under Devlin's leadership they had led the acquiescence to temporary partition. After partition was legislated, many of them quietly preferred that Northern Ireland remain as large as possible—to maximize their prospects of being a part of a larger and more powerful minority, and perhaps thereby enable all-island unification.[40] The rural–urban cleavage was more publicly obvious. Throughout the thirty years from 1921 until the late 1950s the Catholics who voted in rural Ulster usually backed Northern nationalists or socially conservative republicans of one hue or another. By contrast, Belfast Catholics, when they voted, often voted for republican labor candidates or republican socialists, and sometimes for socialists who claimed to transcend both orange and green. This urban–rural cleavage made difficult the creation of a strong pan-nationalist party.

Catholics also displayed dependence, which made them vulnerable. Rural Northern Catholics had been relatively disadvantaged compared with Protestants since plantation times—in landownership, and in the quality of land owned. They were on average poorer and more inclined to migrate after the 1840s. The Irish Catholic family structure on the land—the stem family—encouraged this migratory dynamic. But, given that industrializing Belfast quickly proved an inhospitable milieu, rural Ulster Catholics often preferred to migrate to British or American cities, or elsewhere in the Anglosphere. This pattern preserved the vulnerability of those who remained. By comparison with Ulster Protestants, Ulster Catholics lacked a large and substantial landowning class, or a large professional bourgeoisie. In consequence, they were more likely to be influenced, or led, by politically quiescent bishops and clerics who were professionally obligated to place the organizational interests of their church ahead of the national and ethnic sentiments of their flock. Though there were passionately nationalist clergy who did not always follow their theological or organizational obligations, they were certainly easier to encourage toward conformist and nonconfrontational—if not supine—politics. "Priests," writes Jennifer Todd, "provided the central intellectual and political cadre of the community," until the

---

[40] Devlin himself would have preferred a "home rule within home rule" formula (Hepburn 2008: 278).

1950s, "transmitting the tenets of their own cultural nationalism, which was reproduced through their membership of the most powerful and extensive all-Ireland organization."[41] True, but the Catholic Church was a Catholic church, not a nationalist organization, and its cadre, to use Todd's words, were not revolutionaries. The Catholic hierarchy had uniformly opposed partition, but decisively backed the pro-treaty side in the Irish civil war. It usually kept itself at least at arm's length from the ethos of militant republicanism. Throughout the 1920s and 1930s the "repudiation of both communism and the IRA" was to be a constant theme of Catholic clergy, North and South.[42] The war of independence, partition, and the civil war also meant that Northern nationalists and republicans lost a significant portion of their emergent political elite—to the Irish Free State's political class, army, or professions, or to exile farther afield.[43] In the 1920s, Northern Catholics retreated inwards in their associational life with consequences for their young—they had their own Young Men's Society, Arts Guild, Boy Scouts, Legion of Mary and Holy Childhood Society, even their own Billiards League. Rafferty notes that "these and a host of other societies contributed to the one end of preserving a distinct catholic ethos," but by isolating Catholics from Protestants the consolidation of control became easier.[44]

Institutionally Catholics were also vulnerable to control. The possibility that the Westminster model would be exploited to construct a party and ethnic monopoly on local political power has been anticipated. In the four counties of the northeast, excluding the districts of South Armagh, South Down, and West Belfast, unionists had been entrenched in Westminster constituencies since the mid-1880s, and at county and district council level since 1898. Here Protestants ubiquitously dominated the land, business, the high professions, the higher civil service, and the judiciary. The political question after 1920 was whether unionists would be able to establish full-spectrum dominance across the rest of the new North. That is why programmatic discrimination would matter, and matter most in west and south Ulster. The UUP was able to take advantage of the Irish civil war to establish a partisan transformation and monopoly over security power—replacing the old and mixed RIC with a highly partisan RUC, and the exclusively Protestant Special Constables. Legislatively and administratively the party then stripped away the limited securities for the minority provided in the Government of Ireland Act. This, in short, was how control could be consolidated. The story of its establishment is elaborated in what follows, along with its maintenance, pathologies, and vulnerabilities.

---

[41] Todd (1990: 34).   [42] Rafferty (1994: 230–1).
[43] Between April 1, 1922, and January 31, 1923, for example, roughly 3,000 men left Belfast to join the army of the IFS; see Staunton (2001: 71), who cites Irish archival sources.
[44] Rafferty (1994: 228).

2.2

Not an Inch

Gaining Control in the North, 1919–1939

What we have we hold.

> Sir James Craig, addressing the Northern Ireland
> House of Commons, May 23, 1922[1]

What do you want the special constables for? He said to preserve law and to maintain order . . . This suggestion is to arm these people in the six counties, especially Belfast. The Chief Secretary told us . . . the other day he was going to rake Ireland from end to end for arms, yet he is going to arm "pogromists" to murder the Catholics. These will be going along as peaceful, law-abiding citizens. Happily we have the character of the men who will be these special constables. One of them was arrested in the midst of the riots at Belfast for looting. I put a question to the right hon. gentleman today about Lisburn. Three of the special constables were convicted . . . [interruption] Three hundred special constables resigned their position because the three looters, belonging to their class, were arrested by the police. And it is to the mercy of these men that . . . we Belfast Catholics are to be left. The Protestants are to be armed, for we would not touch your special constabularyship with a forty-foot pole. Their pogrom is to be made less difficult. Instead of paving stones and sticks they are to be given rifles. That is how civil war is to be prevented in Ireland and in Ulster.

> Joseph Devlin, MP for Belfast Falls, Westminster House of
> Commons, October 25, 1920[2]

"In the twentieth century as in the seventeenth God was a Protestant," writes a historian of the partition of Ireland.[3] The leaders of Ulster unionism did not leave their fate in the hands of their supreme being, however. They had ruthlessly abandoned their fellow Protestants outside the six counties in a collective display of *sauve qui peut*, but a carefully downsized garrison land could not be easily secured because it contained native adversaries. Were they to be integrated, assimilated, invited to share power, or expelled beyond the new boundary, as well as from the shipyards? Neither the most benign nor the wholly malign paths

---

[1] Hansard (NI), HC, vol. 2, col. 598 (May 23, 1922).
[2] Hansard, HC, 5th ser., vol. 133, cols 1505–6 (October 25, 1920).
[3] Laffan (1983: 23).

were followed; instead permanent vigilance became the motto of the new regime. Sir James Craig promised David Lloyd George that there would be exemplary good government in the new North. "We are resolved to set such an example of good government and just administration within our jurisdiction, as shall inspire the minority in our midst with confidence, and we hope lead eventually to similar conditions being established throughout the rest of Ireland."[4] Such commitments had not been part of his persona to date, which had envisaged Northern Ireland as "a new impregnable Pale," reconcentrating the descendants of Britain's loyal settlers.[a] He had mostly been silent about the fate of the others, the natives, and even if his letter to Lloyd George expressed sincere intentions he probably would have been unable to bind his followers to these pledges and retain their support.

Exemplary good government and just administration did not materialize. To avoid "Rome Rule," Unionists created rule by Calvin and Hobbes, but whether they did so with full malice aforethought remains at issue. Did the conduct of their nationalist adversaries oblige them to be unreasonable, or was unreasonableness toward the natives already hardwired into their political culture? Nationalists had no doubt. The much-shrunken Ulster was immediately dubbed the Orange Free State by William O'Brien;[5] that would be abbreviated to the Orange State by, among others, the 1960s civil-rights radical Michael Farrell.[6]

Northern Ireland's formation marked an Irish nationalist failure as well as a British state-building failure. Irish nationalism had neither won over nor divided the Unionists of the northeast, who believed that Irish cultural nationalism suggested that the English language, the Protestant religion(s), and the British identity were its exact antitheses—*Irish Irelanders* said as much.[7] Civic nationalism was the official line of the Irish Parliamentary Party (IPP) and Sinn Féin, but remained unheard or disbelieved by Ulster loyalists. Every statement of exclusionary ethnic or religious nationalism, representative or otherwise, especially from the South, was taken to reflect the real sentiments of the Irish—hardliners are often assumed to represent the entire group's authentic beliefs. Partition was not, however, primarily an Irish nationalist ideological or cultural failure, and the particular borderline selected owed most to power politics. Electorally, militarily, and organizationally, republicans were weakest in East Ulster. Making that equally true in all of the new Northern Ireland became a Unionist imperative.

UNCERTAIN PARCHMENT AND FIERY BEGINNINGS:
INSPIRING THE MINORITY IN OUR MIDST

Government formation formally occurred after the elections held for the new Belfast parliament in May 1921. Northern Ireland, however, had the dubious privilege of two legislative births, in the 1920 Act, and in the 1921 Treaty—ratified in

---

[4] The full correspondence between Lloyd George and Craig between 10 November 1921 and December 5 1921 is reprinted in O'Leary and Maume (2004: 146–56).
[5] Mansergh (1991: 73).   [6] Michael Farrell (1980).   [7] Moran (1905/2006).

1922. Lloyd George wrote to Craig in December 1921, in the letter dispatched after his ultimatum to the Sinn Féin delegation and their signature of the treaty, that

> there are two alternatives between which the Government of Northern Ireland is invited to choose. Under the first, retaining all her existing powers, she will enter the Irish Free State with such additional guarantees as may be arranged in conference. Under the second alternative she will retain her present powers, but in respect of all matters not already delegated to her will share the rights and obligations of Great Britain. In the latter case, however, we should feel unable to defend the existing boundary, which must be subject to revision on one side and the other by a Boundary Commission.[8]

There were multiple bites here. In the treaty awaiting ratification, London had formally placed the newly minted Northern Ireland provisionally within the Irish Free State, without formal consultation or consent, albeit with its parliament and powers intact, and with the right of immediate secession (which could be exercised within a month of the formal establishment of the Irish Free State). The new entity's vulnerability was manifest. What Westminster could legislate in one year it could modify or repeal in the next. To maintain what they had, the Unionists would have to secede from the Free State, accept a boundary commission, *and* full contributions to Great Britain's treasury, which Lloyd George had made plain would imply a locally significant fiscal burden. It is too often forgotten that the Irish and British negotiators had thereby agreed on inducements to encourage Northern Ireland to accept the jurisdiction of the Free State. Craig communicated his anger immediately, rejected a united Ireland, declared that his government would give up none of its territory, and demanded the revision of the implied financial arrangements. To avoid the threat of a higher fiscal burden, Craig had earlier told Lloyd George that he and his colleagues would prefer two dominions on the island—a request that Lloyd George chose to reject rather than to test.[9]

This narration provides the legal parchment and high politics description of the two births of the new polity. But it had much bloodier beginnings on the ground, especially in the streets of Belfast. The most violent events were urban, though numerous skirmishes took place on the new border, and the IRA engaged in guerrilla action in the countryside—cutting communications and attempting to take police barracks. Killings, burnings, and forced displacement—now called ethnic or sectarian cleansing—took place in Belfast and its neighborhood. Catholics numbered most of the victims, both in proportion to their local numbers, and absolutely, and especially in 1920 and 1922, they were the primary subjects of targeted house-burnings by Specials. Tables 2.2.1, 2.2.2, and 2.2.3 show that different investigators agree that Catholics suffered higher casualties of dead and wounded in Belfast, where they were then a local minority of roughly one-quarter of the population. Protestants were killed and wounded in large numbers too, so the pattern was not simply of one-sided violence: Robert Lynch tabulates 812 Catholic and 394 Protestant civilians wounded throughout the new North.[10] Property and house-burnings, and forced displacement, took place in Lisburn, Dromore, and Banbridge, in Belfast's hinterland,

---

[8] Younger (1972: 202); see the full text in O'Leary and Maume (2004: 155–6).
[9] Lloyd George to Sir James Craig, November 14, 1921, in O'Leary and Maume (2004: 151–2).
[10] Lynch (2006: 227).

Table 2.2.1. Numbers killed by political violence, Belfast, 1920–1922

Year	Catholiccivilians	Protestantcivilians	Crown forces	Loyalists	Republicans
1920	31	34		5 not assigned	
1921	65	55	14		5
1922	170	90	18		3
Total	266	179	32		8

Notes: Murray's estimates are from his independent research in contemporary newspapers, and differ from those of Budge and O'Leary (1973), Kenna (1922) and Farrell (1980), but not by enormous magnitudes.

Source: adapted from Russell C. Murray (2006: 222 ff.).

Table 2.2.2. Agents responsible for killings (where known), Belfast, 1920–1922

Agents	1920	1921	1922
Loyalists (%)	14	38	56
Crown forces (%)	69	28	19
Republicans (%)	17	34	25
Loyalists and Crown forces/Republicans as a ratio	**4.2 to 1**	**1.9 to 1**	**3 to 1**

Notes: Tables 2.2.1. and 2.2.2 assume I have followed Murray's text correctly. Significant numbers of deaths are not possible to assign to any clear agency. In 1920 that was nearly one-fifth of those killed. Most killings by Crown forces in 1920 were by soldiers; in 1921–2 nearly all were by police.

Source: adapted from Russell C. Murray (2006: 222–3).

Table 2.2.3. Victims of violence, Northern Ireland, June 1920–June 1922

Victims	Belfast	County Tyrone	Derry City	County Armagh	County Londonderry	County Fermanagh	County Down	County Antrim	Total
Catholic civilians	258	21	16	12	7	6	6	5	331
Protestant civilians	159	7	6	9	4	4	7	0	196
Crown forces	35	7	6	13	5	8	5	1	82
IRA	12	4	2	8	2	5	2	0	35

Source: adapted from Lynch (2006: app.), who provides Kenna (1922) as his source, supplemented by the *Irish Times*, *Newsletter*, and the *Freeman's Journal* (1920–2)

almost entirely against Catholics. With spectacular special pleading the *Banbridge Chronicle* opined in 1920: "No violence has been directed against Roman Catholics as such. It is Sinn Féin that the people are determined to *cleanse* the town from. Surely all right thinking Roman Catholics will approve of this and give it their support."[11]

From 1919 onward the IRA's guerrilla strategy throughout Ireland targeted the Royal Irish Constabulary (RIC), which had become a primarily Catholic force at rank-and-file level outside Ulster, but it was balanced in its proportions of Catholics and Protestants within Ulster, especially among the regular ranks. The

---

[11] July 31, 1920, cited in Lawlor (2009: 76); emphasis added.

IRA targeted the RIC's barracks, to break police morale and surveillance capacities, and to seize armories;[12] it identified political police; it ambushed them; it organized their assassination; and it succeeded in generating mass resignations. In response, the British government reinforced the police with an armed gendarmerie, the "Black and Tans," recruited largely outside Ireland, and also supplied more vicious Auxiliaries, "Auxies," to back up the army. In the North, however, veterans from elsewhere were not required because there was a local oversupply of very different veterans, from the UVF. Recruited as special constables, they became the key instrument of what became a sectarian counterinsurgency. The balanced RIC would soon be replaced by a disproportionately Protestant RUC.

Ireland's experience of violence after 1918 was not unique. After the First World War, many demobilized soldiers with combat experience joined militias throughout Europe either for employment or through political motivation. Veterans were recruited by all parties. Sergeant Tom Barry, veteran of Mesopotamia, joined the IRA, organized its most famous ambush at Kilmichael, and became a commandant in the Irish Army. Ulsterman Colonel Gerald Bryce Ferguson Smyth was seconded to the RIC, where he implemented a new policy of reprisals, for which he was killed in Cork by the IRA. Lieutenant Wilfrid Spender, a Larne gun-runner and hero of the Somme, was appointed by Craig and Carson to reorganize the UVF—and became the first and long-serving secretary to the Northern Ireland cabinet. Between 1919 and 1921, 420 ex-servicemen were killed across the island, constituting nearly one in five of all deaths: 227 (54 percent) were serving policemen, 16 (4 percent) died for the IRA, and 177 (42 percent) were civilians when they died. Of the latter, the IRA killed 56 percent, Crown forces 26 percent, and the organizational identity of the rest of the killers is unknown.[13]

Initially the North was much quieter than the South during the war of independence. The IRA was much less powerful in Belfast than in Cork, and calculated that offensive action might endanger its most supportive constituency. The first significant violence in Ulster occurred in Derry, not long after the city had elected its first nationalist and Catholic mayor since 1689. In January 1920, supporters of Sinn Féin and the IPP used proportional representation to coordinate their voters and overturned the Unionists' previous majority on Londonderry Corporation. Rioting occurred in April after the British Dorset Regiment's soldiers fired on a nationalist crowd; and events escalated into mutual evictions of Protestants and Catholics from their homes, and shooting matches between republicans and the city's UVF veterans. British troops restored order after four Protestants and fifteen Catholics had been killed. An RIC Special Branch officer was killed, and the son of the leading figure in the loyalist Apprentice Boys. The latter's death prompted loyalist shipyard workers in Belfast to send Carson a telegram, asking him to mobilize the UVF in revenge.[14] Not all the UVF had been recruited into the British Army in the First World War; the rump had become a home defense force, awaiting the renewal of conflict over home rule. Spender took charge of them.

---

[12] On October 20, 1920, the UK Foreign Secretary reported to the House of Commons that 675 RIC barracks (vacated or occupied) had been destroyed (513) or damaged.

[13] O'Halpin (2012: 154). Responsibility for half of the twenty-six civilian ex-servicemen killed in Antrim can be attributed to Crown forces, mainly shot in sniping or during riots (O'Halpin 2012: 154).

[14] See accounts in Michael Farrell (1980, 1983).

On July 12 speakers spoke from Orange Order platforms to demand that the UVF be made into a police force, an idea that shocked the mainstream British press, but that the British cabinet resolved to implement in the autumn.[b]

By the summer of 1920 the IRA's attacks on police barracks had started to move north. Demobilized loyalist veterans were already embittered by stories of Catholics who had obtained "their" jobs and "their" (modest) prosperity during their absence. Afraid that the IRA would be successful, they had registered Sinn Féin's electoral triumphs in 1917–20 with foreboding. Spender used Orange Halls as recruitment centers, and distributed the UVF's pre-1914 weaponry. Loyalist newspapers consistently reported "outrages" in the South, which included the assassination of Colonel Smyth on July 17. Workers returned to their Belfast employments after their regular July holidays on the day of Smyth's funeral in nearby Banbridge. Loyalist activists, after public meetings, decided to expel all "disloyal" workers—that is, Catholics and "rotten Prods"—the name given to socialist Protestant workers. These expulsions were violent. Some Catholic workers had to swim for their lives from the shipyards while being pelted by "Belfast confetti." Loyalists in engineering factories and foundries adopted the same policy of violent exclusions—though they had fewer Catholics to expel. Approximately 10,000 men and 1,000 women were eventually evicted from their workplaces.[15] The July 21 attacks triggered inter-communal violence throughout the docks and the center of the city, leading to confrontations between physically well-armed mobs of Protestants and Catholics. Soldiers were used to restore order, lethally; by the weekend thirteen civilians had been killed by soldiers and one by police, and in all eighteen civilians were dead, ten Catholics, and eight Protestants.

In the workplace expulsions, loyalist workers were often encouraged by their upper class. Colonel Smyth's mother, for example, demanded the exclusion of republicans from her linen mills. In Banbridge, Dromore, and Lisburn, up to 1,000 Catholics were expelled from work in the Bann valley, and loyalty pledges were coercively extracted from those who remained. On July 24 loyalists mobs attacked and burned the Central Hall of the AOH in Lisburn, a Protestant majority town then distinctly separate from south Belfast. Catholic shops, pubs, and grocery stores were wrecked, and an attack took place on a convent. Much fiercer events in the same town ensued a month later when loyalists reacted to the IRA's assassination of police inspector Oswald Swanzy. Collins had ordered his death because he had been (almost certainly correctly) identified by a coroner's jury as one of the police who had organized the assassination of Cork's recently elected Mayor, Tomás Mac Curtain of Sinn Féin.[16] Swanzy was relocated north for his safety, but that did not save him. IRA specialists from Cork assassinated Swanzy— symbolically using Mac Curtain's personal handgun, but loyalists—correctly— assumed that local IRA men had had some role in his death.

Swanzy had recently influenced a Lisburn court to be lenient with those who pleaded guilty to the July burnings and lootings in the town, which ensured that loyalists thought well of him, but that same testimony had advertised his presence

---

[15] Bardon (1992: 191).

[16] Debate continues over whether Mac Curtain's killing was an unauthorized reprisal, made by local police after an RIC officer had been killed in Cork by the IRA a few hours earlier.

to republicans.[17] After Swanzy's assassination, loyalists carried out wholesale collective retaliation and punishment: Catholics were burned out of their bars, spirit groceries (liquor stores), shops, and houses, and over 1,000 of them fled Lisburn; most walked the seven miles of fields and roads to Belfast, where over the next ten days over thirty people died in riots; others went to Dundalk. An "Expelled Workers Relief Committee" was established. Across the Atlantic, the American Committee for Relief in Ireland (ACRI) and the Irish White Cross Society were founded to aid refugees and others.[18] Their reports from 1922 provide evidence of the disbursements paid out to what today are called IDPs—internally displaced persons.

British soldiers in the North were gradually replaced by the new RUC in 1921, but more substantively by the thoroughly Protestant Ulster Special Constabulary, who directly policed Catholic-majority areas. This became official policy from September 1920 but had been unofficial practice for months. Sir Hamar Greenwood, a dogmatic Canadian and apologist for reprisals,[19] and the chief secretary who had co-authorized the Black and Tans and the Auxies, was equally enthusiastic about setting up the Specials.[c] By midsummer 1922 there were 5,500 full-time and fully armed A Specials, based in barracks, backed by 19,000 uniformed, armed, and equipped B Specials, who resided at home but were on call, and 7,500 C1 Specials (and an uncertain number of other C Specials, who kept arms at home).[20] Under Article 4.3 of the Government of Ireland Act "the navy, the army, the airforce, the territorial force, or any other naval, military, or airforce" were reserved to the Crown, and expressly outside the powers of the Northern government, and under Article 9 police powers were not scheduled for transfer to Belfast until May 1923.[21] But the law embedding Northern Ireland's de facto constitution proved no obstacle to the London and Belfast governments. London financed and armed the Specials (the reconstructed UVF); and the Specials were run by Richard Dawson Bates at Belfast's new Ministry of Home Affairs. Craig did not wholly hide their partisan origins when he declared that "it is also from the ranks of the Loyal Orange Institution that our splendid "Specials" have come."[22]

The largest IRA operation in Fermanagh in February 1921 saw the burning of fifteen houses owned by B Specials (or their presumed supporters) in Roslea, and the death of one policeman and one special. This reprisal had been authorized by the IRA's GHQ to avenge the Specials' previous decision to consign much of the Catholic portion of the town to the flames.[23] There was no further local escalation, but the same year saw far more targeted assassinations of Catholics in Belfast, as opposed to reciprocal killings of both sides' adult males in riots and shoot-outs. Improvised bombings also began. The first to be used by rioting Protestants

[17] Lawlor (2009: 99–101).

[18] Working from police reports and press materials Lawlor (2009: 153) argues that the UVF orchestrated the violence in Lisburn, and used Swanzy's murder to implement a plan to drive Catholics from the town.

[19] His technique was formally to condemn reprisals but to explain that he understood why the police carried them out (MacLaren 2015: 189).

[20] Hezlet (1973: 88).

[21] <http://www.legislation.gov.uk/ukpga/1920/67/pdfs/ukpga_19200067_en.pdf>.

[22] Sir James Craig, addressing an Orange Order parade, July 12, 1922, *Belfast Newsletter*, July 13, 1922.

[23] Staunton (2001: 35).

killed a Catholic. Later four Protestants were killed in the bombing of a Shankill Road tram believed to be transporting shipyard workers. Six Catholic females were subsequently killed when a bomb was hurled amid girls who were skipping. Then five men of the Catholic McMahon family, and one of their lodgers, were executed in their home by policemen, probably led by one Inspector Nixon. Sniping and assassinations replaced riots as the primary causes of violent death in Belfast. Throughout 1920–2 "there was widespread 'ethnic cleansing,' especially of Catholics living within or next to Protestant areas. In the riots of August 1920 . . . about 400 Catholic families were forced out. On several occasions entire Catholic streets were burned out. Over the three years as many as 23,000 Catholics may have been driven out,"[24] together with "rotten Prods." The same urban historian estimates that between a fifth and a third of all male Catholic workers were expelled from Belfast's workplaces.[25] From the midsummer of 1920 the city was under an enforced curfew, which lasted until December 1924. The IRA responded by firebombing Protestant and loyalist businesses, and republicans organized a boycott of Belfast business throughout Ireland, demanding the reinstatement of all the expelled shipyard workers. Neither Sinn Féin nor the IRA condoned or carried out burnings of Protestant working-class civilians' homes in the North,[26] but there were IRA reprisals against houses owned by Specials, especially in border regions, and major "big house" burnings of (usually Protestant) landlords' residences, especially but not only in counties Antrim and Cork.[27]

In July 1920 Craig, and Winston Churchill, now Secretary of State for War, prevailed over the senior civil servant in Dublin, Sir John Anderson. The "arming of the Protestants," as Michael Farrell has described the commissioning of the Specials,[28] was intended not just to relieve the army and the RIC, or to oblige Carson's and Craig's requests. It would also, it was claimed by Craig, in unconscious echoes of the 1790s, bring discipline to the loyalist violence from below. All told during these crisis years of regime formation one in five Protestant males are estimated to have become full or part-time Specials. Together with the armed RUC, they were able effectively to repress IRA activity in the North, aided by repressive legislation—including the use of extensive internment without trial.

After pacification had been completed by the winter of 1922, one might have expected the Specials to have been disbanded. But they remained fully mobilized until December 1925, when it became clear that the boundary commission would produce no changes to the border. In the interval, the Specials had been used publicly and noisily to patrol the borders and any areas likely to come within the remit of the Commission, their strength advertising to the Commission that renewed civil war would flow from proposals to make major changes to the border. The Specials became so entrenched that Craig and Dawson Bates faced a mutiny when the time came to disband them after the security crisis had passed. A Specials, notably in Derry and Ballycastle, rejected their dissolution, arrested

---

[24] Russell C. Murray (2006: 224).   [25] Hepburn (2003: n. 54).
[26] Replying to his critics, historian Peter Hart (2005a) acknowledged that "Unionist organizations embraced or acquiesced in sectarianism in a way nationalist ones—to their credit—did not." Members of the AOH seem to have been less disciplined than the IRA.
[27] Donnelly (2012).   [28] Michael Farrell (1983).

their officers, seized their barracks, and demanded improved terms of dismissal, including a tax-free bounty. They were eventually faced down, though there seems to be no record that any were disciplined.[29] Craig decided to keep approximately 10,000 B Specials as a part-time gendarmerie. A subsequent apologia for the Specials, published in 1972 by Vice-Admiral Sir Arthur Hezlet, concludes: "It was sad that a force which had done so well should have ended like this ... Who are we in these days of redundancy pay, much higher employment and the welfare state, to blame them?" Hezlet maintained that the Specials had arrived "in the nick of time to reinforce the disintegrating RIC and to re-establish the rule of law throughout the Province ... In the campaign of 1921 and 1922, forty-nine of [the Specials] were killed and many more wounded ... Far from being 'the agents of imperialism' or the instruments of British power in Ireland, they were the bulwark of the vast majority of the people of the Province."[30] The Specials were certainly the footsoldiers of the new majority of Ulster Unionists, who embraced both the Union and the Empire. All that unquestionably made them imperialists, but to suggest that they re-established the rule of law, or had the support of the vast majority (that is, including Catholics), is risible. Three authors not known for their sympathies with Irish nationalism argue that Unionist leaders preferred unprofessional but loyal security forces because they judged that "Northern Ireland's viability required not 'good' government but its own government, with as much administrative discretion as possible."[31]

POGROMS AND DEADLY ETHNIC RIOTS

In the burnings of commercial premises and homes, Catholic families, especially in the Belfast urban region, were the primary victims of what contemporary nationalists called pogroms.[d] The Russian word originated as a variant on "devastation" or "storm,"[32] and was initially applied to assaults on unarmed Jewish civilians in Russian cities under the Czars, especially in the 1880s.[33] Analogizing from this experience led to the concept's application to any urban ethnic violence, especially of a reactionary and counterrevolutionary character—the victims of such violence did not need to be Jews. This is exactly how "pogrom" was used in nationalist accounts of what transpired in Belfast, Lisburn, and Banbridge between 1920 and 1922, notably in *Facts and Figures of the Belfast Pogrom*.[34] What had happened conformed to this usage.[35]

Another development of the concept emphasizes that pogroms are sponsored by, or occur with the connivance of, public officials, especially politicians, police, and intelligence agents. "When it can be proved that the police and state authorities

---

[29] Hezlet (1973: 116–18).

[30] Hezlet (1973: 118–19).   [31] Bew et al. (1996: 41).   [32] Bergmann (2003: 35).

[33] Debate continues over whether the Czarist government organized pogroms, or whether they came from below, and had a more spontaneous and anarchic character.

[34] Its author used a pseudonym, Kenna. He has been identified as a priest, Father John Hassan, and some suggest he was a member of Sinn Féin—e.g. Lawlor (2009: 184).

[35] See Kenna (1922); McDermott (2001); Lawlor (2009).

more broadly are directly implicated in a 'riot' in which one community provides the principal or sole victims, then, of course, one is confronted with a pogrom, in which the victims were targeted by the state itself or its agents."[36] In applying this definition to a particular case much hinges on the evidence required for "direct implication." At one extreme, there may be overt evidence of ministerial planning (though smoking documents are unlikely to be kept accessibly in the state archives), and, at another, no more than proof of the failure of watching police to halt assaults, or prevent the destruction and looting of the property of an out-group. At Northern Ireland's inception, there was plenty of police failure to protect the out-group, but so far, no smoking documentary evidence links Craig or Dawson Bates personally to assassinations, or directed expulsions—though reprisal burnings by the Specials were authorized. There is certainly evidence of incitement by prominent politicians, such as Carson, and Craig, and of retro-spective support for the pogromists after incitement had worked its effects;[37] uncontested evidence of police involvement in assassinations; of the Specials' enthusiasm in burnings and reprisals; of the failure of the army and the police to cooperate with judicial proceedings; and unquestionable cover-ups of murder by Specials, notably in the Cushendall killings of 1922.[38] In October 1920 Craig told a ceremony at the shipyards that he approved wholeheartedly of how loyalist workers had engineered the mass expulsions of Catholics in July.[39] In the same period there is also evidence of spontaneity, of non-planning, of loyalist crowds reacting immediately to actions by the IRA, such as the killing of prominent counterinsurgency officers (as in the fairly spontaneous reactions to the assassin-ations of Smyth and Swanzy). Sometimes responses occurred, however, after incitement by politicians, and after exaggerated press-reporting frenzies. These descriptions are not intended to minimize the fact that fear and panic were created by IRA actions, but these were mostly, though not exclusively, occurring else-where in Ireland, not in Belfast or East Ulster. The success of the Specials and the RUC in defeating the IRA in the North was accomplished outside the law, including emergency law, with official connivance. Despite inquiries, and some attempted oversight, London decided to leave coercive control in Craig's hands, and not to look too closely into pro-regime outrages. The killing of three civilians in the previously quiet village of Cushendall in 1922 is a telling case. They were the victims of reprisals by B Specials, undertaken immediately after the IRA's assas-sination of Sir Henry Wilson. The killings were covered up by Spender, Bates, and Craig, and eventually colluded in by Churchill.[40]

Donald Horowitz's *The Deadly Ethnic Riot* appropriately influences current thinking about this type of collective violence.[41,e] Two major theories of riotous behavior by crowds have prevailed historically, one emphasizing the collective

---

[36] Brass (1996: 2).

[37] On July 12 at Finaghy field Carson warned the British government: "if you ... are unable to protect us ... we tell you that we will take the matter into our own hands."

[38] Garson (2017).   [39] Boyd (2005: 181).

[40] Archival research conducted by Anna Garson of the University of Pennsylvania, under my supervision, confirms this summary as the most reasonable interpretation of the data. On the significance of Wilson's killing see Vol. 2, Ch. 3, p. 81, and n. 34.

[41] Horowitz (2001).

release of pent-up passions, and another suggesting that crowds may creatively behave as if they were rational super-persons. But both release and creation may be at work in particular riots.[42] Analysis of riots in *Social Psychology* focuses not just on groups, but on individuals within groups.[43] Each individual may decide whether to participate in violence by looking at payoffs that depend on what others do. They may have hostile impulses toward another group, but these are not released into action until the recognition that others share these impulses, and are going to act on them. When all believe that others are going to act within a hostile crowd, then all are likely to act together, in the belief that their joint violence is unlikely to be punished. Confidence in what others want—and will do—is created by communication, which emerges within the often-noted lull that intervenes between a precipitating incident and a violent crowd response. Such lulls happened in Belfast and surrounding suburban towns in 1920 and 1922. The low likelihood of punishment, for most of the perpetrators, is well attested—as seen in Devlin's complaints about the Specials in Lisburn expressed at the head of this chapter. The crowds' confidence that their members would not be punished is easy to explain. The RIC was collapsing, UVF members were the new source of order, and were well represented within the riotous crowds, and the new Specials.

Deadly ethnic riots are usually preceded by a history of group conflict: the longer and more intense the antagonism, then the more likely the violence. The first recorded lethal riot in Belfast had occurred in 1813, triggered by an Orange march. Subsequently, violent events occurred regularly at election time, or during and after Orange marches in the city, notably in 1832, 1835, and 1841. Major riots occurred in 1843, 1852, and even more ferocious events in 1857, 1864, 1872, and 1886.[f] In 1920, and contrary to the *Banbridge Chronicle*, violent loyalist crowds made little distinction between Catholics and Sinn Féin supporters, or between Catholics who had served in the First World War and those who operated in the IRA.[g] Rather, the crowds targeted Catholic institutions, commercial premises, and houses, in revenge for IRA actions elsewhere in Ulster or Ireland. They considered themselves wholly justified in such collective punishments. When a crowd possessed of such beliefs assesses that violence will not be too risky—that is, when local retaliation opportunities are limited, and the likelihood of arrest, trial, and punishment is low—that is when riots may begin. Deadly rioters attack where they have local superiority, and the advantage of surprise. They will rarely attack in the presence of police or soldiers protecting lives and property, *unless* they believe that the police or soldiers sympathize with them, and will not intervene or use force against them. The crowd's consensus dissolves if or when its members harm members of its own group. Horowitz offers many examples of the care with which rioters identify their targets, taking pains to separate houses and shops owned by their own group from those owned by the target group, and to destroy only the latter. Sometimes crowds halt their violence to conduct identity checks: an individual of uncertain identity is likely to be let go. These portraits of deadly ethnic riots fit very well with what happened to vulnerable Catholics in Lisburn, Banbridge, and Dromore, as vividly rereported from contemporary press, court, and police records in Pearse Lawlor's *The Burnings 1920*.

---

[42] McCauley (2001), reviewing Horowitz (2001).   [43] Brown (1986).

To prevent the recurrence of pogroms and deadly ethnic riots it is extremely difficult to revise, redirect, or "improve" the history of inter-group conflict, but no serious efforts were made in these directions by the new Unionist government, or its immediate successors. Instead the capital city of the new polity witnessed sufficient pogromist violence and deadly ethnic rioting to sow long-term bitterness. Loyalists believed they had taught Catholics a lesson, and had prevented what would otherwise have been an island-wide IRA victory; Catholics, by contrast, recalled that their political and religious meeting places had been attacked, and that these assaults were neither adequately halted, nor usually punished by the authorities—mild sentences were passed on the very few who were convicted. In "The Lisburn Mutiny," complained of by Devlin at the Westminster parliament,[44] special constables mutinied to release and reverse court verdicts on loyalists who had already pleaded guilty, and who had been sentenced for riotous behavior, including the looting of Catholic homes. Spender let the mutineers have their way. By comparison, Sinn Féin leaders quickly brought to an end a retaliatory pogrom from below in Catholic-majority Dundalk—though not until after major burnings and three deaths.

The riots, burnings, and killings that started in the summer of 1920 resumed after the truce of the summer of 1921 between republicans and Crown forces. No party to the conflict in the North—the Crown forces, the UVF/Specials, or the IRA—fully respected the truce. Indeed, the Northern Divisions of the IRA increased their recruitment: many new recruits made the mistaken assumption that the IRA had won,[45] and that the London negotiations would register the unionists' defeat, optimism that proved misplaced. Craig's government anticipated the worst—a British withdrawal and an assault by the Irish Free State—and got the bulk of its "retaliation" in first. There were two distinct patterns of violence in the North in 1920-2. One was triggered by IRA offensives, especially focused in areas near the border. This pattern of guerrilla warfare and counterinsurgency petered out after Collins's death. The second pattern, found in Belfast and its neighborhood, and to a lesser extent in Derry, was characterized by pogroms, deadly ethnic riots, inter-communal street fighting, sniping, and assassinations. David Fitzpatrick reports that official data from the six counties recorded the following homicide rates during the revolutionary years:

1919: 8. 1920:114. 1921: 147. 1922: 418. 1923: 13. 1924: 6.

The deaths coded as homicides included "non-political" killings, which normally were very low, and may have risen a little because of the opportunities created by the breakdown in public order, but the bulk were owed to guerrilla warfare and its repression, and to urban ethno-sectarian violence. The peak year of killing was evidently in 1922. A similar pattern of initially low violence, followed by a major outburst over three years, followed by a return to low violence—that is, an explosive ∩ (or inverted U) curve, may be found in data on disturbances to public order and outrages.[46] This pattern exhibited the re-establishment of British state

[44] Hansard, HC, 5th ser., vol. 133, cols 1504–6 (October 25, 1920).
[45] McDermott (2001).   [46] Fitzpatrick (1998: 251, nn. 2, 3).

power in the North under the new Belfast administration; it also showed the limits to the IRA-led rebellion, especially in East Ulster.

The violent events in Belfast and its vicinity had long-lasting effects. Crown and loyalist forces were in overt direct alliance at the formation of the polity, and only the most egregious and publicized of independent loyalist violent assaults on Catholics produced any disciplinary restraint on the part of the authorities. Catholics had unquestionably come off worst in the inter-communal killings, notably in 1922. In the North, the IRA was much less effective as a "defensive" body than the loyalists and Crown forces proved to be—either on the offensive or the defensive. Recollection of their vulnerability to burnings and expulsions helps explain why most Belfast Catholic males were reluctant to consider becoming republican revolutionaries until the late 1960s, when a generation matured without direct memories of the 1920s. Belfast loyalists' collective memories were different. They thought they had established Northern Ireland through self-help, without reliance on the uncertain support of British conservatives and liberals. Their own martial deeds, arms, police, specials, gangs, and militias had defeated the IRA in Belfast. Since pogroms and deadly ethnic riots had worked, they would be tried again, in 1935 and in 1969.

Over 700 people were detained without charges between 1922 and 1924. The immediate trigger for this policy of internment was the assassination of a Unionist MP William Twaddell in May 1922. He had been rumored to be one of the leaders of a loyalist death squad called the Ulster Imperial Guards. Craig's government had been planning large-scale detentions for some time, and a more proximate justification of internment was provided by an IRA offensive against Northern Ireland in the same month. Overwhelmingly, the police lifted Catholic males; the few interned Protestants were republicans. The police successfully targeted many middle-ranking and regular republicans, but also rounded up people with no involvement in the conflict. The conditions imposed on internees were harsh (they were often encaged), isolating, and demoralizing.[47] Many were held on the SS *Argenta* in Belfast harbor. On release, pro-treaty IRA internees (who had been the majority of those held) often moved South, while anti-treaty IRA internees often left Ireland. Many internees or their families lost their livelihoods, and were then subject to permanent surveillance. The organizers of this policy, unionist politicians, believed that internment had worked. There was truth in this estimation, but both unofficial and official violence had combined to pacify violence from Catholics in the AOH and the IRA.

ESTABLISHING THE COLD HOUSE

The common talk in academe and elsewhere of the establishment of the state of Northern Ireland is incorrect. Northern Ireland was not, and never has been, a state.[48] It was not officially styled a state, unlike its southern neighbor;

---

[47] A detailed study has been executed by one internee's granddaughter; it contains much of value, though it is unfortunately poorly copy-edited (Kleinrichert 2001). The case of Malachi McGuone, the father of my late uncle-in-law, a Sinn Féin court judge, farmer, and merchant, is discussed at pp. 274–5, 357.

[48] See *Terminology*, pp. xxix.

and it lacked, and did not seek, sovereignty in foreign affairs; its limited domestic powers were delegated, not constitutionally entrenched, and its limited fiscal autonomy was sharply circumscribed by dependence upon the British Treasury.[49] The Northern Ireland government ran devolved institutions within the British state. The frequent usage of the expression "the Northern Ireland state" shows, however, that unionists felt that they established something like a state.

Conditioned by centuries of settler insecurity, and national and religious intolerance, and reinforced by their experiences of the violence of 1919–22, few Unionist politicians subsequently made efforts to win legitimacy through seeking Catholic or nationalist support. Compliance was what was sought.[50] The new majority "securitized" its new minority, partly because both Unionist leaders and followers had the same fears. Irish nationalists contested the North's right to exist as a distinctive polity; British politicians regarded partition as temporary, or claimed to regard it as such; and the North's boundaries were expected to be redrawn to the advantage of the Irish Free State, a fear that persisted until the end of 1925. The new polity could not afford its "Imperial Contribution," and would soon have gone bankrupt—as the Dominion of Newfoundland did in the 1930s— had Craig not bargained for extensive British subsidies for local security, and unemployment insurance at British standards, using threats of resignation throughout the 1920s.[h] Northern Ireland's devolved status also left it politically vulnerable. It was now underrepresented at Westminster in proportion to its population, so its MPs were unlikely to be pivotal to government formation (especially as ten of the twelve invariably voted with the Conservatives). This unimportance cut both ways, however. After 1925 the major British parties kept an implicit pact to avoid Irish questions disrupting the imperial parliament. As long as Unionists kept their house in order, so much the better for the peace of Great Britain.

This recital describes the birth fears of unionists at Northern Ireland's formation. New fears developed after 1932. As the Irish Free State moved toward full sovereignty, Unionist politicians and press were outraged by what they saw as British appeasement of de Valera. In 1940 these fears would reach unprecedented depths, but the system of control was in place *before* these additional fears materialized to justify such a system. Over six years (1920–5) Unionists, through improvisation, had developed their constrained polity into a system of control, acquired de facto some components of Weber's definition of a state, a local monopoly over policing, significant lawmaking authority, and, eventually, stably demarcated boundaries.[51] They consolidated this control at their moment of peak security in 1929 when efforts might have been made to accommodate Northern Catholics. The grandiose Stormont parliament, completed in 1932,[52] proved that the "tyranny of the majority" was not just a figment of liberal imaginations. Amid formal liberal democratic institutions, constitutional, coercive, territorial, legal, electoral, economic, and cultural controls were progressively consolidated.

---

[49] Lawrence (1965).   [50] Richard Rose (1971).   [51] Weber (1977/1918).
[52] The Stormont parliament's buildings were not completed until 1932, but it is customary to refer to the entire period from 1920 as the Stormont era.

CONSTITUTIONAL CONTROL

For almost half a century the UUP enjoyed de facto domestic constitutional control, punctuated only by the uncertainty created by the boundary commission in 1924–5 and the fall of France in 1940. The new parliament had the power to make laws for the "peace, order and good government of Northern Ireland," a standard British legal formula in its dominions, even though Northern Ireland was not a dominion. It was unable to repeal or alter the Government of Ireland Act, or any act of the Westminster parliament passed after the Act had come into force. "Imperial matters," such as the Crown, currency, control of the armed forces, and the conduct of foreign policy were retained by London.

Northern Ireland's government consisted of the Crown, represented by the Lord-Lieutenant (replaced by a Governor in 1922), and a bicameral legislature, a fifty-two-member House of Commons, and a twenty-six-member Senate. Its cabinet would come from a Northern Privy Council. From 1920 all cabinets and prime ministers were drawn exclusively from the UUP, which won convincing parliamentary majorities in all the general elections held before the suspension of Stormont in March 1972. The lack of alternation in power is starkly demonstrated by the durability of local ministers. Just four prime ministers served between 1920 and 1969: Craig, later Lord Craigavon (1920–40); John Miller Andrews (1940–3); Basil Stanlake Brooke, later Lord Brookeborough (1943–63), and Terence O'Neill, later Lord O'Neill of the Maine (1963–9).[53] The cabinet was equally stable—death was the normal basis for changes in leadership. Under Craig's premiership, concluded by his death in office—after years of poor health in which he spent much of his time on cruises—there was no major change in cabinet personnel. Upon his last election victory, London's *Sunday Times* observed, seemingly without irony, that "Senor Mussolini and Ataturk are his only rivals in the post-war record of continuous office."[54] Craig would have observed that neither of these men had won their status through free elections, but the polity he ran certainly earned the Orange epithet. By 1968 all members of the cabinet were members of the Orange Order; and between 1921 and 1969, 138 of the 149 UUP MPs elected to the Belfast parliament were members of the Order when they became members.[55] The UUP ran an Orange executive and legislature, and Unionist ministers were able either actively to practice political discrimination, through framing appropriate legislation and sanctioning biased forms of administration, or to endorse discriminatory practices by not using their offices to prevent abuses in local-government councils or public bodies. They had no obvious incentives to make concessions to the minority, and every incentive to help their own supporters. The opposition, by contrast, had no prospect of forming the government, especially after 1929.

The nationalist minority, permanently deprived of government office and its benefits, had little stake in the Belfast House of Commons. Initially its leaders and rank-and-file had divided during the 1918 elections, and then over both partition

---

[53] Three are served by biographies by professional historians: Buckland (1980); Barton (1988); Mulholland (2013).
[54] Bardon (1992: 556).   [55] Aunger (1981: 12), citing Harbinson (1973).

and the treaty. In west Ulster strong hopes were held for the boundary commission among northern nationalists; many of those in East Ulster, who knew they would be excluded from sovereign Ireland under any feasible partition, often remained loyal to the diminished powerhouse of the IPP, Joseph Devlin, the former president of the AOH—even though the prospectus under which Devlin had agreed to the temporary exclusion of Ulster counties had disappeared.[56] He had thought that British surveillance of a home-rule settlement in Dublin and the presence of a large contingent of IPP MPs at Westminster would jointly provide protection for Belfast Catholics.[57]

The likelihood of splits among nationalists prepared to work within the new order was evident when Devlin took his seat in the Belfast parliament in 1925, along with Thomas McAllister, in order to represent Catholic educational interests. They did so under the express proviso that fellow nationalist MPs elected from areas likely to be affected by the boundary commission would not take their seats. Devlin's subsequent new nationalist "party," the National League of the North, emerged in 1928 from the UIL and pro-treaty Sinn Féin supporters, the most prominent and intelligent of whom was Cahir Healy. The League, however, represented intermittent protest, was never organized with the discipline of the party of Parnell, McCarthy, and Redmond, and ceased to function shortly after Devlin's death. The various labels under which Northern nationalists ran for office is proof of their disarray. The National League of the North of 1928–35 was succeeded by the Reunion of Ireland in 1936, the Irish Union Association (IUA) was formed the same year, and the National Council for Unity (NCU) in 1937. After 1945 this array of names would be succeeded by the Irish Anti-Partition League, and in the 1960s by National Unity and the National Democratic Party.[58]

Until 1965, nationalists, under whatever label, refused the role of official opposition, which would have meant fully recognizing the legitimacy of Northern Ireland. Moderates like Devlin were frustrated: "We have no place in the administration of the province whose laws we are supposed to accept, and do accept. I do not think the representations we make have the slightest possible effect."[59] Devlin's "underlying strategy" had been to seek to convert the Protestant working class to home rule through advocating social policies to which the Ulster Unionist leaders were opposed.[60] It foundered on the shoals of loyalism, Orangeism, and antipathy to Irish republicanism. Devlin withdrew from parliamentary politics in 1932, partly because of de Valera's victory in the South in that year, briefly returning in the autumn of 1933, before dying the following January. He had done so only after de Valera had privately indicated to him and Cahir Healy that Northern nationalists would have no access to Dáil Éireann.[i] Among the rationales given by de Valera was the fragmentation of Northern nationalists—to which his own conduct had significantly contributed.

---

[56] Good accounts of Northern nationalists' reaction to partition may be found in Phoenix (1994) and Hepburn (2008).

[57] See, *inter alia,* Lynn (1997); Staunton (2001: *passim*); Hepburn (2008); Norton (2014).

[58] See Phoenix (1994); Lynn (1997); Staunton (2001: *passim*).

[59] Statement made in the House of Commons in 1926, cited in Michael Farrell (1976: 149).

[60] Hepburn (2008: 278).

Republicans magnified the incoherence of the nationalist bloc by running abstentionist candidates against the National League in four constituencies for Stormont in 1933 and again in the Westminster elections of 1935. In 1938 the NCU refused to nominate candidates in the latest election to Stormont. T. J. Campbell, the lawyer and former *Irish News* editor, the person closest to being a successor to Devlin, stood and took his seat with his colleague Richard Byrne. Cahir Healey's UIA MPs also stood, but after taking the required oath they then withdrew from Stormont. "Disunited Nationalists" would have been the appropriate label for all these associations. All lacked nominal cohesion, centralized party executives, fee-paying and card-carrying memberships, and all gradually self-corroded through their failure to recruit young activists. Northern nationalists reflected an impotent politics of estrangement.

Their core problem was to find and agree a coherent strategy to terminate partition. Abstention, withdrawal from Westminster, and the establishing of an Irish parliament had worked after 1918 to free much of Ireland, but in conjunction with effective guerrilla warfare. After 1922 abstention in the North could have no effect on the UUP's robust grip on power, because it ran a majority-backed parliament and government. The abstention of Northern nationalists had no impact on either the Westminster or Belfast parliaments, which cared less that nationalists deemed these parliaments illegitimate. Would engagement with the new order work more productively? Would participation remedy what McAteer came to call the "secondary" repercussions of partition—namely, organized gerrymandering, exclusion, and discrimination? Was it better to let these scandals remain as public advertisements that Northern Ireland was unreformable, and to focus the local and international public on the necessity to terminate partition?

Those who attended Stormont experienced almost total impotence. The government rarely accepted substantive opposition amendments, and ministers could be studiously insulting. On Christmas Day 1943 an event occurred that could have showcased cultural coexistence. An Orange Hall at Portrush was used to celebrate a Catholic mass for US armed forces garrisoned in the North, pending their deployment into the continental European theater. When the hall's unusual usage was raised in Stormont, William Lowry, the Minister of Home Affairs, and the father of a future Lord Chief Justice, thought it amusing to declare that "preparations are being made for its fumigation." Though eventually obliged to apologize, Lowry initially claimed that he understood the hall to have been used by members of the AOH, a calculation that suggested it was in order to insult local Catholics, whereas being facetious toward American Catholics serving as allies (indeed as the saviors) of HMG was an intemperate *faux pas*. Quite apart from such regularly ungenerous discourse, which today can be read online for those who doubt it, Unionist backbenchers monopolized parliamentary committee chairmanships, unlike the norms in the Westminster mothership in which the opposition held some of these posts. Stormont functions therefore appeared confined to diverse ways of expressing unionist domination. The invariably divided opposition never numbered more than eighteen out of fifty-two members of the House of Commons.[61] Infamously, the sole legislative achievement of

---

[61] Arthur (1977 10).

nationalists over five decades was the passage of a Wild Birds Act. The uselessness of parliamentary participation periodically persuaded some nationalists that extraparliamentary activity, including violent republican revolution, was more likely to produce substantive change than lobbying or diplomatic engagement. In 1947, for example, one Ciaran McAnally wrote to the Nationalist MP Anthony Mulvey: "The lesson of the Anglo-Irish conflict is that England bows to force and the threat of force. She despises the Irish politician when he starts to play the diplomatic game."[62]

If the functioning of Stormont's House of Commons did little to convince nationalists or Catholics that ballots were efficacious, the Senate was no better as a vehicle to articulate grievances, aggregate interests, or temporarily restrain the passions of the Commons—and deliberative democracy was not the Senators' forte. If the two chambers of the Belfast legislature disagreed, the Governor was empowered to convoke a joint meeting. No such joint meeting was ever necessary.[63] Of the twenty-six senators, two were ex officio, the mayors of Belfast and Londonderry; the rest were elected by the Commons on a proportional basis. This procedure ensured that the elegantly housed Senate was a shrunken—and slightly more disproportional—replica of the Commons. Craig had deliberately negotiated a different design from that which materialized in Dublin. To avoid exact duplication of the party composition of the Commons, elections to the Senate were staggered. Eight-year terms were served, with one half of the body replaced every four years. The Senate in no sense guarded the nationalist minority, human rights, or the separation of religion and politics, but it did protect one national minority: a hypothetical future Unionist minority. That is because a nationalist majority in the Commons would not have been enough to ensure the passage of parliamentary consent for a united Ireland; instead another four years of similar voting patterns would have been required to produce a matching complexion in the Senate.

The protections within the Government of Ireland Act, originally mostly designed to protect southern unionists in a home-rule Ireland, proved ineffective in aiding Northern nationalists. The Act provided for proportional representation (PR), but Craig was quickly allowed to revert to the old electoral system in local government in 1922, and to do the same for elections to Stormont in measures that took effect in 1929. In principle, legislation and ministerial actions could be declared unlawful if they infringed the Act's provisions outlawing religious discrimination, or if they transgressed Westminster's reserved powers, but the courts proved neither effective guardians of rights nor careful regulators of the division of powers. Nationalists judged them unlikely to find in their favor because they were a unionist establishment—though UUP ministers did report formal legal advice to their colleagues that warned them against improper measures.[j] In sovereign Ireland, by comparison, the courts were confronted with challenges far more frequently: ninety-six cases were considered under the two Irish constitutions between 1919 and 1970, by comparison with six in Northern Ireland.[64]

---

[62] PRONI, Mulvey Papers, D. 1862/16.

[63] On the rare occasions when the Senate rejected bills from the Commons, the latter yielded (Calvert 1968: 156–7).

[64] Barrington (1972: 40).

The clauses of the Government of Ireland Act that outlawed discrimination were awkwardly worded. On some interpretations, they made public funding of Catholic education unlawful—as a form of religious discrimination. The fear that such an interpretation might be upheld inhibited Catholic clerics and lay leaders from bringing test cases. The clauses did not protect political opinion, and therefore did not prevent discrimination against nationalists or republicans. Perusal of the cabinet papers suggests that among themselves UUP ministers strategized against nationalists rather than Catholics. The Act did not prohibit discrimination in the private sector, or protect fundamental civil liberties in a bill of rights supporting freedom of speech and expression, of the press, of assembly, of association, of the right to trial by jury or freedom from arrest or to be free of surveillance without warrant. Minority national, cultural, or communal rights were left unprotected. No securities were expressly intended or read to apply to sub-parliamentary organs, such as local councils, frequently visible promoters of discriminatory practices. The minority, defined as Catholic or as nationalist, usually concluded that their complaints could not be judicially investigated, let alone redressed.[65]

Westminster and Whitehall could have supervised the Belfast government more closely. Had home rule applied throughout Ireland, they would probably have sought to supervise the Dublin parliament. The British government could veto Belfast legislation; legislate for Northern Ireland, even on devolved matters; and Westminster's legislative supremacy remained. But the desire that home rule should "work," particularly by keeping Irish quarrels out of Westminster and Whitehall, made Northern Ireland resemble a "quasi-dominion." The British veto was employed just once, and then temporarily, in July 1922. The offending bill, that which abolished PR for local government elections, was delayed for two months.[k] Craig's cabinet decided that it would resign unless the bill was ratified. Faced with this threat, the British government lifted its veto, and Churchill provided an undignified and less than frank explanation to Cosgrave, the Chairman of the Provisional Government of the Irish Free State: "I have come, though most unwillingly, to the conclusion that the Local Government (Northern Ireland) Bill could not be vetoed . . . After full discussion [among the British signatories to the treaty] we came to the unanimous conclusion that for us to veto a measure clearly within the powers delegated to the Parliament of Northern Ireland would form a dangerous precedent."[66]

The precedent of not exercising the veto proved more dangerous. The UUP was allowed to gerrymander local-government councils on the new border; the new minority was convinced at the outset that London was an ineffective court of appeal; and, fortified by its success, the UUP went on to extend the abolition of PR to Belfast parliamentary elections. The precedent established that London did not wish to oversee let alone manage Northern Ireland's internal politics. It "was not prepared to act either as a policeman for the constitution or as a guardian of minority rights."[67] Surveillance of both parts of Ireland during the

---

[65] Campaign for Social Justice (1989/1964).
[66] Churchill to Cosgrave, September 9, 1922, PRONI, Cab. 9B/40/1.
[67] Jackson (2003: 224).

implementation of the treaty gave way to complete inattention to the Belfast government, except when it seemed expensive or embarrassing. A convention developed, stemming from a Speaker's ruling in London in 1923, that questions could not be asked in Westminster on matters for which responsibility had been devolved to Belfast. Nationalists could therefore only exercise parliamentary voice about injustice or maladministration in a forum controlled by a Belfast government usually deaf to their complaints. London's absence of oversight reinforced control, and had numerous long-term repercussions. When loyalist attacks on the civil-rights movement began in 1967–8, London's Home Office had no full-time civil servant monitoring Northern Ireland. Institutionalized amnesia had become a norm that was not confined to politicians. After 1921, "few people . . . noticed that the United Kingdom had lost a greater percentage of its territory than Germany had."[68] Decolonization is felt less painfully than military defeat, and the citizens of Great Britain could have been forgiven for thinking that Lloyd George had resolved the Irish question.

POLICING CONTROL

The RUC was established in June 1922. From its inception, it had more than ordinary policing duties; its role included defending the Union; it was armed and it resembled a centralized gendarmerie, unlike the police forces in Great Britain, and unlike the new police service in the Irish Free State—the Civic Guards—also formed during a civil war. The Guards, however, had the decisive advantage of being legitimate in the eyes of most of the people they policed. Tellingly in the 1920s there were more than four times as many police officers per head in Northern Ireland than there were in England and Wales, or Scotland.[69] This was not because there was more ordinary crime.

Initially, the RUC was not nakedly sectarian. Its predecessor had recruited among both Catholics and Protestants, and it is not immediately clear from the historical record that the new force was deliberately intended to be biased in its recruitment.[70] The Craig–Collins pacts of 1922 had envisaged a mixed police force, especially in Belfast, and a committee to organize the new force recommended that one-third of the recruits be Catholics, drawn in part from the ranks of the disbanded RIC. This pact may have promised a good start, but that was all it was, a promise. Ronald Weitzer has argued that the one-third quota was designed to put a limit on the number of experienced and suitable Catholics eligible for recruitment, given that well over half of the RIC's members had been Catholics.[71] Proportionality certainly never materialized. Catholic representation in the RUC

---

[68] Davies (1999: 906).

[69] Weitzer (1995: 34). The ratios were 1:160 in Northern Ireland; 1:669 in England and Wales, and 1:751 in Scotland.

[70] Archival research shows, however, that the first committee set up under Dawson Bates for an integrated and professional force, free of Specials, had its positions overturned by UUP backbenchers and Bates (Alec Ward 2017).

[71] Weitzer (1990, 1995).

peaked at 23 percent in 1923, fell to 17 percent by 1927, and dwindled to around 10 percent by the late 1960s.[72]

The name of the new force was hardly neutral, though it reflected continuity with the Royal Irish Constabulary, which had won its royal designation in defeating Fenianism. The claim to all of "Ulster" was resented by Northern nationalists, because three counties of the historic province were in the Free State. The new force was expressly royalist, policed part of historic Ulster, and was not a traditional British constabulary, and thereby hardly likely to win the affection or respect of Northern nationalists. The dwindling number of Catholic recruits (sometimes from the South) were concentrated in rural areas where the local majority was Catholic. Elsewhere Northern Catholics did not attempt to join the RUC mostly because they did not regard it as legitimate, and because they faced potential ostracism or worse—this was manifestly true for republicans, but also for many constitutional nationalists. When Catholics did join, the atmosphere was rarely inclusive. Institutional affiliations between police units and Orange lodges confirmed perceptions of the RUC as loyalists with guns. As early as August 1922 the Minister of Home Affairs permitted RUC members to join the Orange Order. The Sir Robert Peel Loyal Orange Lodge was created, displaying a historical sense of humor.[73] Low Catholic representation, overt empathy for Orangeism, cooperation with the Specials, the presence of ex-UVF and ex-Specials in the formation of the force, all reinforced the impression that the RUC was, as a group of academics later described them, "the armed wing of unionism."[74]

The RUC contravened the liberal democratic norm that the police should exercise an arm's-length relationship with the executive. Police should apply the law, and determine the allocation of their resources to do so, whereas politicians should make the law and hold police to account for their management regarding very general policy objectives. This principle exists to prevent the police from being employed to target the opposition to the government, and to prevent politicians deciding which laws get applied and neglected. The RUC's senior officers were quickly subordinated to the Belfast government. The RUC was closely supervised by the Ministry of Home Affairs, whose top officials have been described as "strident defenders of Protestant interests and whose policies with regard to law and order were sometimes purely political and biased against Catholics."[75] The lack of autonomy in the operational conduct of police business was condemned in a National Council for Civil Liberties report published in 1936 after major riots in Belfast the previous year. It demonstrated police partiality toward Orange mobs, but had no impact. Thirty-three years later, when Harold Wilson's Labour government intervened in the management of local security, British politicians described themselves as "stunned" by the lack of police independence from the governing political party, and not just from the governing party, but from the old landed class. Roland Moyle, parliamentary private secretary to James Callaghan in 1969–70, recalled: "The way the old Home Affairs

---

[72] Michael Farrell (1983: 267).
[73] *Belfast Telegraph*, April 13, 1923, first cited in Frank Gallagher (1957: 178).
[74] Brewer et al. (1988: 50).   [75] Weitzer (1995: 32).

department in Northern Ireland ran the police, my God, I mean the police were the creatures of the mini-aristocracy."[76, I]

Moderate nationalists and most Catholics initially distinguished between the RUC and the Specials—the latter being exclusively Protestant, and notoriously partisan—but the distinction became hard to maintain because half the RUC were recruited from ex-Specials in 1923, and one-third as late as 1951.[77] When Northern Ireland was quiescent—that is, when the IRA was not engaged in attempted insurrection, and when the RUC was confined to ordinary policing— relations with the Catholic community could be civil—because ordinary crime was very low. It was political policing, and police partiality during parades, or during riots, which particularly irked Catholics' sense of injustice. After the Flags and Emblems Act in 1951, trouble, which sometimes escalated into riots, would occur whenever the police were directed to remove the Irish tricolor from public places. The first major riot instigated by Ian Paisley occurred in West Belfast during the 1964 Westminster elections. The offices of "the Republican Party" in Divis Street were broken into by fifty RUC policemen, using crowbars and pickaxes, and an Irish tricolor was seized. Paisley had assembled a crowd to protest at the flag being flown. The police initially deemed Paisley the trouble- maker, but by choosing to uphold the law in this manner they triggered riotous disorder. It would be the police's conspicuous but unselfconscious partiality in front of the world's television cameras that triggered the undoing of the UUP's control, but that would not be until the late 1960s.

TERRITORIAL CONTROL: NOT AN INCH

Nine-, four-, five-, and six-county "Ulsters" had been proposed for exclusion from home rule before 1920, but the decision on six counties was resolved within the Ulster Unionist Council—they sought those districts they could control, and successfully lobbied the coalition government to change the Government of Ireland Bill's definition of Northern Ireland. When accused of betrayal by the unionists of Donegal, Cavan, and Monaghan, they cited the "present calamity" clause in the Ulster Covenant.[78] But the treaty upset this settlement through its provisions for a binding boundary commission if Northern Ireland refused to remain within the Irish Free State.

The UUP leadership feared deeply for the integrity of its fledgling regime, irrationally so if the verdicts of several historians are lightly accepted.[m] Such appraisals, however, neglect unionist strategy and tactics—and good luck—in sabotaging this binding provision of the treaty. Even A. T. Q. Stewart, usually keen to emphasize the intelligence of his compatriots, skated over the skill of unionist political sabotage when he suggested: "Because of the troubles [the violence in the North] and the civil war [in the South] the commission was not able to begin its work until the end of 1924. By that time neither the Free State nor

---

[76] Interview with author, London, January 3, 1991.   [77] Weitzer (1995 39).
[78] See Vol. 1, box.1.5.1, p. 262; see also Buckland (1973: 412–16).

Ulster was prepared to cede an inch of territory to the other."[79] There had been no serious hint before 1924 that the Free State might face any significant loss of territory and it was Craig who had immediately rejected the cession of an inch of his new space. His ministers never recognized the treaty as binding on Northern Ireland—an extraordinary and formally disloyal stand, a perfect instance of settler defiance of the metropolitan will. This rejection did not inhibit Craig's ministers from exercising the secession clause within the treaty, or from later berating de Valera's government for breaking the treaty, facts omitted in partisan histories, which prefer to emphasize the fact of violent and lawless tactics adopted by Collins toward the North (which included collaborating with and laundering weapons to the anti-treaty IRA).

The truth, however, is that both new governments initially failed to comply with the letter or the spirit of the treaty regarding their mutual obligations toward the prospective commission. The UUP cabinet not only rejected the commission but subsequently refused to appoint a Commissioner. Only after legal advice was taken with the Privy Council—whose standing was not recognized by the Free State—did the London government legislate to amend the treaty, enabling the British government to propose a commissioner from Northern Ireland. Collins's memorandum of the meeting he had with Lloyd George, on the morning the treaty was signed, had indicated "we would save Tyrone and Fermanagh, parts of Derry, Armagh and Down," and that Lloyd George agreed that this might be put to Craig.[80] Collins was known to believe, with his colleagues, that a much-reduced Northern Ireland would not be economically viable, a belief encouraged by Lloyd George. It was certainly wrong to believe that a much smaller Northern Ireland would be unviable just because it was smaller: Luxembourg, smaller than county Antrim, had just been recognized at the Versailles peace conference, and so had "free cities." But it was *not* false to believe that Northern Ireland would be rendered unviable under the fiscal provisions of the 1920 Act in conjunction with territorial shrinkage through the commission. Unionists certainly feared for the viability of their new entity. Even though controlling a smaller minority might have significantly improved their internal security, they sought to keep what they had—partly in the conviction that a smaller Northern Ireland would be more vulnerable to subsequent (external) republican attacks. When they debated the treaty, Collins, his fellow negotiators, and the members of Dáil Éireann, including de Valera, never considered that the wording of its twelfth article allowed a minimalist interpretation regarding border revisions on economic and geographic grounds; that it did not give a wholly unambiguous priority to the inhabitants' wishes; and that it did not require that the Commission follow those wishes "as closely as possible." They were unfazed that the Commission's composition allowed for the possibility that the British and the Northern Irish nominees could potentially outvote or block the Free State's commissioner's proposals.

Were the Irish signatories and the deputies to Dáil Éireann[81] therefore fools, or closet partitionists (as revisionist historiography tends to suggest)? Legal texts

---

[79] Stewart (1986: 171).   [80] Pakenham (1967: 220–9).

[81] A deputy is a *Teachta Dála* in Irish, abbreviated as TD in English, with TDs as the plural; the plural in Irish is Teachtaí Dála.

must be read in context, and not just parsed by grammarians. The British negotiators, led by Lloyd George in full consultation with his coalition cabinet colleagues, had accepted the unfairness of the existing partition line, and fast-paced implementation of the treaty was expected (not the Irish civil war). Nothing in the correspondence between the Irish negotiators and the Irish cabinet or in the official British cabinet record indicates that the Commission would significantly add and not just subtract people and land from Northern Ireland. It was tacitly agreed that the provisions envisaged a reduction of Northern Ireland: the scope was for the Commission to decide. Were Ireland's plenipotentiaries nevertheless incompetent, and poorly legally advised? They could have secured better drafting in Article 12, should not have assumed fast-paced implementation, and were overconfident that Lloyd George (or his successors) would deliver on commitments not expressly in the treaty. The wishes of the inhabitants, on the most reasonable construction, were to be primary, subject to other constraints—to avoid enclaves, for example.[n] The Irish negotiators should, however, have specified the unit(s) in which decisions would be made or received written assurances on the matter. The British negotiators would have found it hard to oppose plebiscites based on specified smaller units—for example, wards, poor-law districts, parishes, local-government districts, parliamentary constituencies, counties, or commission determinations based on such units with reference to the 1911 census.

The competence and the confidence of the Irish plenipotentiaries in their interpretation of Article 12 was enhanced by the Unionist reaction to this clause and the entire treaty. Carson declared in the Lords that he had been a fool, a puppet in the political game to get the Conservative party into power, and focused his abusive ire on the treaty's financial provisions.[o] In January 1922, in a direct meeting between Craig and Collins, as heads of the respective new entities, Collins showed Craig a map of the areas he believed would be transferred to the IFS. Craig protested that Lloyd George had deceived him.[82] It is unlikely that Craig was playing charades. In the first of what proved to be two Craig–Collins "pacts"—they were hardly binding legal agreements—Collins proposed, and Craig accepted, the idea of cutting out the middleman provided the pact was implemented.[83] The two leaders would mutually agree the future boundaries. Craig would hardly have made this agreement had he expected to do better with a London government or a commission. Collins had made concessions—promising to end the Belfast boycott—and so, apparently, had Craig—promising to try to help reinstate the expelled workers whose fate had triggered the boycott. Craig's reasons for making this pact were obvious—it suggested that Collins was willing to recognize Northern Ireland; Craig and his cabinet would not be at the mercy of a British–Irish Free State coalition in the commission; and what was tantamount to a revision of the treaty might enable Craig to obtain further amendments—especially regarding its financial provisions.

What, by contrast, were Collins's reasons? The provisions in the first pact, which would assist Northern nationalists, were examples of the Dublin government acting as a guardian of their interests, but what of the new proposals to

---

[82] Morgan (1990: 225).   [83] Hopkinson (1990).

resolve the boundaries? Perhaps Collins had realized that the Commission's determination would be decided by its British-appointed chairman, and therefore sought to ensure that the negotiations would be with just one partner, one that he may have believed he could more easily pressure. "Timing" mattered decisively. The Irish side had ratified the treaty in the belief that the British would ratify it in parallel, and fast, recognizing their dominion authority. Instead, the British insisted on "approving" the treaty first before ratifying it later—after the making of the constitution of the Irish Free State, and after fresh elections in the South.[84] The Dublin Provisional Government thereby lost a key negotiating advantage. They had hoped that the costs of the treaty's terms would persuade unionists to stay within the Free State, and that unionists would not prevaricate in the hope of having a more sympathetic—that is, exclusively Tory—government, in London. But the British position on treaty ratification—not anticipated by the Irish side—postponed Northern Ireland's decision on whether to stay within the Free State, and the setting-up of the Commission. Making a pact to resolve the boundary among Irish governments may have seemed like a good idea—at the time. The subsequent death of Collins, the most hawkish of the Irish Free State's leaders on the North, as well as the costs of the civil war, weakened the bargaining power of the Dublin government, a problem it exacerbated by appointing Eoin McNeill as the Free State's Commissioner—as in 1916 he would prove to be more scrupulous than effective, whereas the commissioner appointed for Northern Ireland by the British government proved a wholly unscrupulous and effective leaker—to Craig.

Craig's cabinet certainly acted as if it feared a Commission would conform to Collins's expectations, and prepared accordingly. Refusing to be bound by the Commission bought them time. Knowing the new border was most suspect in South Down, South Armagh, Fermanagh, and Tyrone, and in Derry city, they responded with electoral engineering. Most local councils situated on the new border had nationalist majorities, and the county councils of Fermanagh and Tyrone had declared their allegiance to Dáil Éireann. Craig's cabinet not only changed the election system for local government but gerrymandered the relevant jurisdictions, to reduce radically the local councils held by nationalists (twenty-five out of nearly eighty in 1920). They executed these tasks in sequence. They abolished PR (STV) in 1922, replacing it with conventional winner-takes-all.[85] A new law also required councilors to take an oath of allegiance to the Crown, making it impossible for overt republicans to take or stay in office. The local elections scheduled for 1923 were postponed, and the wonderfully surnamed Sir John Leech appointed to head a one-person commission to reorganize electoral districts. The changed electoral system and "Leeching" had their consequences magnified by nationalists' and republicans' decisions to engage in electoral boycotts. After the 1924 local elections, nationalists held just two councils.[P] When the Commission was eventually seated, a false impression of unionist electoral dominance prevailed throughout the new entity.

---

[84] For the technicalities and the key role played by Lionel Curtis in frustrating the IFS's ambitions, see McColgan (1977).

[85] For a review of electoral systems and their repercussions for minorities, see Brendan O'Leary (2010).

LAW WITHOUT BLIND JUSTICE

The provisional UUP government had moved quickly to counter the threat of republican, nationalist, or Catholic insurrection through forming and arming the Specials. Formally installed as the government, the UUP passed the Civil Authorities (Special Powers) Act of 1922; it was renewed annually until 1928, renewed for five years until 1933, and then made permanent. It was at the time one of the most draconian pieces of legislation passed within a liberal democratic regime. The Special Powers Act, and subsequent regulations developed under it, provided for extraordinary measures. The government had the right to intern people without trial, which it did between 1922 and 1925, between 1938 and 1946, and between 1956 and 1961; to arrest people without warrant; to issue curfews; and to prohibit inquests—which could prevent the investigation of illegal killings by the security forces. The latter were authorized to compel people to answer questions on pain of being guilty of an offense. These powers were used to repress republican rather than loyalist violence, which "rarely elicited any response."[86] The continuation of the Special Powers Act in 1928, and the decision to make it permanent in 1933, was not justified by any current campaign of republican violence. Rather the UUP chose to ensure that Northern Ireland would be governed, like Ireland before 1914, under a permanent panoply of coercive instruments.

Supervising and interpreting the administration of justice was an overwhelmingly Protestant judiciary, integrated into the UUP, and sometimes into the Orange Order, arrangements that reduced the prospects that the law might impartially protect civil liberties. The first Chief Justice of Northern Ireland was a Catholic—an upper-class royalist who was no one's definition of a republican[87]—but after his death in 1925 no Catholic was appointed to the Supreme Court until 1949, when Justice Shiel joined the bench.[88] As late as 1969 Catholics held six senior judicial appointments, and Catholic judges and barristers had to take archaic oaths of loyalty, containing all the trappings of tradition and undemocratic fealty associated with the British (and Protestant) Crown (see Table 2.2.4). Juries were often less than impartial because they were

Table 2.2.4. Senior judicial offices, Northern Ireland, 1969

Status	Protestant	Catholic	Total
High court judges	6	1	7
County court judges	4	1	5
Resident magistrates	9	3	12
Crown solicitors	8	0	8
Under sheriffs	6	0	6
Clerks of the peace	6	0	6
Total(s)	39	5	44

Source: Campaign for Social Justice (1969).

[86] Hogan and Walker (1989: 14).

[87] Sir Denis Stanislaus Henry, 1st Baronet, KBE PC (Ire), QC (1864–1925), had stood as a unionist candidate for parliament in a by-election in 1907, and won a seat in 1916.

[88] Rafferty (1994: 226, n. 13).

often not allowed to be: the Crown's authorities routinely challenged Catholic jurors when Catholics were on trial. After all, they were disloyal.[89]

ELECTIONS AS CENSUSES OF THE LOYAL

Winner-takes-all, combined with gerrymandering, remained constant features of local government for fifty years, especially in councils west of the River Bann, where there were fewer Protestants. Though unionists represented at most two-thirds of the population by the late 1920s, they controlled 85 percent of all local authorities.[90] Their domination was reinforced by the restriction of the local franchise to ratepayers and their spouses—that is, to local-government taxpayers— and by the retention of "company votes," which gave directors up to six votes, depending upon the valuation of their company's liability for local taxation. Local-government boundaries were required by a nineteenth-century UK law to be drawn with regard to "ratable value," which meant that wards with relatively prosperous but small populations could have the same number of councilors as wards with poorer but larger populations. This legal framework enabled unionists to win "majority" control where there were demographic nationalist majorities— for example, in Omagh, Derry, Armagh, and Fermanagh. Unionists took micro-territorial control deeply seriously, especially on the border, and in west Ulster, segregating Catholics into public housing in "their" wards.

At the opening of the twentieth century, universal suffrage did not apply in local government anywhere in the UK, but when Clement Attlee's Labour government was elected in 1945 on a manifesto commitment to reform the franchise in Great Britain, the UUP determined to resist this example of best-British practice. Retaining the old class-biased voting model adversely affected poorer Protestants as well as Catholics, but the UUP calculated that the old franchise was to its benefit, and the party's judgment was not likely to have been badly wrong on such a grave matter. In its Representation of the People Act (1946) the Stormont parliament legislated to make the local-government franchise even more restrictive: the franchise was removed from lodgers who were not ratepayers. The UUP's Chief Whip, Major Curran, declared that the entire measure was necessary to prevent "Nationalists getting control of the three border counties and Derry City," adding that "the best way to prevent the overthrow of the government by people who had no stake in the country and had not the welfare of the people of Ulster at heart was to *disenfranchise* them."[91] The record of these proceedings was incompetently edited in an effort to confine this truth-telling into oblivion: Hansard records opposition outrage at a statement not found in the printed columns.[q]

The decision to keep a class-biased franchise, which excluded roughly a quarter of a million voters, had the dual advantage of disproportionally disadvantaging disloyal Catholics more than loyal Protestants—as long as the former were poorer,

---

[89] Ultach (1943).
[90] Frank Gallagher (1957: 225–6); Buckland (1981: 60). Frank Gallagher is often dismissed as a propagandist today, but his electoral data are wholly accurate.
[91] *Northern Whig*, January 11, 1946, cited in Michael Farrell (1976: 85–6); emphasis added.

on average—and of excluding the Protestants most likely to consider voting for a labor candidate. From 1923 onward labor candidates averaged less than 8 percent of seats won (including all "others" within their seat totals), though they had a high of 13 percent in 1946; nationalists, by contrast, fell back from holding 17 percent of all seats in 1920 to 13 percent in 1923, the figure that they averaged until 1967, with a high of 19 percent in 1967 and lows of 7 percent in 1925 and 1927. In the early 1960s, Brian Faulkner, then the local Home Secretary, defended the property-based franchise and the additional vote among graduates of Queen's University Belfast. As David Bleakley of the NILP observed: "Neither the Minister nor his party considered it incongruous that 80,000 people in Belfast should be denied a local government vote while 12,091 graduates" elected four of Stormont's fifty-two MPs.[92] Later, however, the UUP's party interest in retaining the restricted franchise became a key normative weakness in the public relations of the regime. The slogan of the Northern Ireland civil-rights movement of the late 1960s, "one man, one vote," coming immediately after the successes of the US civil-rights campaigns, proved powerfully persuasive to British and international audiences. The campaigners were aided by the fact that outsiders often assumed that the property-based franchise applied to all elections in Northern Ireland. The archives reveal that the O'Neill cabinet accepted that the restricted property-based franchise was difficult to justify, but was completely preoccupied with the prediction that expanding the electorate was estimated to benefit Nationalists more than twice as much as Unionists.[93]

The most spectacular example of the joint impact of winner-takes-all, gerrymandering, and the restricted franchise in local government was found in Londonderry Corporation. Here a UUP "majority" of councilors of three to two was created by concentrating the Catholic (and therefore the anti-UUP) majority into the South ward, and creating two smaller wards guaranteed to produce winning majorities of UUP councilors (see Table 2.2.5). Roughly two and a half times as many non-Unionist votes were required to elect a non-Unionist councilor compared with Unionist votes required to elect a Unionist. Edward Warnock, a former Attorney General to the UUP government, wrote to Prime Minister Terence O'Neill in 1968: "I was consulted by Sir James Craig, Dawson Bates and R. D. Magee at the time it was done. Craig thought that the fate of our constitution was on a knife-edge . . . and that . . . it was defensible on the basis that the safety of the State was the supreme law," and claimed it "was most clearly understood that the arrangement was to be a temporary measure—five years was mentioned."

In Belfast, the UUP's starting position at the formation of Northern Ireland was much stronger than in Derry. In 1920 under PR (STV) it had taken thirty-seven of the city's council seats, a clear majority of 62 percent. But the elimination of PR (STV) in 1923 dramatically increased UUP dominance (see Table 2.2.6). Unionists' share of overall seats held in the city went up to 83 percent, and thereafter averaged 79 percent in all the city elections until 1967, with a high of 87 percent in 1937, and a low of 66 percent in 1924. The elimination of PR adversely affected

---

[92] Bleakley (1974: 53).

[93] PRONI, CAB/4/1410/24, October 24, 1968, and PRONI, CAB 4/1411/2, first observed by Harris (2003: 226).

Table 2.2.5. The art of the gerrymander: Wards and local-government election results, Londonderry Corporation, 1967

Ward	Non-Unionists		Unionists	
	Votes	Councilors	Votes	Councilors
South	10,047	8	1,138	0
North	2,530	0	3,946	8
Waterside	1,852	0	3,697	4
Total	14,429	8	8,781	12
votes/councilors	1,804:1		732:1	

Notes: Votes required to elect a Unionist councilor = 732, and to elect a non-Unionist = 1804. The franchise was restricted to ratepayers, which disproportionately disenfranchised non-Unionists.

Source: Cameron (1969: para. 134).

Table 2.2.6. Council seats won by local parties in Belfast, showing the impact of the abolition of PR (STV), 1920, 1923, and 1923–1967

Party	1920			1923			1923–67
	S%	S	U	S%	S	U	S% (average)
Unionists	62	37	0	83	50	23	79.0
Labor	22	13	0	3	2	0	7.8
Nationalists	17	10	0	13	8	0	13.2

Notes: S% = percentage of total seats; S = total seats; U = uncontested seats won. Budge and O'Leary aggregate all kinds of unionist, nationalist, and labor candidates into three categories.

Source: calculated from Budge and O'Leary (1973: 186–7, table 6.7).

Labour candidates most of all—their representation fell to 3 percent of all seats won in 1923; they had won 22 percent in 1920. Thereafter their candidates averaged less than 8 percent of seats won (all "others" have been included within their seat totals), with a high of 13 percent in 1946. Nationalists fell back from 17 percent of all seats in 1920 to 13 percent in 1923, which is what they averaged over the entire period until 1967, with a high of 19 percent in 1967 and lows of 7 percent in 1925 and 1927.

The abolition of PR (STV) for the Belfast parliament was defended in the orthodox nostrums of the Westminster model: PR was not British or democratic, prevented strong government, and contributed to indecisiveness and inefficiencies by enhancing the prospect of "hung parliaments." Craig maintained that it was costly, caused confusion, and created constituencies that were too large and "under-serviced."[94] He took astute care to cite the impatience with PR expressed by Kevin O'Higgins and Desmond FitzGerald within the governing party in the Irish Free State, and by Ramsay MacDonald on behalf of Labour in Great Britain. The arguments were nevertheless threadbare, and do not withstand retrospective

[94] Mansergh (1936: 135).

scrutiny. The alleged problem of overlarge constituencies could have been resolved by reducing their size, as the Free State did in 1934.[95] Less than 2 percent of the votes cast in the election of 1925 were invalid, and subsequent elections in both parts of Ireland confirm that familiarity with PR (STV) increases voter competence and sophistication. While the abolition of PR in local-government elections had been driven by Craig's cabinet's fears of the boundary commission, no such rationale justified the abolition of PR(STV) for Belfast's parliamentary elections. The deed was done at the moment of the regime's peak security since its formation. What mattered were both the UUP's party interests, and its determination to retain control through ensuring that a unified pan-Protestant bloc would be ranged against the nationalist adversary.

In 1928 Unionists legislated that no one could be registered to vote in a Stormont or a local-council election unless born in Northern Ireland, or resident there for three years—extended to seven in 1962. Here the UUP took aim at immigrants from the Irish Free State, who were eligible for the Westminster franchise after three months' residence.[96] When university constituencies were abolished for Westminster's House of Commons in 1948, this vestige of class privilege was retained for the Stormont Commons until 1968. The graduates of the Queen's University of Belfast returned four members. In 1929, with Craig's consent, Queen's had kept PR (STV) to elect these members *because* that was the system used in other British universities. The UUP plainly enjoyed the luxury of deciding when British practices were convenient.

The change to winner-takes-all for Stormont elections in 1929 cemented the hegemony of the UUP. There has been a debate on whether the purpose of this change was to weaken organized labor, which threatened unionist solidarity, or to reduce fragmentation within the unionist camp, or to weaken the position of nationalists.[97] Since abolition of PR achieved all these functions, resolving the debate is not crucial. The immediate impact of the change is assessed in Box 2.2.1 using the standard protocols in political science. Summing up the case against, Joseph Devlin warned:

> The hardest task of some of us is to justify our existence here at all. (Hon. Members: Hear, hear.) I am sometimes told by the Opposition Members that, after all, what have we here [is] only the free play of party interests. The Government in power to-day and the Opposition in power to-morrow. That would exist in a normal community under natural conditions. But unless we are fools everybody knows that in the future, and for a long time in the future, it is difficult for us to believe that we will be able or strong enough to turn out this Government. One would think, with a knowledge of their security in office, they would from pure self-interest if nothing else try to conciliate minorities, win their friendship, seek their co-operation, and be glad to have their advice when advice was legitimate. Instead . . . one would imagine that we were creatures who were only allowed to stand on the mat outside and [be] tolerated . . . you ought to rejoice that Proportional Representation has given the Opposition you have got. You might get a far worse one . . . But when it is all completed, are you any safer than you were before? I do not think so . . . you will do the wisest thing for yourselves

---

[95] Mansergh (1936: 130).   [96] Palley (1972: 394).
[97] Bew et al. (1979); Buckland (1979); Osborne (1979); Pringle (1980: 198).

Box 2.2.1. **The impact of the abolition of PR (STV) for elections to the Belfast parliament: The exclusion of small parties**

Party	Vote (%)		Seats (%)	
	1925	1929	1925	1929
Ulster Unionist	55.0	50.6	61.5	71.2
Independent Unionist	9.0	14.3	7.7	5.8
Nationalists (Northern League)	23.8	11.7	19.2	21.2
Independent Nationalist		1.3		0.0
Republicans (SF)	5.3		3.9	
NI Labour	4.7	8.0	5.8	1.9
Independent Labour		0.8		0.0
TT (Belfast Tenants)	0.9	2.4	0.0	0.0
Liberal		6.3		0.0
Local Option (Temperance)		3.4		0.0
UTA (farmers' association)	1.3		1.9	0.0
Independent		1.2		0.0

Notes: The effective number of parties in a competitive electoral system, N, is the reciprocal of the Hirfindahl-Hirschman concentration index, abbreviated as HH, which is defined as Σp_i^2 where p is the fractional share of the ith party, and Σ indicates summation over all parties.

Nv, the effective number of parties in votes, is therefore measured by $1/HH = 1/\Sigma(pv)_i^2$

Ns, the effective number of parties in seats, is therefore measured by $1/HH = 1/\Sigma(ps)_i^2$

All voting systems reduce the effective number of parties in seats won compared to votes won. In political science r is the relative reduction in the effective number of parties in votes to that in seats, expressed as a percentage: it is therefore measured by (Nv-Ns)/Nv x 100/1 (Taagepera and Shugart 1989: 77–91, 273).

In 1925 r was 13.2%, demonstrating how PR (STV) only slightly reduced the effective number of parties in seats. By contrast, with winner-takes-all, operative in 1929, r more than tripled to 45.5%.

Calculations: in 1925 HHv = 0.37; Nv = 1/HHv = 2.7; HHs = 0.4268; and Ns = 1/HHs = 2.343; therefore r = 13.2 per cent; in 1929 HHv = 0.302, Nv = 1/HHv = 3.306; HHs = 0.5546; and Ns = 1/HHs = 1.803; therefore r = 45.5 per cent.

As can be seen in the last column, no fewer than seven parties received no seats.

Source: author's calculations; electoral data from Elliott (1973).

and you will do something, too, to soften the resentment and the bitterness we feel over our treatment in this House, and out of it, if you withdraw this Bill.[98]

Craig's move ensured that Stormont elections were regular referenda on the status of Northern Ireland, exactly what he sought to accomplish: "what I believe we will get very much better in this house under the old-fashioned plain and simple system, are men who are for the Union on the one hand, or who are against it and want to go into a Dublin parliament on the other."[99] Jack Beattie of the Northern Ireland Labour Party (NILP) declared that what Craig wanted was "sectarian elections," but the prime minister brushed this description aside. The institutionalization of national and sectarian divisions, through winner-takes-all, meant that many Westminster, Stormont, and local-government seats were not even contested because the results

[98] Hansard (NI), HC, vol. 10, cols 517–18 (1929).
[99] Hansard (NI), HC, vol. 8, col. 2276 (1929).

were foregone conclusions. Total turnout for Stormont elections fell dramatically in 1929 and 1933 and remained static (despite a slightly rising population and electorate) until 1969, when the crisis surrounding the civil-rights movement and O'Neill's premiership generated a much higher turnout. The percentage of seats that went uncontested rose steeply in 1929, peaked in 1933 at the incredibly high level of nearly two-thirds of all seats,[100] and then hovered at between 40 and 50 percent of all seats until the crisis election of 1969. If we compare the percentage of seats won by a party in Stormont parliamentary elections to the votes won in the same elections, then the UUP's excess of seats in nine out of ten elections after 1929 was over 10 percent. The principal losers by the same measure were the UUP's unionist opponents—the right-wing ultras and the left wing in the NILP. The incentives to participate for republicans or socialists among the nationalist population were also radically reduced by the abolition of PR.

THE POLITICAL ECONOMY OF CONTROL

Unionist control was consolidated through direct and indirect economic discrimination in employment, in both the public and private sectors, and in the distribution of public consumption benefits, especially public housing. The history of economic policy and practice in inter-group relations in the North had largely been one of exclusion—for example, limiting access to employment, or to promotion—rather than one of exploitation—for example, paying Catholics less for the same tasks, or for the same set of skills and experience, or taxing them more (discussion of education is to follow). These historical patterns intensified under the UUP's new demesne, and numerous historians of different dispositions have documented explicit exhortations by Unionist politicians, including prime ministers and prime ministers-to-be, encouraging discrimination.[101] Since this was the message from the top, the employment, promotion, and contracting policies of the public sector could hardly be expected to be models of impartiality. Ministers practiced discrimination in their own offices: in the 1920s Bates "refused to allow Catholic appointments" at Home Affairs; at Labour, John Andrews, a future prime minister, automatically disqualified candidates from the Irish Free State; and at Agriculture, Archdale "boasted there were only four Catholics in his Ministry."[102] Oaths of allegiance were imposed widely across the public sector, even for low-status jobs.

Not all discrimination flowed from the top or from government policy. Ingrained sectarian and ethnic prejudices sustained discrimination in the private sector, as well as informal or indirect discrimination through recruitment through school or family networks. But, crucially, the government collaborated with these prejudices. A famous article by Ultach published in *The Capuchin Annual* of 1943 contains an infamous photograph of an unemployment card indicating that the

---

[100] Elliott (1973: tables 1.02–1.04).

[101] See, e.g., Michael Farrell (1976: 121–49); Bew et al. (1979); Buckland (1981: 55–81). Senator Sir John Davison, Grand Master of the Orange Order, directly linked discrimination in favor of Protestants to Protestant votes, commending the slogan "Protestants, employ Protestants" (Michael Farrell 1980: 136).

[102] Bew et al. (1996 5); reported earlier in Ultach (1943).

reason the person is entitled to unemployment benefit is because he had been rejected on the basis of his religion. The labor department did not query employers who turned down prospective employees because of their religion—and a person thus rejected remained entitled to benefits.[103]

The pattern of male occupations within each community in the 1971 census is shown in Table 2.2.7. Not surprisingly, Protestants dominated the upper occupational classes, while Catholics were found predominantly in the lower classes; Protestants predominated in superior positions within occupations within the same class; and Protestants were concentrated in the higher-status industries and locations. There was "a striking unevenness" in the distribution of Catholics across industries:[104] scarcely present in well-paid engineering occupations, banking, finance, and the insurance industries, they were more likely to be present in lower-status industries with higher unemployment—for example, construction—and they constituted a majority of the unemployed, even though they were less than a third of the economically active population.

Another way of using census data to evaluate the impact of the UUP's regime is to compare the positions of Catholics and Protestants in 1951 with those they held in 1901. In Belfast, while the proportions of "Catholic and Protestant males employed in public and professional services . . . were at parity in 1901, by 1951 the Catholic share had, proportionately, fallen by a third."[105] Given that Irish Catholics were by then doing as well as European Protestants in the labor markets of the USA, Canada, Australia, and Great Britain, it is with regime policy, and the regime's tolerance of its co-ethnics' practices, not the subordinate group's allegedly inferior work ethic, that the major explanation of these disparities has to be found. A. C. Hepburn observed that, although the class and occupational profiles of Irish immigrants in British and American cities eventually converged toward that of the respective cities as a whole, within two generations in Belfast the position of Irish Catholics declined.[106] The earliest research, not technically or quantitatively sophisticated, showed there was segregation in the workplace, but

Table 2.2.7. Occupational class and religion, economically active men, Northern Ireland, 1971 (%)

Occupational class	Protestants	Catholics	Total	Protestants minus Catholics
Managerial/professional	16	9	14	+7
Lower-grade non-manual	17	12	16	+5
Manual (skilled)	27	23	26	+4
Manual (semi-skilled)	24	25	24	−1
Manual (unskilled) and unemployed	16	31	20	−15

Note: The Canadian scholar Edmund Aunger was the first to investigate the 1971 census with care (Aunger 1975). His comparative discussion of Northern Ireland and New Brunswick (Aunger 1981) was also a pioneering evaluation.

Source: adapted from Aunger (1975: 10).

[103] Ultach (1943: 17–18).
[104] Rowthorn and Wayne (1988: 34); and see Table 2.2.8.
[105] Hepburn (2003: 177).   [106] Hepburn (1996: chs 6, 8).

its scale was unknown, and the causal mechanisms were not identified.[r] There were more Protestant-only than Catholic-only firms, and in some mixed firms Catholics were found in lower-status posts or kept in separate departments.[107] There were some mixed firms, by contrast, in which equality of opportunity appeared to apply. The explanation of occupational segregation partly related to separate social institutions: the Catholic middle class serviced its own community as teachers, clergy, solicitors, and grocers. But teachers and clergy composed nearly twice as many of the Catholic middle class as the equivalent professions among Protestants.[108] Aunger showed on the basis of modal averages that Protestants were overrepresented in positions of authority and influence, and that the typical Protestant male was a skilled worker whereas the typical Catholic male was unskilled. Perhaps the most conclusive indicator of Northern Ireland's political economy was comparative unemployment rates by gender and religion (see Figure 2.2.1). In the early 1960s, in what was sneeringly referred to as the "Mrs Mop March," Mina Browne led a demonstration of loyalists against a decision by Belfast corporation to include Catholics on the roll of school cleaners.[109]

Clientelism in both public and private employment invigorated the UUP's position at the core of a system of patronage. It also served to encourage Catholic emigration, which remained absolutely and disproportionately higher than Protestant migration during the Stormont regime (see Table 2.2.8).[110] Catholics were nearly three times more likely to emigrate in the years before and after the Second

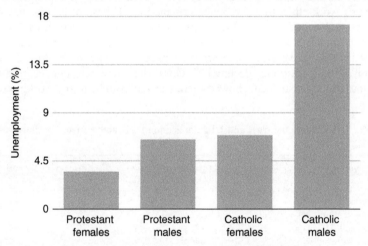

Figure 2.2.1. Religion, gender, and unemployment, Northern Ireland, 1971

Note: Catholic/Protestant male unemployment ratio: 2.62; Catholic/Protestant female unemployment ratio: 1.94.

Source: Smith and Chambers (1987: pt 1, table 2.1).

---

[107] In Richard Rose's loyalty survey of 1968 one in seven Catholics and one in five Protestants reported that all of their co-workers were of the same religion as themselves (Richard Rose 1971: 307).
[108] Aunger (1975: 5).   [109] Boulton (1973 45).
[110] Barritt and Carter (1972/1962: 107–8), Rowthorn and Wayne (1988: app.).

Table 2.2.8. Net emigration rates from Northern Ireland, by religion, 1937–1971 (rate per thousand per annum)

Years	All	Catholics	Non-Catholics	Ratio of Catholicss/non-Catholics
1937–51	3.7	6.5	2.3	2.8
1951–61	6.7	10.8	4.6	2.3
1961–71	4.3	6.8	2.8	2.4

Source: adapted from Simpson (1983: 102).

Table 2.2.9. Estimated impact of emigration on Northern Ireland's religious balance, 1926–1981

Calculations	Catholics		Non-Catholics	
	Number	%	Number	%
1. Population in 1926	420,000	33.4% of total	836,000	66.6% of total
2. Natural increase 1926–81	431,000	102.6% increase	289,000	34.6% increase
3. Hypothetical population 1981	851,000	43.1% of total	1,125,000	56.9% of total
4. Actual population in 1981	588,000	38.3% of total	947,000	61.7% of total
5. Effect of emigration (4–3)	–263,000		–178,000	

Source: adapted from Rowthorn and Wayne (1988: 209).

World War, and nearly two and half times more likely to emigrate in the two decades between 1951 and 1971. Subsequent calculations by economist Bob Rowthorn and trade-union officer and legal researcher Naomi Wayne (see Table 2.2.9) suggest that without this differential migration rate Catholics would have comprised 43 percent of the North's population by 1981. Arguably the prime economic function of discrimination, aside from sating Protestant populist prejudices, was not to exploit Catholics, but to freeze them out, and thereby maintain Protestant solidarity. Catholics were far more likely to leave the "cold house," and thereby maintain the dominance of unionists.[111]

ADMINISTRATIVE CONTROL
AND SEGMENTAL PATRONAGE

The allocation of housing and the manipulation of electoral districts at the local governmental level were connected in an intimate example of political control.[112] Housing segregation maintained predictable electoral outcomes and prevented the development of mixed communities. The pathologies of using planning controls to hem Catholics into "their wards" increased the density of Catholic

[111] In his Nobel laureate acceptance speech David Trimble accepted that Northern Ireland had been "a cold house" for Catholics. www.davidtrimble.org/speeches_toraiseup8.htm (accessed October 2017)
[112] Cameron (1969: para. 140).

living spaces in gerrymandered urban councils. Local authorities under UUP control west of the River Bann, where Catholics were far more likely to be the local majority of the electorate, were zealous in using planning controls and allocation systems to maintain their domination. By contrast, East of the Bann, where Protestants were far more likely to constitute a local electoral majority, housing allocation patterns were less influenced by sectarian electoral considerations.

How control over housing operated at the intimate individual level may be illustrated by Omagh Rural Council in 1944, during the Second World War. George Logue, a Catholic with twenty-one years' service in the British Army, had been invalided out of his profession. After his application for council housing, two Nationalist party councilors, Donnelly and McCullagh, nominated him to rent a vacant cottage in the discretion of the council, on the grounds of merit (service), and need (the veteran had a large family). Omagh Rural Council had been gerrymandered (despite having a population that was over 60 percent Catholic, it was controlled by a UUP governing majority). Two Unionist councilors, McCollum and McDowell, proposed that the tenancy be given to a Protestant laborer, Kyle. Accused by Donnelly of anti-Catholic bigotry, McDowell riposted: "Send Mr Donnelly to the Free State!" A vote was taken: twenty-five Unionist councilors voted for Kyle, twelve Nationalists for Logue. Earlier, in 1936, UUP councilors in Omagh had told their party headquarters that they were determined not to allocate houses to political opponents, who might then outvote them.[113] Twenty years later, George Elliott, the UUP chairman of Enniskillen Housing Committee, declared that his council would build houses to let to the "right people." A Unionist council had no obligation to "cut a stick to beat itself," and, as he put it a year later, was "not going to put people into houses who are going to vote against them at the next election."[114]

The public-employment patterns in policing were mostly self-selecting after the ethnic character of the RUC and the Specials had been established; eventually intentional discrimination was not really required here, except regarding promotion. The same, however, could not be said of employment patterns in the civil service, local authorities, and quasi-governmental agencies (see Table 2.2.10). The first head of the Northern Ireland civil service was Wilfrid Spender, former Larne gun-runner, former head of the UVF, and the organizer of the UVF's transformation into the Special Constabulary. Unionist politicians were appointed to civil-service selection boards, and by 1943 in the higher grades of the civil service Catholics made up a total of 5.8 percent of those employed. Patrick Buckland quotes this figure from the official records of an inquiry conducted by the local Ministry of Finance at the request of Prime Minister Andrews.[115] The petty case of the dismissal of a Catholic gardener from the Stormont grounds, because of pressure from the Orange Order, demonstrates the pervasiveness of Orange surveillance of the civil service.[116] The man in question had a worthy army record *and* a reference from the Prince of Wales, but to no avail. In local authorities, the

[113] This story is taken from the *Irish News* of May 15, 1944, thanks to Dr Eamon Phoenix's column in the current version of that newspaper.

[114] This story is taken from the *Belfast Telegraph*, 19 November 19, 1963, and November 25, 1964, and reported by Mulholland (2004: 204).

[115] Buckland (1979: 20).   [116] Bew et al. (1979: 97, n. 12).

Table 2.2.10. Catholic representation in the Northern Ireland civil service, 1969

Occupational grade	Protestants (%)	Catholics (%)	Total (%)
	(N = 492)	(N = 36)	(N = 528)
Senior administrative	94	6	100
Professional, technical	93	7	100
Senior administrative positions	**Protestants (%)**	**Catholics (%)**	**Total (N)**
Administrative secretaries (elite positions)	98.1	1.9	53
Principal officers	89.2	10.8	102
Deputy principal officers	93.3	6.7	164
TOTAL	92.8	7.2	319

Sources: Campaign for Social Justice (1969); Aunger (1981: 126–7).

Cameron commission of inquiry in 1969 found that unionist-controlled councils had systematically discriminated in favor of Protestants, especially in key administrative posts.[117] In public enterprises and public utilities Catholics were also grossly underrepresented at all levels.[118]

WHY CONTROL DESCRIBES THE STORMONT SYSTEM

This appraisal of the regime is not, it needs emphasizing, confined to radical outliers on the political fringe, or republicans, be they supporters of the IRA or not. The doyen of revisionist historians, Roy Foster, judged the Stormont regime a "Protestant supremacist statelet."[119] The evidence surveyed here suggests the darker systematicity of control, as conceptualized by Lustick, not the paler portrait provided in the review of John H. Whyte.[120] There was segmentation of Catholics at the start of the regime, which was encouraged rather than discouraged—through electoral, residential, and workplace discrimination; the initial greater dependency of the minority was politically exploited; and there was some absolutely minimal co-option when that was deemed prudent. Unionists did not generally seek "to crush catholics, rather to keep them in their place."[121] Catholics intent on upward mobility were largely confined to servicing their own, unless they emigrated. Working-class residential segregation was cemented by a cross-class electoral pact among unionists, and reinforced, where deemed necessary, to maintain pro-regime electoral alignment. Once consolidated, the system prevented effective armed insurrection, disorganized the opposition, and kept the controlled generally pacified.

Intermittently the regime failed to restrain or to punish riots and pogroms organized by its supporters. Craig's government was indulgent toward loyalist mob attacks—for example, those against Catholic pilgrims attending the

[117] Cameron (1969: para. 138).   [118] Aunger (1975).
[119] Foster (1988: 592). Without an argument, however, he claims no "irrelevant colonial 'parallel'" could act as a guide to understanding its present.
[120] Whyte (1983).   [121] Mulholland (2004: 206).

Eucharistic Congress in the South in 1932, or in the Belfast riots of 1935, triggered by an Orange march in North Belfast on July 12, that led to ten days and nights of violence.[122] The Ulster Protestant League may have been the most active loyalist agent in the riots; they regarded Craig's government as soft on Catholics.[123] Ten people were killed, and over fifty Catholic homes were torched on July 13. These riots, which triggered flights and expulsions, were "a phase in the process, partly ongoing and partly cyclical, of ethnic segregation in the city."[124] The lower levels of lethal riotous violence in the North between 1923 and 1969, by comparison with the late nineteenth century, or 1920–2, owed most to the fact that Unionists— and Orangemen—were usually in full local control, with their police, and their magistrates.

The regime conformed to most but fell short of the plenitude of minimal standards of electoral democracy. It did not meet the higher standards of pluralist democracy. The full adult suffrage did not apply at local government level. A de facto one-party regime restricted the national, cultural, and linguistic freedoms of its opponents. Emergency powers were preserved irrespective of the level of security threats. The security forces were ethnically unrepresentative and partisan. The nominal overseer in Westminster collaborated with the local restrictions on citizenship and electoral rights, thereby curtailing the accountability requirements of democracy.[125] Parliamentary speech and ministerial responsibility in Great Britain were restricted by the convenient convention that prevented matters related to powers devolved to Northern Ireland from being raised at Westminster. Broadcasting freedom of expression was also materially restricted within the North—in pre-internet days and before multi-channel TV and radio, public broadcasting mattered more in the exercise of control. A reputable analysis of the BBC archives demonstrates that from 1924 until 1948 the BBC's directors were openly absorbed into the unionist establishment and sought to suppress the fact that Northern Ireland contained two politically, ethnically, and religiously opposed communities. The reporting of GAA sports results was stopped in Sunday news broadcasts after loyalist protests. There was no discussion of "the constitutional question," and, remarkably, no reporting of events south of the border.[126] There was little need to censor the press, however, because each community read its own newspapers and magazines, and showed few signs of according credibility to what was printed by the other side, except when it demonstrated group hatred.

This picture is not intended to imply that the regime was among the most oppressive in the world. African Americans in the southern states of the USA, for example, were subjected to much more brutal and oppressive local control,

---

[122] In the latter case Bates lifted a ban on Orange parades in Craig's absence, thereby precipitating the conflagration.

[123] Its leading light, a former B Special, was later involved in arson and bomb attacks against AOH halls and Catholic churches (Staunton 2001: 147).

[124] Hepburn (1990: 96).

[125] For a useful discussion of definitions of democracy and their empirical and normative implications, see Collier and Levitsky (1997).

[126] Cathcart (1984: 67, 116–21, 148).

including active and widespread disenfranchisement across all elections.[127] But the picture suggests more than mere sub-par performance to be excused as the conduct of a polity that regarded itself as under siege. The regime that was consolidated around Stormont allowed the colonially established ethos of the superiority of Protestants over Catholics to be restructured. All of the defects in its democratic standards can be traced to the institutional legacies of colonialism. A hermetic system had emerged, which seemed incapable of internal change or reform before the mid-1960s.

PARALLEL SCHOOLS: CONTROL
OR THE PRICE OF FAITH OR BOTH?

If politics conformed to tidy models, then, in a civic nation-state, public schools would be secular, and fully funded by the taxpayer, whereas private schools, including religious schools, if permitted, would be exclusively funded by a combination of for-profit enterprise, parental fees, the endowments of religious orders and churches, charitable donations from supporters of such schools, and not-for-profit schools. Great Britain and Ireland, however, have never conformed to the civic nation-state model of schooling, such as that found in France before 1920, or in the historically typical American model of public-school education.

A frequent misunderstanding assumes that the civic nation-state model was available to Northern Catholics after 1920: their clergy opted out of generous offers from Lord Londonderry, at the expense of capital equipment and salaries for their schools, and at the expense of the educational skills of the children of their flock, who then, allegedly, became less competitive in the labor market, and thereby lost out to better-educated Protestants. It is more accurate to simplify matters in a different way. In the latter half of the Union, Ireland had unofficially developed parallel denominational educational systems, in which Catholics and Protestants, through geography and choice, largely went to schools run by their own clergy, mostly funded from taxation. An unofficial system of educational autonomy based on group equality had emerged, in which schools were largely taxpayer-funded, regardless of denomination. Similar systems, with full and proportionate funding for Catholics and Protestants, were officially put in place in Scotland during the First World War, and in Ontario within the federal dominion of Canada. But at the foundation of Northern Ireland, the new parliament modified the inherited system.

That system certainly merited reform, but, against the wishes of its patrician elites, including Lord Londonderry, the UUP allowed a biased system of funding to emerge, in which state schools became de facto Protestant, and received full taxpayer capital funding and salary costs, whereas Catholic schools, as religious schools, had their funding significantly reduced by comparison with what they had enjoyed under government from Dublin Castle—and by comparison with the

---

[127] For a comparison between Northern Ireland and other locations in Europe and North America where ethnic communities were subject to domination in the last two centuries, see Wright (1987).

resources allocated to Protestants.[5] These changes began with the Lynn Committee appointed in 1921.[128] It was boycotted by Catholic clerical and nationalist political leaders, who were then either refusing to recognize Northern Ireland, or objecting to proposals that appeared to aim at "public control" (read as unionist control) over their schools. When the Education Act of 1923 significantly reduced public funding to religiously run schools, the Catholic Church called on nationalists to reconsider their policy of abstention from Belfast's parliament.[129] The Act provided for the continuing payment of salaries and some maintenance, but not for the capital costs of those schools staying outside public control, which were almost entirely Catholic. By contrast, schools that were to come under public control— most of the historically Protestant schools—were to be fully funded. Mindful of the anti-discrimination provisions of the Government of Ireland Act, however, the publicly controlled schools were forbidden to engage in bible instruction in school hours, or to apply a religious test in appointing teachers.

The last-named provisions antagonized many Protestant clerics and laity who wanted the taxpayer's pound *and* their bible. Mirroring Catholic clerical anxieties, ultra-Protestants claimed to fear that in (admittedly diminishing) nationalist majority local-government jurisdictions, local councilors would control Protestant schools—a diabolical vista. Under this pressure, Craig's government folded. The Education Act was amended twice, first in 1925 and then in 1930, to appease these Protestant clerics and their lay enthusiasts, *and*, to be fair, to make some partial amends to Catholics (though these modifications were largely driven by fears of court action rather than generosity of spirit). The "publicly controlled" or state schools effectively became Protestant, in their staffing, and in provision for biblical instruction, and had full funding. The Catholic clergy had considered legal action, despite their fears that the Government of Ireland Act could have been interpreted adversely to their interests. On one of the few occasions in which Craig's cabinet made concessions to Catholic interests, it was proposed and legislated that Catholic schools and other schools under private management would receive half of their capital costs as grants. Had the cabinet not feared loss in the courts, it would have ended up allowing public schools to be run for, by, and with Protestants, fully funded by the taxpayer, while leaving Catholic schools without any capital funding at all.

These concessions enabled Catholics to have some religious and cultural autonomy in their schools, but at the cost of a double burden. They paid in taxation toward what were de facto Protestant schools, while having to find half of the capital funding for their schools out of their own resources. Moreover, they were now in a legal trap. If they sought judicial review to achieve full funding, they could lose the concessions Craig had been prepared to make. Devlin described matters passionately, eloquently, and accurately in 1930, before these concessions were made.

---

[128] Its chair was regarded as an ultra by his own premier; shortly after his appointment to this committee he declared in parliament that there were "two peoples in Ireland, one industrious, law-abiding and God-fearing, and the other slothful, murderous and disloyal" (Denis Kennedy 1988: 97)— perhaps not the best ethos with which to consider the reconstruction of education.

[129] See Harris (1993); McGrath (2000: *passim*).

At first it was thought that the Catholics had been dished, and that everyone else was satisfied... [But] the militant leaders of the churches suddenly discovered that there was a flaw in the ministerial masterpiece... their leaders joined with the Orange Lodges in organizing an agitation for religious instruction in the schools. The Government anxious to placate every aggrieved section of the Protestant community ... found a formula... what is known as simple bible teaching... [It meets] what they regard—and I do not dissent—as the just claims of the Protestant body... By the Act of 1923 the Catholics had already been robbed of the rights which they enjoyed under the British regime, namely, a grant of two-thirds of the cost of the building of their schools... Catholics do not in the least degree object to what you are doing in the building, extension and lighting, and cleaning, of schools for the Protestant children... and they do not desire directly or indirectly in any shape or form to interfere with Protestant schools or with the teaching of religion as they conceive it in their schools. But they do claim, and claim emphatically and justly, a similar right for themselves... This [governmental] performance is bad enough... [but what is worse] is the pretense that all this is caused by the fact we will not accept popular control. Under the Act of 1923 you created what is called four-and-two committees... Under this system of so-called popular control... four of the committee are appointed by the manager and two are chosen by the elected [local] authority. This popular control is mere empty camouflage... the humbug of all this talk about "we will not give public money without public control." [Yet] without public control you are paying the teachers' salaries...[130]

Overall control, the disorganization of Catholics, was partially achieved through exploiting the impartial discourse of public control.

WHAT MOTIVATED CONTROL?

The motivations of the Unionists who created and sustained this system are easy to establish, and are visible in the historical record of Hansard and the press. Ranking their salience is more controversial. Negatively, unionists dreaded coerced incorporation into an all-island parliament that would become a Gaelic, Catholic Irish republican nation-state; betrayal by Great Britain; insurrection by the new Catholic minority left after partition; and disunity and fragmentation within their ranks—divided by sect and class. Positively, they saw the retention of the Union as an affirmation of their now stoutly affirmed British identity and of continuing membership of the world's most powerful empire. Some also hoped to sustain the local ethos of superiority established since plantation times, and to avoid the costs of equal citizenship, a perspective common to Protestant land-owners and loyalist shipyard workers. Unionists subsequently argued that the evolution of the Irish Free State and the Irish Republic confirmed all their prophecies about home rule.

Their hostility toward Irish irredentism remained unabated—even though the defeat of the republicans, South and North, and the burial of the boundary commission in 1925 should have created a temporary relaxation of their security

[130] Joseph Devlin, Hansard (NI), HC, vol. 12, cols 714–20 (April 9, 1930).

assessments. The interval between 1925 and 1932 was not used, however, to accommodate Northern nationalists. Aversion remained the prevalent psychology, and PR for elections to the Belfast parliament was abolished in this interval. The new mobilization of republicans under de Valera's Fianna Fáil restored unionist security anxieties, especially after this party came to power in Dublin in 1932. Later the constitution of 1937, drafted under de Valera's supervision, declared: "The national territory consists of the whole island of Ireland, its islands and the territorial seas."[131] Unionists believed this wording breached the treaty that had granted the Northern parliament the right of secession, and the international agreement made in 1925, when the three governments had agreed not to implement the boundary commission's report. "Pending the reintegration of the national territory," the following article limited the authority of the Dublin parliament to the Free State's jurisdiction, but without prejudice to its right to govern all of Ireland. Unionists and their supporters would later insist that these articles incited the IRA to enforce the territorial claim violently.[t] Unionists portrayed the Irish Free State's evolution toward a republic, achieved de facto by de Valera in 1937, and de jure in 1949, as treason, disloyalty, and dishonest breaching of the treaty—it had been long forgotten that the same treaty that had split de Valera's first cabinet had been unanimously rejected by Craig's cabinet.

Independent Ireland, in unionist eyes, was subject to Vatican doctrine and government, coercively Gaelicized, and economically retarded: Protestants were its prime victims. The rapid fall in their numbers between 1911 and 1926 was submitted in evidence.[132] The contrary verdict that independent Ireland treated its Protestant minority well, qua Protestants, by international and especially by Northern Irish standards of minority treatment, was never accepted by Ulster unionists.[133] They emphatically claimed that their own polity outperformed the Irish Free State and justified their resistance to Irish nationalism. Craig announced:

> I am an Orangeman first and a politician . . . afterwards . . . In the South they boasted of a Catholic State. They still boast of Southern Ireland being a Catholic State. All I boast of is that we are a Protestant Parliament and a Protestant State. It would be rather interesting for historians of the future to compare a Catholic State launched in the South with a Protestant State launched in the North and see which one gets on the better and prospers the more.[134]

Had there actually been peaceful competition over better minority-rights protections historians would have reported their verdicts by now. On comparative prosperity, objective evaluations have varied over time, and by sector. But by the late 1920 and 1930s Northern Ireland's traditional industries were beginning to crumble, and its public sector and citizens were increasingly dependent upon British subventions. Yet Ireland's slow rate of economic growth between the 1920s and 1958, the creation of customs posts and tariff barriers across the island following the "economic war" with Britain in the 1930s, and continuing high

---

[131] See Vol. 2, Ch. 3, pp. 108–18, especially 117–8.
[132] See Vol. 2, Ch. 3, pp. 86–104.   [133] Kurt Derek Bowen (1983: 324–37).
[134] Lord Craigavon (previously Sir James Craig), Hansard (NI), HC, vol. 16, cols 1091–95 (April 24, 1934).

out-migration, were all claimed as vindications of the Union and of Craig's assignment to historians.

Fears of betrayal wed unionists to their own parliament and to programmatic control. They persistently surmised that British governments—liberal, socialist, and even conservative—would abandon them and hand them over to the Dublin parliament, if it seemed expedient.[135] They dreaded that Great Britain would pay less heed to the needs of loyal Ulster than to appeasing American opinion, twisted by Irish–Americans, or to its relations with the South from 1926 onward.[136] These fears of betrayal would rise to coronary level within the UUP elite following the fall of France in 1940, when the London government secretly offered to support Irish reunification in return for Ireland's entry into the war on the side of the British Empire.[137]

Ulster unionists never ceased to remind one another to maintain vigilant surveillance of the "enemy within." Catholic Ireland, whether in constitutional or revolutionary guise, had always threatened Protestant ascendancy. The IRA had engaged in active combat in the North, during the truce of 1921, and after. Collins and his colleagues had been willing to subvert the 1920 Act and the treaty by force—though they held that Craig had fulfilled neither of the Craig–Collins's pacts of 1922. The IRA never surrendered, and its underground militants would launch offensives again in 1938–41 and 1956–62.[138] The IRA's persistence, despite its weakness, made the case for vigilant and repressive security self-evident to Ulster Protestants who regarded independent Ireland as a safe haven for militant republicans. In short, Catholics were disloyal, so there was no case for authentic equal citizenship.[139] That unequal treatment would reinforce their disloyalty did not matter, just as long as they could be controlled.

Colonial legacies therefore survived into the second half of the twentieth century. Loyal Protestant settlers were under siege, and were justified in controlling potential and actual rebels with the means to hand.[140] The programmatic practices of electoral, coercive, legal, and economic domination codified control. Culturally control was expressed through sectarian organizations, like the vibrant Orange and other loyal orders, and in assertive, intimidatory, and triumphalist marches through Catholic areas, accompanied by intermittent acts of "representative violence" against the minority. The accompanying vitriolic rhetoric revealed the insecurities—and aggression—of those who articulated it.[141] Control demanded sustained solidarity among Protestants. To inhibit or co-opt heretical or dissident Protestant voices, whether socialist, liberal, humane Protestant, or otherwise, it was imperative to have all Protestants rally around one party, the UUP. The Lundy fixation expressed the fears of betrayal from within:[142] the

---

[135] Laffan (1983: 82).   [136] Alan J. Ward (1969); McMahon (1984).

[137] Fisk (1985: 186–219).

[138] J. B. Bell (1979: 73–336); Cronin (1983: 169–73); Coogan (2002).

[139] Doyle (1994).

[140] Aughey (1989) and Follis (1995) provide respectively philosophical and historical vindications of Ulster unionism; they revealingly use the "under-siege" theme that has now become an intellectual defensive trope, a justification as well as an explanation.

[141] Wright (1987: 11–20). See also Clayton (1996); Haddick-Flynn (1999); Bryan (2000); McKay (2000); Kaufmann (2007).

[142] Nelson (1984); Stewart (1986). Under siege Governor Lundy proposed surrendering Londonderry in 1688–89: effigies are annually burned in his dishonor.

capital crime of Ulster loyalism.[143] Lundyism "from below" was manifest among some socialist and trade-union activists who threatened to transcend sectarianism. The threat they posed was usually easily handled. Loyalist workers called socialists of their own religious origin "rotten Prods," and explicit accusations of disloyalty, reminders of the dangers inherent in splitting unionist solidarity, and overt renewals of ethnic appeals usually elicited the required responses. Lundyism "from above" would be another matter. Terence O'Neill appeared to Ian Paisley to be Lundy reincarnate, a man ready to surrender the citadel without a fight.

These intermeshed fears, anxieties, and aversions, deeply rooted in historical experience, describe the motivations that drove the establishment of control, but these motivations were overdetermined. In a recent survey, entitled "Why did Unionists Discriminate?," Marc Mulholland has reviewed triumphalism, anti-Catholicism, social prejudice, populism, cabals, security, and sectarian electoralism as distinct dispositions that drove discrimination.[144] The first three of these traits are historically associated with settler colonialism and its sectarian character in Ireland. Populism and security considerations were key components of organizing the majority and disorganizing the minority, which we have shown were integral to the control system. Mulholland places special emphasis, however, on the UUP's conviction that it could never afford to lose an election—this imperative drove many of the features that characterized Northern Ireland until 1972. He concludes by speculating that, had a majority veto on reunification been recognized by Dublin as well as London—in 1925?—the orchestration of discrimination to preserve a one-party regime would have been less virulent. Such a veto, however, would only have been willingly conceded had there been a far more just and defensible partition, or a more reasonable outcome from the boundary commission.

Unionists' criticisms of the Irish state—some of which were factually accurate, as we shall see—would suggest that they were, or would become, sincere exponents of equal and civic citizenship, and more tolerant of their minority's religious, cultural, and economic liberties than their counterparts. But that was not so. Long before the emergence of an organized home-rule movement, but certainly from the 1880s until the 1920s, Unionists not only exhibited fears, but expressed the ubiquitous justifications of settler colonial minorities threatened by democratization, modernization, and decolonization.[145] These may continue to be read without hermeneutic difficulty in twentieth-century speeches, texts, and acts, articulated both by their leaders and by their rank and file, and applied as policy.[146] By 1940 the system of control was entrenched and had a logic of its own. The improvised steps the UUP had taken to control Catholics, nationalists, and republicans had created vested interests in their maintenance. They created deep reservoirs of Catholic resentment. The costs would be paid later.

---

[143] G. Bell (1976: 65); Stewart (1986: 48).   [144] Mulholland (2004).

[145] MacDonald (1986); Weitzer (1990); Clayton (1996). There is evidence of such mentalities among Belfast Tory leaders from the 1860s, evident in the work of Kerby Miller and David Miller, whose common surnames hide different perspectives.

[146] See, e.g., Clayton (1996: *passim*); McKay (2000: *passim*).

2.3

Digesting Decolonization

From Declared to Undeclared Republic, 1919–1940

Nobody in Ireland of any intelligence likes Nationalism any more than a man with a broken arm likes having it set. A healthy nation is as unconscious of its nationality as a healthy man of his bones. But if you break a nation's nationality it will think of nothing else but getting it set again. It will listen to no reformer, to no philosopher, to no preacher, until the demand of the nationalist is granted. It will attend to no business, however vital, except the business of unification and liberation.

> George Bernard Shaw, Preface for Politicians, Preface to the
> First Edition of *John Bull's Other Island,* 1906[1]

Empire, a term now used to denote a state of large size and also (as a rule) of composite character, often, but not necessarily ruled by an emperor—a state which may be a federation, like the German empire, or a unitary state, like the Russian, or even, like the British empire, a loose commonwealth of free states united to a number of subordinated dependencies.

> Ernest Barker, Entry in the *Encyclopedia Britannica,* 1911[2]

THE CIRCLE OF DECOLONIZATION: STATE-BUILDING IN THE SOUTH

The trajectory of the Irish Free State (IFS) may be briefly summarized. It first became a state, and then it became free. This epigram does not tell the entire story, however. Statehood was accomplished through institution-building during and after a civil war. Freedom flowed from a successfully pursued strategy to achieve recognition as a sovereign state, and the systematic, peaceful, and diplomatic erosion of the features of the treaty that had been obnoxious to Irish republicans—except partition. The IFS's trajectory therefore describes a full constitutional circle. Formed as a dominion because the British insisted that the Republic be disestablished, it initially developed sufficient independence to achieve equality of sovereign status with Great Britain and the other dominions,

---

[1] Shaw (1930: 41).   [2] Barker (1911: 347).

then eventually made its own constitution without British interference or
approval, renaming itself as Ireland (Éire in the Irish language), and removing
the monarch as Ireland's head of state, becoming a de facto republic in December
1937. Later it officially declared itself a Republic, a change that took effect in 1949.
The external dimension of this elliptical path to full independence is narrated
in two complementary diplomatic histories, David Harkness's *The Restless
Dominion*[3] and Deirdre McMahon's *Republicans and Imperialists*, which are
relied on here.[4] The domestic trajectory of the early IFS is the subject of numerous
scholarly studies that buttress what follows.[5]

The Ulster unionist press, according to a sympathetic journalist and historian,
perceived the IFS's evolution as a complete vindication of its warnings against
Irish home rule. Irish statehood proved republican, Catholic, and Gaelic, period.
Dennis Kennedy's *The Widening Gulf: Northern Attitudes to the Independent Irish
State, 1919–1949*, treats the accounts in the unionist press as so well founded that
uncritical readers will conclude that the Orange smoke always derived from Papist
fires.[6] Kennedy's judgment is not singular, however. Other authors portray two
equally squalid sectarian polities emerging North and South after 1920–2, as
mirror images, exhibiting the carnival of reaction that James Connolly had
predicted would flow from partition.[7] Such portraits, however, go too far toward
false equivalence.[8] A Catholic ethos did pervade the Irish Free State, and de
Valera's constitution, but the Irish state neither evolved as Rome prescribed, nor
sanctioned or engaged in systematic anti-Protestant discrimination. The Free
State was Green, but it did not maltreat its minority with comparable acerbic or
malice aforethought to that pursued by the Unionist government in the North.
There were unauthorized and harsh communal violent acts enacted against some
southern Protestants, especially in 1922, and the British cultural identity of many
Irish Protestants was not institutionally respected after the monarch ceased being
head of state in 1937.[a] The depth of disrespect was not, however, of the same
magnitude as that exhibited in the North toward the Irish cultural identity.

The numbers, proportions, and social characteristics of the respective new
minorities explain the bulk of the difference in minority treatment by the new
regimes established in 1920–2. The larger northern minority that flowed from the
partition that was overly territorially generous to unionists posed a greater threat

[3] Harkness (1969).

[4] McMahon (1984). The works of Harkness and McMahon are usefully supplemented by Canning
(1985) and Fisk (1985); and by a recent monograph by Keown (2016).

[5] Notably the works of Macardle (1965); Fanning (1978, 1983); Joseph M. Curran (1980);
Lee (1989); Alan J. Ward (1994); Garvin (1996); Laffan (1999); Kissane (2002, 2005); Maguire
(2008); Townshend (2014).

[6] Denis Kennedy (1988: *passim*). The subtitle of his book should have been *Northern Protestant
Attitudes to the Independent Irish State*. The book's several virtues include its revival of forgotten
moments—e.g., in 1934, thousands of Protestants in Donegal petitioned to be allowed to join Northern
Ireland; and he documents attacks on Protestants that took place in the Free State after the Belfast riots
of 1935.

[7] See, notably, Conor Cruise O'Brien (1974); Fitzpatrick (1998); Patterson (2006).

[8] Bloomfield (2007: 153) expresses this perspective as follows: "The unionists were the more greatly
to blame in that they disposed of the ultimate political power. Yet in truth, each side was the mirror
image of the other. An Orange, Protestant, and anti-Irish unity faction confronted a Hibernian,
Catholic and anti-partition faction."

to Ulster Unionists than the much smaller and often more socially advantaged Southern minority posed to the Free State and its successor. The arguments advanced here therefore do not assume a different allocation of political virtue among the political classes on the two sides of the new border. Rather, the demographic distributions created by a biased partition paved the way toward different outcomes: control of the new minority in the North; integration and assimilation of the new minority in the South.

REPUBLICANISM, IMPERIALISM, AND THE TREATY DEBATE

The proposed Irish Free State was neither free nor a state according to its republican critics, who protested its formation in the treaty ratification debate,[b] and later opposed it in civil war. To use later phraseology, they saw the proposed IFS as a neo-colonial dependency. Over time, however, the IFS accomplished full political decolonization—that is, sovereign independent statehood. But the manner of its achievement had deep consequences for the North. Irish state-building was prioritized at the expense of pan-Irish nation-building, and, often unintentionally, entrenched partition, and thereby consolidated unionist hegemonic control. Some historians detect early and persistent "Southern" state nationalism, and would question whether these effects can be treated as unintended.[9] They tend, however, to focus simply on Irish governmental agency.[10] The damage done to the possibilities of accommodation with Ulster unionists is seen as deliberate, executed with conscious if not callous "collateral damage." These perspectives have some merit, but typically neglect the conduct of British imperialists, which is what they still called themselves in this era, especially British efforts to restrain the Free State's independence. The diplomatic record is plain. The British sought to treat the IFS's dominion status as inferior to that of Canada, despite what had been signed in the treaty. Harkness and McMahon, who cover the relevant diplomatic history from 1922 until 1940, show that Irish republicans were not alone in their obsession with the Crown and empire.[11] The distinction between allegiance to the Crown and maintaining Ireland within *the* Empire, on the one hand, and an independent republic externally associated with the Crown, on the other, was important enough that the Liberal imperialists (Lloyd George, Churchill, and Worthington-Evans), and their Conservative allies (Balfour, Birkenhead, Bonar-Law, and Chamberlain), threatened renewal of war if their preferred alternative was not accepted. Equally, the distinction between a dominion and a sovereign republic was important enough to trigger a civil war between those Irish who accepted versus those who rejected the treaty. Neither the imperialists nor the republicans were mad to think that these distinctions mattered.

---

[9] O'Halloran (1987) and Regan (1999, 2013) from different perspectives see the IFS as intentionally but hypocritically partitionist.

[10] Or, on the person and policies of Éamon de Valera, see especially Bowman (1982).

[11] Harkness (1969); McMahon (1984).

Dáil Éireann debated ratification in University College Dublin between December 14, 1921, and January 7, 1922.[12] De Valera protested that the delegates had signed before consulting the cabinet, but accepted that the text should be debated and voted on its merits. The assembly then went into private session to discuss the history of the negotiations, and to attempt to restore some unity among republicans.[13] Here de Valera introduced his alternative proposal, Document No. 2, which Griffith and Collins vigorously maintained had already been rejected in substance by the British. De Valera had misjudged hopes that this document would generate consensus, though it emphatically showed that he was willing to embrace key compromises, including over the monarchy and partition, compromises rejected by harder-line republicans, notably Austin Stack,[c] Liam Mellows,[d] and Séamus Robinson.[e] De Valera withdrew his proposal, but asked that it be kept confidential until he introduced it to the Irish public. Griffith and Collins objected that the public should know that another compromise, already rejected by the British, was an already defeated alternative to the proposed treaty, not the pristine republic.

The key speakers in the public debate in the key session of December 19 enable us to understand the deep controversies that marked independent Ireland until 1949.[14] Proposing, Griffith recognized:

> We took an oath to the Irish Republic, but, as President de Valera himself said, he understood that oath to bind him to do the best he could for Ireland. So do we...If the Irish people say "We have got everything else but the name Republic, and we will fight for it," I would say to them that they are fools, but I will follow in the ranks...But the Irish people will not do that.

The treaty provided the substance of independence, and Ireland's voters would endorse it given the chance, even though the name (and symbolism) of a republic would be absent. Most deputies recognized that this judgment was true during the Christmas recess in which they met their constituents. Griffith defended the treaty as an honorable bargain, and as a "final" settlement: the split was fundamentally a quibble over words, between those who wanted to go into the Empire with their heads up, and those who wanted to half-recognize the British king and Empire. Griffith was seconded by Sean Mackeon,[f] spared execution by the truce that made the treaty possible:

> To me this Treaty gives me what I and my comrades fought for...[For] the first time in 700 years the evacuation of Britain's armed forces...[15] [and] our own Army, not half-equipped, but fully equipped, to defend our interests. If the Treaty were much worse in words than it is alleged to be, once it gave me these two things, I would take it and say...we can develop our own nation in our own way.

[12] The extracts cited here follow the online version published at <http://oireachtasdebates.oireachtas.ie/debates%20authoring/debateswebpack.nsf/takes/dail1921121900003?opendocument> (accessed summer 2014).

[13] T. P. O'Neill (1972).

[14] Sources as in n. 12: I have edited regarding tenses, and indicated where passages are left out, through ellipses, but have carefully avoided any changes in meanings.

[15] Like many British people, Irish nationalists often forget that Great Britain, even as a Union of Crowns, did not exist before 1603.

Opposing, de Valera maintained that the treaty

makes British authority our masters in Ireland. It was said that [deputies] had only an oath to the British King in virtue of common citizenship, but you have an oath to the Irish Constitution, and that Constitution will be a Constitution which will have the King of Great Britain as head of Ireland. You will swear allegiance to that Constitution and to that King; and if the representatives of the Republic should ask the people of Ireland to do that which is inconsistent with the Republic, I say they are subverting the Republic.

The treaty would deliver neither peace nor freedom, and would betray Parnell's spirit because it set bounds to the onward march of the nation. By de Valera's later standards it was an unimpressive speech. Seconding him, Austin Stack expressed the absolutist republican position, which de Valera could not in conscience follow, and vehemently rejected the proposed oath that deputies would have to take under the treaty's provisions.

In [clause] No. I England purports to bestow on Ireland, an ancient nation, the same constitutional status as any of the British Dominions, and also to bestow her with a Parliament having certain powers... [England] tries to limit you to the powers of the Dominion of Canada... I for one cannot accept from England full Canadian powers, three-quarter Canadian powers, or half Canadian powers. I stand for what is Ireland's right, full independence and nothing short of it... Australia, New Zealand... can put up with acknowledgments to the monarch [of] Great Britain as head of their State, for have they not all sprung from England?... This country, on the other hand, has not been a child of England's... England came here as an invader, and for 750 years we have been resisting that conquest. Are we now... to bend the knee and acknowledge that we received from England as a concession full, or half, or three-quarter Dominion powers? I say no... This question of the oath has an extraordinary significance... no member of my family has ever taken an oath of allegiance to England's King... I was nurtured in the traditions of Fenianism... [Was it] for this our fathers have suffered... our comrades have died on the field and in the barrack yard[?]

Count Plunkett, the father of the executed signatory to the 1916 Proclamation, also admonished the deputies: "We have taken an oath of fidelity to the Republic ... Under no conditions will I sacrifice my personal honour..."[16]

Michael Collins made the most influential pro-treaty speech, beginning with a defense of the delegation, mixed with grim humor: "It is scarcely too much to say [we] have been blamed for not returning with recognition of the Irish Republic." The delegation had gone into "conference not on the recognition of the Irish Republic." Indeed,

had we all stood on the recognition of the Irish Republic as a prelude to any conference we could very easily have said so, and there would [have been] no conference... [The] acceptance of [Lloyd George's] invitation [by de Valera]... formed the compromise. I was sent there to form that adaptation, to bear the brunt of it. Now as one of the

[16] In correspondence, Kerby Miller suggests that "the Treaty's symbolic demands had long-lasting corrosive effects on Irish republican morale and morals—and that that, along with their practical consequences, was likely the British intention... to create a colonial regime 'with which we can still do business.'" This interesting suggestion credits the Lloyd George coalition with more Machiavellian cohesion than it possessed, but Miller is right about the consequences.

signatories of the document I naturally recommend its acceptance. I do not recommend it for more than it is. Equally I do not recommend it for less than it is.

Collins differentiated himself from Griffith by articulating a stepping-stone theory of the treaty:

"In my opinion it gives us freedom, not the ultimate freedom that all nations desire and develop to, but the freedom to achieve it [applause]." He went on: I am not a constitutional lawyer . . . [but] I will back my constitutional opinion against the opinion of any Deputy, lawyer or otherwise, in this Dáil . . . (*Reading*): The status as defined is the same constitutional status in the "community of nations known as the British Empire," as Canada, Australia, New Zealand, South Africa. [In] my judgment it is not a definition of any status that would secure us that status, it is the power to hold and to make secure and to increase what we have gained. The fact of Canadian and South African independence is something real and solid, and will grow in reality and force as time goes on. Judged by that touchstone, the relations between Ireland and Britain will have a certainty of freedom and equality which cannot be interfered with. England dare not interfere with Canada. Any attempt to interfere with us would be even more difficult in consequence of the reference to the "constitutional status" of Canada and South Africa. They are, in effect, introduced as guarantors of our freedom, which makes us stronger than if we stood alone. In obtaining the "constitutional status" of Canada, our association with England is based not on the present technical legal position of Canada. It is an old Act, the Canadian Act, and the advances in freedom from it have been considerable. That is the reply to one Deputy who spoke today of the real position, the complete freedom [that] equality with Canada has given us. I refer now not to the legal technical status, but to the status they have come to, the status which enables Canada to send an Ambassador to Washington . . . enables Canada to sign the Treaty of Versailles equally with Great Britain . . . which prevents Great Britain from entering into any foreign alliance without the consent of Canada, and . . . that gives Canada the right to be consulted before she may go into any war. It is not the definition of that status that will give it to us; it is our power to take it and to keep it, and that is where I differ from the others. I believe in our power to take it and to keep it.

Collins argued firmly that the treaty would terminate Britain's military occupation and enable Ireland to develop its own economy.

Of the famous speakers that day, Collins alone addressed the provisions on Northern Ireland.

[Face] facts . . . We have stated we would not coerce the North-East . . . officially in our correspondence . . . What did we mean? Did we mean we were going to coerce them or we were not going to coerce them? What was the use of talking big phrases about not agreeing to the partition of our country? Surely we recognise that the North-East corner does exist, and surely our intention was that we should take such steps as would sooner or later lead to mutual understanding? The Treaty has made an effort to deal with it, and has made an effort, in my opinion, to deal with it on lines that will lead very rapidly to goodwill, and the entry of the North-East under the Irish Parliament [applause]. I don't say it is an ideal arrangement, but if our policy is, as has been stated, a policy of non-coercion, then let somebody else get a better way out of it.

Here too was a stepping stone: the boundary commission would oblige Northern Ireland's leaders to reconsider their position, a theory not borne out by events, unlike his other argument. Collins argued that the will of the people needed to be considered by the deputies, as they had the right to decide between peace and war.

The best-argued anti-treaty speech was made by Erskine Childers, secretary to the delegation, and one of the constitutional lawyers that Collins had in mind.[8]

This Treaty [he declaimed] does not give you what is called Dominion status. The Minister for Finance [Collins] passed lightly over this clause concerning the occupation of our ports... Clause No. 6 in effect declares that the people of Ireland... have no responsibility for defending [their] island from foreign attack... This clause declares that Ireland is unfit, or rather—for we all know the real reason—too dangerous a neighbour to be entrusted with her own coastal defence. And, therefore, in that clause is the most humiliating condition that can be inflicted on any nation claiming to be free, namely, that it is not to be allowed to provide defence against attack by a foreign enemy. There is, it is true, a little proviso saying that the matter will be reconsidered in five years, but there is no guarantee whatever that anything will result from that reconsideration, and the most the reconsideration will amount to is that she is to be allowed to take over a share in her own coastal defence. Clause No. 7 declares that permanently... some of our most important ports are to be occupied by British Forces. Here there is no question of Dominion status, no question of constitutional usage—these qualifying words that are used in the second clause of the Treaty. For ever that occupation is to continue, and in time of war, says sub-section B, or strained relations with a foreign Power, such harbour and other facilities as the British Government may require for the purpose of such defence as aforesaid. In other words, when she pleases to announce that there are strained relations with a foreign Power, or when England is actually in war with a foreign Power, any use whatever can be made of this island whether for naval or military purposes. [No] such conditions or limitations attach to any dominion, least of all Canada... What is Canada? Half a continent. The closest part is nearly 3,000 miles from Britain, and the furthest part 7,000 miles, a great, immense nation, absolutely unconquerable by England, and, what is even more important, attached to England by ties of blood which produces such relations between them that there is no desire on England's part to conquer—two great factors, the distance which renders Canada unconquerable and the blood tie... What is the position of Ireland? After 750 years of war, lying close up against the shores of her great neighbour, what guarantee has she, what equal voice can she have in the decisions of these questions, with England actually occupying her shores, committing her inevitably, legally, constitutionally and in every other way to all her foreign policies and to all her wars?... English interests... will govern and limit every condition and clause in that Treaty now before you. It is useless to point to the words in Clause 2—'constitutional usage'. Supposing that these words... are going to be construed as conferring on Ireland the same power as is held by Canada, how can they be so construed if a question arises as to the construction of a clause? Under the Canadian Constitution Canada has always the power to say, 'Very well, we differ about its construction. I shall put my own interpretation upon it and I shall give up my relation with you altogether.' That is the strength of Canada's position. The blood tie with Canada which naturally produces loyalty and sentimental affection to England cannot reasonably, cannot possibly, cannot humanly be expected from the Irish nation after its 750 years.

Childers questioned whether a treaty was being ratified:

Under what title will Ireland hold her position under this Treaty? It was not signed as a Treaty. It has since been called a Treaty. I don't lay stress on that distinction of words, but what I do lay stress on is this, that the constitution of Ireland and the relation of Ireland to England are going to depend, so far as Ireland is concerned, on the Act of a British Parliament. Nobody knows yet what form that Act is going to take... no undertaking or guarantee has been obtained . . . as to exactly how [the treaty] was going to be carried out by the British Government; but that it must depend upon the Act of the British Parliament is certain. Canada's Constitution depends upon the Act of 1867, and unquestionably Ireland's position will depend upon it too. What does this assembly think of that? Do you . . . think that the freedom and liberties of Ireland are inherent in the people of Ireland . . . and can only be surrendered by the people, or do you think your liberties, your right to freedom, are derived from the act and will of the British Government? [Here there was an interruption and clarification regarding the Irish parliament's right to draft the constitution] . . . I . . . wish to warn the members of the Dáil [not to ratify this treaty] under any foolish and idle illusions . . . The first thing that will appear will be that the legislature of Ireland will be no longer Dáil Éireann . . . it will consist of King and Commons and Senate of Ireland. The King will be part of the legislature . . . and the King will have powers there. If not the King himself, there would be the King's representative in Ireland, the Governor-General, or whatever he may be. The King, representing the British Government, or the Governor-General, will have power to give or refuse assent to Irish legislation. Now I know very well . . . that power is virtually obsolete in Canada. Do you suppose that power is going to be obsolete in Ireland? How can it be?"

Here he was interrupted by a deputy who heckled, "40,000 bayonets," but was not deterred:

If Ireland's destiny is to be irrevocably linked with England . . . if the association . . . is that of a bond slave, as it is, under these Clauses 6 and 7, do you suppose that that supremacy of England is going to be an idle phrase . . . [Every] act and deed of the Irish Parliament is going to be jealously watched from over the water, and that every act of legislation done . . . will be read in the light of that inflexible condition that Ireland is virtually a protectorate of England . . . And here again what does the King mean? The functions of the King as an individual are very small indeed. What the King means is the British Government, and let there be no mistake, under the terms of this Treaty the British Government is going to be supreme in Ireland [cries of "No!"]. It is useless again to refer to Canada. Canada is 3,000 miles away."

Heckled once more when a deputy reminded him "We cannot help that," Childers was getting into his stride:

Pass that Treaty admitting the King to Ireland, or rather retaining him as he is in Ireland now . . . recognise the British Government in Ireland, and your rights and independence are lost for ever . . . It is useless for the Minister for Finance [Collins] to say certain things are necessary because Ireland is nearer England, and at the same time to say that Ireland would get all the powers of Canada which is 3,000 miles away. These two proposals are contradictory. The Governor-General in Ireland will be close to Downing Street. He can communicate by telephone . . . Every executive act . . . every administrative function in Ireland, would be performed—you cannot get away from it—in the name of the King. And the King and the Government behind the King would be barely 200 miles away . . . And if anyone were to raise in any particular matter the status of Canada in connection with the Government of Ireland, what would he be told? Canadian status? . . . It is useless for you to pretend that the King's authority and British authority are not operative in Ireland, when it is actually occupied by British Forces and you are forbidden to have Irish defensive naval forces . . . The Treaty promises Ireland to have an army, and a letter of Mr Lloyd George's says the British Army is to evacuate Ireland if this Treaty is passed, within a short time. But do you suppose under this Treaty, your Irish Army is going to be an independent army? Do you really suppose if British troops are evacuated from the country in a short period, there is anything to prevent them returning under full legal power? Constitutional usage would have nothing to do with the matter. It has in Canada. The British Government would never dare to land a British regiment in Canada without the consent of the Canadian Government. Do you suppose that would be so in Ireland? [A Voice: "Why not?"] I will tell you why not. Under Clauses 6 and 7 you abandon altogether . . . to the British Government responsibility for the defence of Ireland. There is something about a local military defence force [but] if you place under a foreign Power responsibility for the defence of the coasts of Ireland, inevitably and naturally you place responsibility for the defence of the whole island on that foreign Government. How can you separate the coastal defences of an island from its internal defences? Are you to have two authorities? . . . What will be the Irish Army? It will be His Majesty's Army, and . . . whatever character the Irish flag takes, His Majesty's flag will fly in Ireland. Every commission held by every officer . . . will be signed either by His Majesty, or by his deputy in Ireland. How are you going to prevent more troops coming in? I do not know if it is really supposed that under this Treaty the evacuation of troops now means that there is no power to re-occupy Ireland in the future? How could you prevent it? Your ports and coasts belong to the British Government . . . [They] can land what troops they like to reinforce [them] . . . That dependence upon England taints and weakens every clause of the Treaty . . . In its most hopeful aspect . . . it is an instrument placing Ireland in the position of a Dominion of the British Crown. I do not wish to be unfair . . . Clearly and on the face of it, it gives Ireland powers never offered her before, and, in certain respects, important powers. But about the fundamental nature of the Treaty, there should be no doubt . . . It places Ireland definitely and irrevocably under British authority and under the British Crown.

Childers's peroration finished with this recital:

I profoundly regret this Treaty was signed [and] . . . that the alternative proposals of the Irish Delegation were not adhered to . . . [It] is possible to associate Ireland with the British Commonwealth on terms honourable to Ireland . . . [The] specific proposals prepared by the President will at a future time have your consideration [Document No. 2 had been drafted with Childers's assistance] . . . Beyond and above all these questions there lies the paramount and overmastering consideration of all: Are we, by our own act, to abandon our independence? . . . No such act was ever performed before, so far as I know, in the history of the world or since the world became a body of democratic nations. Certainly no such act was ever taken before in the history of Ireland, and I, for my part, believe you here will inflexibly refuse to take that step [applause].

Childers met his match in the young Kevin O'Higgins, the Minister for Local Government.[h]

Deputy Childers, to my mind, took a lot of unnecessary time and trouble in explaining how much nicer it would be to get better terms than these. He did not tell us, as an authority on military and naval matters, how we are going to break the British Army and Navy, and get these better terms [applause]. A sovereign, independent Republic was our claim and our fighting ground, and I think we will all admit that men who decided to fight would be fools to fight for less than the fullness of their rights. But the fact that we were willing to negotiate implied that we had something to give away. If we had not, we should have stood sheer on unconditional evacuation, adding, perhaps, that when this had taken place, we would be willing to consider proposals for treaties on trade, or on defence. We did not do so. We selected five men to negotiate a treaty and there was a clear implication, I contend, that whatever, in view of all the circumstances, these men would recommend, would receive most careful consideration here.

O'Higgins questioned the feasibility of Document No. 2:

As the negotiations developed and the rocks began to appear, our team was advised by the [Irish] Cabinet to work towards an objective which would give to Ireland the status of an external associate of the Commonwealth of Nations known as the British Empire. This phrase external associate has caused some trouble. In explanation... someone used the simile of the limpet and the rock. Ireland would be outside and attached, not inside and absorbed. We were prepared to enter as a free and equal partner into treaties on such matters of common concern as trade and defence. On the question of the Crown, the Cabinet, as its last card, was prepared to recommend to the Dáil a recognition of the King of England as the head of the group of States to which the Irish Free State would be attached, and as the outward and visible sign of that recognition, to vote a yearly sum to his civil list.

These remarks triggered a protest that cabinet (for which read also de Valera's) papers were being publicly discussed, but O'Higgins went on:

I would have wished to examine the difference between the Treaty and the proposals a united Cabinet would have proposed. I would have asked to what extent it affected the lives and fortunes of the plain people of Ireland, whose fate is in our hands. I would have asked you to consider the prospects the rejection of this Treaty opens up and come to a decision with a view to your tremendous responsibility.

Backing Collins, O'Higgins emphasized:

I do not wish to be forced into a stronger advocacy of the Treaty than I feel... I do say it represents such a broad measure of liberty for the Irish people and it acknowledges such a large proportion of its rights, you are not entitled to reject it without being able to show them you have a reasonable prospect of achieving more [hear, hear]. 'The man who is against peace,' said the English Premier in presenting his ultimatum, 'must bear now and for ever the responsibility for terrible and immediate war.' And the men there knew our resources and the resources of the enemy, and they held in their own hearts and consciences that we were not entitled to plunge the plain people of Ireland into a terrible and immediate war for the difference between the terms of the Treaty and what they knew a united Cabinet would recommend to the Dáil... [This treaty...] gives to Ireland complete control over her internal affairs. It removes all English control or interference within the shores of Ireland. Ireland is liable to no taxation from England, and has the fullest fiscal freedom. She has the right to maintain an army and defend her coasts. When England is at war, Ireland need not send one man nor contribute a penny... This morning the President [de Valera] said the army of the Irish Free State would be the army of His Majesty. Can His Majesty send one battalion or company of the Army of the Irish Free State from Cork into the adjoining county? If he acts in Ireland, he acts on the advice of his Irish Ministers [applause]. Yes, if we go into the Empire we go in, not sliding in, attempting to throw dust in our people's eyes, but we go in with our heads up. It is true that by the provisions of the Treaty, Ireland is included in the system known as the British Empire, and the most objectionable aspect of the Treaty is that the threat of force has been used to influence Ireland to a decision to enter this miniature league of nations. It has been called a league of free nations. I admit in practice it is so; but it is unwise and unstatesmanlike to attempt to bind any such league by any ties other than pure voluntary ties. I believe the evolution of this group must be towards a condition, not merely of individual freedom but also of equality of status. I quite admit in the case of Ireland the tie is not voluntary, and in the case of Ireland the status is not equal. Herein lie the defects of the Treaty. But face the facts that they are defects which the English representatives insisted upon with threats of war, terrible and immediate. Let us face also the facts that they are not defects which press so grievously on our citizens that we are entitled to invite war because of them . . .

O'Higgins then attacked the sovereignty of the dead, and addressed the pending oath:

There has been too much talk of what the dead men would do if they were here and had our responsibility. There are men here . . . who carried their lives in their hands for Ireland during the last four or five years, men who but for a fortunate accident might well be dead; they are here to speak for themselves. When I hear it quoted 'What would so and so do if he were here?' I think of the men who risked daily for the last three or four years and who will vote for the Treaty. The men who died for Irish independence never intended that the country should be sentenced to destruction in a hopeless war, if all its rights were not conceded . . . Now I come to King Charles' head—the Oath of Allegiance. Some call it an oath of allegiance. I do not know what it is. I can only speak of it in a negative way. It is not an oath of allegiance. There is a difference between faith and allegiance. Your first allegiance is to the Constitution of the Irish Free State and you swear faith to the King of England. Now faith is a thing that can exist between equals; there is, if I might coin a word, mutuality, reciprocity. It is contingent and conditional, and I hold if you had sworn allegiance to the Constitution of the Irish Free State anything that follows on that is not absolute but conditional on your Constitution being respected, and conditional on the terms of the Treaty being adhered to. In the second clause of the Treaty you have two words of which Deputy Childers took very little stock—he waved it aside: 'The position of the Irish Free State in relation to the Imperial Parliament and Government and otherwise shall be that of the Dominion of Canada and the law, *practice* and constitutional *usage* governing the relationship of the Crown or the representatives of the Crown, and of the Imperial Parliament to the Dominion of Canada shall govern their relationship to the Irish Free State.' Now, those two words 'practice' and 'usage' mean much more than Mr Childers was prepared to attribute to them. They neutralise and nullify 'law'. They were put in with that purpose. The English representatives offered to embody in the Treaty anything to ensure that the power of the Crown in Ireland would be exercised no more than in Canada—in other words, that there would be no power of the Crown in Ireland. Mr Childers says who is to be the judge, who is to decide, where is your court? Everyone knows we will be represented in the League of Nations. That's the Court. For another thing, I take it we ourselves will decide. If we consider our rights are infringed, then we stand solely on our allegiance to the Constitution of the Free State, and nothing else [hear, hear] . . .

O'Higgins finished by slaughtering Stack's sacred cows:

We have responsibilities to all the nation and not merely to a particular political party within the nation. If I felt that by resuming war we had even an outside chance of securing the fullness of our rights, that consideration would scarcely deter me, but I am not prepared to sacrifice them for the sake of handing on a tradition to posterity. I take it that we are the posterity of the generation that preceded us, but they do not seem to have worried much about handing on a separatist tradition intact to us— we had to go back to '67 to dig it up . . . It is possible to be oversolicitous about posterity . . . I do not wish to be flippant about . . . a sacred ideal . . . an ideal sanctified by the best blood of our countrymen . . . but I do ask for a frank admission that in face of tremendous odds we have gone as near the attainment of that ideal as is possible in the existing circumstances [and] for a frank and fearless recognition of political realities . . . for an endorsement of the view of our plenipotentiaries that embodied in this Treaty you have a measure of liberty that may honourably be accepted in the name of our people, not indeed a complete recognition of what we have held, and still hold, to be their right, but at least a political experiment to the working of which we are prepared to bring goodwill and good faith . . . I do the English people the justice of believing that they would gladly have endorsed a more generous measure. I hardly hope that within the terms of this Treaty there lies the fulfilment of Ireland's destiny, but I do hope and believe that with the disappearance of old passions and distrusts, fostered by centuries of persecution and desperate resistance, what remains may be won by agreement and by peaceful political evolution. In that spirit I stand for the ratification of this Treaty—in that spirit I ask you to endorse it . . . on that basis and because of the alternative and all it means for these our people, I ask your acceptance of and your allegiance to the Constitution of Saorstát na hÉireann [applause].

Over subsequent days the other delegates spoke. Robert Barton, Childers's first-cousin, confessed that he and Gavan Duffy had opposed the treaty's terms, but did not want, as a minority in the delegation, to be responsible for war. He did not resile from his signature and commended the treaty. Duffy had been the last delegate to sign. Eamonn Duggan argued that he had signed because Great Britain was more powerful and that the alternative was war, rejecting Duffy's claim that intimidation and demoralization had driven their joint decision. He enumerated the treaty's merits and argued that, under its terms, "if the Irish people cannot achieve freedom it is the fault of the Irish people and not of the Treaty."[i] William Cosgrave joined the criticism of Childers—Ireland lacked a navy, so the treaty's defense provisions were appropriate—and used Childers's former arguments, first articulated in *The Framework of Home Rule* (1911), against his current position: Canada was equal in status to Great Britain; Canada alone could legislate for Canada; in practice, only Canada could change Canada's constitution; the Governor-General was the joint nominee of the Ottawa and London govern-ments; and Canadians owed obedience to only their own constitution. Cosgrave placed his emphasis, however, on letting the people decide between accepting peace or rejecting the treaty.

The delegates and the treaty were denounced at length by Mary MacSwiney, the sister of Cork's mayor who had died on hunger strike. She appealed to honor, world opinion, and against giving in to the trickster Lloyd George.[17] She was later echoed by Liam Mellows, who thought the people's fear of war was damaging their real will for a republic—perhaps an unconscious echo of Rousseau's "will of all" being pitted against "the general will." In 1926 de Valera retrospectively, but accurately, described the republicans' dilemma as "the conflict between the two principles, majority rule on the one hand and the inalienability of national sovereignty on the other."[18] Majority rule implied accepting the treaty; national sovereignty required its rejection. Mellows's speech contrasted with that of Richard Mulcahy, who coolly restated the realists' case. Accepting that de Valera's alternative

---

[17] All the female deputies in Dáil Éireann opposed the treaty, leading to the sexist (and untrue) joke that its opponents were "the Women and Childers' party." Constance Markievicz made the socialist republican case, arguing that the treaty betrayed James Connolly's ideals; Mary MacSwiney declared herself a rebel against the new Free State, and became a staunch spokeswoman of the "Second Dáil," which insisted it remained the legitimate sovereign body in Ireland; while Pearse's mother insisted that Pearse would not have signed the treaty.

[18] Fanning (1977: 14), citing Longford and O'Neill (1970: 186).

had not been treated fairly, he maintained that its supporters had shown no way to achieve it. The treaty was defective, but the IRA could not expel the British armed forces from the designated ports: it had not been able to drive them out of anything, apart from some large police barracks. The treaty gave Ireland command of its resources; these should not be wasted on an unwinnable war.

These lengthy extracts demonstrate that the treaty divided Irish nationalists for rational not just emotional or symbolic reasons.[j] The treaty overturned Ireland's two declarations of a republic—that of 1916 in arms; and that of 1919, in its elected parliament; and could be read to imply that authority in Ireland would now derive from the Crown, not Ireland's people. Ireland was obliged to remain in the Empire; minimally, with a constrained foreign policy, preventing the choice of neutrality let alone taking sides with Britain's enemies; and it granted Great Britain naval bases and other military rights on Irish soil. The British interpretation did not repudiate Westminster's right to legislate for Ireland; to the contrary, they would later insist that the constitution of the IFS would be legislated by the imperial parliament, not just that in Dublin—following dominion, including Canadian, constitutional usage.[19] It was not a treaty of equals (and coerced treaties are now invalid in international law). The British government did not recognize the treaty as one with an independent state; though dominions could conduct external relations, Great Britain did not then recognize the Irish Free State's affairs with Great Britain as foreign.[20] The integrity of de Valera's and Childers's criticisms and their alternative to the treaty, Document No. 2, are recognized by those who do not caricature de Valera.[21] Equally evident, however, is the integrity of the assessments of Collins, Griffith, Mulcahy, and O'Higgins. Time, not logic, proved them right. Collins's core stepping-stone theory proved correct. The worst fears of the anti-treatyites proved incorrect. There was a Dáil Éireann within the IFS; the state's flag was the republican tricolor; there were no royal visits, merely royal correspondence; over time, thanks to both Cosgrave's and de Valera's governments, the IFS developed its full sovereignty; and, by exploiting its treaty powers, especially through facilitating the reconstruction of the Commonwealth, the IFS eventually removed all of the treaty's constraints, aside from those relating to partition—and even these would be formally constitutionally repudiated.

The conflict personified by de Valera and Childers, on the one hand, and Collins and O'Higgins, on the other, confirms Hegel's argument that tragedy is properly defined as a conflict between right and right.[22] The long fellow, as de Valera was known, was correct that the treaty would split republicans and produce a civil war; the big fellow, as Collins was known, was correct that the British appetite for compromise was exhausted, yet the treaty would enable most of

---

[19] McColgan (1977).

[20] It sought to block the IFS's diplomatic accreditation, not conceding the point until 1924 (Whelan 2015).

[21] Lee (2001). The two texts are printed together in one biography (Coogan 1993). Regrettably, de Valera, who had many faults, is now mostly known through Alan Rickman's caricature in Neil Jordan's film *Michael Collins*.

[22] The idea is articulated in Hegel's *Phenomenology* and his *Lectures on Aesthetics*. Many Irish historians, by contrast, treat the treaty debates and the Irish civil war simply as a clash of right and wrong, or of democrats versus dictators. It is generally agreed that class differences do not account for the positions taken by the protagonists (Garvin 1987: 142).

Box 2.3.1. Carsonia: Seán MacEntee's contribution to the treaty debate

---

"First of all, within a month six counties, or more than six counties as it may ultimately turn out to be, have a right to vote themselves out from under the operation of your Treaty, and you are making no provision whatsoever to bring them in." Citing Lloyd George's defense of the boundary commission before the House of Commons, predicting that it would likely lead to a "re-adjustment of boundaries," MacEntee insisted that the real purpose of Article 12 was to ensure that "Ulster—secessionist Ulster—should remain a separate unit," to ensure that "Carsonia shall secure a homogeneous population which is necessary for her, in order to develop as England intends, and as the Orange politicians intend it should develop into a second state and a second people usurping Irish soil."

MacEntee refuted the conviction that the new Northern Ireland would be economically obliged to reunify with the Irish Free State.

Does [deputy Milroy] tell me that material or economic facts are the determining factors in nationality? Would he have said that when we were asking the people of Ireland to risk their economical welfare on the question of nationality three years ago?... there is more in nationality and history than mere materialism... You will say: 'What of the heavy taxation under this Act?'... Show me anything in the bond that will compel England to tax Northern Ireland more heavily than the Free State will be taxed. Show me anything in the Treaty or in the Government of Ireland Act. You cannot show me anything there, and I say as England has found it profitable to subsidise the [Emir] of Afghanistan, she will find it much more profitable to subsidise Northern Ireland to remain out and weaken the Free State; and that is my answer to those who say the economic factors are going to bring about a united Ireland under this document...

This Treaty is the most dangerous and diabolical onslaught that has ever been made upon the unity of our nation, because... we are going to be destructive of our own nationality—[its] provisions... mean this: that in the North of Ireland certain people differing from us somewhat in tradition, and differing in religion... are going to be driven, in order to maintain their separate identity, to demarcate themselves from us, while we, in order to preserve ourselves against the encroachment of English culture, are going to be driven to demarcate ourselves so far as ever we can from them... They will be driven in their schools to hold up the English tradition and ideal. We will be driven in our schools to hold up the Gaelic tradition and ideal...

And yet you tell me that, considering these factors, this is not a partition provision... I am voting against it because I believe it will be a final settlement, and it is the terrible finality of the settlement that appals me... Under this Treaty Ulster will become England's fortress in Ireland—... as impregnable as Gibraltar... England... has robbed you of your territory to settle it upon her new Cromwellians and is asking you now to give her the title deeds. That is what this document means.

[All] those who are sitting for Ulster constituencies, and all of those who vote for the acceptance of this Treaty... will be guilty of a double betrayal—the betrayal of not only our own rights but of the pledge to the Ulster people—a people who, under conditions that those who have not endured them can have no conception of, have stood for us and have suffered for us in the hope that in our day of triumph we should not forget them.

Note: Sean McEntee's contributions are found under both McEntee and Macentee. Then deputy for Monaghan, Seán MacEntee (1889–1984) was a Belfast-born engineer, a participant in the 1916 Rising, member of the Belfast IRA, Sinn Féin TD 1918–23; and later Fianna Fáil TD 1927–69. The longest survivor of the first Dáil, he served as Minister for Finance, 1932–9, 1951–4; Industry & Commerce, 1939–41; Local Government & Public Health, 1941–8; Health & Social Welfare, 1957–65; and as Tánaiste (deputy prime minister), 1959–65.

Source: Deputies of Dáil Éireann, Debate on the Treaty between Great Britain and Ireland, signed in London on December 6, 1921: Sessions December 14. 1921–January 10, 1922, pp. 157–8, published as an electronic text by University College Cork, <https://celt.ucc.ie/published/E900003-001.html> (accessed: 2012).

Ireland to achieve sovereign independence. Ireland's sovereignty was the principal subject of the treaty debate, and the ensuing civil war, not the terms that referred to Ulster or the boundary commission. Most who fought either for the IFS or for the Republic assumed that the Ulster question would be satisfied by the boundary commission, which would make Northern Ireland unworkable.[23] Seán MacEntee was the sole leading deputy to diagnose Article 12 of the Treaty in any depth—see Box 2.3.1—and his arguments were not decisive or picked up by other deputies.

The civil war was provoked by the scope and extent of Irish statehood; its degree of substantive and ritual subordination to the British Empire; its geographical extension was not the key issue. The failure to achieve consensus among Irish nationalists after the vote was held to ratify the treaty was a proximate cause of the civil war, which was not inevitable.

THE PROVISIONAL GOVERNMENT, THE CONSTITUTION OF THE IRISH FREE STATE, AND THE IRISH CIVIL WAR

The Declaration of Independence in 1919 had ratified "the establishment of the Irish Republic" of 1916, and ordained that the people's elected representatives "alone have power to make laws binding on the people of Ireland."[24] That is why Mellows argued that the Irish plenipotentiaries "had no power to agree to anything inconsistent with the existence of the Republic... If the Republic exists, why are we talking about stepping towards the Republic by means of this Treaty?" The question had a point. The IFS took until 1937 to become a republic in all but name, and until 1949 to be a republic in formal name. The Provisional Government of the IFS was obligated to reconstitute the parliament of Southern Ireland, established by the Government of Ireland Act of 1920. Childers was correct that Griffith and Collins had asked Dáil Éireann "to vote its own extinction in history," but wrong to predict an Irish House of Commons and Lords under the King. A new Dáil Éireann, known as the third Dáil, would be confirmed under the constitution of the Free State.

The second Dáil Éireann approved the treaty by sixty-four votes to fifty-seven on January 7, 1922. De Valera promptly resigned but stood for the presidency

[23] Wall (1966); Lyons (1973a). De Valera shared with his pro-treaty adversaries the failure to recognize how the boundary commission's composition and terms of reference might have minimal consequences.
[24] Mitchell and Ó Snodaigh (1985: 58).

again. On January 10, Griffith defeated de Valera for this post by sixty votes to fifty-eight, and thereafter many republican TDs boycotted sessions of the Dáil. Collins became Chairman of the Provisional Government, scheduled to exist for a maximum of one year, and took over the Castle administration, symbol of British power in mid-January. The two governments—Dáil Éireann's under Griffith and the Provisional administration under Collins—ran in parallel with almost identical cabinets, which eliminated executive confusion, until the Autumn. Sinn Féin's pro-treaty TDs met with the Trinity College MPs elected to the parliament of Southern Ireland, on one occasion, to ratify the treaty. They thereby disestablished the Republic. Not, however, according to those subsequent militants who would claim that their authority to represent and govern the Irish Republic (and to fight to unify Ireland) flowed from the second Dáil. In their developed doctrine, the second Dáil vested them with such authority, but it had no right to ratify the treaty (because it had no right to do wrong).

Griffith wanted an early general election to underline the public legitimacy of the treaty. Collins was more reluctant, and sought both to conciliate the losing republicans, and to build up the new army of the IFS by winning officers and regular IRA volunteers to the pro-treaty camp; and in February he agreed with de Valera to postpone elections for three months. IRA forces, led by pro- and anti-treaty officers (and some neutrals), took over different military barracks and installations from the evacuating British Army, and the anti-treaty forces sought to infiltrate the new army of the IFS. Civil war loomed. An IRA convention in March ended in a split. Militarist hardline republicans, led by Rory O'Connor and Mellows, rejected the authority of Dáil Éireann, and sought to postpone or reject elections because the threat of war with England still existed.[25] On April 14, they took over the Four Courts, a provocative challenge to the Provisional Government.

In May 1922, however, Collins and de Valera made a pact, whose details still provoke curiosity. The election would now take place in June. The two factions in Sinn Féin would be represented on a national panel in proportion to their existing strength in the Dáil (66:58). After the election, it was promised, there would be a coalition cabinet: five from the majority faction, four from the minority, with each faction to select its own ministers. Quite how this pact was to be executed without the cooperation of the electorate was not clear, though Collins ensured that other parties (all pro-treaty) would be able to compete. The British government, which had handed supervision of the implementation of the treaty to Churchill, as Secretary of State for the Colonies, was outraged—claiming that the pact violated democratic principles (in which the British were so well versed in Ireland and across their empire). Collins put two defenses to Churchill: the new Dáil would be a constituent assembly rather than a normal parliament, and it was necessary to ensure that elections were held. Constitutional-drafting was underway, but the latter argument suggested that the pact was cunning—it was intended to slow the march toward civil war, and opened an opportunity for moderates among the anti-treaty camp, like de Valera in some moods, to distance themselves from the hardline militarists.

---

[25] Macardle (1965: 633).

Collins hoped to achieve a constitution that would look sufficiently republican to win over more of the anti-treaty faction.[26] But in private negotiations in early June the British government rejected the draft put forward by the Irish constitutional team—itself a compromise. The proposed draft was a republic in all but name: though it accepted the treaty, it included no oath for deputies or ministers, granted full treaty-making powers to the IFS, made Irish courts the final source of legal decisions (with no right of appeal to the privy council, the imperial supreme court). It was essentially kingless and devoid of a governor-general, aside from this clever proposal: "The Representative in Saorstát Eireann of His Majesty King George V, his heirs and successors shall be styled the Commissioner of the British Commonwealth and shall be appointed with the previous assent of the Executive Council of Saorstát Eireann."

The British government, led by Lloyd George and Churchill, declared the draft non-treaty compliant. Its provisions went way beyond dominion usage, and implicitly the threat of a return to war was raised. British cabinet committee minutes suggest that action would initially, at least, have been confined to retaliation on Irish revenues rather than war, but the Irish leaders did not know that. The British government demanded and received clarity that a revised draft would ensure that Ireland was within the Empire, that the Crown's authority would conform to that in other dominions, that the IFS's treaty-making power would not exceed that of Canada, and that both the intensely controversial oath and the office of governor-general would be openly in the draft text.[27] Though the democratic character of the draft eventually approved by British ministers was clear—including the vesting of authority in the people[28]—it did not meet Collins's hopes. Article 2 declared void any article or amendment repugnant to the treaty. Collins and his advisors had been defeated in their ambitions—partly because Griffith, who had opposed their maximalist strategy, insisted on honoring the treaty, thereby potentially opening a chasm within the pro-treaty ranks.

In what has been called "a piece of sharp practice,"[29] Collins did not publicly issue the revised draft of the constitution until the morning of election day—he pled drafting delays, but that lacks credibility. Even more ruthlessly he repudiated the pact with de Valera two days before the election, giving the latter no chance to respond. Collins must have calculated that there was no point in keeping to the concessions made to the anti-treaty TDs, since they could not be won to the revised draft constitution. He had made the treaty the sole important subject of the election, exactly what the pact had originally been designed to avoid. In *The World Crisis, 1918–1928: The Aftermath* (1929) Churchill maintained that the draft to which the IFS leaders had agreed successfully precluded de Valera from being part of a coalition government. As Akenson and Fallin observe, "another way of expressing the same idea would have been to state that an Irish civil war was certain."[30] Yet another way to put matters is that the British government was

---

[26] Two authors speculate that Collins and de Valera may have agreed the text of a draft constitution of the IFS as part of their electoral pact (Akenson and Fallin 1970: 36).

[27] On the drafting of the IFS constitution, see Brian Farrell (1970a, b, 1971a, b). See also Akenson and Fallin (1970) and Harkness (1988); for early commentary on the text, see Kohn (1932).

[28] The Weimar intellectual Leo Kohn (1982) thought highly of its democratic and liberal character.

[29] Lee (1989: 59).   [30] Akenson and Fallin (1970: 66).

willing to risk both an Irish civil war and a return to a war with the Irish to keep the IFS within its "red-lines" of the Empire and the Crown.

The election took place on June 16, 1922. The numbers have been definitively treated by political scientist Michael Gallagher (see Tables 2.3.1–2.3.3). Over 70 percent of those returned as deputies supported the treaty; and the ratio of pro-treaty to anti-treaty SF deputies returned was over 3:2, compared with a ratio of less than 6:5 in the ratification vote. The pro-treaty SF TDs lost eight seats compared to the second Dáil; the anti-treaty SF TDs lost twenty-two. The new competitors, Labour, Farmers and Others, accepted the treaty, so in contested districts almost 80 percent of voters endorsed candidates supporting the treaty. Eight constituencies out of twenty-eight were uncontested, and returned previously arranged SF joint panel candidates—except in Trinity College. These contributed 38 of the total of 128 TDs: 17 pro-treaty SF, 17 anti-treaty SF, and 4 Independents from Trinity. Not one anti-treaty SF candidate headed the first-preference poll in any contested constituency. Supporters of each wing of SF tended to transfer their lower preferences to the other, suggesting some determination

Table 2.3.1. General election, Irish Free State, June 16, 1922

Parties	Pro-treaty SF	Anti-treaty SF	Labour	Farmers	Others
First-preference votes won in contested districts (%)	38.5	21.3	21.3	7.8	10.6
Seats won (%)	45.3	28.1	13.2	5.5	7.8
Seats won (N)	58	36	17	7	10

Note: All figures rounded to one decimal point, so totals may not add to 100. For reasons given by Gallagher, the figures exclude 0.5% of the votes.

Source: Gallagher (1979; 1993: 1–21).

Table 2.3.2. General election, Irish Free State, June 16, 1922: Outcome of non-panel transfers, when both pro- and anti-treaty panelists were available to receive them (%)

Parties	Labour	Farmers	Independents	All non-SF
Pro-treaty SF	44.1	39.5	33.6	39.1
Others including independents	28.1	47.0	56.9	42.6
Anti-treaty SF	27.9	13.5	9.5	18.3
Total (rounded)	100	100	100	100

Source: Gallagher (1979: table 5).

Table 2.3.3. General election, Irish Free State, regional breakdown by first-preference vote in contested districts, June 16, 1922

District	Pro-treaty SF	Anti-treaty SF	Labour	Farmers	Others
Connacht–Ulster	52.2	31.4	4.2	4.9	7.4
Dublin	40.9	11.7	13.4	2.7	31.3
Rest of Leinster	35.6	15.6	37.4	10.3	1.2
Munster	30.6	28.4	21.0	11.2	7.0

Source: Gallagher (1979).

among the party's supporters to preserve unity, but, by contrast, transfers from non-SF candidates broke decisively toward pro-treaty SF (see Table 2.3.2). The breakdown of votes and deputies returned suggests that pro-treaty SF support was very high in Connacht–Ulster and rural Ireland; that voters in Leinster (including Dublin) were the least supportive of SF candidates; and that only in Munster, where the IRA had fought most effectively against Crown forces, did anti-treaty SF candidates come close to parity with pro-treaty SF candidates (see Table 2.3.3). Given the spatial distribution of the vote it may reasonably be suggested that the anti-treaty vote was concentrated among the less well-off, but Labour had also done well in its first competitive election.[31]

The numbers do not entirely speak for themselves. John M. Regan has unforgettably insisted both in *The Irish Counter-Revolution, 1921–36* and in *Myth and the Irish State*[32] that no evaluation of the treaty split and the election of 1922 may ignore or downplay the threat of renewed British violence. The electorate did not have an abstract choice between a republic or a dominion kingdom, or between external association and internal association. Its uncoerced constitutional preferences, if any, cannot be definitively assessed. Irish voters were confronted with a choice between a compromise peace and the renewal of war, with their recently elected leaders in deep disagreement. The debate and election over the treaty was conducted under the shadow of a credible military threat from the world's most powerful empire, which had just shown locally what it was capable of doing on behalf of counter-insurgency, and which was vigorously repressing other anti-colonial rebellions, and would continue to do so over the next two decades, notably in Iraq, Egypt, India, and Palestine. Regan documents historians who downplay or elide this threat, suggesting that too many retrospectively line up with the pro-treaty side, portraying them as democrats facing down a potential elitist dictatorship. Regan's core point and his historiographical notes are accurate. The counterfactual implication is that the anti-treaty/pro-republican vote would have been higher had there been no threat of war, but here, as with many forms of counterfactual reasoning, there is no obvious end to potential regress. Had there been no threat of war, then either any treaty would have been closer to Irish leaders' preferences (a republic) or the negotiations would not have concluded in the winter of 1921 (and the War of Independence would have been renewed). It is certainly wrong, however, to portray the conflict that unfolded as simply one of democrats versus dictators. The British government, electorally mandated, was dictating an outcome to an Irish government, electorally mandated. Within Sinn Féin there were elitists on both sides—after all, with the conspicuous exception of Griffith, the major SF leaders were largely veterans of 1916. It is therefore better to see the conflict among the Irish as one between pessimists (or realists) and optimists (or idealists). That said, many anti-treaty leaders expressly objected to the public being consulted on the treaty, or publicly took the view that the people did not have the right to be wrong, and included, at various junctures, O'Connor,

---

[31] E. Strauss (1957) and Rumpf and Hepburn (1977) were pioneers in left–right and class-based readings of pro- and anti-treaty positions taken by voters; there is definitely something to this idea, even if the straightforward derivations from the election returns are subject to what political scientists call the ecological fallacy.

[32] Regan (1999, 2013).

Mellows, Lynch, and de Valera. The first named infamously responded with a careless "if you like" to a journalist who suggested that his position amounted to setting up a military dictatorship.

Within two weeks of the June elections the Irish civil war began in earnest. Chronological precedence does not prove causation. It was not fought over the election results, which were not seriously disputed. In a Dublin convention of the anti-treaty IRA, held immediately after the elections, initially designed to deal with the consequences of the pact, a proposal, backed by those in occupation of the Four Courts, was put to attack British forces still evacuating from Ireland. It was defeated, but O'Connor and Mellows persisted, and they and their supporters again broke ranks. They had now repudiated both the authority of the (divided) second and the third Dáil Éireann, and, temporarily, that of the anti-treaty IRA convention and its Army Council, including its chief-of-staff, Liam Lynch.[33] What immediately triggered the civil war, however, was not the divisions within the anti-treaty ranks, but the assassination of Sir Henry Wilson, and the reactions to this event, first in London and then in Dublin. Wilson, encountered earlier as the British Army's chief of staff *and* as a supporter of the UVF's militancy against His Majesty's Government, had become a Field Marshal during the First World War. In "retirement" he had become the military advisor to Craig's government in the North and an MP for North Down. He was shot dead on the doorstep of his London home, by two members of the IRA in England—perhaps under instructions from Collins, who had held Wilson responsible for the treatment of Catholics in Belfast, possibly out-of-date instructions.[34]

The London government may have been convinced that the assassination was organized by the IRA in the Four Courts. It certainly publicly chose to believe that. The alternative explanation, that Collins, their pro-treaty ally, was playing a complex double game, was too difficult to contemplate. Whatever drove the actual assessment, Churchill decided to make an opportunity out of Wilson's assassination. Initially, the British government had ordered General Macready, in charge of the evacuation of British troops, to attack the Four Courts. He (wisely) prevaricated, and persuaded the cabinet to modify its orders. Churchill now demanded that the Provisional Government take action against the anti-treaty faction of the IRA in occupation of the Four Courts—or else the British Army

---

[33] Ryan (1986) provides a spare biography of this militant whose civil-war leadership on the anti-treaty side seems almost accidental.

[34] Hart (2003, 2005b) believes that Collins may have given such instructions earlier, but if so, they were as likely to have come from Rory O'Connor; and in his conclusion (2003: 220) maintains that the evidence best supports independent action by the two assassins, Reginald Dunne and Joseph O'Sullivan, who were subsequently tried, convicted, and hung. An earlier biographer of Collins is cautious (Ó Broin 1991), whereas Hopkinson (1988) fits the assassination into Collins's Northern policy. Keith Jeffery (2006) provides the most professional biography of Wilson, an able, gossipy, careerist, and curious Francophile from Longford who, as Chief of the Imperial Guard Staff, managed security policy across the four storm zones of India, Iraq, Egypt and Ireland, 1918-22. He had a state funeral in recognition of his role in the UK's victory over Germany in the Great War. Commentators directly quote Wilson commending ferocious repression in Ireland, but also as regarding both the Black and Tans and Craig's sectarian Specials as counterproductive. Jeffery absolves Wilson of Orange bigotry but not of Irish unionist bigotry toward the southern and Catholic Irish. He argues that Wilson sought to ensure that the armed forces were religiously impartial in conducting their duties in Northern Ireland.

would perform the task. Collins's hand was forced, or, like the British, he chose to have it forced, but only after the Four Courts IRA faction had kidnapped J. J. (Ginger) O'Connell, the deputy Chief of Staff of the IFS's new army. An ultimatum was dispatched to O'Connor to release O'Connell and to evacuate the Four Courts. When O'Connor refused, the Provisional Government under Collins's instructions attacked the Four Courts—and availed of British heavy weapons to do so. De Valera reported for duty to the anti-treaty IRA, though he would play no military role in the civil war. The Four Courts, in ruins, was surrendered on June 30.

The civil war was won by the pro-treaty forces, with British material assistance, but also because they had a better military strategy, and greater public support. Within forty days the IFS army, with Collins as Commander-in-Chief, cleared urban Ireland of what it now called the "irregulars." By mid-July it outflanked the republican ground forces by land and sea in their stronghold of southwest Munster. The Provisional Government successfully recruited soldiers in massive numbers. It was therefore almost immediately clear what the outcome of the war would be.[35] August 1922, however, provided a double blow to the pro-treaty leadership. Griffith died, probably of heart failure, on the 10th, and on August 22 Collins was killed in an ambush in west Cork (he had been careless with his own security). The repercussions of the civil war, whose military course is not narrated here, were immediate and long run, and are critical to understanding the consolidation of Northern Ireland, and the development of North–South relations.

The two key makers and champions of the treaty on the Irish side were dead. Northern nationalists had lost their most effective champion in the new state: Collins's death removed both the most potentially progressive member of the Provisional Government, and the most interventionist toward the North. What-ever his motivations, he had been the most determined to protect northern nationalists—including through reprisals and secret war against the new Northern Ireland. He had been most willing to coerce Craig's regime after the two pacts had failed, and would have been determined to deliver an expanded Irish Free State through the boundary commission.[k] Yet controversy over how Collins's northern policy would have evolved had he lived will continue.[36] Throughout 1922 he wavered between a peaceful and a coercive policy—responding to the UUP's conduct in the North, the plight of northern nationalists, and his strong need to keep the IRA in the North on the pro-treaty side. He largely succeeded in the latter endeavor—the 1st, 2nd, 3rd, 5th Northern and Midland divisions were all pro-treaty, with some exceptions at officer level, while the 4th Northern led by Aiken was originally neutral before it switched to the anti-treaty side. The 3rd Western, which had a small portion of Fermanagh in its jurisdiction, was the sole unam-biguously anti-treaty division.

The successors to Griffith and Collins, led by William Cosgrave and Kevin O'Higgins, were much less conciliatory toward republicans than Collins had been

---

[35] For a pioneering comparative survey of the politics of the Irish civil war, see Kissane (2005); for a historian's treatment, see Hopkinson (1988); for how it is commemorated see Anne Dolan (2003).

[36] Key contributions include Coogan (1990: ch. 11); Staunton (1997); Phoenix (1998); Regan (1998); and Lynch (2006: 87–8, 97–9, 100–5).

prepared to be.[37] They resolved to terminate the civil war with ruthless repressive rigor.[38] The Public Safety Act of September 1922 enabled military courts to impose the death sentence, and put paid to efforts to initiate a peace process. The cabinet later authorized the execution of seventy-seven republicans, over three times as many as the British carried out during the war of independence, and jailed over 10,000 republicans under emergency legislation.[39] In November 1922 eight Republican prisoners, including Erskine Childers, were executed. In a move that was both morally and strategically inept, Liam Lynch, the anti-treaty IRA Chief of Staff, ordered any IRA volunteer who could do so to kill any TD or senator who had voted for the "Murder Bill." Judges and journalists were also threatened. On December 6, 1922, the Irish Free State was formally established by British statute, and within days the last British troops in Dublin had left for Great Britain, but that did not end the civil war. On December 7, two TDs were shot, Seán Hales and Padraig Ó Máille—Hales died, Ó Máille was badly wounded. The Irish cabinet deliberated all night, and decided on retaliatory executions, publicly defended as such. Four Republican leaders who had surrendered at the Four Courts—O'Connor, Mellows, Dick Barret, and Joe McKelvey, the commanding officer of the 3rd Northern Division of IRA—were selected, and shot within hours. The cabinet's leading light defended the executions as an impersonal decision: O'Connor had been O'Higgins's best man at his wedding, and O'Higgins was the last to approve his friend's execution. In February 1923, expressing sorrow if not regret, Cosgrave judged the executions remarkably effective. He told a neutral IRA delegation: "I am not going to hesitate if the country is to live, and if we have to exterminate 10,000 Republicans, the 3 million of our people are bigger than this ten thousand."[40] Official executions were justified by Mulcahy because they would restrain freelancing reprisals on behalf of the IFS, but that was not the case: there may have been twice as many unauthorized executions. The Ballyseedy massacre of 1923 was the most notorious: when five Free State soldiers were killed in an explosion at Knocknagoshel, nine republican prisoners were tied to a landmine that was then detonated—astonishingly a survivor was blown into a neighboring field.[41] The IRA's leadership was demoralized by the time Lynch was killed in flight in April 1923. His successor, Frank Aiken, always a reluctant participant and more amenable to de Valera than other IRA leaders, ordered the IRA to end the struggle and to dump arms (rather than formally to surrender).[1] The IRA noticeably did not disband; it was less noticed that de Valera and Aiken had stated that majority-rule decisions should be adhered to, not necessarily because they were right, but because this rule made for peace, order, and unity.

---

[37] Peter Hart (2005b: 33) correctly observed: "It was the Treaty-based Provisional Government that actually started the Civil War and was the more violent of the two 'sides' in that struggle."

[38] G. B. Shaw, who saw Collins before his death, reported him as being in a bellicose disposition toward the anti-treaty republicans (Kissane 2005: 102).

[39] One political scientist observes that the execution rate was low in comparison to other civil wars (Kissane 2002: 92).

[40] Mulcahy papers p 7/B//284, cited in Jordan (2006: Kindle location 2122).

[41] Unauthorized reprisals continued after the formal cessation of hostilities—e.g., Noel Lemass, brother of the future prime minister, was killed in the mistaken belief that he had been responsible for Hales's assassination.

The war of Green against Green had obscured and relegated the importance of the Ulster question in southern politics in 1922–3, and thereby facilitated the UUP's consolidation of its control in the North.[42] The new IFS government emerged shattered militarily, financially, and diplomatically. Cosgrave's cabinet was in no mood to renew instability through an aggressive northern policy, let alone prosecute a war over the details of partition. In a foretaste of things to come in October 1922, a northern nationalist deputation arrived in Dublin, including priests, solicitors, and local councilors, looking for funds to counteract unionist propaganda. They got short shrift from O'Higgins: "We have no other policy for the North East than we have for any other part of Ireland and that is the Treaty policy." He crisply suggested that what northern nationalists needed was not just funds but a great deal of strenuous voluntary work—which had worked elsewhere. The washing of southern hands could hardly have been more apparent. An interned teacher in Belfast in January 1923 wrote to Eoin MacNeill that "the bitter part is the reflection that when I do get out I shall probably be forgotten." He was right. After the civil war neither Griffith nor Collins was available to hold their British counterparts to their formal (or informal) pledges on partition, and when the civil war was won Lloyd George's coalition had fallen from office.

The Conservatives would govern Great Britain from October 1922 until June 1929 under Bonar Law and Baldwin, aside from a brief interval of ten months in 1924 when there was a minority Labour government led by Ramsay MacDonald, which made no substantive difference to the British preference to see no major changes in the North. Cosgrave's cabinet pursued the implementation of Article 12 of the treaty, but, as seen, was outmaneuvered by Craig and the British government. Its reputation was damaged when MacNeill proved an inept commissioner and Feetham's unpublished report recommended that both the Free State and Northern Ireland should lose and gain small quanta of territory and citizens. Facing a no-confidence motion in Dáil Éireann, Cosgrave led a delegation to London. In return for burying the boundary commission's proposals in December 1925, the Irish Free State accepted British relief on some of Ireland's debts. This treaty amended the original treaty, accepted partition, and recognized Northern Ireland.[43] Northern nationalists could be forgiven for thinking that they had been literally sold out.[44]

The longer-run consequences of the Irish civil war worked throughout the diaspora and within domestic southern Irish politics. The war of brothers and sisters deeply disturbed and disorganized Irish American associations, and reduced their potency for politics in the Isles for decades. The old Fenian John Devoy considered de Valera a monster, meriting punishment for his crimes, lamenting that the savage civil war had revived "the old English theory . . . that

---

[42] For studies of the civil war, see Hopkinson (1988); Garvin (1996); Augusteijn (2002); Kissane (2005).

[43] See Kissane (2005).

[44] And perhaps sold out cheaply. Eoin MacNeill in an unpublished memoir recorded his conviction that the London government was at least as panicked as the Dublin government in 1925, and he had "very little doubt that if the Irish government had demanded at the same time the remission of the land annuity payments it would have been readily conceded" (Hand 1973: 272). This thought suggests an interesting counterfactual: had MacNeill's conjecture materialized, there would have been no economic war in the 1930s, or at least it would have required a different trigger.

when England's firm hand was removed, the Irish would start to cut each other's throats."[45] The diaspora, both in America and in Great Britain, was effectively demobilized. Within the South, the civil war entrenched itself as the enduring axis of party competition: two major blocs emerged.[46] Both had originated in Sinn Féin and the divisions that triggered the civil war, though they were to draw adherents from other parties. These pro-treaty and anti-treaty parties would never subsequently share power in a coalition government—even in 2016 the idea was resisted by both camps. Cumann na nGaedheal ("Association of the Irish") was the initial name taken by the pro-treaty party that governed under Cosgrave's leadership until 1932.[47] After a series of mergers with smaller parties, including former supporters of the IPP, the southern unionists, the National Centre, and the National Guard ("the Blueshirts"), in 1933 it became Fine Gael ("Clan of the Irish"—the United Ireland party). The anti-treaty side initially successfully claimed the title deeds (and some of the funds) of Sinn Féin, through its majority on the party's executive.

However, the rump Sinn Féin, like the anti-treaty IRA, could not remain unified. Abstention from an Irish parliament guaranteed it had no influence—including over decisions related to the civil war and the treaty. When the Dáil addressed emergency legislation, framework legislation, or the débâcle over the boundary commission, Sinn Féin was impotent. Had the party's deputies entered the Dáil in 1925 to vote against Cumann na nGaedheal's deal with Great Britain and Northern Ireland, as encouraged by the Irish Labour Party, that treaty would not have been ratified. Sinn Féin's insistence on principle had, perversely, led to the recognition of Northern Ireland and the entrenchment of the border it opposed. These episodes provided an instructive education for an anti-treaty party willing to work within the system to change it. Fianna Fáil ("Soldiers of Destiny") was founded in 1926 by de Valera, with "The Republican Party" as its English title. Its members constituted the bulk of the losers of the civil war, but now prepared, albeit reluctantly and truculently, to participate in the IFS. They left behind the ineffective "activists" in Sinn Féin, many of whom would not be integrally reconnected to the IRA for decades, and thereby consigned themselves to total ineffectiveness.[m]

The electoral competition between Cumann na nGaedheal/Fine Gael and Fianna Fáil had one supreme virtue. It pacified the civil-war cleavage into a democratic parliamentary rivalry: the two parties now primarily competed over which of them would best establish Irish freedom. This competition eventually increasingly focused on left–right, and economic and social policy questions not directly related to the treaty.[48] Their struggle had two mutually reinforcing effects before 1949 for the North. The external activities of the governors of the IFS were directed towards the reform, repeal, and outright abolition of the treaty provisions regarded as intolerable violations of Irish sovereignty. Both parties competed

---

[45] Cited in Jay P. Dolan (2008: 205).

[46] See Mair (1978, 1987). On the names of Irish parties, see Coakley (1980). Garvin (1981) provides an introduction to the origins of the party system, while Carty (1983) provides the implied antithesis to Mair's account, in which policies matter.

[47] The name had been used by Arthur Griffith for the immediate organizational precursor of SF.

[48] Impressive analyses of the Irish party system, from a perspective sympathetic to Irish Labour, may be found in Mair (1987, 1992); for opening guidance, see Coakley and Gallagher (1993).

vigorously to remove the last vestiges of British imperialism and colonialism, even if one was more comfortable with dominion and monarchical forms. Until 1932 Cumann na nGaedheal worked to prove that Collin's stepping-stone theory was correct, and vehemently rejected Fianna Fáil's accusations that its leaders were pro-British royalists, or neo-Redmondites. After 1932, de Valera steadily implemented the agenda of Document No. 2, because he genuinely believed in it. The internal actions of the governments run by these parties, by contrast, sought to establish independent Irish public policy—that is, distinct cultural, social, and economic programs suited to the needs and demands of Irish citizens, and they reflected the historic agenda of Sinn Féin, from which both had sprung.[49] These complementary external and domestic state-building activities, almost inevitably, cut against the logic of accommodating Ulster Protestants as part of the Irish nation. Neither of the two principal parties developed consistent and stable policies to persuade Ulster Protestants of the merits of reunification.

Since neither Ulster unionists nor northern nationalists could vote in the South (unless they moved residence), no electoral incentive encouraged a strong accommodationist stance by the two major parties—though most southern Protestants rallied to Cumann na nGaedheal as the party of order. In addition, though each party claimed to guard or advance the best interests of northern nationalists, no institutionalized consultation with these co-nationals occurred, and frequently their interests were ignored. In short, party competition in the IFS ensured that state-building took place at the expense of pan-Irish nation-building. It would culminate in Ireland's exit from the Commonwealth under a Fine Gael-led coalition government intent on outflanking Fianna Fáil's claim to be *the* republican party. The same pattern was illustrated in the erection of a formal constitutional claim to island-wide national territory under de Valera's freshly drafted constitution of 1937. Neither move was obvious if the intent was to win Ulster Protestant consent for reunification. As for northern nationalists, one of their most significant leaders came to an early judgment that has stood the test of time: "Out of power, they [the southern political parties] would use us. In power, they would find a hundred reasons for leaving us to paddle our own canoe."[50]

SOUTHERN PROTESTANTS: EXPULSIONS, EXODUS, DEMOGRAPHIC COLLAPSE, OR THE NORMAL FATE OF A NATIONAL MINORITY?

When George Bernard Shaw declared during the home-rule controversies in 1914 that he "would rather be burned at the stake by Irish Catholics than protected by Englishmen,"[51] he was not writing as a typical Irish Protestant. Within a

---

[49] For a Durkheimian and culturalist account of Cumann na nGaedheal/Fine Gael as the party of the Irish Enlightenment and Fianna Fail as the party of Gaelic romanticism, see Prager (1986: esp. 27–66), though he recognizes that to say that the enlightened endorsed the treaty whereas the romantics opposed it would be "inaccurate" (p. 51).

[50] *Ulster Herald*, October 20, 1926, cited in Staunton (2001: 73).

[51] Jack White (1975: frontispiece).

decade his people would become a formerly dominant minority within the Irish Free State, no longer directly protected by Englishmen. Though never likely to be burned at the stake, they believed that the question of their fate under Irish majority rule was genuine. Amid the Irish civil war, a worried deputation, led by the Church of Ireland Archbishop of Dublin, enquired of the Provisional Government "if they were to be permitted to live in Ireland or if it was desired that they should leave the country."[52] They received the necessary assurances, and appeared to have believed them.

The social power of the Protestant landed caste had been broken by nativist land movements and by Gladstone and his successors' land policies, and with partition the unionists in the south, especially those in counties Monaghan, Cavan, and Donegal, were abandoned by the UUP leadership in a collective act of *sauve qui peut*. The remainder, contra Ian Paisley Sr, did not experience genocide. Although British military power, on and off island, quietly insured Irish Protestants against their professed nightmares of extirpation or expulsion, any such ambitions had *not* been programmatic components of any Irish nation-alist movements or prominent persons since the seventeenth century. Neverthe-less, the descendants of settlers often fear that the natives will do to them what their ancestors did to the natives, and episodes during the Irish revolution gave Irish Protestants cause for deep concern. Significantly, however, the rump UK never saber-rattled on behalf of its former co-nationals in the Free State or the subsequent republic—though Craig argued for an invasion from his Belfast redoubt.[53] No public or diplomatic remonstrances took place over alleged expellees or refugees, or over claims of governmental discrimination, for good reason. Irish Protestants, or the Anglo-Irish elite—as they were sometimes still called—never actively sought British intervention in Irish affairs, and London governments after 1922 did not see it as in their interests to exploit their abandoned co-nationals, except for surveillance and intelligence-gathering.

Republicans and nationalists, both in Sinn Féin and the IPP, countenanced self-government for varying definitions of Ulster between 1922 and 1937 as long as it would remain within Ireland (home rule within home rule for the IPP; a subor-dinate Northern parliament under Southern Ireland, as in the treaty and Docu-ment No. 2; and under Dáil Éireann in de Valera's constitution). The secession of Northern Ireland from the Irish Free State ended any prospects that southern Protestants would participate in any scheme of territorial autonomy. Their com-paratively small numbers and lack of concentration rendered them unsuited to territorial autonomy, and no representative leaders among Irish Protestants ever made territorial demands on the Irish Free State. Given their demographic and geographic fate, small and dispersed, Irish Protestants after 1922 therefore had five likely trajectories. They could be integrated into a civic Irish citizenship: their ethnic and religious origins would be irrelevant to their rights; their cultural and religious identity would be privately and institutionally secure, and expressly exercised without fear of repressive consequences. Such integration might foretell full-scale assimilation into the new Irish polity—through public and private practices—through acculturation, desegregation, and long-term fusion through

---

[52] Kurt Derek Bowen (1983: 24).　　　[53] See Vol. 2, Ch. 4, pp. 126–7.

intermarriage. The subsequent data on intermarriage certainly suggest this story. The rate of intermarriage of native-born Irish Protestant women with Catholic men was 6.1 percent of the marrying cohort born before 1926; by the mid-1970s the intermarriage rate had risen to 19.1 percent; and by the years 1984–91 over a third of female Protestants born in the early 1960s were marrying Catholic males.[54] Industrialization, urbanization, and increased educational participation reduced social barriers in the South. Voluntary segregation in schools and universities, clubs and workplaces, was reduced, facilitating interaction and marriage. Integration and assimilation are variations on forms of equality. But assimilation was admittedly accelerated by Catholic pressure—that required Catholics to try to convert their Protestant marriage partners until the Second Vatican Council. Much worse fates than integration or assimilation were possible, however. They could have been expelled, and Irish Protestants could, like Northern Catholics, have been subjected to control—that is, targeted for ethnic and religious disorganization and discrimination. If they experienced the former, then in the last instance they could choose to emigrate.

Recently debate has occurred over which of these trajectories—integration, assimilation, expulsion, control, or emigration—or permutations among them, best describes the collective experience of southern Protestants. It bears emphasis, however, that the subject had not previously been a matter of serious argument among historians or social scientists. The fate of southern Protestants after the Treaty was once a settled subject in professional historiography. Both external and internal observers—though not Ulster unionists—agreed that southern Protestants had been a well-treated minority after 1922–3, especially by comparison with northern Catholics, and by the standards of interwar and postwar Europe. Unlike many previously dominant minorities in European history, they were not expropriated. No inhibitions were placed on the exercise of their religious freedom: their churches, church lands, and church organizations were not interfered with. The two Irish constitutions (1922 and 1937) positively expressed and supported formal religious freedoms, and these provisions were generally respected, especially within education. Protestants were not actively displaced by political decisions from high-status positions in the public or private sectors or the professions in the cities. Openly welcomed by Griffith on behalf of the Provisional Government, they were integrated with full citizenship rights, with the active consent of their best-known political leaders—for example, Lord Midleton. Kevin O'Higgins insisted Irish Protestants were "part and parcel of the nation," not alien enemies or planters.[55]

No parallel occurred to the systematic gerrymandering or active disenfranchisement in the North. There was no banning of minority political parties. Protestants were treated as equal citizens, with full private cultural rights, and their religious institutions did not experience discriminatory public policy—for example, Trinity College Dublin was not nationalized, nor coerced through intrusive regulation. Until the late 1930s, southern Protestants were overrepresented in Dáil Éireann and the Senate, and long remained overrepresented among economic elites, and among political, legal, scholarly, and professional top

[54] Richard O'Leary (1999: table 2).   [55] Jack White (1975: 91).

positions (though most of their community was not upper class or professional). The Free State's first senate had half of its sixty members nominated by the government. W. B. Yeats was a distinctly non-party Protestant senator; but in all twenty were of Protestant origins; sixteen were ex-unionists. Initially the British identity of Irish Protestants was respected. Between 1922 and 1937 the symbolism of the monarchy and formal linkages to the mother state through dominion status remained. Famous social organizations, founded during Protestant dominance, were not renamed—the Royal Irish Academy, the Royal Irish College of Surgeons, the Royal College of General Practitioners, the Royal Irish Academy of Music, and the Royal Dublin Horse Show[56]—and that remained so even after the monarch was no longer Ireland's head of state. Most of the professions remained tied to accreditation bodies headquartered in London. They were very slowly nationalized, and not in acts of national, ethnic, or religious revenge. No public policy of overt cultural erasure was applied—English was not replaced, though that had been the ambition of some cultural nationalists. Though distressed by the loss of monarchical symbolism, increasingly eroded after 1932, and by the exit of Ireland from the Commonwealth, eventually the overwhelming bulk of southern Irish Protestants politically integrated, becoming loyal citizens of the Republic.[57]

In 1983 Kurt Bowen, reflecting the local historiographical consensus, wrote a book about southern Protestants subtitled "Ireland's privileged minority," without a question mark.[58] The Minority Rights Group, reporting in 1975, under the authorship of Jack White, did not go as far, but produced no major indictment.[59] Well-known surveys published during the armed conflict in the North between the late 1960s and the early 1990s, such as F. S. L. Lyons's *Ireland since the Famine* (2nd rev. edn,1973), Máire and Conor O'Brien's *A Concise History of Ireland* (3rd rev. edn, 1985), or Roy F. Foster's *Modern Ireland* (1988), contain no reports of systematic oppression of southern Protestants, whether at the hands of the Irish state, or society.[n] In "The Minority Problem in the 26 Counties," first published in 1967, Leland Lyons, a future Provost of Trinity College, described southern Protestants as a dog that had not barked since the treaty.[60] He added that "a minority may not bark because it is afraid to bark, or it may not bark because it has no cause to do so. Both these interpretations are in a measure true of the southern minority."[61] Politically ex-unionists divided between those who isolated themselves, and those who chose loyalty to the new order, most of whom became supporters of Cumann na nGaedheal and its successor Fine Gael. Reactionaries aired British or imperialist sentiments in private clubs, but no Protestant party formed to unwind dominion status, or to

---

[56] Brendan Behan memorably described the Anglo-Irishman as a "Protestant on a horse," a quip that reflected upper-class participation in the British aristocratic cult of horses.

[57] Very few would have thought it proper to spy for Great Britain, Elizabeth Bowen was a prominent exception (Bowen et al. 2009).

[58] See, e.g., Kurt Derek Bowen (1983).   [59] Jack White (1975).

[60] Lyons (1923–83) was born in Derry, but grew up in Roscommon, and had a distinguished academic career in Ireland and England.

[61] Lyons (1967).

restore the Union. Lyons mentioned the operation of the *Ne Temere* decree,[62] and the censorship of books and other media as matters that "irked" (liberal) southern Protestants, but judged that, "given the historical background, things could have been very different and it is only proper to acknowledge here that the almost total absence of religious discrimination in the new state must stand out as one of the major achievements of a self-governing Ireland."[63]

The Free State implemented cultural nationalist projects, especially the promotion of the Irish language, which were distasteful to Ulster unionists' sensibilities, and to those of many (though not all) southern Protestants. Yet facility in Irish was not retrospectively applied to exclude Irish Protestants or anyone else from public office. It was, however, applied going forward. The application of the (often tweaked) language policy in schools and public institutions applied to all. Strikingly, Lyons made no mention of it in the essay under discussion. Was he afraid to bark on the subject? It seems more likely that he politely resisted the temptation to describe the policy's failure. One consequence of the pro-Irish policy may have been to increase the numbers of middle- and upper-class Irish Protestants educated in English private schools, who then did not return; and it may also have increased the propensity of border Protestants in Donegal, Cavan, and Monaghan to send their children to school in Northern Ireland.

The Free State's Catholic majority, both its clergy and its laity, quickly affected lawmaking on matters related to divorce, family law, and what are now rightly regarded as women's rights. Initially, however, Catholic perspectives on these matters scarcely differed from those of most Irish Protestants. In 1925 Senator Yeats remonstrated that the practical banning of divorce, which would follow from the removal of the right of private petition to the UK Privy Council, a procedure available to the wealthy, would be disastrous.

> If you show that this country, Southern Ireland, is going to be governed by Catholic ideas and Catholic ideas alone, you will never get the North. You will create an impassable barrier between North and South, and you will pass more and more Catholic laws, while the North will, gradually, assimilate its divorce and other laws to England. You will put a wedge into the midst of this nation . . . [64]

[62] *Ne Temere* took its name from a declaration of Catholic matrimonial law issued by Pope Pius X that took effect from Easter 1908. It applied to every marriage of a Catholic; it renewed and reinforced old Catholic decrees since the Council of Trent that rendered marriages invalid for Catholics unless celebrated by an authorized priest. Impliedly, it rendered null and void in the eyes of the Church any marriages by Catholics (by birth, or converts) to non-Catholics under state or non-Catholic auspices, unless there were dispensations. But, contrary to the Protestant spin immediately placed upon it, the *Ne Temere* decree was about the validity of all marriages involving Catholics; it contained no reference to the religious upbringing of children, as can be verified by reading the text, which many historians seem not to have done. The demand that children of mixed marriages should be raised as Catholics was *already* a requirement under dispensations granted by the Catholic Church to ensure what it deemed a valid marriage, either when *disparitatis cultus* (the non-Catholic not being Christian) applied or *mixtae religionis* (the non-Catholic being a baptized Christian) applied. It is fair, however, to see the issuing of the decree as evidence of increased Catholic discipline of its flock, and of careless insensitivity to those married to Protestants. See Vol. 1. Ch. 5, p. 363, and 409 endnote w, and Vol. 2, Ch. 3, p. 101.

[63] Lyons (1967: 97).   [64] Denis Kennedy (1988: 159–60).

On this occasion Yeats did not help his honorable cause by misnaming the state that had placed him in its upper house. His magnetism is such, however, that the Free State's evolution is often read solely through the prism of this speech. It is forgotten that the Church of Ireland, to which the overwhelmingly majority of southern Protestants were affiliated, then fully opposed divorce,[65] or that a decade more would elapse before Great Britain's row over Edward VIII's intended marriage to his divorced American fiancée ended in the king's abdication. In the same speech Yeats declared: "We are no petty people. We are one of the great stocks of Europe. We are the people of Grattan; we are the people of Swift, the people of Emmet, the people of Parnell. We have created the most of the modern literature of this country. We have created the best of its political intelligence."[66] The literary eminence was and remains clear, and would be enhanced in the twentieth century by Sean O'Casey (1880–1964), Rosamund Jacob (1888–1960), Molly Keane (1904–96), Samuel Beckett (1906–89), Louis MacNeice (1907–63), Iris Murdoch (1919–99), and Jennifer Johnston (1930–) among others. But the case for the concentration of optimal political intelligence was not as obvious.

Fianna Fáil's electoral rise from the mid-1920s, Lyons noted, generated fears among southern Protestants, notably in the *Irish Times* then the house organ of their upper class.

> Sullen resentment [among ex-unionists greeted] the Anglo-Irish economic war, the whittling away of the outward and visible signs of dominion status, the revision of constituencies increasing the number having less than five members and therefore making it more difficult for minority interests to gain seats, the abolition of university representation in the Dáil, and above all the abolition of the Senate [which took place in 1936].[67]

The Senate was, however, revived in the constitution of 1937. Even five-seat constituencies for the Dáil guaranteed Protestants' representation as Protestants only if they constituted a quota of the relevant electorate (that is, 16 percent plus 1), and voted solidly along sectarian lines. Nowhere was this true after the mid-1930s, except in some local-government districts, especially near the border. In any case, it is agreed that the modification of the seat numbers per electoral district was not targeted at Protestants. Rather the two leading parties had an interest in reducing the seats won by third parties and independents. It is fairer to suggest that the change was careless of Protestant interests. There is little in the public record, however, to suggest that these changes were significantly protested, and Protestants have continued to be present in significant numbers in Irish public life. In 1923, in the first elections after the civil war, they constituted 14 of the 153 deputies (TDs)—that is, roughly 9 percent of the entire body; in 1927, 14 Protestant TDs were elected, 11 not affiliated with any political party.[68] Subsequently, two of Ireland's nine Presidents have been Protestants: the first,

---

[65] It still does: "marriage is in its purpose a union permanent and life-long, for better or worse, till death do them part, of one man with one woman" (Canons of the Church of Ireland, 31, 1), though it did come to believe that the Irish constitution should permit civil divorce.

[66] Lyons (1967: 94).

[67] Lyons (1967: 102–3). The contrast with the North was not stated by Lyons: there PR (STV) was abolished outright; see Vol. 2, Ch. 2, pp. 44-8.

[68] Kurt Derek Bowen (1983: 48).

Table 2.3.4. Religious denominations, Independent Ireland, 1926–1991 (%)

Religious denomination	1926	1936	1946	1961	1971	1981	1991
Roman Catholic	92.6	93.4	94.3	94.9	93.9	93.0	91.6
Church of Ireland	5.5	4.9	4.2	3.7	3.3	2.7	2.5
Presbyterian	1.1	0.9	0.8	0.7	0.5	0.4	0.4
Methodist	0.4	0.3	0.3	0.2	0.2	0.2	
Jewish	0.1	0.1	0.1	0.1	0.1	0.1	0.004
Other	0.3	0.2	0.3	0.4	0.2	0.3	1
No religion					0.3	1.2	1.9
Not stated					1.6	2.1	2.4

Notes: (i) The 1951, 1956, 1966, and 1979 censuses did not include religious questions.
(ii) From 1911 until 1961 "no religion" and "not stated" were aggregated under "other religion.'
(iii) Until 1991 Protestants of no specific denomination were classed as Church of Ireland.

Source: Census of Ireland.

Douglas Hyde (1938–45), and the fourth, Erskine Childers (1973–74). Its seventh, Mary Robinson (née Burke) (1990–97), is married to Nicholas, a Protestant, historian, author and cartoonist. Lyons's concluding note suggested that in the fifteen years preceding his essay (1951–66) the reconciliation of southern Protestants to the new regime had been completed, and speculated that future historians would credit de Valera and his party with that accomplishment.

That has certainly not been the case. From the late 1980s some historians implied or overtly stated that Irish nationalism in power in Dublin mirrored the exclusivism and the sectarianism of Ulster unionism in Belfast.[69] Southern Protestants too, it now appeared, had lived under a tyranny of the majority. The large decline in their numbers, of over 30 percent, between 1911 and 1926 (there was no census in 1921) has been attributed to sectarian expulsions, and the slow decline in their numbers from the mid-1920s—see Table 2.3.4 and Map 2.3.1 —has been read as a mixture of attrition and coercive assimilation. It is usually conceded that Irish nationalism was less extreme and unjust in its majoritarian exclusivism and sectarianism than Ulster unionism, because few scholars have argued for full equivalence.[70] The possible triggers for this major shift in the historiographical framing of the fate of southern Protestants are various. Those who wish a speedy oblivion to all past Irish quarrels, the outlook of self-described post-nationalist intellectuals,[71] are keen to encourage an impartial plague on all houses of religion. The victories of secular anti-clericalism in the South have (rightly) repudiated the numerous authoritarian excesses, abuses, and crimes of the Catholic Church, but have also encouraged the view that the southern pot had no right whatever to blacken the reputation of the northern kettle. Today's southern ex-Catholic secular individual may conclude that southern Protestants were as oppressed as northern Catholics.

[69] See, e.g., passages and asides in Bowman (1982), O'Halloran (1987), Fitzpatrick (1998), and Patterson (2006), especially the latter three.
[70] Arguments that come close to the claim of equivalence may be found in O'Halloran (1987), Fitzpatrick (1998), and Patterson (2006).
[71] See, e.g., Kearney (1997).

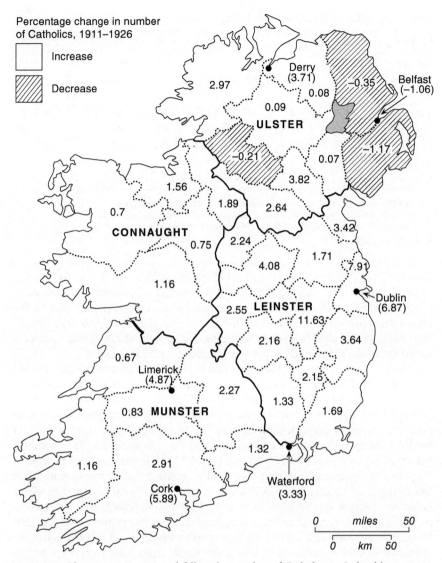

Map 2.3.1. The percentage rise and fall in the number of Catholics in Ireland by county, 1911–1926

In the early 1990s another possibility was suggested: the recovery of repressed facts. Those persuaded by the doctoral thesis, essays, and books of the Newfoundland-born historian Peter Hart (1963–2010) advanced this perspective.[o] In 1993, in an opening salvo, Hart argued that IRA gunmen in County Cork who killed thirteen Protestant men in Dunmanway and Ballygroman over several nights in late April 1922 had wanted revenge for the killing of one of their local leaders, but also wanted to exterminate or drive away all local Protestants. He insisted they were killed because they were Protestants, not because they were loyalists or informers. This contribution was republished under the heading "Taking it Out on the

Protestants," in 1998—the title adapted a quotation from a remark by a Cork IRA leader.[72] Hart's writings strongly suggested that a violently anti-Protestant animus had existed in the southern IRA, certainly in its stronghold of Cork, knowledge of which had been too long suppressed or forgotten. If so, it had been unconscionably overlooked by professional historians, including, we may add, in the books of Lyons, Cruise O'Brien, and Foster. Could this have been true?

By 1996 Hart maintained that "what may be termed 'ethnic cleansing'" had occurred in parts of nine southern Irish counties—Cork, King's County (Offaly), Leitrim, Limerick, Louth, Mayo, Queen's County (Laois), Tipperary and Westmeath.[73] In a chapter republished as "The Protestant Experience of Revolution in Southern Ireland" Hart asserted that a Protestant exodus had occurred between 1921 and 1924 "in a sudden, massive upheaval . . . The rate of departures apparently began to slow again in 1924, but by early 1926 nearly 40 per cent had gone for good."[74] He concluded:

All of the nightmare images of ethnic conflict in the twentieth century are here: the massacres and anonymous death squads, the burning homes and churches, the mass expulsions and trains filled with refugees, the transformation of lifelong neighbors into enemies, the conspiracy theories and the terminology of hatred. Munster, Leinster, and Connaught can take their place with fellow imperial provinces, Silesia, Galicia, and Bosnia, as part of the post-war "unmixing of peoples" in Europe.

Hart then paused mid-paragraph, to exercise some self-control: "We must not exaggerate. The Free State government had no part in persecution. Cork was not Smyrna, nor Belfast. Nevertheless, sectarianism was embedded in the vocabulary and syntax of the Irish revolution, north and south. Any accounting of its violence and consequences must encompass the dreary steeples of Bandon and Ballinasloe as well as those of Fermanagh and Tyrone."[75] The IRA, he suggested, had targeted all minorities; first, Protestants, but also ex-soldiers (often Catholics), tinkers, and tramps, and others seen as social deviants. He calculated that 36 percent of the 204 civilians killed by the IRA in Cork were Protestants, well above their share in either the 1911 or the 1926 censuses. While they comprised 17 percent of those listed as suspected informers in IRA documents, they were but 10 percent of the actual informers according to British and other documentation.[76]

Hart's reconstructions from archival and interview sources seemed compelling: introduced by well-composed stories that were intimate and harrowing, they were read and praised beyond academe, and included some enterprising social science.[77] They seemed persuasive to those like this author who have traveled in (and immersed themselves in the literature on) the contemporary Balkans, Iraq, Kyrgyzstan, and Sudan; and especially vivid for anyone who has seen twentieth-century ethnic conflict through documentaries or television news screens. Indeed, the latter may have inspired Hart to paint his canvas, because

[72] Hart (1998: ch. 12). [73] Reprinted in Hart (2003: 237).
[74] Hart (2003: 239). [75] Hart (2003: 240). [76] Hart (1998: 293–315 *passim*).
[77] "The Social Structure of the IRA" published in Hart (2003: ch. 5) should retain recognition: it builds upon previous work by David Fitzpatrick and Tom Garvin to provide a compelling quantitative and qualitative picture of the IRA Volunteers. It should be read alongside the important work of Augusteijn (1996).

some of his stories have turned out, on scrutiny, not to be fully accurate, to exaggerate, and to display more grave flaws. John M. Regan had initially been impressed by Hart's work,[78] but more careful readings, including those of allegedly amateur historians, sometimes self-described as republicans, and often pilloried for their rudeness, have obliged the recognition that Hart's scholarship was, minimally, sometimes contradictory, confused, and hasty. Worse still, some of his publications, notably on "the Boys of Kilmichael," are now charged with inventions, in which suspect and conceivably fabricated reports of interviews with IRA survivors supported preconceptions about what had happened in the 1920s, conceptions that conformed with British counterinsurgency propaganda of the day.[79]

Though Hart's critics are accused of *ad hominem* attacks, both his doctoral examiners have subsequently found fault with his work. In *The Republic: The Fight for Irish Independence 1918–1923*, Charles Townshend noted "some flaws in Hart's use of evidence," particularly that he ignored that the British Army's *Record of the Rebellion in Ireland* had openly declared that many Protestants "in the Bandon area" gave information to the military;[P] and that Hart failed to acknowledge that British soldiers, including intelligence officers—who had broken the rules of the truce, though Townshend does not expressly say this—were held by the IRA immediately before the Dunmanway killings, in the vicinity, and were later executed by the IRA.[80] This "elision," the term is Regan's, avoided discussion of a different explanation from Hart's—namely, that the assassinated civilians had included informers (or that the captured British officers had divulged their sources under interrogation).[q] The executed officers may have been killed because they were British. Townshend accepts that the Cork units had the best intelligence operation within the IRA—something Hart should have considered before claiming that those assassinated in the Bandon valley were killed solely because they were Protestants.[81]

David Fitzpatrick strongly qualified rather than repudiated his former student's work; he has not publicly criticized his methods. *Descendancy: Irish Protestant Histories since 1795* (2014) presents careful studies of the demographic collapse of southern Protestants between 1911 and 1926. His chief innovation is assiduous labor in constructing and exploiting available data on Methodists, whom he uses as a proxy for the southern Protestant population as a whole—justified because there are no census data for Ireland between 1911 and 1926, when the major fall in that population occurred. Fitzpatrick concludes:

> the main source of Protestant malaise in the nascent Irish Free State was not excess migration but failure to enroll new members, presumably as a consequence of already low fertility and nuptiality, exacerbated by losses through mixed marriages and conversion. If any campaign of "ethnic cleansing" was attempted, its demographic impact was fairly minor. Statistical analysis therefore suggests that the spectre of Protestant extermination [by which Fitzpatrick means expulsion] has distracted

[78] <http://www.history.ac.uk/reviews/review/416> (accessed August 2016).
[79] See Niall Meehan (2014); Murphy and Meehan (2008: *passim*).
[80] See Townshend (2014: 369–76).
[81] See also John M. Regan's "The 'Bandon Valley Massacre' as a Historical Problem" (Regan 2013: 176–205).

debate about revolutionary Ireland for too long, and should be laid to rest. It would seem that the inexorable numerical decline of southern Protestantism was mainly self-inflicted.[82]

In "The Spectre of 'Ethnic Cleansing' in Revolutionary Ireland," which finishes the same book, Fitzpatrick provides further light. Basing his judgments on careful studies of records in Cork, he describes west Cork Methodists, mostly of British stock, as something of an occupational elite (not large landowners or civil servants)—for example, drapers, shopkeepers, tailors, and chemists.[83] His findings on their fate may be summarized though the following extracts:

> The statistical imprint of revolutionary disruption [on Protestant and Methodist demography] was perceptible but fairly minor . . . revolutionary turmoil did not lead to a massive exodus of Methodists from west Cork . . . [and] had limited impact on long-established patterns of heavy emigration and inadequate recruitment . . . Latent resentment [against Irish Protestants] only exploded into violence intermittently when passions were inflamed by external events or released by breakdown of civic controls . . . The 'spectre' of extermination was real, in the sense that many feared for short periods that vulnerable southern Protestants communities would be expropriated and uprooted. Yet fear typically succumbed to hope, and panic to common sense. The outcome was not 'ethnic cleansing,' but a concerted attempt to rebuild Protestant communities and establish a satisfactory *modus vivendi* in the Irish Free State.[84]

Cumulatively these judgments must inter Hart's most provocative suggestion, which Fitzpatrick kindly describes as "a tentative hypothesis." Fitzpatrick's data suggest that "the proportionate decline in [Methodist] membership in West Cork between 1911 and 1926 was close to that for Southern Ireland as a whole."[85] The decline was unexceptional despite what he calls "the unsurpassed ferocity and frequency of attacks against Protestants" in this county. That the said ferocity and frequency did not have the major demographic impact suggested by Hart must make readers wonder whether they are being rhetorically inflated alongside Fitzpatrick's otherwise admirable statistical caution. Only 230 of the 811 [Methodist] members who emigrated from the Cork district between 1911 and 1926 left during the revolutionary years.[86] Differently put, there was an average emigration rate of fifty-four people per annum in these intercensal years. Moreover, their emigration rate was higher in 1911–14 (248) than in the revolutionary years 1919–23 (230). The same data suggest that their average emigration rate during the latter years was fifty-seven persons per annum—that is, three persons more per year than in the entire intercensal period. These redescriptions of Fitzpatrick's data are not intended to minimize the fear or horror experienced by the victims of violence and their families, which he conveys well, but they imply that any talk of "ethnic cleansing" is wholly disproportionate.

Two implications flowed from Hart's "tentative" arguments: first, that the nine (southern) counties in which he found *prima facie* evidence of "what may be termed "ethnic cleansing" would have had higher death tolls (inducing higher flights levels), and therefore, secondly, there would have been higher increases in

---

[82] Fitzpatrick (2014: 180).   [83] Fitzpatrick (2014: 183).
[84] Fitzpatrick (2014: 190, 234, 240, 220, 240).   [85] Fitzpatrick (2014: 186).
[86] Fitzpatrick (2014: 188).

Table 2.3.5. Nine counties where Hart suggested "ethnic cleansing" had occurred 1911–1926

County	Total fatalities during the War of Independence	Rank in number of fatalities out of 32 counties in Ireland	% rise in Catholic population 1911–1926	Rank in number of fatalities out of 32 counties & 6 urban boroughs
Cork	495	1	2.9 (County) 5.9 (City)	8/32 2/6
Tipperary	152	4	2.3	13/32
Limerick	121	6	0.7 (County) 4.9 (City)	24/32 3/6
Mayo	43	10	0.7	26/32
Louth	26	16	3.4	7/32
King's (Offaly)	21	19	2.6	11/32
Westmeath	18	22	4.1	4/32
Leitrim	15	26	1.9	16/32
Queen's (Laois)	10	29	2.2	14/32

Sources: for columns (2) and (3), O'Halpin (2012: 152); for columns (4) and (5), see Map 2.3.1.

the Catholic shares of these respective counties between 1911 and 1926 than in other counties.[87] Data gathered in Table 2.3.5 show negligible support for either implication. Six of the nine counties suggested as possible sites of "ethnic cleansing" were outside the nine most violent counties—namely, Mayo (10th), Louth (16th), Offaly (19th), Westmeath (22nd), Leitrim (26th), and Laois (19th). Moreover, just three of the counties, Cork, Westmeath, and Louth, were among the top nine counties that showed most growth in their intercensal Catholic populations. The other six—Offaly (11th), Tipperary (13th), Laois (14th), Leitrim (16th)—were clustered where there was medium net growth in the share of the Catholic population, though Mayo was placed last in the Irish Free State (26th). The cities of Cork and Limerick experienced a significant increase in their Catholic populations, but that is overwhelmingly attributable to the loss of their British (Protestant) garrison populations, and to demographic collapse and migration among urban Protestants rather than rural expulsions in their respective counties. If Hart merely advanced a tentative hypothesis, it had scant foundation in the geography of the violence of the Irish revolution.

Fitzpatrick also quietly dismisses *The Year of Disappearances: Political Killings in Cork 1921–1922* (2010), whose author, Gerard Murphy, has advanced numerous speculative claims, including "what amounts to a pogrom on Methodists in [Co.] Cork,"[88] a claim incompatible with Fitzpatrick's data: "All told, Methodists accounted for three of 22 Protestant civilians known to have died in Cork, as a result of political violence, by July 1921." In the April 1922 Bandon valley killings,

---

[87] On the importance of the empirical implication of theories and hypotheses, see, among others, King et al. (1994).

[88] Gerard Murphy (2010: 236); for Fitzpatrick's withering review of Murphy's book as a disorganized dossier, which uses devices associated with bad fiction, see "History in a Hurry" in the Dublin Review of Books, <http://www.drb.ie/essays/history-in-a-hurry> (accessed August 2016).

two Methodists were killed, and one was subsequently killed during the Irish civil war.[89] Though Murphy may be right to speculate that some victims may have been omitted from the records, an average of 1.5 Methodists killed per annum, over the revolutionary years does not constitute a "pogrom"—not even an "almost pogrom"—not least because Methodists were not targeted *qua* Methodists. When they were targeted, it was generally as loyalists, as informers, or indeed as Protestants. Arguments such as Murphy's, and Hart's more enthusiastic interpreters, appear to seek to establish a rough equivalence in the scale and intensity in the violent experiences of the two new minorities created by partition, northern nationalists and southern unionists, or to situate Ireland in 1919–23 amid the literature on contemporary ethnic conflicts in the Balkans and elsewhere. Neither temptation, however, has warrant in the evidence, a verdict that does not, of course, exonerate the Bandon IRA.

In a mostly sober appraisal Fitzpatrick raises the temperature by asking the question: "Even if southern Protestants as a community were not subjected to 'ethnic cleansing,' is it not credible to apply such a term to the Methodist families actually displaced from revolutionary west Cork?" In a virtuoso display of forensic skills, he calculates that 26 families (105 persons) were displaced, 13 leaving in 1921, and 11 in 1922. He concludes that "violence and intimidation did not necessarily lead to a panic-driven unplanned, terminal, and irreversible exodus." Indeed, "most Methodist families either resisted the pressure to leave home or subsequently returned. Even the permanent emigrants seldom abandoned their properties without strenuous efforts to secure a fair price for their assets."[90] The "ethnic-cleansing" hypothesis is, in short, falsified—once again. Fitzpatrick defends Hart for his "intellectual rigour, thorough research, [and] fair judgement," but whoever reads through Fitzpatrick's work must find it difficult to concur.[91] Fitzpatrick is least persuasive when praising his former student for his "lucid, unexcited prose."[92] The lucidity is not in dispute, but the brio of the prose, which helped win his work public attention, sometimes led him off the scholarly path into selection bias and contradictory use of evidence.

Hart's conclusions about the killings in the Bandon valley in April 1922 were extrapolated to the rest of the Irish Free State but "unburdened by credible evidence." These words are Regan's, who had positively reviewed Hart's *The IRA At War*,[93] but later observed that "Hart presented no verifiable evidence of widespread religious violence in Southern Ireland."[94] Hart had maintained that a "veil of silence" was drawn over the "continuing persecution and dispossession of the Protestants of West Cork,"[95] and that most of his "Cork interviewees refused to admit, or remember, that any such [sectarian] killings had taken place."[96] His critics complain about Hart's use of anonymous oral interviews, which cannot be verified, whereas in other stories narrated by Hart, especially regarding the

---

[89] Fitzpatrick (2014: 209, 197).   [90] Fitzpatrick (2014: 235, 237, 240).

[91] O'Halpin (2012: 153) concludes that Hart's estimate "that 64% of deaths in [Ireland in] 1921 were civilian is excessive." Differences in counting and coding are not in O'Halpin's view the source of the difference, but rather the restricted range of sources then available to Hart.

[92] <http://www.drb.ie/essays/history-in-a-hurry> (accessed August 2016).

[93] <http://www.history.ac.uk/reviews/review/416> (accessed August 2016).

[94] Regan (2013: 21).   [95] Hart (1998: 290).   [96] Hart (1998: 292).

Kilmichael ambush, the critics have observed that at least one of the relevant interviewees cannot have been alive, or available for interview at the dates he specifies. These doubts have raised questions of integrity, and they matter because the oral evidence appears to have been pivotal to the arguments being advanced.[97]

Without questioning the integrity or accuracy of Hart's oral sources, however, his accounts, descriptions, and replies to his critics suggest that the Bandon valley killings were exceptional, rogue, and uncharacteristic actions of some anti-treaty IRA volunteers in West Cork; did not lead to Balkan-style mass expulsions; and did not compare in scale or duration to the killings in Belfast in 1920–2. A recital of alternative accounts would include the following. The thirteen men who were killed were all Protestants, but not all of the men who were wounded or targeted for assassination in this episode were Protestants, though most were.[98] A high proportion of those "unsympathetic loyalists"[99] killed or assassinated were informers, were sincerely believed to be informers, or were merely alleged to be informers—though Hart judged the claims worthless, not all are persuaded. The motivations of the killers who were never tried or identified with certainty have been much discussed and are probably undecidable.[100] Arguments have been made for four clusters of motivations: (i) *reprisals* for the local killing of local IRA commander O'Neill or for faraway killings of Belfast Catholics, or both; (ii) *greed, grievance, and long-term revenge* (allegations were made of land-grabbing by at least one of the victims' relatives); (iii) *organizational security fears* (triggered by O'Neill's killing);[101] and, lastly, Hart's preferred conclusion (iv) *ethnic or sectarian violence*. Endorsing any of these rival accounts does not apologize for the IRA, does not excuse any killings or attempted assassinations, which were conducted without anything remotely resembling a judicial process, revolutionary or otherwise—they were killings of civilians, none of whom had recently held political or military office. But the verdict of simple sectarianism remains unproven.

Curiously, however, sectarianism *was* the verdict of most non-Protestant contemporaries of the victims, a fact one would not gather from Hart. Dunmanway was "widely regarded by contemporary observers as a sectarian campaign by what now might be termed 'dissident' republicans."[102] The Belfast *comhairle ceanntair* of Sinn Féin expressed horror at the brutal extermination of our Protestant fellow-countrymen in Cork.[103] The killings were registered throughout Ireland and condemned by "innumerable public bodies," including Dáil Éireann, because "these murders" were "violently in conflict with the traditions and principles of the Republican army" and "created shame and anger throughout Ireland." These quotations are from Dorothy Macardle's *The Irish Republic*, generally held to be

[97] Dr Niall Meehan of Griffith College has been Hart's most thorough and persuasive critic, see especially his contributions to Murphy and Meehan (2008) and his full statement in Niall Meehan (2014).

[98] See, e.g., Keane (2014: *passim*).   [99] The phrase is that of Bielenberg et al. (2014: 53).

[100] Files on spies, informers, and agents are not always kept, or kept in their integrity, for the future benefit of historians.

[101] But it has been noted that "no such counterintelligence justification emerged from the IRA at the time of the 1922 killings" (Bielenberg, et al. 2014: 53).

[102] Fitzpatrick (2014: 195).

[103] *Cork Constitution*, May 4, 1922, cited in Fitzpatrick (2014).

the most orthodox republican author of standing in the historiography of the Irish revolution. She cited de Valera's speech on April 30, 1922, after the killings: "The German Palatines, the French Huguenots, the English Protestants flying from the fires of Smithfield, later the Wesleyans and the Jews, who were persecuted in every land, in this land of ours always found safe asylum. That glorious record must not be tarnished by acts against a helpless minority."[104] Ireland's past and subsequent record of minority protection may not have been glorious, and the Protestant minority was certainly more resilient than this phrasing implied, but Hart's provocative accounts have not survived scrutiny.[105]

Hart sometimes adopted the style of a crime-writer, leading with shocking assertions, before making more judicious qualifications. For example, in "Ethnic Conflict and Minority Responses," a chapter published adjacent to "The Protestant Experience of Revolution in Southern Ireland,"[106] he maintained:

> What happened in southern Ireland did not constitute "ethnic cleansing," and there were at least four necessary factors missing to make this so: a state with its resources and authority in the hands of one group directed at another; a plan or an enabling or mobilizing racial or sectarian ideology; any real threat or provocation on the part of the target group; and violence at totalizing or eliminationist levels . . . The nightmare images were there, but they should not be confused with very different realities elsewhere.[107]

We might quibble with these necessary conditions—militias, for example, can organize expulsions, and without any threat or provocation from the target group—but the conclusion was reasonable. Earlier Hart recognized that "Republican organizations were officially non-sectarian, [which had] played an important part in damping down southern ethnic violence, even though the IRA were its main practitioners."[108] Later he acknowledged that, within the Free State, "there was certainly no institutional discrimination or constraints on identity, employment economic activity, education, or movement. There were no purges of the civil service, and Protestants were free to take part in politics. There were even minority safeguards built into the new constitution, although largely on behalf of the social elite."[109]

The local historian and geographer Barry Keane summarizes the Cork controversy to date:

> There is little evidence that there was a coordinated campaign of murder and intimidation against Protestants in the area; nevertheless, the Protestant population of West Cork declined by approximately 1,200 people over the fifteen-year period for non-economic reasons. These include the impact of the Great War, influenza, the change of administration, *Ne Temere* and, of course, fear. Given what happened in Ireland between 1911 and 1926, the surprise is not how many native Protestants left but how many remained. Perhaps those involved on both sides of the ongoing historiographical controversy would join together in seeking the publication of the manuscript of the 1926 census as a matter of urgency to establish certainty in place of speculation.[110]

---

[104] Macardle (1965: 795).
[105] Efforts to achieve balanced overviews may be found in Bielenberg et al. (2014: *passim*).
[106] Hart (2003: 242–58).   [107] Hart (2003: 246).   [108] Hart (2003: 22).
[109] Hart (2003: 252).   [110] Keane (2012).

It is unlikely, however, that full publication of the census will resolve all disputes, though it is highly improbable that it will revive Hart's initial hypotheses—which, lest we forget, he repudiated. As Keane's recital reminds us, the First World War and the withdrawal of "garrison Protestants" to Great Britain and Northern Ireland initially had nothing to do with Irish revolutionary violence. The departure of the military garrison, the disbanding of Irish regiments, and the emigration of their families accounted for about a quarter of Protestant émigrés from Ireland between 1911 and 1926.[111] The exit of civil servants, police officials, and their families added further numbers—the administrative garrison. Their careers, or their unwillingness to serve new masters, drove their departures rather than the policies of the new government.

But exit was not the universal choice: some transferred their loyalties to the Irish Free State, and others exercised voice in efforts to shape its trajectory. The subsequent fall in the proportion of Irish Protestants after the civil war, reflected in Table 2.3.4, cannot plausibly be attributed to genocide (Ian Paisley's charge), ethnic cleansing (Hart's "hypothesis"), or coercive assimilation. Mostly it reflected the different demographic structures of Protestants and Catholics at the start of the Free State: Catholics were far more numerous, younger, and had significantly higher birth rates. On average, Irish Protestants had higher educational attainments and greater international networks, and appear to have disproportionately sought employment elsewhere in the Commonwealth—they *may* have emigrated more partly because they were better networked to do so to their perceived advantage. The received understanding of the *Ne Temere* decree reinforced these trends.[112] The Catholic Church obliged its flock to assimilate the offspring of mixed marriages—though in the North working-class Protestants agreed that the products of mixed marriages should be treated as Catholics, and in Dublin, as we shall see, the decree's interpretation probably confirmed existing trends in mixed marriages (the children were already being brought up as Catholics).[113] The new governing elite in the Irish Free State supported the maintenance of denominational schools, Protestant as well as Catholic. It aided the survival of Protestant hospitals long after the numbers of Protestants had made a case for closure on economic grounds. Isolated incidents of overt discrimination against Protestants in public administration were not endorsed by the governments of the day. An extensive literature has been generated by the case of the Co. Mayo Library Board, which refused to sanction the appointment of a Protestant woman, Letitia Dunbar-Harrison, a graduate of Trinity College, to the job of local librarian, a decision strongly criticized by the Dublin government, which enforced the appointment on merit—though it later transferred her with her consent—and dismissed the discriminatory local board. The most disgraceful conduct on this occasion certainly was displayed by de Valera, then the leader of the opposition, who endorsed the local Mayo bigotry. But it later became part of the pride of his governments, as of those led by his party competitors, that they did not discriminate against Protestants in public appointments. The political integration of Irish

[111] Kurt Derek Bowen (1983: 22).   [112] See Vol 2. Ch. 3, p. 89, n.62.
[113] See, however, Vol. 2. Ch. 3, p. 89, n. 62 As late as 1957, Catholics at Fethard-on-Sea were encouraged by a local priest to boycott local Protestants to enforce what were understood as the *Ne Temere* provisions on a mother who had resiled from them.

Protestants as Irish citizens certainly took place at the expense of their British national identity, but that development was mightily assisted by the departure of the British state after 1922 and their abandonment by Ulster Unionists in the six counties.

A fitting penultimatum on "the Hart controversy" is that, as it unfolded, little attention was paid to the pioneering demographic investigations of Martin Maguire, whose first major contribution was also published in 1993. He initially specialized in the history of Protestant working-class Dubliners, mostly composed of migrants from Great Britain and their descendants.[114] His analysis of census data between 1861 and 1911, and micro-studies of Dublin wards and parishes, show that the numerical decline of this class started in the nineteenth century—well before the Irish Revolution. Maguire emphasizes three developments: the decline of manufacturing led to migration to Great Britain;[115] the decline of working-class sectarianism—a powerful contrast with Belfast—was expressed in residential integration, and facilitated Protestant and Catholic intermarriage, especially between Protestant men and Catholic women; and, lastly, the large number of working class Protestant women who married soldiers who were disproportionally Protestant or not Irish (and who later left Ireland): between 1871 and 1911, in over one third of marriages in Dublin Protestant working class parishes, the groom was in the military. In sum, by the early twentieth-century, the Dublin Protestant working class was less sectarian than its forebears, remote from elite Protestant power networks, and living among and marrying into the Catholic working class. When exiting through emigration, they did so in search of better employment, or to live with their soldier husbands. The conjunction of these developments was demographic decline. Combined with Fitzpatrick's analyses of Cork, Maguire's evidence obliges the conclusion that the exit of Protestants from what became the Irish Free State was not caused by revolutionary violence. Rather, their demographic collapse was well underway before the General Post Office was captured by the Volunteers.

In preparing his ministers for key negotiations in 1938, Sir Henry Batterbee, a key official in London's Dominions Office, observed that de Valera's government had won over many unionists and Protestants to the southern government, and that Protestants were disproportionately advantaged in senior government positions: "Contrast this with Northern Ireland, where it is impossible for anyone to obtain a Government appointment higher than that of a policeman unless he belongs to an Orange Order."[116] While this statement simplified matters, it was a sounder comparison of northern and southern treatments of their respective minorities than that in some recent historiography.

What then might be a fair and non-polemical assessment of the respective treatments of their largest minorities by the two new regimes created in the 1920s?

---

[114] Maguire (1993); and for an array of his studies, see <http://eprints.dkit.ie/view/creators/Maguire=3AMartin=3A=3A.html> (accessed July 2014). Maguire's findings are consistent with the work of Kerby Miller and Liam Kennedy on NW Ulster, and the work of Breandán Mac Suibne and David Dickson on North Donegal–according to Dr Mac Suibne.

[115] Skilled Catholic workers also migrated to Great Britain, but Catholic numbers in Dublin were replenished by rural migration.

[116] Cited in McMahon (1984: 235).

The argument advanced here, so far, confirms that, whereas northern Catholics were subjected to a control regime, southern Protestants were not subjected to postcolonial expulsion. Balance, however, requires a proper assessment of the experience of the Protestants who stayed—as opposed to reciting accurate negations: they were not expelled, expropriated, or discriminated against in public employment—that do not tell the whole story. The key "ugly scars on Kathleen's face," to employ D. H. Akenson's phrasing, relate to Ireland's cultural policy.[117] His assessment is that "Protestants were tolerated and well treated as a religious minority but were penalized and ill-treated as a *cultural* minority."[118] Penalized is the wrong expression, if it suggests legal penalties, equivalent to the penal laws, and the ill-treatment has to be elaborated. Akenson's monograph on Irish educational policy emphasizes that the Irish government generously sustained Protestant schools with fewer children on their rolls than was permitted for the Catholic majority: by 1962–3 Protestant children were less than 3 percent of enrolled children, but 9 percent of all elementary schools were Protestant.[119] A special program was developed to bus Protestant children to Protestant primary schools. Even though the downside of this policy may have been a proliferation of small one-teacher schools among Protestants, there can be little doubt that sovereign Ireland was far more generous in its educational provision to its religious minority than its northern counterpart—it overprovided on a proportionate basis, whereas the UUP government underprovided.

Akenson emphasizes, however, that the Irish state's Gaelic revival policy was not equivalently tolerant or generous. Teaching of Irish in state-aided schools was made compulsory. Irish-medium teaching, though not compulsory, was incentivized with grants and scholarships. By the mid-1920s there was an ambitious plan to teach infants in Irish, irrespective of the language at home: by 1928 1,240 infant schools were taught in Irish-medium, 373 solely in English, and 3,570 in both English and Irish. Teachers' salary, seniority, and promotion prospects were deliberately enhanced by qualifications in Irish—and, since Protestants were present but much less present than Catholics in the Gaelic revival, these incentive structures placed a burden on their teachers' recruitment and careers. In 1925 high-school students required a pass in Irish to pass their overall intermediate certificate; in 1936 the same policy was applied to the leaving certificate (the high-school diploma). An even more severe policy was contemplated. In 1942 a measure backed by de Valera's government passed the Irish parliament: it would have held all children of Irish parents, whether in private or state-aided schools, to the same curriculum (with undisguised implications for obligatory Irish-language education). President Hyde, however, referred the bill to the Supreme Court, which correctly found it repugnant to the constitution.

Successive Irish governments undoubtedly pursued a Gaelic revival policy. They acted as normal nationalists, intent on constructing a culturally specific nation-state. But, their language policies were targeted at the entire public sector, and at all citizens: Protestants *qua* Protestants were not expressly targeted. Some Protestants complained, however, that Irish phrasing, texts, and especially history texts were saturated with Catholic assumptions, so that a

---

[117] Akenson (1975: 134).   [118] Akenson (1975: 118–19).   [119] Akenson (1975: 117).

pro-Irish policy was in fact religiously discriminatory. The Irish government was not, however, linguistically coercive on the French republican model, to the consternation of its Gaelicist hardliners, who wanted it to be otherwise. English was and remained an official language, protected in the constitution of 1922 and the new constitution of 1937. Until the Supreme Court ruled against what may have become ubiquitous linguistic coercion in education—and would have required parents to notify the police before they sent their children abroad, in the words of Richard Mulcahy—successive Irish governments pursued what might charitably be recognized as a normal integration strategy—that is, they aimed to create a common public domain, with a free private cultural domain. That common public domain was to be one in which Irish was elevated to the status of the national language. Given that the linguistic shift from Irish to English had already occurred throughout most of Ireland, and that English was a global lingua franca that strongly benefited Irish migrants, this revivalist project was probably doomed to limited success. No revival policy could have worked without some incentives for parents, children, and teachers in favor of Irish. In its efforts to achieve its distinctive common public domain—in which Irish was the national language and English an official language—successive Irish governments necessarily impinged upon the linguistic British identity of Irish Protestants. Irish had never been the language of most of their forebears, and when it had, that had been forgotten. The revival policy may have damaged the human capital of all young citizens, because education in other subjects suffered as a byproduct of the efforts to revivify Irish. In this domain, breaches of cultural rights claims occurred, if not constitutional or legal breaches: there was no international law protecting the language rights of national minorities, and the constitution had functioned to block the most majoritarian assimilationist moment in de Valera's government. Irish cultural nationalists, reflecting their self-understanding as members of an imperially wounded nation, and holding strongly exaggerated conceptions of the role of British coercion in explaining the loss of Irish, gave little thought to how their linguistic policies were perceived by the Irish Protestant minority in the South and the Ulster Unionist majority within the North. When challenged, they either believed that a "one-nation, one-language" policy was justified, or that majority-rule decision-making was appropriately extended to all aspects of culture. Neither principle, however, was ever democratically tested. Had precise referendums on the subject ever been held, it seems unlikely that the majority of the English-speaking citizens of the Irish Free State, Catholic or Protestant, would have voted for many of the incentives to revive Irish, especially if they had worked against their own prospects of public-sector employment. The cultural fanatics in civil society were most intrusive in sport: in 1943 the GAA proposed the sacking of the Minister of Defence, Oscar Traynor, a hero of the war of independence, not, as Seán Ó Faoláin pointed out, because he had been incompetent in his administration of the army or air force, but because he had allowed members of the army to play foreign games.[120]

---

[120] "The Stuffed Shirts" (June 1943), in Kent (2016: 225). Ó Faoláin deemed the episode "the most lunatic" of recent Celtic lunacies. Myles Dillon, a champion of both the language and of a tolerant Catholicism, later noted that the language policy was "turned into an instrument of discipline . . . [and] as a means of transferring power—or rather authority" over cultural institutions (1960: 24). His plea for

ESTABLISHING A SOVEREIGN STATE AND
ATTAINING EXTERNAL ASSOCIATION

The treaty had made the Irish Free State a constituent dominion of the British Commonwealth of Nations with the same constitutional status as Canada. What that meant was a work-in-progress.[121] An Imperial Conference of 1907 had defined the self-governing British colonies as dominions, but how self-governing were they? In domestic politics the Crown acted upon the advice of the government of the dominion, but in 1911 Asquith had rejected the idea that Great Britain should share its authority in making foreign policy with the dominions. The title of the British Commonwealth of Nations—in preference to the British Empire— was pioneered by the South African Jan Smuts, who emphasized its two core institutions, the shared monarchy and the system of conferences. By 1917 he wanted to formalize the status of the dominions as equal sovereign states: domestically, each dominion should be recognized as having the power to amend its own constitution, and be free to control appeals to the privy council as part of the confirmation of the supremacy of its own legal system (and thereby overturn Westminster's Colonial Laws Validity Act of 1865); externally, each dominion should have the same status and recognition at the postwar peace conference, and the dominions' treaty-making powers and right to appoint "ministers" to foreign countries should be clarified. In Smuts's confederal vision, the dominions would become coordinate but equal governments of the king and not be under the jurisdiction of the Colonial Office or any other British department. They would have direct access to the monarch, who would act on their advice without any British ministerial intermediary; with the same logic, the governor-general was to become simply and solely a representative of the sovereign. Plainly, however, until Smuts's vision was realized, the sovereignty of the dominions was constrained. In 1921 Great Britain still administered its relations with dominions under the jurisdiction of the Colonial Office. Churchill, the Duke of Devonshire, J. H. Thomas, and Leo Amery successively dealt with the IFS and other dominions as Secretaries of State for the Colonies. A separate Dominions Office was not created until 1925, but its first three secretaries, Leo Amery, Sydney Webb (Lord Passfield), and J. H. Thomas, simultaneously held the Colonial Office portfolio— until 1931. These dull facts of administrative history embarrass those who deny the longevity of colonialism in British–Irish relations.

Collins had observed in the treaty debate that the dominions' presence at the Paris Peace Conference indicated their novel and evolving international standing. The power to make treaties was being acquired by Canada, which had announced its intention to appoint an ambassador to Washington. But the British government formally retained the right to reserve and veto dominion legislation. Its formal powers of reservation were still applied over shipping and London's finance market (on the grounds that a single regulatory structure was required).

---

an idea of the Irish nation as a river fed by many streams was made in a vigorous but courteous reply to Ernest Blythe. My thanks to Professor Paul Bew for the reference.

[121] What follows is indebted to Harkness (1969).

London could legislate to bind the empire (albeit with the consent of the dominions), and its officials maintained that the judicial committee of the privy council (not mentioned in the treaty) could hear appeals from any colonial (or dominion) court. They insisted that, as well as being a channel of communication, and the monarch's representative, the governor-general in each dominion be appointed and instructed as its agent by the British government—instructions that included the right to reserve bills (though not in the IFS). The constitutions of dominions, even if drafted in the dominions, were enacted in London, and each had reserved areas that required the Westminster parliament to modify them. Great Britain presumed a common external relations and defense policy under its hegemony, though that was under strain, as both Canadian and South African ministers increasingly demanded the right of consultation over the declaration of war and peace, and the right to neutrality.

The first article of the constitution of the IFS defined the state as a coequal member of the British Commonwealth of Nations. The second defined all powers of government as derived from the people of Ireland (not the Crown). It stripped the governor-generalship of the historic powers it had held in other dominions—the Dáil determined the opening and closing of parliament; the president of the executive council was nominated by the Dáil, and other ministers by the president; and the governor-general could not dissolve parliament. The power to amend the constitution—subject to the treaty, a schedule to the text—was kept within Ireland. The Irish deputy took an oath of allegiance to the constitution and to the king in his role within that constitution. On the Irish understanding, the king was Ireland's king, not the British king—a change eventually accepted in the alteration of the king's title from "King of Great Britain and Ireland . . . " to "King of Great Britain, Ireland . . . " The vital punctuation became known as the O'Higgins comma. The right of appeal to the Privy Council from Irish courts had not been part of the treaty, but, despite assurances given to Ireland's delegation by Lloyd George's team, its inclusion within the draft constitution had been demanded—but placed there in a highly constrained and indeed contradictory form, which would allow appeals only in cases that affected other dominions.

The Irish Free State played a key role in the constitutional decolonization of the British Empire, though the latter's transition into the British Commonwealth of Nations and then the plain Commonwealth, was neither linear nor without strain.[122] Until 1936 British officials stubbornly sought to read the treaty minimally—sometimes trying to freeze the Free State's status to that of Canada's in 1921. The IFS's first major initiative to confirm its status as a sovereign state was its successful application to join the League of Nations in 1923. It applied as Saorstát Eireann, a fully self-governing state, not as a dominion, and would go on to play a distinguished role within the League, especially for a small state. It was elected to the Council in 1930 and de Valera would serve as one of its presidents.[123] Overcoming British protests, the IFS successfully registered the treaty as

---

[122] This discussion of the Commonwealth depends on Mansergh (1966, 1991), Harkness (1969), and McMahon (1984).

[123] He was President of Council of the League of Nations at its 68th and Special Sessions, September and October 1932, and President of the Assembly of the League of Nations, 1938.

an international one with the League—putting at least one controversy to rest.[124] The British held to the eventually untenable position that relations between and among the dominions were not international, even though the dominions had international status—an argument held to flow from the unitary theory of the Crown. In the same year, 1924, the IFS appointed a minister plenipotentiary to Washington—with which the British government cooperated—and started to issue its own passports, opening passport offices in Washington and New York.[125] Along with the Canadian government, the IFS also refused to accept responsibility for or sign the Treaty of Lausanne.

The IFS delegation played a subdued role in the 1923 Imperial Conference, but the run-up to that conference saw novel evolutions in constitutional "usage" and "practice." Canada and other dominions refused to support Lloyd George's threat to go to war with Turkey in 1922, and in 1923 Canada signed a fishing treaty with the USA, without involving the London government, or allowing the UK to sign on behalf of Canada—Britain's previous insistence on its responsibility for imperial foreign affairs, and its right to conduct foreign policy on behalf of the dominions, including signing collectively binding treaties, had been dispatched. IFS ministers and officials deliberately regarded imperial conferences as intergovernmental meetings, without federal or confederal powers to bind the member states, except through their unanimous consent—a view with which the Canadians and South Africans generally concurred. The strategic object of the IFS was precisely to prevent such conferences evolving into a confederal or federal government while chipping away at the unitary theory of the Crown. At the Imperial Conference of 1926, led by O'Higgins, the IFS, along with the Canadian and South African delegations, played a major role in constitutional modernization.[126] The king's title was altered to recognize Ireland's statehood, the role of the governor-general clarified, and the treaty-making powers of the dominions recognized. The conference culminated in the Balfour declaration, now a less infamous declaration than another that bears the same man's name. It defined the dominions as autonomous communities, equal in status, and in no way subordinate "in any aspect" of their domestic or external affairs, and as freely associated members of the British Commonwealth, united by a common allegiance to the Crown. Balfour, however, appended a controversial explanation in which he distinguished between equality of status and equality of function—Great Britain was to remain paramount in diplomacy and defense.[127]

The Balfour declaration led logically though not inevitably to the Statute of Westminster of 1931, in which the British parliament permanently renounced its right to legislate for the States of the Commonwealth, including the Irish Free State, and recognized each state's full constitutional independence and equality.

---

[124] The British government, informed with less than a week's notice, later objected to its registration, employing a unitary sovereignty theory of the Commonwealth, but its objections were not accepted by the League.

[125] See Whelan (2015), who records that both Irish republicans in the USA and FCO officials in London initially wanted to block the IFS's diplomatic presence in Washington DC.

[126] O'Higgins wrote to his wife that New Zealand "must be like Northern Ireland—it produces the same type of Jingo reactionary" (Harkness 1969: 91).

[127] Harkness (1969: 97).

The legal uprooting of British paramountcy from the dominions had been preceded by a technical committee, which met in 1929. Among other matters it declared British governmental reservation and veto powers obsolete, and commended their abandonment, sought to confirm the extraterritorial effect of dominion legislation, proposed the repeal of the Colonial Laws Validity Act of 1865, commended the full domestication of the governors-general under the appointment and instruction of the dominion governments, and defined the Crown as a symbol of free association. In 1931 the IFS separately removed the final figleaf in the external supervision of its foreign policy—it replaced the British Great Seal, and the protocols attached to its use, with its own.

The culmination of this sustained and skillful diplomatic route to recognized statehood, including an autonomous foreign policy, under what was now clearly an Irish (not British) constitutional monarchy, was not, however, widely hailed at home, in a land suffering from the repercussions of the great depression. At best it was regarded as a belated confirmation of Ireland's official understanding of the treaty—de Valera would later have sufficient manners to acknowledge that the stepping-stone theory of the treaty had been correct. That treaty still stood, however, and remained, so it seemed, superior to Ireland's constitution, according to its text; Great Britain certainly read the treaty as unilaterally unamendable by Ireland. Whether the Statute of Westminster had repealed Ireland's constitutional obligations under the treaty seemed uncertain to British lawyers. Irish officials, however, argued that the Irish constitution had not expressly limited the power of the Oireachtas to legislate contrary to the treaty; and had not limited its power of constitutional amendment; and that constitutional usage and practice in the dominions had evolved in accordance with the Balfour declaration and the Statute of Westminster. It followed that the British government had no authority or veto power over the constitution of the IFS, which was therefore free to amend or end the treaty, and indeed to secede from the Commonwealth. Exactly these fears precipitated a British reaction. During the passage of the Statute of Westminster through the mother of parliaments, Churchill and other diehards sought to amend it to safeguard their reading of the treaty. They failed, after a public letter from Cosgrave affirmed that his government's policy was that the treaty could be altered only by mutual consent. To the defenders of the IFS, the oath of allegiance and the standing of the Privy Council remained the outstanding indignities to be excised before the constitutional independence and integrity of the IFS would be complete. Cosgrave's Cumann na nGaedheal government was engaged on both these matters when it lost office to a Fianna Fáil minority government in 1932.

The constitutional and diplomatic achievements of the IFS that are emphasized in Harkness's *The Restless Dominion* cannot be denied. Its leaders catalyzed and hastened changes afoot among at least some of the dominions. Its policy of incremental advance was aided on crucial occasions by alliances with other dominions, two weak and divided Labour governments (in 1924, and in 1929–31), and the general economic and imperial management difficulties faced by Conservative-dominated governments—which reduced the rationality of allowing obsessed diehards to block the dynamic implications of the treaty. Moreover, for an entire decade a pro-treaty government held power in Dublin (1922–32). London governments were more inclined to ratify or acquiesce in changes insisted upon by Cumann na nGaedheal governments—in the hope that would assist them in heading off the electoral advance of Fianna Fáil, which was opposed to the treaty. That hope expired after 1932, though it was not instantly extinguished.

THE CONSTITUTION OF 1937:
THE UNDECLARED REPUBLIC

In April 1932, in his second month of office, de Valera introduced what became the Constitution (Removal of Oath) Act. Its legislative stages in the Dáil were completed by May, but it was delayed in the Senate for a year. This obstruction of a manifesto commitment prompted him to legislate to abolish the Senate, which would later be restored in a modified form, but it would be conveniently absent during constitutional reconstruction. The new act deleted the oath itself, and removed the constitutional provision that blocked amendments repugnant to the treaty, and the restriction on amendments to the constitution.[128] Accusations of unilateral treaty-breaking were predictable from the British political class, but the Statute of Westminster tied their hands—the constitutional usage and practice of the dominions had moved on, including in UK law. When de Valera subsequently won exactly half the seats in the Dáil for his party in 1933, he then proceeded incrementally, in the style of Cosgrave's government, to abolish appeals to the Judicial Committee of the Privy Council, and the office of governor-general. After Governor-General James McNeill had resigned—after being insulted, intentionally or otherwise, by ministers from the new government—de Valera appointed Donal Buckley as his successor. This non-upper-class man would conduct his minimal office business in an unimpressive suburban dwelling devoid of regal pretension, and would later happily sign the abolition of his own office on behalf of the king.[129]

George V died in January 1936. His son and heir, Edward VIII, had as his first priority marriage to Wallis Simpson, a previously divorced American woman, yet to be divorced from her second husband. Marriage to a previously divorced person was then a major religious and social taboo in England and elsewhere, and Mrs Simpson suffered from a double dose of the alleged affliction, and the impossibly vulgar status of being an American commoner. Under pressure from the British cabinet, Edward chose love and abdicated in December 1936. De Valera, unlike other moralizing dominion premiers, expressed no formal views on the king's marital intentions, or their validity, but drafted and passed the Irish Free State's External Relations Act of 1936, which took effect immediately after the king's abdication.[130] The diplomatic and consular representatives of Saorstát Eireann would now be appointed by the Irish cabinet, and every treaty would be concluded by Irish ministers. It also declared:

---

[128] <http://www.irishstatutebook.ie/eli/1933/act/6/enacted/en/print.html> (accessed May 2016).
[129] See Vol. 1, Ch. 2, p. 114, n. 25. He was also known as Daniel, and by his name in Irish.
[130] McMahon (1984: 198–202) shows that de Valera was reactive and hesitant in this crisis rather than brilliantly proactive in shaping the opportunity.

so long as Saorstát Eireann is associated with the following nations, that is to say, Australia, Canada, Great Britain, New Zealand, and South Africa, and so long as the king recognised by those nations as the symbol of their co-operation continues to act on behalf of each of those nations (on the advice of the several Governments thereof) for the purposes of the appointment of diplomatic and consular representatives and the conclusion of international agreements, the king so recognised may, and is hereby authorised to, act on behalf of Saorstát Eireann for the like purposes as and when advised by the Executive Council so to do.[131]

In short, the role of the king, for Irish purposes, was now externally confined to his capacity as head of the Commonwealth, and as the head of state of Ireland's allies.

De Valera then proceeded to draft a new constitution, driven by neither Anglophobia nor personal resentment: self-vindication would be a more accurate psychological description. The timing, however, was linked to the coronation of the new king, George VI, and a subsequent imperial conference of the dominions from which de Valera excused his government. When Fianna Fáil had first taken power, the constitution of Saorstát Éireann had already been multiply amended, and, contrary to its founders' intentions, had become an Irish exemplar of the (domestic) sovereignty of parliament. The reason was partly procedural. The constitution's transitional provisions permitted amendment by ordinary legislation in its first eight years, and, through the Constitution Amendment No. 16 Act of 1929, the period during which amendments could be made in this way was extended for another eight years. When the IFS constitution was eventually superseded, it had been formally amended no less than twenty-seven times— roughly twice per year. The amended text, now including the (temporary) abolition of the Senate, bore increasingly little resemblance to the original document. A court judgment of 1924 (*R. (Cooney)* v. *Clinton*) had arguably reduced the constitution to absurdity: the Court of Appeal held that any Irish legislative act inconsistent with the constitution would supersede the constitution, because it would be deemed a constitutional amendment! This ruling effectively re-created the sovereignty of parliament—rendering the idea of the constitution as fundamental law redundant—at least as long as the transitional provisions remained. Notoriously, the provisions enabling a popular initiative to propose a constitutional amendment had been removed in 1928 after Fianna Fáil had successfully organized the requisite petition to propose having the oath removed. The Cumann na nGaedheal government deleted the relevant constitutional provision through ordinary legislation, and then allowed the transitional provisions to continue for another eight years.

There was therefore a strong case for a fresh constitution, both to function as a check on the authority of the government, and to imbibe lessons since 1922. Such considerations coincided with de Valera's determination to remove the stain the treaty had imposed on Irish freedom, and to implement his Document No. 2: Ireland would choose its own constitution, free of British supervision or impediment, and freely externally associate with the Commonwealth.[132] The adoption of this new constitution was meticulously planned, so that it would not be seen as an

[131] <http://www.irishstatutebook.ie/eli/1936/act/58/enacted/en/print.html> (accessed May 2016).
[132] What follows draws upon J. M. Kelly (1980); Kelly et al. (1987); and Morgan (1990). See also Bromage (1937a, b), and Bromage and Bromage (1940) for contemporaneous assessments.

amendment of the old one—and thereby construed, however indirectly, to flow from the authority of the imperial parliament and the treaty. A constitutional rupture was required. The draft text was therefore separately ratified in a plebiscite. It met with modest approval from the citizens on July 1, 1937. Legal scholar D. G. Morgan reports that 38.6 percent of the electorate voted in favor of *Bunreacht na hÉireann*, 29.6 percent against, and 31.8 percent either abstained or spoiled their votes. Alternatively put, on a 75 percent turnout, the constitution was approved by 56 percent of the electorate, and, unlike the sharp practice of 1922, citizens had two months to consider the draft, and were not threatened with war by a British prime minister. The constitution was a major subject of the election, and de Valera canvassed actively for it—while pompously deploring that its provisions had become the subject of partisan debate. He had supervised the drafting process; and personally, and frequently persuasively, shepherded the text through Dáil Éireann—accepting few amendments. The electorate was asked: "Do you approve of the Draft Constitution which is the subject of this plebiscite?" Ten percent more of the electorate answered affirmatively than gave Fianna Fáil candidates their first preferences in the general election held on the same day, facts that permit—even if they do not prove—the conclusion that the constitution was endorsed by most Fianna Fáil and Labour voters, and, perhaps, by some previously abstentionist republicans.

Bunreacht na hÉireann[133] warrants attention not just because, as amended, it remains in force, but because it was a critical moment in constitutional decolonization.[134] Sovereign Ireland made its own constitution without British impediment, oversight, or approval. Some provisions also had consequences for Ulster Unionists and northern nationalists; probably serving to make Irish reunification less likely. The constitution of 1937 also needs to be treated without caricature: it is now typically read as a Vatican-drafted clerico-fascist and patriarchal specimen of corporatism, replete with regressive linguistic coercion and aggressive ethnonational territorial irredentism.[135] In the first place the new constitution incorporated many features of the 1922 constitution: the jurist J. M. Kelly called it the rebottling of wine that was by then quite old and of familiar vintage. Yet the new text had more vim and vigor. Article 1 needs no gloss: "The Irish nation hereby affirms its inalienable, indefeasible, and sovereign right to choose its own form of Government, to determine its relations with other nations, and to develop its life, political, economic and cultural, in accordance with its own genius and traditions." Article 5 declared Ireland a sovereign, independent, democratic state; Article 6 (1) that "all powers of government, legislative, executive and judicial, derive, under God, from the people, whose right it is to designate the rulers of the State and, in final appeal, to decide all questions of national policy, according to the requirements of the common good;" and 6 (2) that the powers of government are "exercisable only by or on the authority of the organs of state established by

---

[133] One translation might be "Foundational Legislation" of Ireland, or Fundamental Law of Ireland.

[134] See Brian Farrell (1988); Keogh and McCarthy (2007).

[135] The English Conservative Michael Oakeshott (1939: 45–72), who enjoys a reputation as overblown as that of his avatar Edmund Burke, placed passages from the 1937 constitution under "catholic" rather than "democratic," and compared Ireland to Salazar's Portugal; for his errors in these respects, see Kissane (2007: 222–3).

this constitution." This last clause precluded Westminster from legislating for Ireland, and the Crown from any role in Irish lawmaking. The institutional arrangements were familiar—parliamentary and cabinet government headed by a prime minister, to be named Taoiseach (Irish for chief);[136] weak bicameralism (the new Senate had no ability to veto or significantly to delay legislation passed by the Dáil); and with proportional representation (STV) entrenched to elect Dáil Éireann.[137] Importantly, however, the Dáil could no longer amend the constitution on its own: amendments drafted by the Dáil would have to be ratified in a referendum. The most novel office was that of an elected president. Fears that it would be the instrument through which de Valera would become an Irish *Führer* or *duce* proved wildly misplaced: the first incumbent was the non-party Protestant and Gaelic League scholar Professor Douglas Hyde. The president would be a largely symbolic head of state, mostly directed by the cabinet as the governor-general in the dominions was advised by dominion ministers. Other consequential novelties included the protection of human rights. Though Articles 6–10 of the 1922 constitution had been the first among the dominions expressly to document such propositions as fundamental law, they were not as elaborate as in the new text, nor as effective. The new bill of rights protected the civil liberties of the individual. The governmental institutions—the president, and the Oireachtas (Dáil Éireann and the Senate)—may not amend or restrict such rights; the judiciary is required to uphold them; and only the people of Ireland can modify them through a referendum.

By 1939 under this constitution Ireland was "the sole successor state [created] after the end of the First World War to have retained a democratic form of government."[138] Other questions mattered more to contemporaries. Was Ireland now a republic? The constitution carefully did not say, but the text met all known dictionary definitions.[139] In an emphatic silence, no king of Ireland was mentioned. The head of state was a president; and the head of government a prime minister: one was elected by the people, the other elected by the first house of the legislature elected by the people. There was no hereditary or clerical second chamber or offices of state with these traits. But Ireland had not left the Commonwealth, of which it remained a voluntary member, though not by constitutional obligation. The External Relations Act of 1936 remained in force, and Ireland's authorities were empowered to remain in or to join appropriate leagues of nations. The king's status as the head of the Commonwealth was therefore indirectly recognized, and de Valera, locked into his vision of Document No. 2, persuaded himself that this might be a useful vehicle through which Ulster Unionists would accept Irish reunification.[r]

---

[136] On the choice of title, see Murray Smith (1995).

[137] Some Fianna Fáil ministers would have liked to abolish PR, but MacEntee, a northerner, observed that it would weaken the case against the abolition of PR in the North, while de Valera clearly feared it would weaken the constitution's prospects of popular ratification (McMahon 1984: 216).

[138] Kissane (2007: 211).

[139] Later, in response to being needled by James Dillon of Fine Gael, de Valera invoked numerous dictionary entries to affirm that Ireland was a republic (Dáil Éireann Debates, vol. 27, no. 23, Committee on Finance, Vote 65—External Affairs (July 17, 1945))—a speech worth reading. Brooke commented that Unionists "do not have to look at a dictionary to see what our Constitution means. That Constitution is in our hearts" (Hansard (NI), HC, vol. 29, col. 79 (July 24. 1945)).

In short, Ireland was now an undeclared republic, but had it become a Roman Catholic state? Article 40 forbad the publication or utterance of blasphemous, seditious, or indecent matter—application being left to the courts to determine (probably to be mostly staffed by Catholic judges). But English law did the same, and English rule was not Rome rule. Under Cosgrave's government, the IFS had established a censorship board in 1929, which acquired an unenviable skill in banning works that would achieve worldwide recognition for outstanding literary merit. But all of this was arguably routine mid-century Christian censoriousness, shared by most Irish Catholics and Protestants, albeit now regrettably given constitutional force. Fianna Fáil had identified itself with public Catholicism: turning Catholic feast days into public holidays; displaying crucifixes in Dáil Éireann; and banning the import of contraceptives.[140] And both the tone and the substance of the constitution displayed a Catholic ethos—notably regarding the family, marriage, religion, and private property—but subject to democratic control and amendment. The state would protect the family as the indispensable basis of the welfare of the nation and the state, and be the watchdog of the institution of marriage—declaring that no law could be provided to dissolve a marriage. Not only was divorce forbidden; so was the remarriage of those divorced elsewhere. The former Edward VIII could not have married Wallis Simpson in Ireland, just as he could not do so in the Church of England. The constitution acknowledged that persons have the natural right, antecedent to positive law, to private property, following Aquinas rather than Bentham or Marx. But it also recognized that private ownership rights, and the rights to transfer, bequeath, and inherit property, should be regulated by principles of social justice, and it allowed for public ownership of natural resources and public enterprises (thereby making the text compatible not just with Catholic social teaching, but also with social liberalism and social democracy). Article 44, more controversially but ambiguously, recognized "the special position" of the Holy Catholic Apostolic and Roman Church as the guardian of the faith possessed by the great majority of citizens. But the state guaranteed not to endow any religion. This formula was neither papist nor republican rule: neither Rome nor Paris. The Vatican's preferred established church was not ceded, but neither was the wholly unambiguous separation of church and state characteristic of French republicanism.[141] What was special about the Catholic Church's position remained to be seen.

The constitution recognized, named, and protected the other religious denominations and associations already existing in Ireland—including Jews. The entire formula was a version of Napoleon's concordat, which had recognized the special position of the Catholic Church, and had recognized other religions—including that of the Jews. De Valera had held off demands for the establishment of the Catholic Church, and the religious minorities seemed to have been content with the new constitutional articles.[142] Ireland was the sole place where Jews

---

[140] Inglis (1987); Patrick Murray (2000: 257–62).

[141] The archives at Armagh demonstrate that the Cardinal Archbishop MacRory sought to have the state recognize Catholicism as the religion of 97 percent of the people of the twenty-six counties and as that established by our Divine Lord; and that he disliked the acknowledgment of other Christian sects and Jews, and sought to strip the Church of Ireland of its title (Rafferty 1994: 238).

[142] Patrick Murray (2000: 293).

improved their constitutional standing in Europe in the 1930s. Every citizen was guaranteed freedom of conscience, and the free profession and practice of religion, subject to public order and morality. Article 44.3 guaranteed that "the state shall not impose any disabilities or make any discrimination on the ground of religious profession, belief or status." The recognized religions all then opposed divorce. Neither the other religious denominations nor de Valera sought to protect the irreligious, whose freedom of expression did not appear to encompass the allegedly blasphemous or the indecent.[143] The failure unambiguously to separate state and religion—and not merely to prevent establishment or endowment—left the Catholic Church as the dominant societal organization in schools, orphanages, workhouses, and hospitals, powers it would use and abuse.

A Catholic ethos was palpable in two further respects—patriarchal sexism and communitarianism. Article 42.1 and 42.2 specified that "the State recognises that by her life within the home, woman gives to the State a support without which the common good cannot be achieved," and that it "shall, therefore, endeavour to ensure that mothers shall not be obliged by economic necessity to engage in labour to the neglect of their duties in the home." Patriarchalism built on the theme of two spheres—the tacitly male public and the expressly female private— was not invented by Irish Catholics, but Irish Catholics would not be in the vanguard in its demolition. The National University Women Graduates' Association criticized these provisions, as did republican feminists. They successfully achieved some amendments, highlighting formal equality without distinction of sex. In J. J. Lee's view, the traditional model of the woman's role was probably supported by traditionalist females, who outnumbered their professional and more liberal sisters. He also points out that the state proved very unsuccessful in promoting marriage by west European standards—and not just because there was no divorce for a marriage that failed. Communitarianism was evident in the "Directive Principles of Social Policy," which were not justiciable. They were an early example of placing aspirational goals in constitutions—to provide ambitions for the legislature and governmental agencies.

Was Ireland still bound by the treaty ratified in 1922? No treaty articles affecting Ireland's domestic law and sovereignty remained in the text, and important provisions for the future specified that no treaty could be made in the same way as that ratified in 1922—including financial arrangements.[144] The text was, however, silent on the treaty: it was neither incorporated, nor expressly repudiated. Article 29.2, however, provided that "Ireland accepts the generally recognised principles of international law as its rule of conduct in its relations with other States," and Article 29.6. that "no international agreement shall be part of the domestic law of the State save as may be determined by the Oireachtas." Since the treaty was an international agreement, the defense and ports provisions of the treaty remained binding, *and*, despite the tenor of Articles 2 and 3, the provisions regarding Northern Ireland arguably remained in force. De Valera had been faithful to Document No. 2, in which Ireland was to be externally associated

---

[143] The import and sale of contraceptives had been banned under *criminal* law—which would later lead to long-running sagas.

[144] See Article 29.5 and 29.6.

with the Commonwealth, including in matters of defense, peace, and war, and to recognize "His Britannic Majesty as head of the Association." After the constitution had been ratified, he sought to negotiate away the British presence in the treaty ports, and to end partition. The right of the dominions to be neutral was already implicitly recognized, insisted upon by Canada and South Africa. Neutrality was not, however, proclaimed in the constitution.

Was sovereign Ireland now a *Gaelic* nation-state? The state had a new name, Éire in Irish, Ireland in English. In constitutional adjudication, the Irish text was to have precedence over the English. Article 8 enabled provision to be "made for the exclusive use of Irish or English" for any official purposes, throughout the state, or any part of it. This article reassured citizens that mono-Gaelicization would not be compulsory in public life—though it did not exclude language requirements from being made obligatory for public office. English was a fully protected official language: the constitution did not inaugurate a monolingual Irish polity. Ireland was officially bilingual, but with an overwhelmingly English-speaking majority, including in the Oireachtas and the courts. Public policy favored Irish, but those who sought a Gaelic polity were to be disappointed.

Was Ireland now bound by an aggressive ethno-national and irredentist constitution? The answer has to be a qualified "no." The constitution was made in the name of "the people of Éire." These, however, turned out to be the people of the state, rather than the nation of the whole people of the island. Or did they? The preface, reads:

> In the Name of the Most Holy Trinity, from Whom is all authority and to Whom, as our final end, all actions both of men and States must be referred,
> We, the people of Éire, Humbly acknowledging all our obligations to our Divine Lord, Jesus Christ, Who sustained our fathers through centuries of trial,
> Gratefully remembering their heroic and unremitting struggle to regain the rightful independence of our Nation,
> And seeking to promote the common good, with due observance of Prudence, Justice and Charity, so that the dignity and freedom of the individual may be assured, true social order attained, the unity of our country restored, and concord established with other nations,
> Do hereby adopt, enact, and give to ourselves this Constitution.

This phrasing is not theologically neutral; it invoked trinitarian rather than Arian or unitarian convictions, but the opening lines are not solely Roman Catholic and may have been expressly modeled on the constitution of Poland.[145] That sovereignty appeared to have been located in the Holy Trinity was as metaphysical as the three-in-one deity itself. The preface is not a justiciable part of the constitution, however, and Article 6.1 vesting sovereignty in the people is what matters. But who were the fathers whom Christ had sustained through centuries of trial? The reference was not to Catholic priests, because, contrary to rumor, they did not constitute the people of Eire. Those who underwent centuries of trial at unnamed hands must either be the nation of Ireland (broadly understood), or Irish Catholics, or Irish Catholics and dissenters (who also went through

---

[145] Irish Jesuits submitted a preamble modeled on Poland's constitution, though only the first clause is in the Bunreacht (Keogh 1988: 14, 16, 18).

persecution), and the males thereof. Perhaps all three meanings were intended. But Churchmen, Irish Anglicans, and mothers could be forgiven for thinking they were not defined as part of the people giving themselves this constitution. Elsewhere, however, the constitution made plain that for legal purposes the authority granted by the people applied to the citizens and territory of the Irish Free State. The whole people of the island of Ireland were not those adopting, enacting, and giving themselves the constitution. Neither Ulster Unionists nor northern nationalists were formally consulted in the making of the constitution (though northern bishops were). Had they been granted votes on the matter the draft text would not have been ratified.

Section 1 of the constitution, entitled "The Nation," did not define the nation, thereby leaving hanging the ambiguity in the preface. Article 2, however, defined "the national territory" as "the whole island of Ireland, its islands and the territorial seas." By implication the Irish nation—whose territory this was—has to be read as the entire people on the whole island, its islands, and the territorial seas. Article 2, however, was qualified or explained by Article 3 as follows: "Pending the re-integration of the national territory, and without prejudice to the right of the parliament and government established by this constitution to exercise jurisdiction over the whole territory, the laws enacted by the parliament shall have the like area and extent of application as the laws of Saorstát Éireann and the like extra-territorial effect." The phrasing "pending the re-integration of the national territory" recognized partition as a fact, a legal fact, because the final part of the clause confines the jurisdiction of the laws of the parliament created under the new constitution to those of the outgoing Irish Free State. Equally, however, the reintegration of this divided territory was made a key goal of the constitution—a later ruling deemed it an imperative.[146]

Did these two articles derecognize Northern Ireland, or repudiate the 1925 tripartite agreement that had interred the boundary commission? That was how they were understood, and allowed to be understood, by its advocates, by Ulster unionists, by popular opinion, and by many of the imperial lawyers of Great Britain. *But* no such express or implied derecognition or repudiation took place in the text. According to Article 29.2, the new constitution bound Ireland to international law, and the agreement of 1925 was an international treaty. The function of the controversial component of Article 3—"without prejudice to the right of the parliament and government established by this constitution to exercise jurisdiction over the whole territory"—was to allow the constitution of 1937 to apply to the whole island after unification. Quite why unionists would accept, let alone welcome, this premise was neither obvious then, nor since. "Without prejudice to the right" is lawyer's language. It allowed the new constitution to apply to all of Ireland, but did not oblige that method of incorporation to be the sole route through which unification could take place (for example, constitutional amendments could have been made). Much grief and amateur textual construction, paranoid or otherwise, would have been avoided had another clause stated that the reintegration of the national territory would require the negotiation of a new constitution. As drafted, the two articles could be misconstrued—and were so

---

[146] See Vol. 3, Ch. 3, p. 92.

read, and perhaps were intended to be so misread—to suggest not only that Ireland sought to redeem lost territory, which it could incorporate within its new constitution without modification, but that, even before this reintegration, the Irish parliament could in principle legislate for the whole island, its immediate islands, and territorial waters.

Over sixty years later the modification of these articles—on the grounds that they constituted a contentious sovereign territorial claim, the removal of which were regarded as a *sine qua non* by unionists—would become a key part of the Irish peace process. The new Article 2 now expressly defined the Irish nation, as follows:

> It is the entitlement and birthright of every person born in the island of Ireland, which includes its islands and seas, to be part of the Irish Nation. That is also the entitlement of all persons otherwise qualified in accordance with law to be citizens of Ireland. Furthermore, the Irish nation cherishes its special affinity with people of Irish ancestry living abroad who share its cultural identity and heritage.

The new Article 3 also specified the procedure through which Irish reunification could take place, while allowing for the creation of north–south bodies with legal powers:

> 3.1. It is the firm will of the Irish Nation, in harmony and friendship, to unite all the people who share the territory of the island of Ireland, in all the diversity of their identities and traditions, recognizing that a united Ireland shall be brought about only by peaceful means with the consent of a majority of the people, democratically expressed, in both jurisdictions in the island. Until then, the laws enacted by the Parliament established by this Constitution shall have the like area and extent of application as the laws enacted by the Parliament that existed immediately before the coming into operation of this Constitution.

> 3.2. Institutions with executive powers and functions that are shared between those jurisdictions may be established by their respective responsible authorities for stated purposes and may exercise powers and functions in respect of all or any part of the island.

The Irish nation is now defined geographically, and through naturalization, in a manner entirely consistent with the definition of the national territory as originally specified in the 1937 constitution (the island, its islands, and seas), but now it is the nation that is expressly defined, not the territory. What matters to unionists, however, is that the mechanism through which partition may be reversed is now specified—namely, majority consent in two distinct jurisdictions. This expression rules out not only conquest, but also the possibility that peaceful diplomatic negotiations between the British and Irish governments could on their own lead to the territorial transfer of the North into the jurisdiction of the South.

This parsing should help today's reader understand what was implicit in de Valera's constitution. Consistent with international law, Articles 2 and 3 allowed for the possibility that Irish unification could take place through an agreement between the London and Dublin governments, bypassing the Belfast government (and its voters). This was the strategy de Valera was intent on leaving open for adoption. By contrast, today's versions of these articles were negotiated with Ulster Unionists, and did not antagonize their leaders—unlike de Valera's provisions. Replying in the last Dáil debate on the draft text to a protest at the absence from the text of recognition of the feelings and aspirations of "the people in the North . . . whom we wish to reconcile," de Valera declared, "you cannot go further than we have gone in this Constitution to meet the views of those in the North without sacrificing, to an extent that they are not prepared to sacrifice, the legitimate views and opinions of the vast majority of our people here."[147] These alleged limits to astounding southern generosity were now entrenched.

One last semi-technical construction is required. The original Articles 2 and 3 implicitly assumed that Ireland should be reunified as a unitary not a federal state. Article 15.2 allowed that provision could "be made by law for the creation or recognition of subordinate legislatures and for the powers and functions of these legislatures." This clause permitted the recognition of the Northern Ireland Parliament within a decentralized unitary state, as a subordinate legislature of the Oireachtas; by contrast, a federal or confederal Ireland could not have been negotiated without constitutional amendments. Why Ulster Unionists would consider subordinating their parliament to Dublin, when they had rejected that option in 1922, and why they should be expected to accept a constitution over which they had not been consulted—and given no express encouragement to negotiate entry through amendment—was neither addressed, nor answered by de Valera, except in his scarcely credible claim that the constitution reached the very limits of accommodation with the unionist minority on the island.

Ulster Unionists were not alone in not being formally consulted. The same was true of northern nationalists—though many approved of the content of the new constitution. One Ulsterman, Eamon Donnelly, a Fianna Fáil TD, moved deferral of the drafting of a new constitution until partition had been ended, and until the whole people of Ireland could ratify it. He had no success—he was also a hardline advocate of the view that if there was to be a new constitution it should declare a republic. Donnelly correctly anticipated, however, that apparent constitutional closure, after a debate primarily among Catholics in the South of various hues, would make ending partition more difficult. The new constitution provided no mechanisms for the state's transformation into a federation, for a confederal process of integration of the North, or for openly allowing the state's authorities to negotiate an institutional settlement with the representatives of Northern Ireland. Here de Valera locked in his party's ideological opposition to partition, and acted as if he could roll back the negotiating clock to 1921. With a straight face he drafted a constitution for the whole island while initially limiting its application to the twenty-six counties. Ulster unionists understood the message to mean: "This entire island is our national land, and you are part of our people, whether you like it or not. Once you work out that you made a major mistake in 1920–22 we will allow you to subordinate your parliament to ours." Not inclined to contemplate subordination to what they deemed a Catholic and Gaelic Republic, or to reverse the control they had established, Unionists renewed their guard, and Craig successfully called and won the last election of his life on February 9, 1938, within six weeks of the entry into force of the Constitution of Ireland. The vehemence of the unionist rejection of the new Irish constitution was reflected

---

[147] Moynihan (1980: 304).

in Craig's official request to be able to rename Northern Ireland as Ulster—a counterblast that Whitehall and British ministers refused.

THE ANGLO-IRISH AGREEMENTS OF 1938

Only "in the summer of 1936 did the implications of the constitutional developments of the last two decades dawn upon the British government," writes the author of a well-crafted and copiously documented history of Anglo-Irish relations in the 1930s.[148] Deirdre McMahon portrays a British coalition government vacillating and uncertain on its Irish policy after 1932, slow to absorb the implications of the Statute of Westminster, or to accept that de Valera and his party were now the dominant agents in southern Irish politics, and much slower to take de Valera at his word. The British coalition equivocated over whether to accept an Irish republic that would secede from the Commonwealth but in which Britain's strategic defense interests could be preserved. They were skeptical of de Valera's intent to design a constitution that would keep Ireland within the Commonwealth and externally recognize the king—combined with its aim to end partition. The diehards refused to contemplate any unwinding of partition, or of the standing of the Crown, and found it unthinkable that the Commonwealth could encompass republics.

British policy attained greater clarity after 1935, when Malcolm MacDonald, the son of Ramsay MacDonald, became the Secretary of State for the Dominions. This charming, eloquent, and intelligent diplomat, who would play a major role in the decolonization of the empire after 1945,[149] was eventually able to break free of the anxieties of the Conservative diehards and the shibboleths of Labour's deferential royalists, and develop a constructive working relationship with de Valera and his officials. He could do so because he found an unexpected ally in Neville Chamberlain, the chancellor of the exchequer, and soon to be prime minister. Today Chamberlain is a much-reviled figure, and historians generally side with his nemesis Winston Churchill on almost all matters, but Chamberlain should be recalled as one of the fathers of Irish freedom—an honor not to be bestowed on his father or brother, nor on Churchill.[150]

Between 1932 and 1938 the Irish Free State and Great Britain engaged in what was called "the economic war." The two places were one another's closest trading partners, and the Free State continued to use the pound sterling. The Free State's dependency was strikingly evident in two respects: 90 percent of its agricultural exports went to Great Britain, and its producers and households were almost entirely dependent on imports of British coal. The trade war was sparked by de Valera's fulfillment of his manifesto pledge to refuse to send the land annuities to Great Britain—the repayment of the loans that had been made to Irish tenants to buy their land. Fianna Fáil had been shocked to discover that Cosgrave had

---

[148] McMahon (1984: 188).   [149] Sanger (1995).
[150] See the references to Joseph and Austen Chamberlain, and to Winston Churchill in Vol. 1. McMahon (1984) shows that Warren Fisher, the Treasury secretary, also followed a rational line: following British national interests as consistently as possible with Ireland's goal of sovereign self-assertion, thereby acting as the gravedigger of the treaty's non-partition provisions.

secretly agreed to make such repayments in 1924. These annuities were a significant drain on Irish agriculture. They were portrayed as continuing tribute from past conquests—and linked by Fianna Fáil to Ireland's overtaxation under the Union.[151] Northern Ireland had been allowed to retain its annuities, and de Valera maintained that the Irish Free State should be treated equally—whatever the Cosgrave government had agreed. In another measure of postcolonial retribution, de Valera's government refused to pay the pensions of some retired RIC officers and former British civil servants.

The coalition government of MacDonald and Baldwin responded by imposing a 20 percent import duty on all goods from the Irish Free State, and subsequently imposed quotas on Irish livestock. The Irish then retaliated by putting import duties on goods from Britain and Northern Ireland—including coal, cement, electrical goods, iron and steel, and machinery. De Valera called a snap election in 1933 to rally the Free State's citizens in the economic war. The enterprise was successful: his party significantly increased its vote and seat share, leaving it one seat short of a single-party majority. The Irish government had begun an improvised import-substitution development program. It hoped to achieve increased agricultural self-sufficiency and diversification and develop Irish "infant industries."

In 1935 a coal-in-exchange-for cattle pact eased the negative consequences for both governments, but the trade war remained mutually hurtful, even if not equally so. The Free State's cattle industry suffered severely—probably hitting big farmers who voted Fine Gael more than Fianna Fáil's, but many farmers went bankrupt. Emigration and unemployment rose, and the balance of trade and the national debt worsened, though it is difficult to divorce the effects of "the economic war" from those of the global great depression. Diversification in agriculture was limited, and, amid a worsening international environment, few new markets were won, and conditions were not propitious for a surge in domestic investment (though peat usage developed, and small farmers benefited from not paying toward annuities). Great Britain was hurt much more than it expected, as McMahon's account of the deliberations of Irish Situation Committee of the British cabinet confirm.[152] Unemployment was triggered at ports, in mining, and in agri-business linked to Irish cattle. The British share of the Free State's markets fell by approximately one-quarter, and its consumers of beef and dairy products were adversely affected. Northern Ireland was severely affected—the sole obvious benefit for the locals was that its farmers displaced some of the Irish suppliers to the British market. Cross-border trade across the Ireland was disrupted by hard customs and tariffs barriers—and smuggling increased.

The Anglo-Irish Agreements of 1938 linked and resolved three interrelated disputes. Financially, Great Britain agreed to end its demand to be compensated for the land annuities, in return for a lump sum of £10 million to be paid by the Irish Free State in settlement of all claims—Britain believed it was owed at least £78 million. In trade, the two governments agreed to remove all import duties applied to one another's goods and services in the previous five years, and guaranteed better treatment of each other's exports for three years. Some quotas

---

[151] Fianna Fáil's use of the land annuities question has been read as mobilizing Anglophobia (Foster 1988: 553–4), but a subsequent demonstration of its economic and political rationality is more persuasive (O'Rourke 1991).

[152] McMahon (1984: *passim*).

and tariffs remained, however, and Ireland was allowed to impose duties to protect its new industries from British imports. Politically, the treaty ports were ceded to Dublin's jurisdiction, and evacuated in early 1939—without military or diplomatic preconditions. The treaty of 1921–2 was modified by mutual consent.

Economic historian Kevin O'Rourke, in a compelling article entitled "Burn Everything British but their Coal," has a crisp and satisfying account of the war, rooted in both economics and politics. The economic war was settled on terms highly favorable to the Irish, but the domestic welfare costs of the war were not so great as has been thought, and the dispute helped de Valera electorally. He estimates that if, "3 percent of the GNP was lost in the seven years between 1932 and 1938; this amounts to roughly £4.5 million per annum, or £31.5 million in all. Against this a capitalized £100-million liability was settled with a £10-million lump-sum payment, and Ireland gained the Treaty Ports." The results of O'Rourke's modeling suggest:

> (1) the aggregate welfare cost of the economic war was less than has been claimed by some, and (2) the dispute shifted income to workers and the towns, thus helping de Valera electorally. Both factors help explain de Valera's tough bargaining stance, which in turn largely explains the eventual Irish victory in the dispute. The fact that de Valera won the economic war does not mean that his trade policy was blameless . . . In particular, Ireland lagged behind in the general move to free trade after World War II . . . [but] the search for policy failures in the de Valera era should focus on that issue, rather than on the economic war per se.[153]

De Valera's government was the beneficiary of Chamberlain's general appeasement policies, which were not acts of abject cowardice, but pragmatic responses intended to buy the overstretched British Empire time to prepare for the probable renewal of war on the European continent. Chamberlain and MacDonald hoped that postcolonial detente with the newly self-baptized Éire would reduce historical animosities, and make it more likely that the Irish could be won voluntarily to a full diplomatic and military alliance. They were, therefore, willing to return the deep-water ports.[154] Articles 6 and 7 of the treaty were deleted. While critics of the British government, including Churchill, believed that the ports were vital to British security, Chamberlain was advised by defense officials—including the military—that the ports were run down, expensive to maintain, and underemployed—four ships were regularly anchored—and not "absolutely vital" to British defense forces.[155] More astutely, it was thought that the ports could not be easily used in a major war without the cooperation of the Dublin government. For de Valera's cabinet, the return of the ports marked the elimination of the last noxious feature of the treaty of 1922—except partition. It made future neutrality feasible, no longer merely a technical constitutional right, because Ireland would no longer be obliged to make the ports available to the British navy, army, or air force in time of war. For de Valera the agreements were a triumph. He went to the polls to reverse the weakened performance of 1937, and secured a governing

---

[153] O'Rourke (1991: 366).
[154] The complexities of the negotiations are dealt with in McMahon (1984: chs. 11–12).
[155] McMahon (1984: 232).

single-party majority in June 1938 for Fianna Fáil, the first time a party had won such a majority in the history of the state.

Before and during the negotiations, de Valera had sought a British declaration against partition, but this was refused, and the issue was not pressed—though the Home Office made half-hearted, complacent inquiries into the condition of northern nationalists. To London's surprise, however, Dublin refused to allow Northern Ireland to be a special beneficiary of the prospective trade agreements— Chamberlain was obliged to make side payments to the northern government to free him to close the deals with the Dublin government.[5] These included agricultural subsidies being put on a par with Britain's, an agreement to assist in the event of budgetary difficulties, and the imperial contribution to Northern Ireland's unemployment insurance fund no longer being scrutinized, even if it breached £1 million. Unionists protested that the British Isles had been endangered by the return of the ports and feared that the next step would be a London–Dublin agreement to end partition. Northern nationalists, by contrast, were disappointed that partition had not been the core subject of the negotiations, but hoped that it would be de Valera's next priority. That would not be so—except nominally and rhetorically. His anti-partitionist campaigning was not entirely cynical, but it had no immediate prospect of success precisely because of his earlier constitutional closures, and because Chamberlain, by offering no obstruction to the return of the ports, prevented de Valera from trying to link ending partition to a defense agreement. Chamberlain had agreed to confirm Ireland's sovereignty, and de Valera's previous strategic choices ruled out quick progress on achieving unionist consent to end partition. To keep his party and northern nationalists happy, he embarked upon a press-driven anti-partition campaign in which hope temporarily triumphed over experience.

DECOLONIZED IRELAND: NEUTRALITY, STATEHOOD, AND NATIONHOOD, 1938–1940

The impact of the Second World War throughout Ireland is considered in Chapter 4. Here it is appropriate to consider the first major strategic choice faced by the decolonized and undeclared republic, which had just eradicated the constraints imposed by the treaty, won the economic war, and completed economic detente with Great Britain. These achievements, and the idea of progress toward reunification, were punctured by the outbreak of a new and eventually global war, which would serve to deepen North–South differences, and weaken the detente that de Valera and Chamberlain and MacDonald had established. The fall of France between May 10 and June 22, 1940 left Hitler's Germany ascendant in western Europe. Churchill replaced Chamberlain as the prime minister of Great Britain on May 10; the British Empire was isolated in its core; its major European ally would shortly surrender to Hitler; and it stared defeat in the face, despite the successful evacuation of Dunkirk. The air battle for Britain began at the end of June.

At this nadir in Great Britain's fortunes, was there a possible trade-off in which Great Britain would have guaranteed the end of partition in return for Ireland's participation in the war on the side of the Allies? Negotiations to that end were managed by Chamberlain, now demoted to Lord President of the Council (but still leader of the Conservative party until October 1940), and by MacDonald— that is, by the men who had conducted the negotiations that had led to the return of the treaty ports in 1938, but who now reported to Churchill.[156] On June 25, 1940, the British War Cabinet approved a paper for presentation to de Valera. In return for Ireland's decision to join the war with the Allies, the British government would "forthwith" issue a declaration accepting the principle of a united Ireland, and establish a joint body, including delegations from the two Irish governments, to consider the constitutional and other practical details of the Union of Ireland.[157]

MacDonald met de Valera, Lemass, and Aiken on June 27. Lemass was favor- able, but Aiken was vigorous in insisting upon both unity and neutrality, as was de Valera, though less so. The Irish cabinet had already voted to reject the proposals. Suspicion about British sincerity was evident, which MacDonald attempted to rebut. A revised British offer, signed by Chamberlain, was delivered on June 28. The key novelty was that, *in addition* to facilitating (but not enforcing) Irish unity, the British agreed to drop the requirement that Eire enter the war, in return for an invitation to British forces to cooperate in securing Eire's security "against the fate which has overcome neutral Norway, Holland, Belgium, Denmark and Luxem- bourg." The Irish cabinet deliberated at length. A week later, on July 4, de Valera replied that his colleagues rejected the proposals because they envisaged "the immediate abandonment" of neutrality but gave "no guarantee of unity."[158]

Debate over de Valera's strategic reasoning—and that of his divided cabinet— in rejecting the British offer will probably continue. John Bowman and J. J. Lee argue that de Valera and his colleagues doubted the British commitment to deliver on Irish unity, and had good grounds for doing so, because Churchill's position required Northern Ireland's negotiated consent to Irish unity (and, we might add, given Churchill's past volatile record on Ireland, including the fact that he had spent much of the previous two decades as a diehard imperial guard dog, implacably committed to a narrow reading of the treaty of 1922—on the Crown, the boundary commission, the oath, Ireland's constitution, and the return of the treaty ports). The Fianna Fáil government also had to consider its interests in continuing neutrality given Ireland's abject military weakness.[159] The legacies of the First World War were not far from Irish ministers' minds: Irishmen, like Redmond, who had allied with the British, had been repudiated by their co- nationals. This time there was a much stronger and worldwide expectation that Germany would defeat Great Britain—France was prostrate; the USA was neutral; and the Hitler–Stalin pact still held.[160]

---

[156] The historiographical confusion on these matters is such that one historian has Neville Cham- berlain as the British prime minister on June 28, 1940 (Bew 2007: 469), when Churchill had been prime minister since May 10—perhaps it is difficult to recall Churchill as an appeaser of Irish nationalists.

[157] Longford and O'Neill (1970: 365–6).   [158] Bowman (1982: 236).

[159] Lee (1989: 234–6) describes Ireland as totally unprepared for war with untrained troops and obsolete equipment—by comparison with the Swiss and the Swedes, the Irish at most had pursued a policy of "half-armed neutrality." Of course, had Ireland developed a proper army, it is easy to imagine the reactions in Great Britain and among Ulster Unionists.

[160] Bowman (1982: 266); Lee (1989: 248).

Commenting on Lee's appraisal, the late Cornelius O'Leary argued that the British offer was sincere, and that the British government could have delivered the consent of the younger unionist leaders.[161] But neither British sincerity nor the delivery of the unionists was tested, and the younger unionists were not in charge. Since these evaluations, more archival material has emerged that generally confirm Bowman's and Lee's assessments, while Malcolm MacDonald's biographer has published the following extract from his subject's memoir of the three meetings he had with de Valera.

I did my best to persuade him to accept our proposals. He was extremely friendly but adamant. He dismissed the suggestion about a United Ireland as a promise which, however, sincere, might produce no effective result ... He said emphatically that he and his colleagues wanted us to win the war; and he argued that one reason why Eire should remain a neutral land was that this would reduce the danger of us being defeated in the struggle. He feared that, if his government now declared war against Germany, Hitler's forces would immediately invade militarily weak Eire and, in spite of our offer of military help, quickly overrun it. That would not only be disastrous for the Irish people but also increase the prospect of a powerful invasion of Britain. This threat to Britain would probably be avoided if Eire remained neutral. The use of Eire's territories and coasts would be denied not only to us but the enemy. Regarding our defence against submarine warfare in the Atlantic, he commented that we had full use of the ports in Northern Ireland, and he hoped that this helped us considerably. As for Eire's government attitude, he assured me that it would continue to be entirely benevolent to us in every possible open-and secret-way.

I did my best to persuade him [otherwise] ... I personally thought there was a lot to be said for his arguments. When I reported my failure to Churchill, however, he showed anger against de Valera.[162]

Reviewing the historiography clarifies the three available choices before de Valera's cabinet members: A, B, and C in Figure 2.3.1.[163] The status quo, A, involved the persistence of neutrality and the continuation of partition, with the serious risk that neutrality would be violated by either Great Britain or Germany—or both. The British offer conveyed by MacDonald, B, offered a mildly improved version of the status quo on partition. Churchill's government was offering to nudge the northern government into constitutional negotiations, albeit in return for Eire immediately joining Great Britain in the war against the Axis powers, directly or indirectly.[164] The offer met what de Valera had sought in the 1938 Anglo-Irish negotiations—namely, a vigorous British declaration in favor of unity, though under a formulation that would have encouraged any compliant Unionist negotiators—if they could be found—to demand major modifications of *Bunreacht na hÉireann*. Lemass would have accepted the British offer, but the

---

[161] Cornelius O'Leary (1990)—Brookeborough's biographer suggests the same (Barton 1988).

[162] Sanger (1995: 199–200). The diaries of the then permanent under-secretary at the Foreign Office record that Churchill thought of MacDonald as "rat-poison" because of his role in the return of the treaty ports (McMahon 1984: 234).

[163] Key treatments are in Bowman (1982); Canning (1985); Fisk (1985); Lee (1989).

[164] Bew (2007: 464, n. 74) reports second-hand exchanges in which Craig was "all but ordered to end partition on the best terms that he could" (Dwyer 1977: 54). If this is accurate, then strong nudging is an appropriate description.

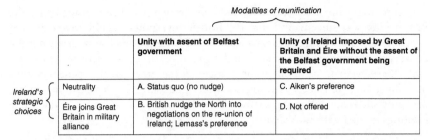

Figure 2.3.1. The actual choices facing de Valera's cabinet, summer 1940

majority of the Irish cabinet resolved in favor of Aiken's preference to the status quo, and also preferred the status quo to the British offer—that is, the cabinet's majority ranked their preferences C > A > B. The cabinet sought *both* neutrality and a firm British commitment to terminate partition. It seems clear, however, that the Irish cabinet never believed that the British would close on such an offer. Differently put, nationalist Ireland's continuing protest over the de facto unionist veto on ending partition was used by de Valera's government to legitimate sticking to neutrality. Option D was not available on the British side—urban legends notwithstanding. Option D would have meant an enforced override of the unionist veto on Irish reunification, along with Ireland's accession to a shared military alliance. It was *not* offered by the British government—at best it was hinted at. Albion managed to seem perfidious even at its darkest hour.

Craig, however, may have believed that he would be forced to accept Irish unity—or that he would be induced to make his followers believe that was necessary. He dictated a "proud, impertinent, explosive" telegram to Chamberlain: "AM PROFOUNDLY SHOCKED AND DISGUSTED BY YOUR LETTER MAKING SUGGESTIONS SO FAR REACHING BEHIND MY BACK AND WITHOUT ANY PRE-CONSULTATION WITH ME. TO SUCH TREACHERY TO LOYAL ULSTER I WILL NEVER BE A PARTY."[165] British policymakers were prepared to betray loyal Ulster; but they deliberated over the price—that is, over whether the betrayal would bring them sufficient net benefits. Faced with the costs of imposing Irish unification, and with de Valera's apparent determination to stick with neutrality, they did not offer option D, because they preferred A, the status quo—in which they could use the ports and airspace of Northern Ireland *and* keep in reserve the option of reinvading Ireland if that was deemed necessary.

In international relations, the subsequent joke has been that Ireland is always neutral—against Great Britain. But it is not true; de Valera never contemplated an alliance with Britain's enemies, either explicitly or secretly; and he and his cabinet repressed the members of the IRA who did. He calculated that the British offer on unity was a postdated check of uncertain currency that left intact the unionist veto: a "deferred payment" for immediate entry into the war.[166] He could not trust the offer. Craig, by contrast, thought the British were intent on betrayal.[167] The joint but opposite suspicions of Craig and de Valera toward London's intentions

[165] Fisk (1985: 207).   [166] Fisk (1985: 202).
[167] Telegrams cited in Canning (1985: 285); Fisk (1985: 207–8).

are telling. The London government's offer pledged to seek the assent of the Belfast government to an Irish Union, but it was left hanging what would happen if that assent was not forthcoming.[168] In writing the official rejection of the British offer, de Valera stated:

> Our present Constitution represents the limit to which we believe our people are prepared to go to meet the sentiments of the Northern Unionists, but on the plan proposed, Lord Craigavon and his colleagues could at any stage render the whole project nugatory and prevent the desired unification by demanding concessions to which the majority of the people could not agree.[169]

In the summer of 1940, de Valera, along with his cabinet, clearly chose what they perceived as the best security option for their decolonized state, and its citizens, rather than risking both in an uncertain enterprise to reunify the national territory through negotiations with men who had well-deserved reputations for being at least as hardline as ardent republicans.[170] And when a version of the British offer appeared to be repeated by Churchill—after Pearl Harbor—shortly before the USA entered the war on Great Britain's side, de Valera's cabinet made the same choice.

Neutrality would be persisted with, after the USA had joined the war, even though many US officials, including the US envoy to Dublin, a relation by marriage of President Roosevelt, strongly encouraged an Irish policy reversal.[171] An unspoken assumption lay behind this persistence. When the chips were down, the Irish state, as they had designed it, mattered more to de Valera and Fianna Fáil's leaders than a hazardous and uncertain project to reunify Ireland though negotiations with Ulster unionists. They never tested whether their voters thought the same way, but it seems fair to assume that they thought they did. As the Second World War began, it had been clear to those who wanted to examine the matter that northern nationalists were second-class citizens in the North. Now, however, it was clearer than ever that sovereign Ireland ranked them as a second-order interest, though, among northern nationalists themselves, it took the generation that came of age in the 1960s to make the deduction.

---

[168] Amid MacDonald's negotiations with de Valera, Churchill annotated a telegram from the former: "But all contingent upon Ulster agreeing & S. Ireland coming into the war" (Fisk 1985: 206).

[169] Fisk (1985: 212–13).

[170] By the time Ireland had officially rejected the British proposal, Craig had publicly offered defense cooperation with the South *provided* that Axis diplomats were expelled, and provided that constitutional questions should not be raised (Harkness 1996: 69). That is, partition was to continue, *and* Ireland was to abandon neutrality.

[171] For a defense of the neutrality policy, see the spirited if narrow memoir of Ireland's leading diplomat in Washington from 1938 until 1947, Robert Brennan (2002). Brennan's daughter Maeve become a leading editorial light in the *New Yorker*, and an accomplished writer.

2.4

The Unexpected Stabilization of Control

The Second World War and its Aftermath, 1940–1957

> We are the children of the Empire, we Ulster people ... we have done more
> than our fair share in upbuilding those great communities that own Britain as
> their mother.
>
> Hugh Pollock, Northern Ireland House of Commons, 1921[a]

> I'm not Irish, I'm an Ulsterman—my family came here in '97, I mean
> 1597 ... My principle was always to be fair as far as you could, but you
> can't be entirely fair politically; there's always somebody who gets a rough
> deal ... I was very lucky. I had a completely united Unionist party, barring the
> odd crank or two, loyalist party I call 'em.
>
> Lord Brookeborough, spring 1972[1]

No consensus existed in Northern Ireland on how to respond to what became the
bloodiest conflagration in human history. The war transformed neither local
interethnic nor cross-border relations but had profound repercussions. The
Unionists were "King's men," according to Craig, and in the run-up to and after
the war began, the visibly aged prime minister publicly pressed London to extend
conscription to his jurisdiction. Mindful of what had happened in the First World
War, and the express hostility of Northern nationalists, the Catholic hierarchy,
and de Valera's government, the idea was politely declined. No conscription in the
North remained London's policy, vivid testimony to the local depth of division by
nationality. Even Churchill, Britain's most aggressive bulldog, retreated within a
week after his coalition cabinet ruminated on extending conscription to the North
in May 1941. His ministers admitted they had no reliable data on the rate of
enlistment among Northerners.[b]

Northern nationalist leaders solidly opposed conscription, and backed the
South's neutrality—though an unrealistic micro-minority within the minority,
among the IRA and its supporters, saw Britain's newest danger as the latest
opportunity for reunification, under Nazi auspices. Unionist extremism, by contrast, came from the top, and its depth was not fully appreciated at the time.
In June 1940, a few months before he died, Craigavon wrote to Churchill to argue
that Scots and Welsh regiments should be used to overthrow the Irish

---

[1] VanVoris (1975: 7–8).

government, and install a military governor in Dublin—he claimed that de Valera had fallen under Nazi influence. Craig's perhaps demented aggression was compounded by comic ignorance: he advised distributing propaganda in Gaelic and English to persuade the Irish that the Celtic regiments would defend them. It is too magnanimous to assume that illness, shock, or senility precipitated this missive—censors closed it to public access for seventy-five years.[2] The letter was entirely in keeping with Craig's past, which has been too kindly treated by historians.

One major episode of cross-border humanitarian solidarity occurred during the war. Luftwaffe air raids in April 1941 left Belfast on fire and with at least a thousand dead. Irish fire brigades were dispatched at de Valera's bidding after a request for help from the North.[3] But Craig's successor, Prime Minister J. M Andrews (1871–1956), spoiled the prospects for North–South détente by re-expressing the call for conscription. Previously best known for overt anti-Catholic bigotry, Andrews proved an inept leader of a cabinet radically in need of renewal.[4] His old guard, to whom he was loyal, were crumbling around him, and not fit for the challenges of wartime administration. Indeed, for the first time the UUP's regime looked vulnerable to collapse from within. Its factotums on Belfast Corporation were so mired in corruption that the city was placed under direct administrative controls throughout the war. The UUP lost a Stormont by-election for the first time in March 1941—humiliatingly in Craig's constituency—and another in the following November. One of its junior officials described the North as being only half-in the war: its civil defense capacities were woefully organized; wartime strikes were ineptly handled; the region's full industrial capacity, especially in war munitions, was never reached; quality controls in armament production were criticized; and at the end of 1940 unemployment was as high as during the great depression in Great Britain.[5]

Timing matters in politics. Andrews prematurely sought to commit his government—and the London Treasury—to major expensive postwar reconstruction programs, precisely to head off perceived discontent among the Belfast Protestant working class, expressed in the by-elections and in vigorous trade unionism. Advance cashing-in on loyalty, however, occasioned disapproval from the UK Chancellor and Treasury officials, who crisply suggested that the programs would bankrupt the Northern government. A backbench revolt simmered within the UUP from January 1943, and by May Andrews was forced to resign. He was succeeded by Basil Brooke (1888–1973), an aristocrat from Fermanagh, who had founded the Specials in his home county, and was one of twenty-six of his family who had fought in the First World War. Previously notorious for public advocacy of discrimination against Catholics in employment, Brooke was then much more energetic, disciplined, and politically astute than either Andrews or Craig (in his later years). He formed a fresh cabinet. A fully

---

[2] Fisk (1985: 210).

[3] Barton (1989) provides a clear account; his writings are among the most judicious of treatments of Northern Ireland during and after the Second World War.

[4] "Though by no means a total nonentity, Andrews is best remembered for his remark that he had counted the number of Catholics among the porters at Stormont. The exercise did not require a command of higher mathematics" (Lee 1989: 257).

[5] Barton (1996: 47).

inclusive coalition of all the major parties, like that in London, was beyond the pale of UUP thought,[6] but Brooke co-opted the Protestant laborite Harry Midgley (1893–1957), who had started political life with an unwarranted reputation for Bolshevism, before graduating to the Northern Ireland Labour Party (NILP).[c] An opponent of conscription at the start of the war, Midgley had left the NILP because he could not accept its policy of neutrality on "the constitutional question," and had founded the short-lived Commonwealth Labour Party. Between 1941 and 1947 it had some success in by-elections and general elections in the Belfast region. The co-option proved effective: Midgley would later join the UUP.

But Brooke made some mistakes in his appointments. In February 1944, he demanded the resignation of the Revd Professor Robert Corkey (1881–1966), a teacher of ethics and theology at the Presbyterian College of Belfast and subsequently the Moderator of the General Assembly of the Presbyterian Church in Ireland. He had held a Queen's University seat in the Stormont House of Commons until Brooke had made him a senator and Minister of Education. Corkey, according to Craig, had failed to perform his duties. Given the tasks the reverend had accumulated both from the deity and from his fellow man, the suggestion was convincing, but Corkey protested that he was being fired on principle—Brooke allegedly opposed compulsory religious instruction in schools—and that an anti-Presbyterian bias animated the education ministry, colluded in by Brooke, a member of the Church of Ireland. This event brought intra-Protestant sectarian tensions to the surface within the UUP—Craig and Andrews had been Presbyterians. It also suggested that Brooke was moderate in the scope of his bigotry;[d] he wanted to run an effective wartime government.[7]

The UUP incumbents would gradually benefit from Ireland's neutrality, especially from the strategic enhancement of the North's ports and airspace, and the furnishing of a safe location for stationing American troops on their way to continental Europe. Inquisitorial British reviews of unjust unionist administration were filed away.[8] Loyalists eventually basked in the glory of those dubbed Churchill's Ulster generals: Field Marshal Alan Brooke, from Fermanagh, Chief of the Imperial General Staff through the key years of the war, was related to the Northern Ireland prime minister; Field Marshal Sir John Dill was from Lurgan, and forged a special relationship with the USA's George Marshall; Field Marshal Claude Auckinleck hailed from Fermanagh, and his Chief of Staff, Major General Eric Dorman-Smith, was a Cavan Catholic; Field Marshal Harold Alexander had Ulster–Scots aristocratic roots in Tyrone; and the most famous of these Ulster generals, and the one who put the most effort into being famous, Field Marshal

---

[6] As he put it in a retrospective interview in the spring of 1972: "You obviously can't take a man who's opposed to you politically and put him in a key position. It would be very rash . . . as if the British in the last war put a German in the Admiralty and another in the War Office" (VanVoris 1975: 8).

[7] Evident earlier in his role as Minister of Commerce, <https://www.youtube.com/watch?v=pUgbTnqGzGo> (accessed July 2015).

[8] McMahon (1984: 264–71) judges the responses of the Home Office officials to evidence of discrimination against Northern Catholics to exude "a cosmetic complacency," and "ignorance" and "myopia," which even then did not withstand empirical scrutiny, and were subject to a withering evidence-based review by Batterbee at the Dominions Office.

Bernard Montgomery, came from a Donegal family.[9] Loyal Ulster, meaning Protestant and Unionist Ulster, won praise from British ministers, notably Churchill and Herbert Morrison, the Labour Home Secretary.[10]

Remarkably, however, the depth of loyalty in "Ulster"—among loyalists—was debated during the war. There is no subsequent historiographical consensus. Irish and Northern Irish men volunteered for the British military, but who contributed more volunteers, absolutely or proportionately—that is, did Irish Protestants volunteer more than Catholics? Ireland's neutrality was berated in unionist and British media, but Brian Girvin and Geoffrey Roberts have shown that by 1944 Ireland's societal contributions to Britain's war effort started to be publicly and privately praised,[11] even in Irish official circles.[12] Press stories, diplomats, and Northern nationalists suggested that southern Irishmen enlisted at a proportionally higher rate than the Northern Irish (Protestants). The Dominions Office was tasked with collecting the data. Its first tally suggested nearly 3,500 officers from the South, compared with just over 2,400 from the North, and a total soldiery of nearly 28,000 from the South compared with roughly 26,500 from the North. At the end of 1944 figures for the three services were provided. Approximately 37,500 men and 4,500 women from the South were in the armed forces, whereas the respective numbers for the North were about 37,500 and 3,100. During 1945, however, the official figures for the South were increased to 50,000. These data cannot be used confidently to estimate the proportionate contributions of Catholics and Protestants, but do *not* suggest strikingly disproportionate Protestant contributions. In April 1946 General Sir Hubert Gough, founding president of the Irish Servicemen's Shamrock Club, once involved in the Curragh mutiny, wrote to the *Times* insisting that the official figures were misleading: "I have confidential, but trustworthy information that in August–September 1944, the official lists of next-of-kin notifiable in case of casualties contained upward of 165,000 addresses in Éire." Historical demographer Enda Delaney describes this number as a "useful top-of-the-range figure."[13] Brian Girvin's treatment of "The Emergency"[14] reviews the numbers of Irish recruited, and draws on the scholarship of Yvonne McEwen, who has suggested a possible figure of 60,000 (southern) Irish recruits into British forces.[e] No accurate total or sectarian breakdown seems likely, so this particular "whataboutery" remains unsettled. What we do know is that the losses of the First World War—in which Gough was one of Haig's most controversial generals— made many Irishmen, northern and southern, Catholic and Protestant, reluctant to enlist after 1939.

For the long run what mattered was that the contributions of Ireland's soldiers to Great Britain's (and America's) war effort did not compensate for the loss in diplomatic strength caused by the Dublin government's choice of neutrality.

---

[9] His memoirs record that he was asked to prepare plans to seize Cork and Cobh in the summer of 1940 (Montgomery 1958: 70); he had fought against Ireland's independence in 1921–2.

[10] Harkness (1996: 73).

[11] Girvin and Roberts (1998) point out that Ireland's High Commissioner wrote to the *Spectator* in March 1944, replying to an editorial hostile to Irish neutrality, indicating that no difficulty or hindrance had been placed in the way of those who wished to join the British Army and observed the high proportions of military age who had left.

[12] Girvin and Roberts (2000).   [13] Delaney (2000: 149).   [14] Girvin (2006).

Ireland ended the war in diplomatic isolation. The subsequent all-party anti-partition campaign demonstrated the triumph of hope over rational appraisal of evidence. As Lee has observed: "The most frequent official justification for neutrality was the border. Yet neutrality reinforced partition."[15] It did so because it gave the British and the Americans strong strategic reasons to want sustained access to the ports and air space of Northern Ireland—most easily obtained through the maintenance of partition—and because having different alignments in total wars has lasting effects on perceptions in high politics. The deepened development of Derry as a naval base occurred because of the denial of the Irish treaty ports. Neutral Ireland could not be an ally of the US in the way that the UK (and Northern Ireland) was. Neutrality had other repercussions. In 1946 the Soviet Union vetoed Ireland's application to join the United Nations—even though the Potsdam conference of 1945 had made clear that the USA, USSR, and UK were willing to accept the membership of wartime neutrals. The Soviet motivation was doubtless primarily driven by the desire to avoid the balance of membership becoming more pro-American. Ireland was excluded from member-ship until December 1955, when it was admitted amid a balanced entry of Eastern bloc states, pro-Western states, and wartime neutrals.[16]

DE VALERA, NEUTRALITY, AND
THE IRA'S SELF-DESTRUCTION

De Valera's government delivered on the pledges of benign neutrality given to Malcolm MacDonald and Chamberlain in 1940. Though Churchill believed that de Valera and his colleagues were driven by Anglophobia, Dublin consistently interpreted neutrality in ways that quietly leaned toward the UK's interests—and toward the USA when it joined the war in December 1941. Allied pilots and crew who crashed on Irish territory were silently allowed to head North, while German airmen were interned. Irish citizens served in large numbers in Britain's armed forces, and in its factories, and with no effort made to restrain these employment decisions. Girvin and Roberts estimate that over 8 percent of Ireland's population emigrated to Great Britain during the war, a stunning figure. If children (<14) and the elderly (>65), and travel restrictions on youth, are factored in, their estimate rises to as high as 15 percent of the relevant population.[17] This was extraordinary economic migration—people typically do not move into war zones for work.

Initially, the Irish government did not want to be directly implicated—to avoid diplomatic damage to its neutrality policy. Administrative cooperation between London and Dublin was therefore presented as minimal, though it was deep and extensive. Great Britain benefited from augmenting its labor supply when war-time mobilization led to full employment—and from Irish agricultural exports. Ireland benefited from remittances from its émigré workers, soldiers, sailors, and airmen, and saw its unemployment reduced. It depended upon Great Britain's shipping—and navy—for imports. Southern volunteers in Britain's armed forces

---

[15] Lee (1989: 270).   [16] See MacQueen (1983).   [17] Girvin and Roberts (1998).

may have included loyalists, but most were patriots of the new Irish state who saw enlistment as fully compatible with the defense of Ireland. Most veterans interviewed in a project run by Girvin and Roberts believed that neutrality had been the best policy for Ireland.[f]

De Valera's government enjoyed a cross-party consensus on neutrality, enabling him to recover the status of national leader that he had enjoyed between 1919 and 1921, and his popular esteem did not start to diminish until the privations of the emergency began to bite. Like Brooke, however, he never contemplated forming a wartime grand coalition government. One decision he had reached before the war's outset, however, was to secure "the safety of the people" through the repression of the IRA. Though defeated in the civil war, the anti-treaty IRA had never conceded the legitimacy of the Free State, nor that of Ireland after 1937. After its ceasefire in 1923, de Valera had proposed that the IRA agree to destroy its weapons in return for the abolition of the oath. The IRA accepted, but Cosgrave's government rejected the proposal. On recovering power in 1932, de Valera set about implementing Document No. 2. His critics have often portrayed this conduct as cynical, hypocritical, and inconsistent, enjoying the irony that the principal politician on the anti-treaty side would use the Free State's powers to accomplish what he and Childers had said could not be done. Equal relish accompanies commentary on de Valera's evolution into the nemesis of the IRA. Though not without his inconsistencies, hypocrisies, and (religious) bigotry, as an office-holder de Valera was generally consistent toward the IRA. Quite deliberately he exhausted persuasion before resorting to repression.[g] Repealing the oath, enacting an Irish-made and ratified constitution, and winning back the treaty ports, he successfully beat a path toward republican goals (except terminating partition, which in de Valera's view required diplomacy).[18] When this path was established, he insisted that no normative reason could justify the IRA's continuing existence.

Frank Aiken was appointed as de Valera's first Minister of Defence. He had been the IRA Chief of Staff who had ordered volunteers to dump arms in 1923. He reactivated the ceasefire proposals of 1923—that is, the trading-in of weapons for the removal of the oath—but the IRA did not engage. Initial governmental patience was manifested in the pardoning and release of IRA prisoners. Then, with increasingly emphatic clarity, de Valera insisted state authority applied to IRA volunteers: they had no right to carry arms in public, let alone assassinate people. Ireland was a state in which "every nationalist who had any aspirations for the independence of the country" could "pursue these aspirations in a peaceable way." Majority rule had to apply; the alternative was the rule of the strongest.[19] The Blueshirts were the first to experience the rigor of public safety and emergency laws—and a revamped police special branch. Then the IRA's volunteers had their collars tugged, often by former IRA men who had joined Ireland's security services. Over 300 men were convicted by military tribunals between 1934 and 1936, and that summer the IRA was declared an unlawful association. Thereafter, de Valera rarely referred to it by name.[h] His new constitution established

---

[18] For discussion on De Valera, Fianna Fáil, and partition, see Vol. 2, Ch. 4, pp. 136–40.
[19] Moynihan (1980: 239–40).

special courts for civil emergencies. The right to peaceful assembly was expressly protected, but "without arms." Article 39 defined treason to "consist only in levying war against the state . . . or attempting by force of arms or other violent means to overthrow the organs of government established by this constitution, or taking part . . . with any person to make or take part or be concerned in any such attempt."

In January 1939 the IRA's declaration of war on the governments of Great Britain and Northern Ireland in the name of "the Republic" jeopardized de Valera's promise that he would never allow Ireland to be used as a base of attack against Great Britain. He regarded it as an intolerable usurpation of the Irish state's authority. An embarrassingly successful IRA ammunition raid doubled the insult. The IRA's constitutional doctrine, to which de Valera had once lent his prestige, regarded the surviving republican deputies of the second Dáil Éireann, who had rejected the treaty, as the valid government of the (virtual) Republic. At the end of 1938 its surviving seven-person executive council, including Mary MacSwiney, delegated the government of this Republic to the IRA's Army Council. Duly advised, Taoiseach de Valera set out to demonstrate that there was but one government in independent Ireland. The Offences Against the State Act was legislated, and, when its sixth part was held unconstitutional by Justice Gavan Duffy, an amendment to the Emergency Powers Act was passed—enabling internment without trial.[20] Responding to incarcerated IRA hunger-strikers in 1939–40, de Valera declared his government faced "the alternative of two evils. We have to choose the lesser, and the lesser evil is to see men die rather than that the safety of the whole community should be endangered."[21] They were allowed to die—though not before other prisoners had benefited from release or modification of their terms.

The hanging of IRA men for a bombing that (accidentally[22]) killed five civilians in Coventry in England had earlier prompted calls for mercy by many Irish nationalists, based on procedural grounds. These were rejected by the London government. Before long the Dublin government followed suit for IRA actions on Irish soil. Wartime censorship and a cross-party consensus enabled the repression of the IRA to proceed with subdued public reactions. The right of appeal from the military tribunal was eliminated from the Emergency Powers Act. After August 1940, the tribunal was charged with imposing and executing the death sentence where appropriate—with no right of appeal regarding such conviction or sentence.[23] Patrick McGrath and Thomas Harte of the IRA were executed by firing squad in September 1940, having been found guilty of killing an Irish policeman. The crushing defeat of the IRA was imminent, and was completed by its own disarray and internal disputes. The major internal feud, driven by paranoia about the organization's penetration by informers, led to the kidnapping and torture of Stephen Hayes, the IRA's Chief of Staff, by his own men, from Belfast. Hayes escaped, claiming that he had not been an informer. Since he was sentenced for five years of penal servitude in an Irish court in the summer of 1942—without

---

[20] Coogan (2002: 136–8).   [21] Moynihan (1980: 422).
[22] Cronin (1987: 75) reports the IRA's O/C (Officer Commanding) for Britain as suggesting otherwise.
[23] Coogan (2002: 148).

reprieve—it seems likely he was telling the truth. Years later an IRA volunteer Tarlach Ó hUid, who had been imprisoned in Derry by the Northern government, spoke for many when he told Tim Pat Coogan, if "Hayes was a traitor . . . the IRA was a lousy organization for having such a man at the top, or else he was innocent, in which case the IRA was a doubly lousy organization . . . [having extracted an incredible false confession through torture]. Either way I was finished."[24]

The IRA's ideological myopia and volatile opportunism in its alliances, evident both in its schisms and in its sequential decisions to seek allies on the far left and the far right in the 1930s and 1940s, had cost it dear. Its most socialist left, for whom Connolly remained an icon, peeled away to form the short-lived Republican Congress in 1934, having earlier formed a front organization, Saor Éire, that had rapidly faded. The Congress did not last much longer. Its retrospectively most prominent figure, Frank Ryan, took its leading cadres to fight for republican Spain. They were outnumbered, perhaps by three to one, by Blueshirt volunteers who went to fight for Franco. In short, some pro-treaty IRA men became fascists, while some anti-treaty IRA men became allies of communists. After fighting courageously for the republican side in Spain, Ryan was captured and imprisoned by Franco's regime, though it subsequently permitted his "escape" to the German government, which believed it could exploit him.

The rump IRA in Ireland was neither ideologically fascist—though Dan Breen had become an overt admirer of Hitler—nor communist—though Mick Fitzpatrick had sought Soviet contacts. But it was militarist, and locked in several time warps. The militarists had not updated their knowledge of effective sabotage, their materiel, or their enemies' capabilities. With the brief exception of Seán MacBride, who was won over to de Valera's constitution in 1937, the IRA was bereft of politically talented leaders. Its organizational élan and morale were at their nadir, a condition that prompted fantasy to displace strategy. Sean Russell, the IRA's latest Chief of Staff, sought support from Clan na Gael in the USA, still run by Joseph McGarrity, but otherwise much weakened, to fund a bombing campaign in English cities—targeting military and industrial installations. The idea was that this policy would eventually oblige the British to end partition; it had been preferred to Barry's advocacy of a direct assault on the North.[25]

The bombing campaign proved a fatal if not farcical repeat of the escapades of the dynamiters in the 1880s. After initial hits on declared targets without loss of life, bloody and incompetent actions and outcomes took the headlines, with some seven civilians killed and two hundred injured. The Prevention of Violence Act of 1939, which allowed deportation, internment, and the registration of all Irish men living in Britain, proved sufficient to repress the IRA in Great Britain, where its volunteers enjoyed no significant support among the Irish diaspora.[26] Undaunted by the futility of this "campaign," Russell made the hapless Hayes his successor, before making his way to Berlin from the USA in the summer of 1940, reactivating connections he had explored five years earlier. Together with German military and intelligence figures, he planned sabotage and insurgency in the North.

---

[24] Coogan (2002: 156).

[25] It prompted at least one resignation from the IRA's Army Council (Cronin 1987: 89).

[26] The Act went through its first and second readings in the Lords in five minutes, and its third stage was waived (McGuffin 1973: 37).

He died, however, on a German U-boat on his way back to Ireland. Ryan, who had accompanied him, returned to Germany, where he died in a hospital in Dresden in 1944. Some have imagined that Ryan poisoned Russell (the left-wing socialist sabotaging the Nazi collaborator's mission would fit a film script), but the record suggests that Ryan was not informed of the German planning until after Russell's death from an untreated ulcerous condition.[27]

A Northern "campaign" by the IRA in 1941-2 in the wake of its failures in England proved no more effective, either in sabotage or in assassinations. Tom Williams was executed in Belfast Crumlin Road Gaol for his role in the death of an RUC officer; his fellow youthful co-conspirators, including Gerry Adams Sr, had their death sentences commuted. The military prospects of a handful of men against both the Northern regime *and* hundreds of thousands of Allied troops had this forlorn enterprise ever made some headway had evidently not been judged by any serious calculus. The sole rationale available for such action was the hope of redemption by Nazi Germany—a catastrophic misjudgment by 1942, and argu-ably since well before 1933. In sum, between 1939 and 1946 the IRA was crushed by deportation and standard policing in England, and by police and intelligence operations combined with internment in both parts of Ireland.[28] Perhaps a thousand men were interned without trial on the island, and by war's end few remained in the organization. In 1944, after the execution of Charlie Kerins in Dublin's Mountjoy Jail, the IRA had no Chief of Staff for the first time in its history. Its sole leader of standing, who assumed the role while briefly free, was Harry White, now more famous as the uncle of Danny Morrison, Sinn Féin's publicity officer in the 1980s. One recital of the IRA's losses confirms that more of its men had died in prisons during the Second World War than in active combat:

> Apart from Russell and Ryan, twenty-six IRA men lost their lives between April 1939[29] and May 1946. Of these, nine were executed, five killed in gun-battles with the police on both sides of the border; six died in prison hospitals; three died on hunger-strike; two were killed in explosions and one was shot dead by military police at the internment camp in the Curragh.[30]

Joseph Lee remarks that the dead IRA men could have claimed "to be the logical products of the official political culture which now sought to suppress them."[31] There is some justice in this evaluation of de Valera's Ireland, but it does not extend to Northern Ireland or Great Britain, where officials were not in the habit of glorifying Irish republicanism. Whatever its sources of inspiration, at war's end militant Irish republicanism had few volunteers and no recent deeds of which to be proud. A future member and sympathizer subsequently wrote: "If the mem-bership of the IRB in 1912 could have been seated comfortably in a concert hall, the IRA in 1949 would have managed quite well in a school class-room."[32] It had also lost much of its previous public esteem: "The German threat to Britain, and

---

[27] Ryan's biographer (Fearghal McGarry 2002) portrays him as moving among European ideologies (socialism and fascism) while staying much the same character.

[28] For the IRA in the 1920s and 1930s, see J. Bowyer Bell (1979); Coogan (2002); English (2003); and especially Hanley (2002).

[29] In my paperback edition of Lyons's book there is what must be a misprint: April 1930 rather than 1939.

[30] Lyons (1973b: 557).   [31] Lee (1989: 224).   [32] Cronin (1987: 273).

Ireland too, changed the popular attitude towards the IRA. By mid-May 1940, there could be no doubt any longer that Hitler was the enemy of small nations. The IRA was seen as pro-German and therefore dangerous."[33]

WAR'S END, DE VALERA, HITLER, AND URBAN LEGENDS

In May 1945, de Valera called upon the German legation in Dublin to convey his government's condolences to the German people on the death of their late head of state. This decision—minimally bound to irritate both the USA and the UK—is typically, and correctly, explained by de Valera's martinet-like adherence to diplomatic protocol. Conor Cruise O'Brien, however, believed that electoral calculations were at work.

> There was a presidential election due in the following month, and although the Irish presidency is mainly a ceremonial office, it was important ... that his candidate, Seán T. Ó Ceallaigh, should defeat his challengers [to set] a seal of popular approval on [the] neutrality [policy]. [He] knew that that gesture would generate a great volume of abuse from the British against himself and neutrality, and that this could only do him good with the Irish electorate. It worked like a charm. Churchill himself rose to the bait. He delivered a scornful, scalding attack on De Valera and on Irish neutrality. Dev replied, over Irish radio, in a dignified, sweetly reasonable speech, with a gentle, almost subliminal, evocation of Ireland's past sufferings at the hands of the English, combined with an appreciative acknowledgment of Britain's respect for Irish neutrality in the Second World War.[34]

The speech was a major success with the Irish public, and Ó Ceallaigh won the contest.[35] Perhaps all politics is local, and the short-run vote motive usually trumps broader political rationality among politicians, but if this was de Valera's calculus, it was as myopic as his own eyes were becoming. His party had won a "handsome election victory in 1944," and it was because he was so confident of a victory for Ó Ceallaigh (also known as O'Kelly) that he had picked his friend and party loyalist to run.[36] Securing the symbolic presidency for a close confidant was scarcely worth a very bad start in the international relations of the postwar world. It is therefore simpler and more accurate to believe that the former star performer in the League of Nations, intent on emphatically affirming Ireland's neutrality, had made an unnecessary major public-relations blunder, which he was able to redeem to his domestic advantage in replying to a denunciation by Churchill.

---

[33] Cronin (1987: 82).   [34] Conor Cruise O'Brien (1998: 105).

[35] Churchill's speech is summarized, and the key passage in de Valera's is reported, with commentary, in Dudley Edwards (1987: 146–7), who deems the speech, broadcast on the radio, de Valera's finest hour. The full text may be found in Moynihan (1980: 474–5). One of its memorable rebuffs, silently referencing the Melian dialogue of Thucydides, went as follows: "It is, indeed, hard for the strong to be just to the weak, but acting justly always has its rewards." This was a polite commentary on Churchill's boast that he had resisted the temptation to invade Ireland.

[36] Lee (1989: 239).

Whereas O'Brien reinterpreted this episode as evidence of de Valera's "crafty fingertips," Paul Bew, by contrast, sees evidence of de Valera's "somewhat closed mentality." He expressly states that de Valera had made no such visit "to the US embassy on the death of Roosevelt."[37] In fact, the *Irish Press* of April 14, 1945, under the heading "Many Calls to the US Legation," reports visits by the Taoiseach, and every member of his cabinet, including Frank Aiken, who had been personally roasted by Roosevelt in Washington, when he had visited the USA during the war, and had resisted pressure for Ireland to join the allies.[38] The front page of the same edition reports a eulogy to Roosevelt by de Valera and the adjournment of Dáil Éireann with the support of all present. That so many decades after de Valera's decision to pay his respects to the German legation this story can be so casually embroidered, like an urban legend, by intellectuals of O'Brien's and Bew's standing is testimony to the lasting adverse reception of the story among observers of Irish nationalism. Today it is often correctly said that the first person who invokes Hitler has lost the argument—de Valera's customary critics do not abide by this maxim.[39]

DE VALERA, PARTITION, AND THE ANTI-PARTITION LEAGUE: THE CHIEF OUTFLANKED

De Valera's critics have a stronger case when they scrutinize his record on partition.[40] As a revolutionary republican leader, he had initially demonstrated a stance toward Ulster Protestants that was unexceptional, though before the treaty he had briefly entertained ideas of an Irish federation or confederation—without being clear on the distinction. He had reacted to the enactment of partition by supporting the Belfast boycott in the belief that economic pressure would modify Unionist minds—illustrating the common republican assumption that unionists are driven by material interests whereas nationalists are not. During and after the treaty negotiations, however, he privately and occasionally publicly revealed himself to be a compromiser: he supported a county opt-out—that is, he was willing to see four counties go. In the debate over the treaty he proposed no changes to the provisions on Ulster—that is, he accepted the border's resolution by boundary commission if Northern Ireland opted out of independent Ireland. He evidently expected the commission would produce either a very similar outcome to a county opt-out—namely, Fermanagh and Tyrone would go south—or an even better one, in which Newry and Derry, and their hinterlands, and south Armagh, would also join independent Ireland.

After the civil war de Valera re-emerged as an apparently vigorous hardline anti-partitionist. As the Sinn Féin leader, and as a candidate for office, in 1924 he was arrested for illegally entering Northern Ireland, and refused to recognize the court.

---

[37] Bew (2007: 478).   [38] *Irish Press*, April 14, 1945, p. 3, col. 4.
[39] Tom Garvin (2011: 27), who usually has better judgment, declares that "it seems probable that the reason" condolences were sent to the German Legation was de Valera's "wish to outflank the Germanophile and pro-Nazi elements of the IRA and his own greener Fianna Fáil supporters."
[40] The section draws especially upon Bowman (1982); Ryle (1983); Ó Beacháin (2014).

- Sinn Fein > (anti-treaty) Sinn Féin
- Sinn Féin ≥ (pro-treaty) Cumann na Ghaedheal > **Fine Gael** (1933–) — Sinn Féin

- **Sinn Féin ≥ Fianna Fáil (anti-treaty)** (1926–) ≥ Progressive Democrats (1986–2009) — Sinn Féin

- **Sinn Féin** > Official Sinn Féin (1969–) > Sinn Féin the Workers Party > **The Workers Party** ≥ Democratic Left [merged with the Irish Labour Party] > **Irish Labour Party** — Sinn Féin

- **Sinn Féin** ≥ Provisional Sinn Féin (1969–) aka **Sinn Féin**
- **Sinn Féin** ≥ Republican Sinn Féin (1986–) — Sinn Féin

Figure 2.4.1. The genealogy of Irish parties

Note: Most significant parties in independent Ireland have their origins in Sinn Féin. > = succeeded by; ≥ = split from; parties in bold still exist.

He was held in solitary confinement at Belfast's Crumlin Road Gaol for a month, but treated courteously by the governor, with whom he played chess, according to lore one can hear at the prison, now a museum. The following year, de Valera denounced the failure of the boundary commission and exploited the issue to trigger a debate within Sinn Féin—arguing that the party should take its seats in Dáil Éireann to oppose the tripartite 1925 agreement, which buried the commission. He chose to split and form Fianna Fáil precisely because hardline Sinn Féin deputies refused to consider participation in the Dáil on this question (see Figure 2.4.1). The new party was therefore deliberately identified with a strongly anti-partitionist stance. Discussion of a more reasonable boundary line ceased, though de Valera did consistently indicate, from 1921, that coercion should not be employed to end partition, because it would not be effective. The logical corollary was that reunification would have to be made attractive, sufficiently so to win over at least some unionists. Here de Valera never delivered.

Confirming sovereignty had been the first priority of de Valera and his party: partition was not substantively addressed until the drafting of the new constitution and the opening of negotiations with Chamberlain's government in 1938. This sequencing, as well as his government's responses to the British "offers" of 1940–1, indicate that de Valera, and his most senior colleagues, believed that Ireland's sovereignty, including the right to be neutral, took priority over outreach to Northern unionists (or support for Northern nationalists). Unionists were to be wooed with two formal possibilities: a reunified Ireland would remain within the Commonwealth, externally associated with the Crown, and Northern Ireland could retain its parliament with its current powers if it agreed to reunification.

Between 1932 and 1948 no symbolic let alone substantive efforts were made to achieve rapprochement with Ulster unionists by the Fianna Fáil government. Indeed, the agreements of 1938–9 with Great Britain nearly foundered on de Valera's refusal to give preference to imports from Northern Ireland.[41] The Irish Anti-Partition League was founded by Northern Nationalists in 1945—after de Valera had refused to support an all-Ireland campaign the year before.[42]

The question therefore arises whether de Valera was a perfect illustration of the instrumentalist politician who exploits symbolic ethnicity (in this case, overturning partition) to win votes, but who does not believe his own rhetoric. Though de Valera was skilled at vote-hunting, it is fairer to conclude that at least until 1939 he had hoped to resolve partition as the last of his political objects—through direct negotiations with the London government. This plan, feasible or not, was rendered irrelevant by the outworking of the world war. In 1939 de Valera had opened an anti-partition campaign in Great Britain, which then had to be put on ice. He pledged to return to it after the world war, which overshadowed all matters. But throughout that war partition was deployed to justify Ireland's neutrality: how could Ireland ally with Great Britain when the latter was in occupation of Irish national territory? Even when the USA effectively joined the war in 1942, that remained the position.

When the idea of an anti-partition campaign resurfaced in 1944–5, however, de Valera's room for maneuver had dramatically narrowed. Great Britain, because of both Ireland's neutrality and the recent near-death experience of its empire in the war, was now far more committed to keeping Northern Ireland within the union for strategic reasons; and Fianna Fáil, for the first time, faced a credible party rival on both its nationalist and left flanks, one willing to take its seats in Dáil Éireann, if elected. The end of wartime censorship lifted the lid on accumulated grievances, and the new party Clann na Poblachta (Children (aka Family) of the Republic) seemed perfectly placed to exploit them. Founded by former members of the IRA, angered at the recent treatment of IRA prisoners, it was determined to adopt a more left-wing, health-and-welfare-oriented policy program. Its most prominent figure was the former IRA Chief of Staff, Seán MacBride, the young and attractive son of the executed 1916 leader and Maud Gonne, and who would later morph into a human-rights lawyer. Some Fianna Fáil cadres had joined the Clann, disillusioned with de Valera, and there was a surprisingly widespread expectation that Clann na Poblachta would produce the kind of electoral meltdown of Fianna Fáil that Redmond's Irish Parliamentary Party had once experienced at the hands of de Valera's Sinn Féin.

De Valera, however, was a much more skilled politician than Redmond. Preemptive electoral manipulations took place organized by Seán MacEntee—the average size of each district was lowered, and the Dáil was dissolved early, precipitating a winter campaign (December 1947–February 1948).[i] De Valera had a good track record in electoral timing, and hoped to nip the Clann's rise in the bud because it was organizationally present only in Dublin. The results partly

---

[41] Johnson (1980).
[42] Bowman (1982: 257–8). For a useful account of the Northern origins and development of the APL, see Purdie (1986).

vindicated his judgment: Fianna Fáil obtained almost 42 percent of the vote and won 68 of the available 147 seats, a significant plurality, whereas the Clann won just 10 seats, much fewer than expected, partly because it ran too many candidates in many districts. Though it had won over 13 percent of first-preference votes, the Clann won just less than 7 percent of the seats. There was an unexpected sting in the tail for de Valera, however. An inter-party coalition government was formed to keep his party out of office.[43] The Clann and two Labour factions went into coalition with Fine Gael and two small farmers' parties. This coalition was the first occasion in which personnel from rival sides of the civil war formed a joint government. It is also a rare example of a government formed by small parties to exclude the largest party that was also the most centrist on the left and right dimension of politics. Fianna Fáil was equally the most centrist party on another dimension: its members were ranged between the enthusiasts for the open proc-lamation of a republic in the Clann and those who were still for the Commonwealth in Fine Gael. The Clann's condition for coalition formation was that Fine Gael's leader General Mulcahy—whom its members blamed for civil-war executions and repressions—would not become Taoiseach. As a result, John A. Costello, a pros-perous lawyer, became Ireland's prime minister without being leader of his party, the sole time to date that this has happened.

Seán MacBride became Minister for External Affairs, and was seen both as the driving force behind Ireland's exit from the Commonwealth and an all-party anti-partition campaign. The campaign originated in the response of the Clann, Fine Gael, and Fianna Fáil to questions posed to them by the APL about their policy toward partition. The coherence of simultaneously pursuing both objects was not questioned by any prominent Irish nationalist. Costello's government officially declared Ireland a republic in April 1949, on the thirty-third anniversary of the Easter Rising. The plan had emerged, quasi-chaotically, at a press con-ference in Canada in October 1948, partly driven by Costello's effort to ensure that not all the credit would go to MacBride. In taking this step, both the Clann and Fine Gael had outflanked de Valera's Fianna Fáil, showing that the latter had no monopoly on nationalism or republicanism. The Republic had been recovered by "a strange coalition of renegades and amateurs, led by the traitors who signed the imperialists' Treaty of 1921–22."[44] MacBride and his colleagues also seemed to outflank de Valera on neutrality, refusing an invitation to join NATO because that would obligate Ireland to recognize partition, and offering membership in return for the end of partition—an offer that could only be refused.[45] In declaring the Republic, the External Relations Act of 1936 was repealed, the Act that had capped de Valera's strategy to implement Document No. 2: making Ireland a republic in its domestic affairs, while leaving the king as an ambiguous occultation for symbolic functions connected to the Common-wealth and external relations. The Act's repeal shredded de Valera's constitutional program of accommodation of Ulster Unionists' British identity, such as it had been. Brooke responded by calling an election in Northern Ireland, which put

---

[43] See McCullagh (1998); I benefited from externally examining the Ph.D thesis submitted at UCD that formed the core of this book.

[44] So Garvin (2011: 26) imagines how matters must have seemed in the mind of Fianna Fáil.

[45] For discussions, see Fanning (1979); Cronin (1985).

paid to the Northern Ireland Labour Party's postwar breakthrough, and brought most of the unionist bloc back within his party's fold. None of the parties in the South proposed any program to woo Ulster Protestants from their preference for the Union.[46]

The controversy over the Mother and Child Scheme, a healthcare program opposed by the Catholic Church, brought down the inter-party government and led to the disintegration of the Clann.[47] Many of the party's deputies resigned in solidarity with its health minister, Noel Browne, and the Clann won just two seats in the ensuing 1951 general election, which returned Fianna Fáil to the status of a minority government—it won only one more seat than in 1948. Later, in 1954, the Clann agreed to support a new Fine Gael-led coalition government from the backbenches (when it had just three deputies). Controversy and disunity would prove the abiding feature of the party's brief life, and MacBride was unequal to the task of keeping it together. In 1953, Liam Kelly, expelled from the IRA in 1951, won the Mid-Tyrone constituency for Stormont, which he did not attend, but then followed up by becoming a Clann Senator in the South, where he fulfilled his attendance duties. Kelly was the leading light in Saor Uladh (Free Ulster), a splinter group that had left the IRA and had begun raids in Fermanagh and Tyrone against RUC barracks. Given members with such alignments and sympathies, it was not surprising that the Clann withdrew its support from the second coalition government in late 1956, as the IRA began its "border campaign." The Clann's residual activists sympathized with the IRA's newest campaign and opposed its repression. The party would return just one deputy at the 1957 general election, however, and MacBride lost his seat—though his party lingered on until its dissolution in the 1960s. The Clann's disunity, indiscipline, and its adventurism, especially perhaps its leader's decision to split his party over the Mother and Child Scheme, had contributed to its failure to displace Fianna Fáil, when it was vulnerable. And when de Valera returned to office with a safe majority in 1957, for the first time since 1944–8, his cabinet had no hesitation in introducing internment against the IRA, notwithstanding the mass sympathy expressed at the funeral of Seán South of Garryowen.[48] The young parliamentary secretary to the Minister of Justice who oversaw internment, and who succeeded to the minister's post in 1961, was Charles J. Haughey, the son-in-law of Seán Lemass, de Valera's successor.

NORTHERN IRELAND AFTER THE NAZI EMPIRE

On November 30, 1948, a spectacularly vicious debate took place at Stormont on a Nationalist motion, one to which little attention is paid in the historiography, perhaps because no participant looks well in retrospect. The occasion was triggered by Costello's declaration of intent to create or re-create the Republic the previous month. It should perhaps be called "the Nazis and Rapists debate." Those who think that President Donald Trump has deeply lowered the tone of

---

[46] Barton (1992: 19).   [47] The most judicious treatment is in Whyte (1979: chs 7, 8).
[48] See Vol. 1, Intro, p.3.

democratic dialogue may be saddened to learn that there is no novelty in calling entire nations rapists. The debate's polarized and ructious character almost speaks for itself.

Cahir Healy, describing nationalists as the children of the dispossessed, welcomed the recent declaration of the Republic of Ireland, suggested that unionists were traitors for not joining in this welcome, insulted Churchill in passing, and insisted that unionists should welcome republicanism because it had been introduced to Ireland by Presbyterians. For his pains, he was called "a Hitler man" by a unionist backbencher. Healy's seconder, Jack Beattie, Republican Labour, then issued a barrage against the absent socialist apostate Midgley, the unionist who had once been anti-partitionist. Beattie went on to call unionists the Nazis of the Six Counties.

Replying, Prime Minister Brooke opened by suggesting that Healy had been the Nazis' friend. Called to withdraw, Brooke asked whether Healy had communicated with the German minister in Dublin during the war. When Healy denied the claim, Brooke conditionally withdrew it.[j] He went on to insist that, while unionists were Irishmen, Irishmen were in two communities, not one, and vehemently rejected Dublin's alleged generosity.

> If you are wooing a girl you at least approach her with some pleasantness and you do not go to her father and have a slanging match. You do not approach her father's house with a dagger in one hand, a revolver in the other and, perhaps, a jemmy[49] in your pocket. One goes along making some fairly decent approach; at least that is my experience. What the Free State are after is the rape of Ulster; it is not marriage. It is the rape of Ulster they want, and when they would have done that dreadful deed they would throw the wretched girl on one side and rob her of all her means. And that would be the end of it. We do not believe in that sort of approach. What enticement have we ever been offered? We heard today, I think from the Proposer of the Motion, that the offer which we had was that we should retain a Parliament here in Ulster, but that all the power now retained by the Imperial Government would be transferred to Dublin. My answer to that is, thank you for nothing. They have not got that to offer, and in any case it is ours already. It is clearly, to my mind, a smokescreen to swallow up the Ulster people. Having done so then the position would be created which is already existing in the South, where the whole Protestant population has decreased by no less than 35 per cent . . . [The] only solution to this very difficult situation which exists in Ireland, as a whole, is two Governments . . . I submit that we have got in this country in miniature what exists all over the world. Belgium and Holland parted. Scandinavian countries broke up. Why? Because traditions and sentiments were obviously different. I suggest that that is the only solution until such a day when, perhaps, the Free State may come nearer our form of thought. Then, perhaps, we shall arrive at closer union. But whether that day is in sight I am very doubtful. As far as I can see our traditions and loyalties go further and further away. It is said about us that we are intractable. Hitler said that about the rest of Europe and England. He said that his patience was exhausted by the intractable attitude of Great Britain. The only place his patience was not exhausted was in Eire, because, as we know only too well, through the cost of our ships and the lives of our men by that country's action Hitler found a friend.[50]

---

[49] A jemmy is a short crowbar often used by burglars.

[50] The first day of the debate may be found at Harvard (NI), HC, vol. 32, cols 3641–83 (November 30, 1948).

With the principal leaders of each major bloc, eagerly supported by their backbenchers, calling one another Nazis, or comparing one another to rapists, political accommodation was unlikely to be at hand, and so it proved. The Second World War had apparently stabilized Northern Ireland's status within the Union, but so did the declaration of the Republic. The Ireland Act 1949, passed in response by the Westminster parliament, recognized Ireland's republican status (the other dominions took similar steps). But for the first time in statute law Great Britain officially granted Northern Ireland's parliament a veto on its constitutional status:

> It is hereby declared that Northern Ireland shall remain part of His Majesty's dominions and of the United Kingdom and it is hereby affirmed that in no event will Northern Ireland or any part thereof cease to be part of His Majesty's dominions and of the United Kingdom without the consent of the Parliament of Northern Ireland (Article 1 (2)).

This veto ruled out Irish unification without Stormont's consent, *and* any repartition without its consent. The imperial government's working party had briefed the cabinet with a paper that concluded that the North should stay within His Majesty's dominions as a

> matter of first class strategic importance ... So far as can be foreseen it will never be to Great Britain's advantage that Northern Ireland should form part of a territory outside His Majesty's jurisdiction. Indeed, it seems unlikely that Great Britain would ever be able to agree to this even if the people of Northern Ireland desired it.[51]

This thoroughly colonial, undemocratic, and entirely militarist reasoning was not made public.[52] Indeed the democratic will of the Northern Ireland public, and the North's wartime services, were presented to parliament as deciding the matter. Prime Minister Attlee and Churchill, the Leader of the Opposition, concurred on the veto provision, which closed off the possibility long entertained by Irish nationalist leaders, South and North, that Irish reunification could occur through joint diplomatic action by the Dublin and London governments.

The hopes of the organizers of the Anti-Partition League, which had had some mobilization successes in the North, especially outside Belfast, were crushed.[53] They were to be equally disappointed in their efforts to see admission for their elected officials to Dáil Éireann: the Clann had proposed that rights of audience be given to Northern MPs and Senators. The idea would have required a constitutional amendment, and granting them voting rights would have made them pivotal legislators, especially in the close-fought elections between 1948 and 1954.

The "constitutional assurance" that the Ireland Act gave to the Stormont parliament was not, however, constitutional in any robust conception. Any future Westminster parliament could delete the declaration through ordinary legislation, as Attlee told Unionist ministers in private[54]—and as was later illustrated when

---

[51] TNA: PRO CAB 21/1842, Report by Working Party, January 1, 1949.

[52] Unionist historian Brian Barton (1992: 12) argues that the move was taken because of the Labour cabinet's perception of "Britain's immediate strategic interests." Frank Pakenham (Lord Longford) was the sole member of the cabinet to dissent from the new guarantee.

[53] Purdie (1986).   [54] Barton (1992: 19).

the veto on Irish reunification was transferred from the parliament to the people of Northern Ireland.[55] The declaration was nevertheless correctly seen as a unionist net gain. The first majority Labour government in British history had created an all-party commitment that Northern Ireland should remain within the UK, and affirmed that Irish unity required the joint consent of the two jurisdictions created by partition. The Labour government recognized Ireland as an independent republic that had left "His Majesty's Dominions" (and thereby the Commonwealth), but decided not to treat Ireland, especially its citizens, as foreign,[56] and did not exclude Ireland from Commonwealth trade agreements. Article 2.1 of the Ireland Act declared

> that, notwithstanding that the Republic of Ireland is not part of His Majesty's dominions, the Republic of Ireland is not a foreign country for the purposes of any law in force in any part of the United Kingdom or in any colony, protectorate or United Kingdom trust territory, whether by virtue of a rule of law or of an Act of Parliament or any other enactment or instrument whatsoever, whether passed or made before or after the passing of this Act, and references in any Act of Parliament, other enactment or instrument whatsoever, whether passed or made before or after the passing of this Act, to foreigners, aliens, foreign countries, and foreign or foreign-built ships or aircraft shall be construed accordingly.

This legislation ensured that Irish residents in Great Britain would continue to enjoy full voting rights; indeed, it would be as if Ireland had not left the Commonwealth. A common travel zone would remain within the Isles.

Party interests, not just travel and labor-market requirements, drove this legislation. Irish migrants to Great Britain in the interwar years had been overwhelmingly working-class, unskilled, rural or urban workers,[57] though these traits were not universal—for example, one in ten doctors in England and Wales in 1951 had been born in Ireland.[58] The Irish working-class migrant, male or female, mostly voted Labour, and Catholics in Great Britain—who, in the main, were of Irish extraction—disproportionately voted Labour, irrespective of their class background (see Table 2.4.1).[59] In London's House of Commons, Home Secretary and enthusiastic unionist Herbert Morrison observed that the initiative for constitutional change had come from Dublin, and insisted that the UK was responding generously. Attlee concluded that "the government of Eire considered the cutting of the last tie which united Eire to the British Commonwealth was a more important objective of policy than ending partition."[60] This was fair comment, but it was Attlee's government that insisted that republics could not be members of

---

[55] See Vol. 3, Ch. 2, pp. 53–5.

[56] The comic line in London, as reported by the French ambassador, was that, whereas Ireland had before agreed to be excluded inside the Commonwealth, it was now included outside the Commonwealth (Harkness 1996: 80, n. 34). The remark bears some resemblance to the observation in 2016–18 that the UK government has gone from wanting to be in the European Union with opt-outs to wanting to be outside it with opt-ins.

[57] Delaney (2000: *passim*).   [58] Delaney (2000: 207).

[59] Since survey data began to be collected, they suggest that (self-identifying) Catholics generally have preferred to vote Labour, often by large margins, since 1959 (the exception being in 1979), and have generally shown lower support than other Christian denominations for the Liberals or Liberal Democrats.

[60] Hansard, HC, vol. 464, col. 1858 (May 11, 1949).

Table 2.4.1. Average party vote share by religious grouping, Great Britain, 1959–2010 (%)

Religious grouping	Labour	Conservative	Liberal/SDP/ Liberal Democrat
Catholics	54.3	31.1	12.8
Anglicans	35.5	47.8	15.4
Nonconformists	36.9	41.5	19.3
Church of Scotland/Presbyterian	37.3	37.9	13.3
No religion	43.2	32.6	19.9

Note: Figures for those identifying with no religion cover the years 1970–2010.
Source: Clements and Spencer (2014); BES surveys, weighted data.

the Commonwealth, a stance that would shortly be reversed to retain the membership of an independent India. Within the Labour cabinet there had been some dissent, and a proposal was considered to bring partition before an international tribunal or arbitration body. Attlee himself ruled out bringing the question to the United Nations, lacking confidence that the necessary votes could be won either in the Security Council or in the General Assembly.[61] Only in private did British ministers recognize that world opinion saw partition differently from themselves.

The declaration of the Republic, the Ireland Act, and the failure of the anti-partition campaign led to one unexpected outcome: a rejuvenated IRA and Sinn Féin, especially in the border counties of historic Ulster, on both sides of the partition line. Not, however, because the Republic had been recovered. According to the true believers, care of the Republic remained vested in the IRA's Army Council. Rather it was because the IRA had learned some organizational lessons, and because the overturning of partition now remained the outstanding unfinished political business of Irish nationalism, and there seemed no constitutional path toward that goal. The declaration of the Republic and the Ireland Act had not only seen de Valera outflanked, but had put the kibosh on his claim that a diplomatic path to Irish unity existed through intergovernmental negotiations between London and Dublin. The rhetoric de Valera had indulged in during his worldwide anti-partition tour when he was out of office (1948–51), and the all-party denunciation of the UK's Ireland Act at Dublin's Mansion House in 1949,[62] suggested to some within the younger generation that they would have to imitate their fathers' deeds rather than their current words—that is, the end of British sovereignty in the North would have to be accomplished by force of arms.

The much-battered survivors of the 1940s internment camps passed on the leadership baton and sought organizational renewal. Before long a new set of recruits, from the South and the North, were being trained for a border campaign. They soon had a very intelligent director of operations, who had been a journalist in the USA and had served as an officer in Ireland's army, Seán Cronin (1922–2011).[63]

---

[61] Barton (1992: 16).   [62] Mansion House Anti-Partition Conference (1950a, b, c).

[63] Author of *Notes on Guerrilla Warfare,* and subsequently of numerous texts, both popular and more academic (Cronin 1972, 1983, 1987; Cronin and Roche 1973). Though narrow, his works are refreshingly free of factual error; after his IRA career, he was a successful journalist with the *Irish Times.*

He put his writing and military skills to work, and eventually became the IRA's Chief of Staff. In their naïveté, some of the IRA's fresh recruits expected support from the Southern government. More astutely, in 1954 the leaders of the slowly revitalizing IRA, rearming largely through raids on police barracks, issued General Order No. 8, which instructed IRA volunteers not to engage in any armed combat, in any circumstances, with the police and security forces of the Government of Ireland, which they still called the Free State. This move was very important, even if one journalist (and former politician, academician, civil servant, and historian with a Ph.D), later misrepresented its timing.[k] The order meant that the IRA was no longer in armed opposition to independent Ireland, just to Northern Ireland; it tacitly recognized that what the IRA insisted on calling the twenty-six counties was a republic, even if it was not *the* Republic. This greater realism in grand strategy and tactics did not make the IRA campaign of 1956–62 a success.

IRELAND'S POST-INDEPENDENCE ECONOMIC PERFORMANCE

By 1958 it was widely assumed that Northern Ireland's status within the UK was now triply secure: geopolitically, because of Ireland's neutrality, and Great Britain and America's assessment that the status quo was in their strategic interests; constitutionally, through the Ireland Act, which seemed to give the Northern Ireland Parliament a veto on any move toward Irish reunification; and economically, by the attractions of the British welfare state, and Ireland's apparent comparative economic backwardness—all of which were assumed to entrench Protestant preferences for the Union, and to weaken Catholic preferences for Irish unification.

As all but the last of these subjects have been addressed, it is apposite to deal briefly here with Ireland's economic performance. In 1922 the Irish Free State was cut off from the industrialized Lagan valley, and was overwhelmingly agricultural. Its exports went overwhelmingly to the UK. The distinguished economic historian Kevin O'Rourke has convincingly argued that Ireland's post-independence policy and (growth) performance were "not particularly unusual" in Europe, though they were both "hampered by an excessive dependence on a poorly performing UK economy." Ireland's subsequent EEC membership in 1973, and its single market program successor, were vital for Ireland's economic transformation: Irish independence and EU membership have complemented each other.[64] O'Rourke has no hesitation, however, in referencing "the colonial" backstory, to explain Ireland's poor start, and to account for why mass emigration persisted into the twentieth century. He emphasizes that emigration rates were systematically higher in all European countries with higher birth rates, that were poorer, and with previous histories of emigration. The Irish therefore unsurprisingly

[64] These paragraphs rely heavily on my notes of Kevin O'Rourke's lecture at the 1916–2016 National Centennial Conference, November 2016, National University of Ireland–Galway: any "plagiarism" is therefore intentional.

remained highly mobile after independence. In consequence, the domestic labor supply was restricted, raising Irish wages, which sustained living standards but deprived the economy of the (grim) advantages of cheap labor.

O'Rourke underlines that all newly industrializing states, in continental Europe and North America, developed through protectionism, a policy not available to pre-independence Ireland. Irish nationalists were sane to think that Ireland could and should have industrialized with protectionist policies, but perhaps by the 1950s they had overcommitted to its permanent merits.[65] Over the century 1911–2010 countries within western Europe that were initially poorer grew much more rapidly than countries that were initially richer—mostly through adapting best practices and technologies already adopted elsewhere. Within this comparative framework, O'Rourke argues Ireland's economic performance during 1926–2000 has culminated exactly where one would predict, given Ireland's initial income level. What was initially unusual, however, was that it took so long for Ireland's policymakers to try protectionism. The Fianna Fáil government's shift toward protectionism was not idiosyncratic, let alone impulsive—even the British switched to protectionism before the Irish in the 1930s. Ireland was not subsequently a protectionist outlier, and the policy probably helped maintain employment when jobs were internationally scarce. The "economic war" was a distinctive episode, but, as previously noted, O'Rourke has shown it was settled on very good terms, which facilitated Ireland's neutrality.[66] The Second World War was economically difficult: Ireland did not benefit from the demand for war products like Scotland or Northern Ireland, and Great Britain was able to exploit its bargaining power as a monopoly purchaser of Irish agricultural products. But after it was over Ireland had briefly shared in the postwar boom (1945–50). Its subsequent economic performance, from 1950 until 1975, was what was so striking—plainly below the west European average.

Three coherent explanations that fit the facts are offered by O'Rourke, none of which, strikingly, references cultural accounts.[67] These are recurrent balance-of-payments crises; delayed liberalization; and excessive dependence on the poorly performing British economy—all of which were interlinked. The first, the "stop–go" phenomenon, was shared with Britain, and aggravated by Ireland's decision to keep the Irish pound at parity with the pound sterling. Ireland was slow in "liberalizing" some of its trade policy as the postwar European boom took off, but O'Rourke emphasizes that it was an early mover in seeking to attract foreign direct investment. Nevertheless, the constraints of British policy mattered. British economic diplomacy in the 1950s and 1960s was one of volatile failure, vacillating between the Commonwealth, EFTA, and the EEC, until Macmillan decided that the UK's interests lay in joining the EEC. Ireland had prepared to opt for EEC membership with the UK in 1961, but was blocked by General de Gaulle. Irish trade liberalization remained focused on the economic relationship with Great Britain, a dependency that hamstrung the Irish economy until the mid-1970s.

---

[65] For an elegant study of Friedrich List's influence on European economic development, see Szporluk (1991).

[66] See O'Rourke (1991) and the discussion at Vol. 2, Ch. 3, pp. 119–21.

[67] For the best of such accounts, see Garvin (2005), proof that collective self-criticism can be overdone.

Its postwar isolation and dependency partly explain why Ireland had no association agreement with the EEC nor membership of EFTA, but after 1973 Ireland was selling into the EEC as a whole, and, argues O'Rourke, that made all the difference—both for exports and in attracting inward investment.

O'Rourke also observes that Ireland's growth performance was similar to that in Northern Ireland and Wales during the two decades 1954–73, suggestive of shared problems, rather than the tale of Southern backwardness and Northern modernity advanced by Ulster Unionists in the 1950s. These problems included multiple and fragmented trade unions inhibiting the corporatist coordination that was successful elsewhere in Europe. Yet simply being linked to the sluggish British economy may have been what mattered. O'Rourke's argument is that Irish independence was essential to exploit EU membership, and the latter was vital for Ireland to become one of the small states capable of responding flexibly to changing international conditions.[68] Its independence, in his view, would not have worked as well without the EU, and, just as importantly, EU membership would not have worked as well without independence. As we shall see, Unionist confidence about the economic merits of the Union for Northern Ireland would later lose its objective foundations, but in 1958 geopolitical, political, and economic complacency among Ulster Unionists made sense of the facts. That complacency would not survive another decade.

---

[68] O'Rourke presumably has in mind the literature initiated by Katzenstein (1985), to which the major Irish contribution has been the work of Niamh Hardiman, starting with Hardiman (1989).

2.5

Losing Control, 1958–1972

Fish vary . . . and the same can be said of subversive organizations. If a fish has got to be destroyed it can be attacked directly by rod or net . . . But if rod and net cannot succeed by themselves it may be necessary to do something about the water.

Frank Kitson, 1971[1]

You have the old racial–colonial struggle going on, and this is the key to the whole problem.

Eddie McAteer, last leader of the Nationalist Party, 1972[2]

Victory can be the prelude to defeat. Ulster Unionists would experience this truism soon after their period of unchallenged dominance between 1949 and 1956. The rapid blunting of the IRA's offensive of 1956–7 hid the structural brittleness of the Unionist regime. Defeat, on the other hand, obliges the losers who survive to reconsider their strategy and tactics. Northern nationalists and Irish republicans exemplify this maxim in the years after 1958, and it is with their disorganization and defeats that this chapter commences before considering how some Ulster Unionists sought to modernize Northern Ireland to respond to new challenges.

THE DISORGANIZATION AND DEFEAT OF NORTHERN NATIONALISM AND REPUBLICANISM

In the decade after the Ireland Act, the Unionist regime was largely unconcerned by the campaign of the Anti-Partition League. Mobilizing the B Specials, it coped easily with a largely southern-led small-scale cross-border IRA campaign that started in late 1956, and that confined itself to the border region. The IRA's offensive was effectively over within a year. Internment without trial was reintroduced against its volunteers on both sides of the border. The campaign did not finally terminate until 1962, when an order was given to dump arms. It had begun

---

[1] Kitson (1971: 49). General Sir Frank Kitson (1926–) was a participant in counterinsurgency and peacekeeping operations in Kenya, Malaya, Oman, Cyprus, and Northern Ireland, a writer on counterinsurgency, who culminated his career as Commander-in-Chief UK Land Forces. See Vol. 1, p. 38, n. 28, 73 n132, 181.

[2] VanVoris (1975: 14).

with high hopes among IRA volunteers. Imprisoned Sinn Féin candidates had won seats for Mid-Ulster and Fermanagh–South Tyrone in the Westminster parliament elections of 1955, and had gone on to win an enforced by-election in one of the seats. In Leinster House in January 1957, Seán MacBride had proposed a vote of no confidence in the Fine Gael–Labour government, targeted at Taoiseach Costello's measures against the IRA that had included the arrest of key leaders. The government fell, and in the general election in March Sinn Féin candidates had some success. They elected four deputies to Dáil Éireann—John Joe Rice in South Kerry, John Joe McGirl in Sligo–Leitrim, Ruarí Ó Brádaigh in Longford, and Éighneachán Ó hAnnluain in Monaghan. But the election of these four deputies scarcely compared to those won by Fianna Fáil, which had seventy-eight seats, an absolute majority—and MacBride had lost his seat. De Valera was resolved that there could not be two armed forces in Ireland—even if one was targeted at Northern Ireland. That was among the reasons the IRA was soon defeated. Another was that it conducted itself according to the laws of war. Yet another was that it had not fully evaluated whether votes for Sinn Féin in the North had expressed alienation rather than support for armed combat. The campaign was not underpinned by any mobilization of Northern nationalists.

Even before the IRA's incursions were defeated by the B Specials, the UUP had begun to relax into a calmer dominance. Intellectuals reflected this newfound complacency. "The Irish question ... was almost as dead as Captain Boycott," wrote the author of the first serious study of London–Belfast financial and constitutional relations published in 1965.[3] A notorious illustration of complacency was Thomas Wilson, an Ulsterman, a professor of political economy at Glasgow, and future drafter of urban and transport plans in the O'Neill era. Wilson edited *Ulster under Home Rule* in 1955. Catholic grievances were dismissed with a comparative thought before he reflected upon modes of inferiority:

> they have less to complain about than the US Negroes, and their lot is a very pleasant one as compared with the nationalists in, say, the Ukraine ... For generations they were the underdogs, the despised "croppies," the adherents of a persecuted religion, who were kept out of public affairs by their Protestant conquerors. They were made to feel inferior, and to make matters worse they often *were* inferior, if *only* in those personal qualities that make for success in competitive economic life.[4]

The economist provided no data to confirm Ulster Catholics' inferior aptitudes for economic success, and signally failed to consider whether being conquered, despised, persecuted, and discriminated against might have had consequences for the formation of Catholic aptitudes or attitudes—or for Protestant perceptions about these same dispositions.[5]

Ulster under Home Rule was a period piece, evidence of tranquil domination, in which the inferior could be safely held responsible for their own inferiority. But the Orange polity appeared secure when Captain Terence O'Neill replaced Lord Brookeborough as prime minister in 1963. Until then there had been just three prime ministers, two of whom had served for two decades. But between 1969 and

---

[3] Lawrence (1965: 75).   [4] Thomas Wilson (1955: 208–9); emphasis in original.
[5] His reasoning scarcely improved with age—see Brendan O'Leary (1989).

1972 three prime ministers would resign: O'Neill in April 1969; his distant relation and immediate successor, James Chichester-Clark, in March 1971; and their nemesis Brian Faulkner in March 1972. This rapid succession expressed a full-blown regime crisis. Faulkner resigned when it became clear that Edward Heath's Conservative government in London intended to remove security powers from the Northern Ireland government. Heath's government prorogued the Stormont parliament, and thereby brought the UUP's domination to an end. The pace and direction of these events, which collapsed the system of control, were not foreseen in 1949, 1955, or 1963, and they prompt important puzzles. How did the UUP lose the support and protection of the UK's governing parties, which had appeared to be secure under the Ireland Act? Why did hegemonic control start to disintegrate within five years of the start of O'Neill's premiership? Why did the London government reintervene in the North to manage its domestic Irish politics? Why did the Irish government contemplate its own intervention in 1969? Why did new loyalist militias and the Provisional IRA emerge? Why did a non-violent civil-rights movement culminate in protracted violence?

Patterns exist in the answers to these questions: some concentrate on exogenous and others on endogenous causes. Unionist commentators, whether Northern Irish or British, blame Stormont's collapse largely on persistent Irish irredentism. An illegitimate, Catholic, and leftist rebellion was allowed to succeed by a feckless Labour government, a path in which the Conservatives apparently colluded.[6] The Catholic minority of the 1960s, disaffected and disloyal, were unreconstructed Irish nationalists—disguised or mildly refurbished in civil-rights clothing, they remained a fifth column of the Republic, the successors to the IRA's 1956–62 border campaign. Their "alleged" grievances were old and recycled exaggerations, fictions, or the self-imposed consequences of their own sustained disloyalty. The civil-rights campaign of 1967–9 was simply a fresh strategic maneuver. The local security forces were provoked by Marxist or Republican (or Marxist–Republican) revolutionaries who had planned to destroy the Stormont government and thereby set the stage for Irish reunification.[7] Northern nationalists were actively and subversively supported by the Republic: ideologically, by the claim to sovereignty embedded in the 1937 constitution; physically, by an undeclared "safe haven" for the planning of guerrilla and terrorist operations from south of the border; and militarily, by shipments of arms from leading members of the Irish government, and other forms of aid, intelligence, and collusion.[8]

Left-wing nationalists have often agreed with these unionist commentators that the Stormont regime collapsed because of a minority rebellion, led by their peers. They have tended, however, to explain the intervention of British troops and the abolition of Stormont as undertaken in the external interests of British imperialism or the British capitalist state.[9] The British had delegated the task of

---

[6] See, e.g., Utley (1975).
[7] See, e.g., Tom Wilson (1989: 154, 157). Brookeborough reflected with world-weariness: "Now, of course, the Coms are mixed up in it. They would find it hard to resist as a good a garden as that to play around in" (VanVoris 1975: 8).
[8] See the discussion of "the Dublin Arms trial" in Justin O'Brien (2000) and Clifford (2009a, b); and see Appendix at the end of this chapter.
[9] See, among others, O'Dowd et al. (1980).

suppressing Irish nationalism to Stormont in the 1920s, but, when it was destabilized by a mass democratic movement, London intervened to shore up Stormont. When reforming Stormont proved futile, only then did the British government opt for direct rule. In the early 1970s many left-wing nationalists and militant republicans expected that the new system of direct rule would quickly go the way of other imperial direct-rule regimes in the mid-twentieth century. They expected or perhaps just hoped to repeat the pattern of 1919–21 and bring the British government rapidly to the negotiating table.

Conventional endogenous explanations, by contrast, account for the break-down of the Stormont system through reference to the region's endemic ethno-religious divisions. Sometimes no attempt is made to explain the timing of the collapse: the emphasis is on the cohabitation of the same space by two antagonistic communities, creating inherent stability—for example, Joseph's Lee's otherwise magnificent panorama of twentieth-century Ireland is full of references to "ancestral animosities" and "hereditary hatreds," and provides a full account, accurate, of mutual blundering and miscalculations in the late 1960s. Another historian, Patrick Buckland, by contrast with Lee, is empathetic toward Irish unionism. He argued that Stormont's collapse was inevitable: "In the face of all these difficulties—a ramshackle political structure, a dearth of political talent, a divided society, a decaying economy and an irredentist neighbour—the wonder is not that the 1920 settlement eventually collapsed in violence in 1972 but that it lasted so long."[10] Others, by contrast, seek to explain precisely why the system shattered in the late 1960s. Sociologists of religion see the ecumenical movement flowing from the Second Vatican Council of the Roman Catholic Church (Vatican II, 1962–5), as a decisive occurrence: it intensified the insecurities of Protestants, and made them more resistant to political change.[11] The "Great Man" theory of history also appears in the historiography. The interaction between the reforming Terence O'Neill, allegedly deeply exposed to liberal and cosmopolitan English culture in his development, and the atavistic, sectarian, and parochial politicians with whom he had to work, unleashed an unanticipated and unintended chain of events that ended in the abolition of Stormont.[12] Another pattern of explanation, also largely endogenous, and compatible with Lee's account, emphasizes a "tragedy of errors;" this is the title of the memoir of the English-born civil servant who advised in Belfast throughout the late Stormont period, and went on doing so until the end of direct rule in 2007.[13]

All these explanations contain pointers toward the truth, but many truths continue to be denied. Some unionists continue to absolve the UUP's control regime of much of the responsibility for the unrest, belittle, or deny, minority grievances, and seek to delegitimize the civil-rights movement as merely an IRA or republican plot, and typically forget that certainly this time around loyalists and B Specials began the killings, whether we choose a starting date of 1966 or 1969. Some nationalists, by contrast, exonerate militant republicans of any blame for the return and quickening of armed violence. They try to cast the IRA, Official or Provisional, in purely reactive and defensive roles. Those focused on endogenous explanations, by contrast, blame local cultures, and the locals, too much. Arguably

---

[10] See Buckland (1981: 30).   [11] See, e.g., Bruce (1986: 89–92).
[12] See Richard Rose (1971: 97); Bruce (1986: 69–71).   [13] Bloomfield (2007).

they generously depict the external agents as indifferent, irrelevant, or benign, rather than as callous, incompetent, or myopic. In short, they leave the London and Dublin governments' culpabilities insufficiently acknowledged. The salience of Vatican II is certainly overstated, and many mistakes have been made about O'Neill, the allegedly great lost reformer. Errors, as we shall see, were certainly made by many agents—to err is human—but more than human folly and incompetence were at work. The collapse of Stormont is better framed in a structural explanation that emphasizes key external changes that affected the motivations of political agents outside and inside Northern Ireland.

THE EXTERNAL BACKGROUND TO WHAT TRANSPIRED IN O'NEILL'S PREMIERSHIP

The transformed development strategy of the Irish state in the late 1950s and early 1960s decisively, if unintentionally, contributed to the collapse of the UUP's hegemonic control, but it took time for this outcome to be evident. Between 1937 and 1949 it had at least seemed possible to some among Northern nationalists and the Irish governing parties that diplomatic constitutional nationalism had prospects of mobilizing international pressure on behalf of Irish unification. Ireland had benefited from Chamberlain's general appeasement policies,[14] and in 1940 at the nadir of Great Britain's war effort, Chamberlain and then Churchill had (tentatively) appeared to offer unification with Northern Ireland to de Valera in return for the Republic's participation on the allied side.[15] The Irish diaspora had not been entirely demobilized in the 1920s, and after 1945 efforts were made in the US Congress, encouraged by MacBride, to link Marshall Aid to the UK and Irish reunification,[16] A number of British Labour party's MPs, participants in the postwar Labour government, were sympathetic to a united Ireland, or regarded themselves as indebted to Irish voters.[17] Yet, when the coalition government in Dublin, led by Costello and MacBride, declared its intention to make Ireland a republic, the Westminster government had responded with the Ireland Act.

The Soviet Union lifted its veto on Ireland's admission to the United Nations in late 1955, and this major change in Ireland's diplomatic relations produced a significant change in tone on the question of partition, strongly expressed by Fine Gael's Liam Cosgrave, the son of William, and then Minister for External Relations. There were

> two points which we must recognize as permanent realities in our approach to the question of Partition: firstly, that it is a problem for which there is no quick and easy solution; secondly, that the first step towards unity lies in more neighbourly relations between the two sections of the Irish people. It is a matter for regret that the actions of the advocates of the illusory quick solution by violence have impeded progress in the development of more neighbourly relations.

[14] See McMahon (1984); see also Vol. 2, Ch. 3, pp. 123–6.   [15] See Vol. 2, Ch. 3, pp. 122–26.
[16] Cronin (1987: 190–8). The definitive account of Ireland and the Marshall Plan may be found in Whelan (2000b); and more briefly in Whelan (2000a).
[17] Purdie (1983: *passim*).

Nevertheless, he insisted:

> The climate in which violence flourishes, which is the inevitable result of loss of faith in constitutional methods, is . . . a predictable reaction to the abuse of constitutional processes whereby the most elementary democratic rights have been denied to the Nationalist minority in the Six Counties by gerrymander, discrimination in housing and employment, and even open provocation by the para-military force usually called the B-Specials. In the past month, we have seen attempts, fortunately abortive, to introduce discrimination into the fields of children's allowances and education. It is in the continuation of repressive and discriminatory actions that we have the soil in which the seeds of violence flourish, and I need hardly say that these measures, apart from their results, make the task of developing neighbourly relations difficult . . . I wish to assure the House that we will continue to expose repressive or discriminatory practices against our fellow-countrymen and use every means appropriate to bring international public opinion to bear on such cases. In the United Nations of which we are now members, we are . . . determined to miss no opportunity of seeking to undo the unnatural division of our country. *We do not, however, propose to raise the issue on inappropriate occasions or to give to the world the impression that we have no interest in any matter of international policy save that of Partition alone.*[18]

Having failed to reunify Ireland by diplomatic means or through international campaigning, the new Republic had emerged protectionist out of the wartime emergency, bereft of any military alliance, or a truly productive engagement with the victorious allies, and still dependent on Great Britain as its primary trading partner, and suffering from constant labor emigration, both skilled and unskilled. Stagnation had blocked social mobility within Ireland, and in Joseph Lee's well-developed account led to "insiders" developing possessor and incumbent mentalities across both public and private institutions.[19] Others have diagnosed cultural as well as economic stagnation, partly owed to the ethos imparted by the social dominance of the Catholic Church, and have linked the two.[20] By the 1950s, Ireland's per capita emigration toll was approaching that of the immediate post-famine years. The need for successful economic development focused the minds of the political and administrative elite, and an international climate of trade liberalization provided an opportunity that had not been present since 1929. The USA was promoting free trade throughout the non-communist world, and two regional projects were competing within western Europe: the British-led free-trade strategy that culminated in the European Free Trade Agreement (EFTA), built around the UK's Scandinavian and Irish partners, and the French, German, Benelux, and Italian-led European Economic Community (EEC), which culminated in the Treaty of Rome, with a customs union and a commitment to a common internal market, which came into force on January 1, 1958.[21]

---

[18] Dáil Éireann Debates, vol. 159, no. 1 (July 3, 1956), <https://www.oireachtas.ie/en/debates/debate/dail/1956-07-03/33/> (accessed September 2018), emphasis added.

[19] See Lee (1989: *passim*).   [20] Garvin (2005, 2011).

[21] See Milward et al. (1992) and Milward (2005) on the UK's failed alternative to the EEC; on the formation of the EEC and discussions of its implications for Ireland and partitioned nations, see Lindberg and Scheingold (1970); Tannam 1999; Elizabeth M. Meehan (2000); McGarry (2001); Anderson (2009); Mabry et al. (2013).

THE IRISH STATE SHIFTS DEVELOPMENT
STRATEGY: LEMASS AND "TECHNOCRATIC
ANTI-PARTITIONISM"

Ireland had choices, and it had to choose. After several false starts among the three brief lived governments of 1948–57, it embarked upon a major change in its strategy in 1958, signaled in two key papers, *Economic Development* and *Programme for Economic Expansion*. Its officials decided to encourage foreign direct investment (FDI) and expose its nascent industries to competition.[22] It would become a partner in the General Agreement on Trade and Tariffs, signed in December 1967 at the end of the Kennedy Round, and, more generally, it would follow the free-trade strategy of its largest partner, Great Britain. The change in direction was solidified in 1959 by the departure of the 77-year-old de Valera from the premiership (he remained President until 1973, twice winning seven-year terms, in 1959 and 1966). His replacement as Taoiseach, the more pragmatic and energetic Seán Lemass, like many of his subsequent peers in the postcolonial world, but earlier than most, fully switched Ireland's development strategy from import substitution toward promoting FDI and export-led-growth.[23] This post-1958 strategy shift was driven by political, electoral, and economic considerations within Ireland, but had significant spillover effects on Northern Ireland.

The new policy regime had implications for irredentism—which was bad for business, especially if it led to violence. Good relations with Northern Ireland, the UK, EFTA, and then the EEC, became imperative for the success of the new focus on FDI and economic growth. The resolution of the national question was subordinated to economic development. Fianna Fáil, the party that managed the transition from protectionism to economic liberalism, rationalized the apparent volte-face in its Northern policy by claiming that without advanced economic development Ulster Protestants would continue to find unification an unattractive prospect. Tom Lyne has persuasively argued that under Lemmas the party initiated a "technocratic anti-partitionist strategy."[24] Its premise was that, through economic growth and prosperity and cross-border functional cooperation, Irish unity would be accomplished. Cross-border cooperation increased in the fishing industry, railways, tourism, and electricity generation, collaboration quietly but effectively encouraged by civil servants in Dublin and Belfast. In the 1950s Northern Ireland and the Republic passed matching Erne Drainage Development Acts, created a Foyle Fisheries Commission, the Great Northern Railway Board, and quietly cooperated on customs control, lighthouse management, electricity supply, and animal health and disease control. In 1959 Lemass is reported to have said that the linkage between neutrality and partition had not been seriously discussed in his time in cabinet, and by 1962 was publicly questioning whether

---

[22] The galvanizing role of the new Secretary of Finance T. K. Whitaker is accepted by all commentators; for the administrative and intellectual politics, start with Lee (1989: 341–59). Whitaker's first biography is provided by Chambers (2014).

[23] Seán Lemass is the subject of a major trade in biographies, a testament to his significance: Bew and Patterson (1982); Brian Farrell (1985); O'Sullivan (1994); Horgan (1997); Garvin (2009); Evans (2011). He is one of the precious few to be admired in Lee (1989).

[24] Lyne (1990).

membership of NATO would automatically amount to recognizing UK sovereignty over Northern Ireland. In the same year, in an interview with the *New York Times*, he recognized that a military commitment would be an "inevitable" component of joining the common market, and in that context he would be prepared to yield on neutrality.[25]

The IRA's small border campaign of 1956–62 did not disturb the strategy of seeking a thaw in north–south relations. To the contrary. The Republic cooperated with Stormont in repressing the IRA, and introduced internment under its Offences against the State Act. "Operation Harvest" and its sequels ended with the IRA dumping arms and berating the Northern nationalist population for failing to give it sufficient support.[26] The campaign fizzled out long before the formal cessation of hostilities. It had not been started on a whim, however. The organization had recovered from its nadir, had internally purged itself, and was able to recruit afresh amid the fervor generated by the Anti-Partition League and the apparent locking and bolting of the Union in the Ireland Act.[27] According to one of its leaders in a position to know, "the recruits of the IRA in the 1950s came out of the anti-partition agitation against the Ireland Act."[28] Northern nationalists had voted for republican candidates in the 1955 Westminster parliamentary elections in the North—giving them over 150,000 votes, or 23.7 percent of the regional poll,—and two jailed IRA men had won the traditionally nationalist seats of Mid-Ulster and Fermanagh–South Tyrone. These results were overread by the IRA's leadership, which deemed the time propitious to launch a military offensive in December 1956. The key leader later diagnosed its weaknesses in his Ph.D thesis, submitted to New York's New School: the Stormont government had been alerted by arms raids; the IRA was poorly armed and resourced; its Northern organization was rudimentary; it had only loose ties with the local Nationalists, "who gave the campaign covert but not open support, and the IRA had no political organization by which it could reach the people with its message." The "campaign" became largely "a matter of armed forays over the border."[29] Its captured volunteers were being released before its campaign formally ended.

In Dáil Éireann, de Valera, bolstered by a large majority,[30] had interpreted his electoral victory as a mandate to repress republicans. Public officials were suspended if they violated the Offences against the State Act; public employees were obliged to sign an oath respecting Ireland's constitution, on pain of dismissal; and, as seen, internment was introduced and applied, matching the policy in the North. The four Sinn Féin candidates elected as deputies had shown their cause retained reservoirs of support. Equally, the refusal of the IRA and Sinn Féin showed that some republicans appreciated the need to have both a political and a military strategy. The Sinn Féin candidates had run on an incredible platform, however. They would form a government if they won a majority, but otherwise would abstain from attendance. When the 1959 Westminster elections took place in the

---

[25] Keatinge (1984: 24, 26). For a full account of Lemass's development on this subject, see Keogh (2000: *passim*), who argues that his two principal foreign-policy goals were to secure Irish membership of the EEC and to normalize the relationship between Britain and Ireland—which meant improving relations with Belfast. The end of neutrality and NATO membership were not to be obstacles to these goals.

[26] J. Bowyer Bell (1979: 289–336); see also Vol. 1, Intro, p. 3.   [27] Lyons (1973b: 561).

[28] Cronin (1987: 273).   [29] Cronin (1983: 171).   [30] Ó Beacháin (2014: 243–8).

North, support for republicans had fallen to 11 percent, largely because the Nationalist Party decided to recontest districts that it had left alone in 1955. In any case, abstentionism was becoming increasingly pointless. In 1958 Stormont passed legislation, targeted at Sinn Féin, regarding its own elections: valid candidates would have to declare in advance that they would take their seats. Ballot-box republicanism seemed futile. So, however, did armed struggle. The IRA had confined its targets to Crown forces, and had initially excluded the B Specials—showing determination to avoid even the appearance of sectarianism—but its "war" was therefore minimal in its consequences.

Lemass directed friendly speeches northwards. In 1963, he conceded that a united Ireland should be federal in form, with considerable autonomy for the northern state.[31] He encouraged the Nationalist Party to abandon abstentionism (toward Stormont) and become the formal opposition. The Northern minority received the consistent signals: it was on its own for now, and it was to engage Belfast and not just entreat Dublin. Improvements in its position would have to come from within the political system, within the UK and Northern Ireland. In 1965 Lemass risked visiting O'Neill in Stormont, a visit that conveyed an implicit recognition of Northern Ireland, even if it aroused the suspicions of loyalists like the Revd Ian Paisley, who threw snowballs at his motorcade. The summit meeting, the first between the two prime ministers on the island for forty years, was accompanied by others at ministerial and official levels. This initiative promised to break the mold in Northern Irish politics. It seemed to deprive unionists of the argument that the Irish state, the IRA, and the northern minority were in a solid coalition against their regime, and expanded the space for O'Neill's rhetoric of "community reconciliation."

Lemass also took a pragmatic, revisionist, and secular approach toward de Valera's constitution. Before he retired from office in 1966, he had established an all-party review committee in Dáil Éireann. The next year the committee proposed a new Article 3 for the constitution.[32] The draft provisions read as follows:

1. The Irish nation hereby proclaims its firm will that its territory be re-united in harmony and brotherly affection between all Irishmen.

2. The laws enacted by the Parliament established by this Constitution shall, until the achievement of the nation's unity shall otherwise require, have the like area and extent of application as the laws of the Parliament which existed prior to the adoption of this Constitution. Provision may be made by law to give extra-territorial effect to such laws.[33]

This wording would have clearly made the reunification of the island aspirational, rather than a matter of legal right, and would have left the door open to negotiations for a confederal or federal Ireland. The review committee also proposed the deletion of Article 44.1, 2, and 3, because "these provisions give offence to non-Catholics and are also a useful weapon in the hands of those who

---

[31] de Paor (1971: 138).
[32] See Vol. 2, Ch. 3, p. 116, for the wording of Article 3 that the new text was proposed to supersede.
[33] Report of the Committee on the Constitution, December 1967, Stationery Office, Dublin, 5–6.

are anxious to emphasise the differences between North and South."[34] It proposed a review and removal of the ban on divorce because it was harsh and rigid, and coercive in relation to Catholics and non-Catholics, whose religious rules do not absolutely prohibit divorce.[35] The review was most successful in the short term in delivering the deletion of sections 2 and 3 from Article 44 of the constitution: the special position of the Catholic Church was deleted in 1972 after a referendum held after the retirement of Archbishop McQuaid of Dublin. Other changes were frozen, however, after the outbreak of renewed conflict.

Ireland's acceptance and promotion of trade liberalization after 1958 also had ramifications for relations with Great Britain. The UK and Ireland began adapting their relationships in preparation for entry into the EEC, signing a bilateral free-trade agreement with one another in 1965. Their simultaneous entry into the EEC, eventually ratified in 1973, would have occurred earlier, in 1967, but for President de Gaulle's exercise of a veto targeted at the British in 1962. Such improvements in British–Irish relations, as free-trading and then as EEC and EU partners, subsequently made it slightly more difficult for the British government to resist the pressure for reform in Northern Ireland, and made Unionist justifications for their control regime seem threadbare and self-serving. Though it may have seemed otherwise, the Irish government did not switch back to full-blooded irredentism when armed conflict broke out in 1968–9—despite the temptations, military contingency planning, and an arms-running scandal involving government ministers.[36] Rather, British policymakers had to explain to the world, and to themselves, why reforming Northern Ireland was so difficult.

SOCIAL DEMOCRACY AND THE DEMOCRATIZATION OF GREAT BRITAIN

The economic and social development of postwar Great Britain also had unintended consequences that undermined the foundations of hegemonic control in the North. The British welfare state, acting on the Beveridge Report, was dramatically extended by the Labour government of 1945–51.[37] Despite the conservatism of the UUP, and widespread beliefs among its members that the welfare state would exacerbate the fecklessness of the Catholic minority, the new welfare programs were applied in Northern Ireland. Straightforward political calculations were involved.[38] Anti-partitionism within the British labor movement suggested prudence was appropriate rather than direct confrontation with a transformative government then judged highly likely to remain in power. The London government made the extension of the new welfare programs to the North extremely attractive: Northern Ireland could provide services at UK standards as long as it

---

[34] Report of the Committee on the Constitution, December 1967, Stationery Office, Dublin, 47.

[35] Report of the Committee on the Constitution, December 1967, Stationery Office, Dublin, 48.

[36] Kelly (1971, 1999); MacIntyre (1971); Clifford (2009a, b); discussed further at Vol. 2, appendix. 2.6.1, pp. 193–6.

[37] The starting if not the endpoint of discussion for this moment is Addison (1994).

[38] Harkness (1977).

imposed tax rates similar to those in Great Britain; if they followed this path, the Treasury in London would make up the shortfall in required revenues. The constraints of the Government of Ireland Act were apparently forgotten: Northern Ireland would be subsidized as necessary to have British welfare standards.

The UUP cabinet eventually calculated that implementing Labour's welfare-state program would be wise, and that refusing to do so would undermine pan-Protestant solidarity. Labour, socialist, and commonwealth candidates had performed quite well in wartime by-elections, and in the 1945 general elections in Northern Ireland; and the UUP feared losing support to the Northern Ireland Labour Party (NILP), which endorsed the program of the Attlee government. Brooke confided to his diary in November 1945 the grim options he and his colleagues faced: "Stay as we are with possible chaos [disagreement with the London government on its socialist policies]; join Eire–unthinkable; back to Westminster—dangerous; dominion status, might lower living standards."[39] Rarely has a unionist politician more succinctly or candidly summarized his party and his people's options. Staying as they were, and détente with the Labour government, proved wise. Cheap talk of preferring dominion status to accepting socialism had persisted among UUP ministers until the Tories returned to office in London. Labour's Home Secretary James Chuter Ede had scornfully assessed that option. It was "like saying we dislike home rule so much we are determined to have it."[40]

The Belfast cabinet's decision to extend the welfare state and apply its social benefits was not pursued to increase support for the Union among Catholics or nationalists. Such a policy shift would have deviated from the UUP's sectarian electoral strategy, and would have been inconsistent with entrenched discrimin-ation and policies that discouraged Catholics from joining the UUP. Mainstream unionists continued to profess that most Catholics were unreconstructed rebels, and the UUP did not even debate Catholic membership of its ranks until 1959, when some of its younger members realized that the welfare state was attractive to Northern Catholics, and may have weakened the lure of national reunification.[41] In fact, hardline UUP ministers tried to distort the application of Westminster's welfare principles by denying benefits to large families—which were dispropor-tionately Catholic. Westminster had made provisions for family allowances, with increasingly larger payments for each child after the second. Though usually firm exponents of parity of service provision with Great Britain, Belfast's draft legisla-tion of 1957 initially reconstructed this flow of funds, so that larger allowances would be paid for the second and third children rather than for subsequent children.[42] The move was blatantly sectarian, and, under serious pressure from

---

[39] Barton (1992: 2).

[40] January 18, 1949, in TNA: PRO CAB 21/1842, cited in Barton (1992: 7). Relying heavily on evidence of civil-service preparation for UK-wide reforms, John Ditch (1988) argues that the modern welfare state was not imposed by Westminster upon a reluctant Stormont administration, but it was clearly the potential NILP/Labour government axis that shaped the decisions of the UUP cabinet.

[41] In 1959 Clarence Graham (Chair of the UUC Standing Committee) and Brian Magginis (Attorney General) advocated both Catholic members and candidates; but Brookeborough supported George Clark, the Grand Master of the Orange Lodge, in opposing the suggestion. No such sectarian exclusion applied within any of the Nationalist parties.

[42] Ivan Neill was the UUP Minister of Labour and National Insurance and was driven by the conviction that Unionists had a disproportionately higher share of smaller families with Nationalists in

Whitehall, on the first occasion since the war, the UUP cabinet backed down,[43] although Brookeborough refused the resignation of his demographic engineer.

Labour's welfare programs, and state support for farmers, were not substantively repealed by the three Conservative governments that held office between 1951 and 1964. This entrenchment of the social-democratic welfare state had unintended consequences, however, all of which served to undermine the UUP's control system. For the first time since 1922 disparities became visible between the average standards of living in the two parts of Ireland, and the public enthusiasm of the entirety of the northern minority's commitment to reunification diminished. The Republic did not experience a significant growth spurt until the 1960s. In 1964, Northern Ireland had 95,000 children in secondary education compared to 85,000 in the Republic, and with a much smaller population. Expenditure on higher education was three times higher in the North; welfare payments were 50 percent higher; and one historian judged that "the difference [in quality] between the health services was so great that little comparison was possible."[44] The conjunction of these changes paved the way for Catholic demands for equal citizenship rights in the late 1960s. They had begun to interact more with British institutions, to be less reliant on faith-based services, and to expect more as citizens from the state within which they lived.

There was highly significant postwar welfare-state legislation in education, but a time lag before its consequences were felt. Lt Col. Samuel Hall-Thompson (1885–1954), educated at Dulwich College in England, the UUP's postwar Northern education minister (1944–50), proved relatively liberal—pushing through a modest increase in capital funding for Catholic schools to 65 percent.[45] Cardinal MacRory had privately indicated that, if support had been raised to 75 percent, then Catholic schools would participate in the "four and two" system,[46] but the minister was constrained, by UUP backbenchers, and, according to his testimony, by the Protestant churches, which had handed over their schools to the state sector. Hall-Thompson's reward for his mild liberalism was to be hounded out of office: Brooke replaced him with Midgley, now a member of the UUP, more right wing, and overtly exclusionary in disposition.[47] Before Hall-Thompson put through the 1947 Northern Ireland Education Act, most adults in the region had experienced only primary education, with a small minority going on to grammar (high) schools. Access to grammar schools required either the payment of fees or success in winning a very limited number of scholarships through competitive examinations organized by the Ministry of Education. Under the new act, high-school education was provided for all pupils, and the age of transfer from primary to secondary education was set at 11 years. Northern Ireland's Act

---

the converse position—and seemed to believe that allowances had already led to a disproportionate upsurge in the Nationalist birth rate (Mulholland 2004: 200).

[43] de Paor (1971: 129–30). This attempted maneuver was the one to which Liam Cosgrave had referred; see Vol. 2, Ch. 5, p. 153.

[44] Buckland (1981: 103).

[45] His son, Robert Hall-Thompson (1920–92), stood successfully as a pro-O'Neill candidate in 1969 and became chief whip for the UUP in the power-sharing executive of 1974, and joined the Conservative party late in life.

[46] See Vol. 2, Ch. 2, pp. 56–7.

[47] For the roles of Hall-Thompson and Midgley regarding Catholic education, see McGrath (2000).

followed the English model of 1944, and recognized three types of high school: grammar, technical, and intermediate. The technical schools attracted few pupils, so that by the late 1950s and early 1960s a dual system had emerged—of grammar and secondary schools. Grammar schools continued to charge fees, but the ministry operated a selection procedure to identify pupils suited for the grammar-school curriculum—an intelligence test administered at the end of primary schooling, "the 11+." Those who passed, irrespective of whether they went on to state or religious schools, now had their fees paid for by the ministry. The grammar schools were also permitted to continue to take a limited number of fee-paying pupils who had not passed the 11+.

Under these transformative arrangements, Catholics went on to secondary education and universities as first-timers in their families in greater numbers in the 1950s and 1960s.[48] Examples abound of Catholic grammar schools benefiting from the Education Act and of the consequences for subsequently prominent pupils who matured in the 1960s. St Patrick's Girls' Academy, Dungannon, taught Bernadette Devlin; St Dominic's Grammar School in Belfast taught Mary McAleese (née Leneghan), President of Ireland 1997–2011; St Patrick's Grammar School, Armagh, educated the poets Paul Muldoon and John Montague; St Mary's Christian Brothers Grammar School numbers Gerry Adams among its alumni; Kevin Boyle, the civil-rights leader, and internationally distinguished human-rights lawyer, went to Abbey Christian Brothers Grammar School in Newry, as did Seamus Mallon, deputy first minister of Northern Ireland 1999–2001.[49] The BBC broadcaster and employment lawyer Vincent Hanna, Gerry Fitt's son-in-law, went to St McNissi's College, Garron Tower, as did the human-rights and anti-discrimination lawyer and professor Christopher McCrudden. The most famous case is St Columb's Derry, a Catholic boarding and grammar school, which graduated a glittering crop in the 1960s—Seamus Heaney, Seamus Deane, and Phil Coulter distinguished themselves in different branches of the humanities, and Eamonn McCann and John Hume were leading lights in the future cadre of activists and politicians.[50] Austin Currie attended St Patrick's Academy Grammar School in Dungannon and described himself as "of the lucky generation, the first to benefit from free second- and third-level education, and it was all due to politics."[51]

The Catholic proportion of Queen's University's student body increased between 1961 and 1972, from 22 to 32 percent, very close to its proportion of the total population.[52] It is widely if not universally acknowledged that the civil-rights movement of the late 1960s was spearheaded by a new Catholic middle class, especially its student cohorts, who had grown up under the British welfare state.[a] The leaders of the civil-rights movement, and the student-based far-left movement, "People's Democracy," were overwhelmingly educated Catholics, or Catholic students. These new organizations, even if their importance may

---

[48] Among the UUP MPs who voted against the increased grants to Catholic schools was the young Brian Faulkner (Boyd 1972: 27–8).

[49] Mallon is also said by the BBC to have gone to St Patrick's Armagh. Boyle's reflections on the cramped atmosphere of Newry were recorded by the US academic W. H. VanVoris (1975: 23–31). Boyle maintained that the "snobs" went to the rich man's grammar school (VanVoris 1975: 27).

[50] *The Boys of St Columb's* is a notable documentary film directed by Maurice Fitzpatrick.

[51] Currie (2004: 37).   [52] Foster (1988: 584).

have been exaggerated in comparison with traditional Catholic and nationalist organizations, were new in rhetoric and objectives, and dominated by graduates. The same had been true of National Unity, which challenged the Nationalist Party in the early 1960s. Austin Currie and his peers had established the New Ireland Society at Queen's University.[53] Their leaders, who eventually attracted public, British, and international attention, developed the slogan of "equal citizenship" that proved corrosive for Stormont's reputation, embracing a civil-rights platform that partially displaced traditional nationalism. One reason they did so was because the youngest among them had been brought up as citizens in the new social-democratic welfare state. The import of Labour's welfare state had made Northern Irish Catholics more British by treating them as equal beneficiaries of programs that the Stormont parliament could not modify.

The growth of the welfare state weakened a key facet of the control system as it had operated after 1921. It reduced the incentives to emigrate among the outgroup. In sovereign and uninhibitedly brutal control systems—for example, in apartheid South Africa—the economic dependency among subordinated group(s) is nearly absolute; co-option is easier and rife; and threats of retribution ensure quiescence, or prompt emigration.[54] But, after 1945–51, no religious or political discrimination could be made in the allocation of welfare cash benefits in the North (as opposed to services), nor in access to grammar and tertiary education, because these citizenship rights were determined by Westminster and Whitehall. Catholics benefited as byproducts of the UUP's decision to follow parity in British service provision. There were demographic implications. The pace of minority emigration slowed, sustaining a larger minority than would otherwise have been the case, and the Catholic share of the Northern population, which had been static in the 1926 and 1937 censuses (at 33.5 percent), started to rise marginally in the postwar years, to 34.4 percent in 1951, 34.9 percent in 1961, reaching 36.8 percent in 1971.[55] The Catholic birth rate remained distinctly higher than that of Protestants. These changes in demographic ratios, accompanied by a bulge in the Catholic youth population, affected Catholic confidence and Protestant insecurities during the protests of the late 1960s and early 1970s, and thereafter.

The growth of the welfare state also led to growing metropolitan interest and the possibility of interventions in Northern Ireland. The Belfast government's failure to develop its economy successfully was evident in an unemployment rate high above the UK average throughout the late 1950s and 1960s, and the subvention from Whitehall—the gap between public expenditure in Northern Ireland and what was raised there in public revenue—became increasingly visible to civil servants and politicians. The inertia of the aging Lord Brookeborough, as Brooke had become in 1952, and his government's apparent capture by interest groups built around declining traditional industries, were noticed in London. Michael MacDonald argues that British officials cooperated with UUP backbenchers in replacing Brookeborough with his "progressive" Minister of Finance, Captain Terence O'Neill.[56] That seems too strong a claim, but increased fiscal dependency

---

[53] Currie (2004: 40–1).   [54] Smooha (1980).   [55] Paul A. Compton (1985: table 1).

[56] MacDonald (1986: 71). O'Neill himself recalled that Brookeborough had resisted British efforts during Macmillan's premiership to respond to Irish prime minister Sean Lemass's calls for North–South dialogue.

made the UUP government much more susceptible to pressure from the new Labour government, which was elected in 1964. It began to be suggested that some of Stormont's powers should be transferred to Westminster.[57]

The incoming Labour government was interested in Northern Ireland for political reasons. The new prime minister, Harold Wilson, had Irish voters in his Huyton constituency; he was aware of his party's sizable Irish support in Great Britain; and he wanted to make his mark by tackling difficult problems.[58] He had expressed interest in reforming Northern Ireland before the 1964 election campaign, and, with other ministers, indicated that he shared the aspiration for a united Ireland. How deep this stance was on Wilson's part may be doubted, but he was intensely irritated by the fact that the Ulster Unionists, who returned all twelve of Northern Ireland's MPs to Westminster in the 1964 election, continued to take, as they always had done, the Conservative whip.[59] Labour's wafer-thin parliamentary majority between 1964 and 1966 was jeopardized by these "Ulster Tories"—usually an unprintable word preceded the phrase. In 1965 the Campaign for Democracy in Ulster, made up of backbench Labour MPs, was founded by Paul Rose to promote concern about abuses of human rights. It could count on as many as 100 Labour MPs for support.[60] In 1966 Wilson informed O'Neill that the subvention was becoming hard to justify if the position of the minority could not be improved.[61]

THE INTERNAL ENVIRONMENT IN
THE O'NEILL PREMIERSHIP

These distinct and novel developments in the Republic and Great Britain impinged upon Northern Ireland in ways that presaged the breakdown of the UUP's control. External developments were transforming both the nationalist and the unionist blocs, but internal forces prompting change were also at work. Traditional nationalism had failed Catholics before and after 1945. Constitutional nationalism, articulated in the Anti-Partition League of 1948–9, had done nothing to alter the North's constitutional status or overtly to improve Catholics' treatment. Electoral abstentionism, or voting for Sinn Féin candidates in elections in the 1950s, expressed alienation but achieved nothing—apart from encouraging the IRA to believe, mistakenly, that an insurrectionary strategy was viable. The apparent futility of either traditional constitutional nationalism or militant republicanism, and the changed attitudes induced by the welfare state, prompted some "revisionism" among the Catholic population.[62]

While not abandoning its nationalist sentiments, much of the Catholic middle class began to prioritize the reform of Northern Ireland, and before long for many

---

[57] Buckland (1981: 107).   [58] Bew et al. (1979: 179–80).   [59] Harold Wilson (1971: 232).
[60] Buckland (1981: 108); Paul Rose (2001).   [61] Harold Wilson (1971: 270).
[62] See the writings of two very different Catholics with the same surname, Ciaran McKeown (1984: 1–15); Michael McKeown (1986: 1–38).

of them it became the overriding goal.[63] A succession of groups and proposed parties emerged seeking both to advertise and to change the position of the minority. In 1958, a conference of Catholics at Garron Tower suggested friendship and cooperation with and within the existing institutions.[64] National Unity was formed in 1959 by Catholics frustrated by single-issue anti-partitionism, and by the Nationalist Party's neglect of social and economic questions.[65] The Nationalist Party was criticized, sometimes unfairly, as a party of publicans and hoteliers. National Unity accepted the existence of Northern Ireland, and demanded reform instead of a focus on anti-partitionism.[66] It forced the Nationalist Party to propose policies aimed at improving the economic and social conditions of Northern Catholics. National Unity spawned a new organization in 1965, the National Democratic Party. Working-class Catholics were intensively focused on their housing needs, and Derry Labour emerged as a principal organizer on that front. Secular leaders with secular agendas were coming more to the fore, seeking social justice before Irish unity.

New attitudes within the Catholic community were expressed in the formation of the small but significantly named Campaign for Social Justice (CSJ) in 1964, which collected data, addressed discrimination, and was especially vigorous in Tyrone.[67] By 1965 the CSJ had affiliated with the National Council for Civil Liberties in London, and cultivated the Campaign for Democracy in Ulster. When no adequate redress of grievances was forthcoming by 1967, the Northern Ireland Civil Rights Association (NICRA) was formed with similar aims to those of the CSJ. Instead of being an intellectual ginger group, however, it emulated the US civil-rights movement.[68] While the CSJ and NICRA were predominantly led by middle-class activists, Belfast's working-class Catholics were also shifting towards individuals, organizations, and parties that appeared to put reform ahead of a united Ireland—electing Gerry Fitt under a Republican Labour ticket to Westminster in 1966, and Paddy Devlin of the NILP to Stormont in 1969. The NILP had been the starting place of several of the most prominent civil-rights leaders of Catholic formation—for example, Eamonn McCann, Erskine Holmes, Michael Farrell, and Paddy Devlin. Yet the party was so wedded to purely parliamentary politics that it failed to benefit from the civil-rights mobilization.[b]

Physical-force republicanism was widely judged to have failed even more abysmally than the constitutional Northern Nationalists. The IRA campaign of 1956–62 was considered a fiasco. The IRA had failed completely to mobilize Catholics or nationalists, especially in urban areas, and acknowledged this assessment in its ceasefire announcement. Its military impact was minimal—perhaps because the collateral damage was so severely controlled. The UUP government had felt so confident of victory that it released all internees even before the IRA

---

[63] For discussions, see Michael McKeown (1986), and for an early treatment by a political scientist, see McAllister (1975).

[64] Then a unionist vigilante, the UUP Stormont MP Brian Faulkner, warned that these polite Catholics "did not want to strengthen the constitution but to overthrow it" (Boyd 1972: 34).

[65] McAllister (1975).

[66] This is the context in which John Hume emerged (McLoughlin 2010).

[67] The memoir by one of its principal organizers is instructive (McCluskey 1989) and usefully reproduces the CSJ's documentation, including correspondence with British politicians.

[68] See Dooley (1998); Arthur (2000a, b).

had announced its formal end to hostilities.[69] After this crushing defeat, many disillusioned republicans had dropped out of the organization while others embarked upon political rather than military activity. Eventually many of them became more socialist, or Marxist-Leninist, than Catholic or nationalist. This new republicanism eventually produced the Republican Clubs, a number of Wolfe Tone Societies, and much later the Workers' Party, all of them indirectly influenced by the Connolly Association formed in Great Britain. These groups supported the reformism of the civil-rights movement, and on some accounts devised its strategy.[70] By 1967, the IRA, as a military organization, was again close to extinction, as it had been in the 1940s—close to extinction but not dead.

The new participatory and reform-oriented attitude among Catholics posed serious problems for the UUP. What if abstentionist defeatism was no longer the strategy conveniently prevalent among the minority? The legitimacy of the UUP's control rested on the premise that Catholics were nationalist rebels who had to be treated as security risks, and maintained in self-earned political, economic, and social inferiority because they were disloyal. Without a plausible national-security justification, hegemonic control was unmasked as naked domination, and more difficult to sustain at home, and to defend in Great Britain and abroad. Controlling republicans who wanted to destroy the polity was much more ideologically defensible than deliberately disadvantaging Catholics who wanted just treatment. In the past, Unionist solidarity had been bolstered by the South's official verbal hostility or bellicose speech, both under de Valera's cabinets (1932–48, 1951–4, 1957–9) and under the postwar coalition governments (1948–51, 1954–7), and by the obvious unwillingness of the minority to accept Northern Ireland. In the 1960s, however, the Republic's elected officials, official postures, and language ceased to provide such easy excuses.

Another factor prompting change was the trajectory of the regional economy, O'Neill's prime focus, as finance minister, and when he became prime minister. Traditional industries, linen, shipbuilding, and agriculture, were in serious decline by the 1960s (see Table 2.5.1(a)). Employment in shipbuilding, the prize of the skilled Protestant working class, fell by 40 percent between 1961 and 1964 alone.[71] Despite finding some new sources of industrial and mainly public-service employment (see Table 2.5.1(b)), Northern Ireland had much higher unemployment than any other UK region. A sympathetic commentator declared that unemployment was the "one problem that had defied solution."[72] Those in employment, however, enjoyed the increasing prosperity of the long economic boom then raising expectations everywhere in western Europe. Relative deprivation (compared with Protestants) and raised expectations proved potent sources of discontent among Catholics.

The NILP had begun to do better in competition with the UUP at the end of Brookeborough's dispensation. After its reorganization in 1949, when the Ireland Act forced it off the fence, and it became a pro-Union party, the NILP had not won a seat at Stormont until it took four at the 1958 election, polling 16 percent of the total vote. It retained these seats with its highest number of votes ever in the

---

[69] Buckland (1981: 105).
[70] See the discussion of Desmond Greaves at Vol. 2, Ch. 5, p. 170.
[71] Bew et al. (1979: 135).
[72] Lawrence (1965: 101).

Table 2.5.1(a). Employment in Northern Ireland's traditional sectors, 1950–1973

Sector	1950 labor force	1973 labor force	Net loss (%)
Agriculture, forestry, and fishing	101,000	55,000	46,000 (45.5)
Textiles	65,000	19,000	46,000 (70.7)
Shipbuilding	24,000	10,000	14,000 (41.7)

Source: Northern Ireland Office (1974: 6).

Table 2.5.1(b). The shifting pattern of sectoral employment, Northern Ireland, 1926–1971 (shares in %)

Sector	1926	1961	1971
Agriculture	29	16	11
Industry	34	42	42
Services	37	42	47

Source: Kennedy et al. (1988: 99).

subsequent election in 1962, when it won 26 percent of the total vote cast (though these figures were flattering because of the low number of contested seats). The NILP posed a threat to the UUP's electoral hegemony, especially in the Belfast urban area.

THE PROMISE OF O'NEILL

In this setting, Captain Terence O'Neill became Northern Ireland's fourth prime minister. Unlike his most famous critics, Faulkner or Paisley, he had served, and been wounded, in the Second World War. He adopted the strategies then being employed in Great Britain to deal with the decline of traditional industries— regional planning, new-town development, and infrastructural investments to boost economic growth: what was once known as "regional Keynesianism." A six-year plan was adopted in 1964 to counter the traditional concentration of industry in Belfast, and to disperse industry and the labor force more widely. Central to the new approach was the construction of new infrastructure, including two motorways, new house-building programs, a series of new growth-centers, including a new city, a second university, and a centralized and rationalized public administration. This modernization also had repercussions for border politics. In a move toward more corporatist industrial relations, O'Neill's government recognized the Dublin-based Irish Congress of Trade Unions, for the first time, in 1964, and, to enhance economic cooperation, friendlier relations were pursued with the Republic. To create an atmosphere conducive to external investment, O'Neill promoted better "community relations."[c]

Various explanations have been offered of O'Neill's avoidance of the overt sectarianism of his predecessors. His time at Eton, and his stint in the Guards, exposed him to more liberal and cosmopolitan British culture, and separated him from the more narrow-minded bigots in the grassroots of the UUP and the

Orange Order.[73] One Anglophile argued that, "because his early family life was primarily spent at school in England, abroad, and in the army, O'Neill lacked the intensely parochial look conventionally found among politicians in the province. Instead of looking in and back, he looked forward and out."[74] Even if the assumptions underlying these arguments are correct, they are not entirely persuasive. O'Neill sought to improve cross-community relations as a byproduct of his determination to ramp up economic development. The superficiality of his liberalism was demonstrated in a condescending speech made a few days after his resignation in 1969:

> It is frightfully hard to explain to a Protestant that if you give Roman Catholics a good job and a good house they will live like Protestants, because they will see neighbours with cars and TV sets. They will refuse to have eighteen children, but if the Roman Catholic is jobless and lives in a most ghastly hovel he will rear eighteen children on national assistance. It is impossible to explain this to a militant Protestant... He cannot understand, in fact, that if you treat Roman Catholics with due consideration and kindness they will live like Protestants, in spite of the authoritarian nature of their church.[75]

These sentences, which were not written by his civil servants, are hard to square with the belief that O'Neill "had no sympathy with what he saw as parochial unionism."[76] O'Neill has been more aptly described: "The Prime Minister's moderation lay in avoiding bigotry."[77]

O'Neill had good manners, but his motivations and actions were more prosaic. Sectarian drum-beating would not have resolved the region's economic problems, and might have discouraged external investors. British subventions for the welfare state and agricultural subsidies increased from £46 million in 1963 to £72 million in 1968, an increase of over 50 percent—though allowance must be made for inflation.[78] The party interest of key members of the Labour government of 1964–70, and its backbenchers—vigilantly watching the UUP's conduct both at Westminster and at Belfast—made the preservation of traditional sectarianism fraught with danger. As memories of wartime loyalties faded, and rapprochement between Great Britain and Ireland proceeded under Lemass, diplomatic initiatives seemed more appropriate than rabble-rousing. Given the acquiescence of the minority, the recent defeat of the IRA, the conciliatory approach of Lemass, and the arrival of the ecumenical movement, a rhetorical alternative to old-line sectarianism was in order.

Economic "modernization" also had the potential to resolve the UUP's problems with its working-class voters. By stealing the NILP's language and policies, O'Neill positioned the UUP as both the natural and the progressive party of government, and in 1965 he won a Stormont general election in which the NILP's vote share fell significantly. Some claimed that O'Neill "sought nothing less than a fully legitimate regime in which Catholics would support the Constitution as well as comply with its basic laws."[79] If so, he proceeded at a snail's pace, and few Catholics, past or present, have swallowed this notion. O'Neill's

---

[73] Bruce (1986: 69). For the same judgment, see Bloomfield (2007: 160).
[74] Richard Rose (1971: 97).   [75] Buckland (1981: 112).   [76] Bruce (1986: 68–71).
[77] Arthur (1974: 17).   [78] Buckland (1981: 103).   [79] Richard Rose (1971: 97).

concessions were symbolic, not substantive, and often forced out of him and his party colleagues—the latter, granted, were the real constraint. In 1964 there was talk of "building bridges" between the two communities, revolutionary language given the intransigence of Brookeborough, but delivering on the promise was more difficult. Even the naming of a new bridge over the Lagan, linking east and central Belfast, aroused controversy. The "Elizabeth II Bridge" was the Governor's choice; Paisley and the unionist right had campaigned for the "Carson Bridge." Neither name would have built a bridge to Catholics or nationalists. However, public condolences were sent to Cardinal Conway on the death of Pope John XXIII in June 1963; Catholic schools were visited for the first time by a Northern premier; and photographs were taken of O'Neill meeting priests and nuns. The invitation to Lemass promised further reconciliation. These gestures and the accompanying rhetoric whetted the minority's appetite for reforms—and alerted the ultras among the majority.

O'Neill disappointed the minority, however. The Lockwood Committee on higher education, established in November 1963 without Catholic representation, recommended in early 1965 that the second new university should be located, not in predominantly Catholic and depressed Derry, the second city of the North, but in a greenfield site, in solidly Protestant and prosperous Coleraine.[80] Archival evidence confirms that leading unionists within the second city lobbied O'Neill not to place the new university near the Foyle—probably because they believed it would weaken the UUP's position in the gerrymandered city.[81] In July of the same year the government accepted the Matthew Report, recommending the construction of a new city, southwest of Belfast, between the then predominantly Protestant towns of Portadown and Lurgan. It was to be named "Craigavon" in honor of the first prime minister. The announcement was made by minister William (Bill) Craig, no relation.[82] This logic prioritized development east of the Bann, where UUP support was concentrated, but the design of the new city was manipulated "with Byzantine cunning."[83] The planners' idea had been to absorb people from the south and west of the region (predominantly Catholic), but a second report envisaged decanting some of Belfast's population—in proportions of families in different community groups that would be the same as that of the whole province. This "balance" would not threaten unionist electoral domination. New urban planning therefore reupholstered sectarian electoral segregation.[84]

Infrastructural improvements did not help nationalist-dominated areas. Not only did Derry lose out on a university, but, along with Newry, it lost rail connections. The unavoidable perception was that the new motorways from Belfast went toward Protestant Ballymena and the new Craigavon, but not to Derry or Newry. Little attempt was made to promote Catholics to public bodies, which the *Belfast Telegraph* observed "made a nonsense of the prime minister and all that is said about a bridge-building policy." In 1967, three out of thirty-three

[80] Ó Dochartaigh (1997: pp. xv, xvi, 22–4, 85).   [81] Mulholland (2004: 195–7).
[82] In the Stormont House of Commons Joseph Connellan acidly riposted to the news: "A Protestant city for a Protestant people."
[83] Mulholland (2004: 197).
[84] Lurgan is now strongly Catholic, while Portadown is strongly Protestant; both are highly segregated; and Craigavon has never achieved urban let alone urbane unity.

people on the Youth Employment Services Board were Catholic; two out of twenty-two on the Hospitals Authority; and two out of twenty-four on the General Health Services Board. In 1969, the membership of twenty-one public boards was estimated to be 85 percent non-Catholic.[85] Catholics simply were not invited into the higher echelons of the regime—either in Belfast or elsewhere. Co-option was extremely limited. The UUP was still tied to the Orange Order, which the young Brian Faulkner described as "the most democratic body in the world . . . the backbone of Ulster."[86] The UUP did not attempt to attract Catholic members or support.[87] O'Neill did not actively seek Catholic endorsement for his party and his programs until three months before his resignation.

The institutions of control were left unaltered. While the commemoration of the fiftieth anniversary of the Easter Rising was allowed in 1966, the loyalist backlash against this event prompted the government to ban the Republican Clubs, and the centenary celebrations of the Fenian rebellion of 1867. No reform of the local government gerrymanders occurred, nor was there an end to the discriminatory housing policies that underpinned gerrymandering. The business and university votes were abolished for Stormont elections in 1968, twenty years after Great Britain, but no attempt was made to introduce universal suffrage at the local level. Marc Mulholland, citing a civil-service memorandum, observes that by the 1960s there were only 3,000 company votes (0.5 percent of the electorate), but a full half of these were in Londonderry Corporation, the gerrymandered maiden city.[88] The UUP told trade unionists concerned about the discrepancy between the local-government franchise in Northern Ireland and Great Britain that Great Britain was out of line![89] *The Reshaping of Local Government: Statement of Aims,* a white paper released in December 1967, was far more concerned with the inefficiencies of the local government system than with minority grievances. No steps were taken to remove or reduce discrimination. The Minister of Home Affairs refused a private member's attempt to process a bill of rights because it would allow "disappointed office-seekers to air their frustrations."[90] The Special Powers Act and the B Specials remained, along with offensive and tendentious legislation like the Flags and Emblems Act. The police actually became more Protestant in the O'Neill years: the proportion of Catholic officers dropped from 12 to 9.4 percent between 1961 and 1972, a fall of over one-fifth. The judiciary remained overwhelmingly Protestant, and two of three judges in the Northern Ireland Court of Appeal had held the post of Attorney-General in UUP governments.[91]

The breakdown of hegemonic control in Northern Ireland exemplifies Tocqueville's thesis that, when a bad government seeks to reform itself, it is in its greatest danger.[92] O'Neill had raised minority expectations, pushed higher by Labour's election victories at Westminster in 1964 and 1966, but O'Neill could not satisfy these expectations, or chose not to do so. In the "Loyalty Survey," carried out in 1968, Catholics felt that Northern Ireland politics were changing for the better, and felt this way more than Protestants. Of all Catholics interviewed, 65 percent believed things were changing for the better, 27 percent saw no change, and only

---

[85] Quotation and data from Harkness (1983: 149).   [86] Boyd (1972: 24).
[87] Darby (1976: 15–16).   [88] Mulholland (2004: 205).   [89] Buckland (1981: 117–18).
[90] Palley (1972: 410).   [91] Buckland (1981: 116).
[92] Arthur (1984: 107); Tom Wilson (1989: 152).

4 percent felt matters had become worse.[93] The reluctance of O'Neill's cabinet to reform led to disillusionment, and growing public protests, and the key transition occurred, we can now see, with the establishment of the Northern Ireland Civil Rights Association (NICRA) in February 1967 out of the joint efforts of the Wolfe Tone Societies and the CSJ.

O'Neill's base within his party was insecure, and charges of "Lundyism" were heard. He was out of touch with the grass roots; he had not been elected by the parliamentary party, but had "emerged" in the manner in which Conservative leaders used to emerge—through "soundings;" it was questionable whether he would have won an electoral contest. He preferred the advice of technocrats and civil servants to his party headquarters, and was aloof: the upper-class English culture of his time may explain this trait better than his alleged liberalism. He was also inept. He did not consult his cabinet before taking the decision to invite Lemass to Belfast—Faulkner later pinpointed this decision as the start of the decline in O'Neill's support.[d] By implicitly recognizing Northern Ireland, Lemass had argu- ably taken the riskier step, but he prepared the ground with his colleagues.[94] O'Neill even set up a new government department while most of his colleagues were on vacation. Style was not his only problem, however; the direction of policy mattered. Modernization threatened the local-government system; rationalization would re- duce the numbers of local councils, and councilors, and their functions, and undermine Unionist clientelism. Those who ran local unionist powerbases, espe- cially in western Northern Ireland, were disturbed, and became key figures oppos- ing O'Neill. By encouraging external investment O'Neill estranged some local capitalists; and Belfast workers, redundant through the decline of traditional indus- tries, were unenthusiastic about the plans to decentralize economic activity.[95]

O'Neill's internal opposition perceived rapid change, exacerbated by Brooke- borough's long and intransigent tenure of office.[96] They believed that the old ways had worked; their siege-mentalities were fully intact; and the 1956–62 IRA campaign was fresh in their minds. The new behavior of the minority and the conciliatory approach of Ireland's government were seen as subtler republican plotting, or as a demonstration of a new self-confidence—either way, it was a cause for concern. Fundamentalists, led by Paisley, were persuaded that the ecu- menical movement encouraged by Vatican II had made Ulster's situation more perilous. They too were in the vanguard of the early opposition to O'Neill.[97] Loyalist anxieties were strengthened when Wilson returned Roger Casement's remains to the Republic. Loyalists sought traditional vigilant solidarity, not concessions.

O'Neill therefore presided over both increased unionist disunity and minority expectations. When Catholic opposition remained letter- and lobby-based rather than "on the streets," his unionist opponents could be held in check, though his decision not to ban republican fiftieth anniversary commemorations of the Easter Rising aroused Protestant opposition. They juxtaposed their sacrifice at the Somme with the republican "stab in the back." His unwillingness to confront republican memorialization was seen as encouraging rebellion. His condemnation

---

[93] Richard Rose (1971: 474 ff.).   [94] Foster (1988: 585).   [95] Wright (1973).
[96] For a revealing post-office retirement interview, see VanVoris (1975: 3–16). Brookeborough believed that order had to take precedence to justice.
[97] Bruce (1986: 89–120).

of those who took the law into their own hands, and the jailing of some ultra-Protestants, like Paisley, reinforced loyalist impressions that he was a traitor. In September 1966 O'Neill disclosed a backbench plot, naming backbenchers Desmond Boal, John McQuade, Austin Ardill, and John Taylor as the culprits. Speculation was widespread that a number of his ministers, including Harry West and William Morgan, and Deputy Prime Minister Faulkner, opposed him.[98] All would subsequently make their names as unionist diehards: Faulkner as the last prime minister under the Stormont regime; West[e] as the intransigent opponent of power-sharing in 1974; Taylor as a key hardliner, future deputy leader, and, as Lord Kilclooney a diehard provincial newspaper magnate; Boal and McQuade became leading lights in the DUP; and Ardill the first deputy leader of William Craig's Vanguard Party.[99] In the spring of 1967 O'Neill sacked agriculture minister West, ostensibly over a conflict of interest, while the RUC uncovered a loyalist plot to kill the prime minister.[100] It was not, however, until the creation of the NICRA and the start of Catholic mass protests that O'Neill came under prolonged fire within the Protestant community.

The platform of NICRA consisted of those grievances that O'Neill had neglected to touch: universal suffrage at the local-government level ("one man, one vote"), anti-discrimination legislation covering public employment, the allocation of subsidized housing according to need, the repeal of the Special Powers Act, and the disbanding of the USC—the Specials. The minority had begun to appeal to the metropole for their rights as British citizens. This appeal to the central government copied the tactics of blacks in the Deep South of the USA. A neglected pioneer of the idea of a civil-rights campaign was the Liverpool communist intellectual of Ulster Protestant roots, C. Desmond Greaves (1913–88), the biographer of James Connolly and Liam Mellows. In the 1950s he "advanced the view that the way to a peaceful solution of the Irish problem was to discredit Ulster Unionism in Britain through exposing the discriminatory practices which occurred under the Stormont regime, in the process winning sympathetic allies for the cause of Irish reunification."[101f] The Connolly Association of Great Britain adopted this perspective in 1955, and campaigned to influence trade-union and labor-movement opinion, organizing the first Irish civil-rights marches in England—the longest being from Liverpool to London in 1962. It influenced the National Council for Civil Liberties, the Movement for Colonial Freedom, and the Labour Party's Campaign for Democracy in Ulster. As his obituarist argues: "Though his work was in Britain, there is a good case for regarding Desmond Greaves as the intellectual progenitor of the civil rights movement of the 1960s."[102] He proposed the idea for a civil-rights conference in Belfast in 1965, in which republicans and labor activists first engaged one another.[103]

---

[98] Harkness (1983: 148). It seems Boal came within one vote of having a majority of UUP backbenchers willing to ask O'Neill for his resignation (Gailey 1995: 115).

[99] Having made or finished their careers, Faulkner, West, and Ardill were subsequently to travel to Damascus. As they aged, they became moderates by experience, either implementing or recommending power-sharing.

[100] Moloney and Pollak (1986: 150).   [101] Coughlan (1990: 7).   [102] Coughlan (1990: 8).

[103] An equally good case can be made that "Ultach" first saw the political potential of a civil-rights movement to undermine the UUP's dominance (Ultach 1940, 1943).

Though the civil-rights movement began with communist and republican participants' engagements, there was an extensive range of opinion within it; it was no mere republican or communist front.[104] Irish nationalism remained important among Catholics in the 1960s, and reductionist economic or deprivation explanations of their attitudes and behavior will not do. Notably, in June 1968 it was the young Austin Currie, a Nationalist MP at Stormont, who instigated a civil-disobedience protest about housing discrimination. He squatted in a house in Caledon that had been allocated by Dungannon Rural District Council to a 19-year-old unmarried Protestant woman, the secretary of a local Unionist politician, ahead of numerous large families, including Catholic families. The protesters were evicted by RUC officers, who included one of the young woman's brothers. The annual conference of the Nationalist Party unanimously approved Currie's action.[g] Those who claim that the civil-rights movement was merely nationalism in tactical guise[105] fail to explain why discrimination motivated people to protest, and they downplay the potential support that existed among the minority to live within a reformed Union (while nevertheless hoping for eventual Irish unification).

Asked in 1968 if they approved or disapproved of the Northern Ireland constitution, admittedly an imperfect and complex question, almost as many Catholics approved as disapproved (33 percent as against 34 percent).[106] A *Belfast Telegraph* poll in 1967 showed that 70 percent of the minority supported the continuation of the link with Great Britain in one form or another, and that only 30 percent wanted an independent united Ireland.[107] In 1969 the Cameron Commission reported that nationalism among Catholics was less important than it had been.[108] Rose's "Loyalty Survey" suggested that 30 percent of Catholic respondents would approve "if nationalists agreed to stop debating partition and accepted the present border as final."[109] While the nonviolence of the civil-rights movement may have been partly driven by tactical considerations, this approach was not being used by all, or indeed by most, to win a united Ireland— though many approved of that as a long-term goal.[h] A peaceful civil-rights movement was supported because it set exemplary standards for future coexistence; it would avoid injuries and death; it would give less excuse to the Belfast government to repress its critics; and it would oblige the majority to listen—in the North, and perhaps in London.[110] It was the violent response to the civil-rights movement that led many Catholics to return to a less complicated nationalism, or to arms.

The civil-rights platform had a different appeal to the Labour government. It was not being asked to downsize the UK, or push unionists into a united Ireland. Redressing minority grievances seemed to entail few costs: the full application of non-sectarian British practices, against the allies of the Tories. However, the civil-rights campaign posed novel problems for the governing UUP, opening up splits

---

[104] Purdie (1988, 1990); Ó Dochartaigh (1997).

[105] Hewitt (1981); Tom Wilson (1989: 153–5).

[106] Richard Rose (1971: 435). Officially Northern Ireland had no "constitution," so the interpretation of this question was not straightforward, and may account for the divided Catholic responses.

[107] Whyte (1990: 77).   [108] de Paor (1971: 171–87).   [109] Richard Rose (1971: 483).

[110] Wright (1987: 165–6).

between reformers and hardliners. Stormont had previously managed armed subversion, by superior force, and a panoply of repressive surveillance and legislation. Such measures were too blunt in the new circumstances, especially given the region's lack of independence and the development of novel national and international broadcasting media in the 1960s, notably television. Independent control regimes, with autarkic economies, could treat nonviolent protest indistinguishably from violent protest, as South Africa did in 1960 and 1976, but Stormont, like the state governments in the southern USA in the 1950s, was more constrained—though many RUC officers and B Specials evidently had not received any advisory memoranda on public-relations management from their superiors.

The first major civil-rights march took place in western Northern Ireland from Coalisland to Dungannon on August 24, 1968.[111] Its success prompted the NICRA to organize another in Derry on October 5, an idea that provoked atavistic outrage among Protestants. Control of sacred territory was being challenged. Unionist opposition now spilled onto the streets. William Craig, the Minister of Home Affairs, happily capitulated to Orange pressure by ordering the civil-rights marchers to keep within traditionally nationalist areas. This attempt to reassert territorial control, effectively dubbing the march as sectarian, escalated tensions, and, when the marchers refused to be cowed, the Protestant-dominated RUC ran amok. The televised scenes were conveyed around the world, and the marks of a political slum within the UK's backyard was brought back to London by an injured delegation of visiting Westminster MPs who had joined the march.[i]

Within weeks, O'Neill announced reforms at Wilson's prompting. In November 1968, he promised the impartial allocation of public housing; the appointment of an Ombudsman to investigate minority grievances; the replacement of the Londonderry Corporation by a Development Commission; the reform and reorganization of the local-government system; the repeal of all or parts of the Special Powers Act; and he pledged that all these reforms would be implemented by 1971. This package antagonized many unionists but did not go far enough for many Catholics. On the unionist right, Craig, who resembled the advocates of states' rights over security in the USA in the 1950s and 1960s,[112] was fired in December after attacking the package. Meanwhile Paisley, using the slogan "O'Neill must go!," stepped up his extraparliamentary campaign. Left-wing radicals, by contrast, were exhilarated by the successes of the NICRA marches, and wanted to press further. The student-based People's Democracy (PD) organized a new march from Belfast to Derry in January 1969, which one of its leaders, Michael Farrell, modeled on the US civil-rights march from Selma to Montgomery (which had exposed the racist bigotry of the Deep South).[113] Its route provided an opportunity for loyalist extremists, including some in the security forces, to ambush the marchers, which they eventually did in large numbers at Burntollet bridge.[114]

[111] de Paor (1971: 170–87).
[112] Bloomfield (2007: 170) mistakenly treats Craig as resembling Southern politicians before the US Civil War—the comparison with contemporaneous Southern Democrats in the 1960s is much more appropriate.
[113] Michael Farrell (1980 248–9).
[114] In their pamphlet *Burntollet* Bowes Egan and Vincent McCormick identified over 250 of the 300 attackers of the march, estimating that nearly 100 had served as B Specials.

Table 2.5.2. The Stormont parliamentary election, February 1969

Party/movement	Votes	% poll	Seats
Ulster Unionist Party (pro-O'Neill)	245,925	44.0	27
Ulster Unionist Party (anti-O'Neill)	95,696	17.1	12
Independent/Protestant Unionists	34,923	6.3	0
Northern Ireland Labour Party	45,113	8.1	2
Republican Labour	13,155	2.4	2
Nationalists/National Democrats	68,324	12.2	6
Civil-rights Independents and People's Democracy	45,622	8.1	3

Notes: (i) The turnout was 71%. (ii) 7 of the 52 seats were uncontested (5 UUP, 2 Nationalist). (iii) The UUP vote was split both between pro- and anti-O'Neill candidates *and* official and unofficial candidates.

Source: Flackes and Elliott (1989: 304–10).

O'Neill reacted by condemning the marchers and threatening the further use of the B Specials, thereby alienating Catholics.[115] A few days later he set up a commission of inquiry, thereby infuriating Protestants and prompting the resignation of two leading ministers, supported by twelve backbenchers. O'Neill's response to his party's palpable disunity was to dissolve parliament and call a general election for February 24, 1969.

The election was not the comprehensive success for which he had hoped, even though the UUP's share of the vote—if we combine the tally of its official and unofficial candidates—was over 61 percent. Official and pro-O'Neill Unionists gathered 44 percent of the vote, but of the thirty-nine elected UUP MPs (thirty-six official and three unofficial), twelve were opposed to O'Neill, including his foremost critics, Craig and Faulkner (see Table 2.5.2). Anti-O'Neill candidates performed best in Fermanagh and Tyrone, and in working-class constituencies in Belfast.[116] The UUP had split, and so had its supporters, but the reforming faction was neither solid nor comfortable. O'Neill was nearly humiliated in his own Bannside constituency, narrowly defeating Paisley (Farrell had stood for the People's Democracy, ensuring that O'Neill won few tactical Catholic votes, if any). O'Neill would resign within two months. The fragmentation of the Catholic vote across parties and candidates was even more extensive than that among Protestants. It permanently weakened the Nationalist Party, already challenged by the National Democrats. Radicalized by the civil-rights movement and by Burntollet, Catholic voters elected three civil-rights leaders, John Hume, Ivan Cooper, and Paddy O'Hanlon,[117] each of whom replaced incumbent Nationalist MPs who had not encouraged demonstrations. The leading Nationalist who had been the major civil-rights activist, Austin Currie, was returned with an enhanced vote. Catholics also voted in considerable numbers for the semi-Trotskyist positions articulated by the People's Democracy—though not for reasons that Lev

---

[115] Bloomfield (2007: 173) honestly recalls the resentment of O'Neill's close advisors and intimates at the PD's "irresponsible initiative," and regrets that they did not properly express contempt for the "loyalist thugs who had assaulted this smaller number of young people."

[116] Lee (1989: 425).

[117] The latter's deathbed memoir is among the best from the SDLP cadre of 1960s leaders (O'Hanlon 2011).

Davidovich Bronstein would have approved. Just over a year later, the Social Democratic and Labour Party (SDLP) of Northern Ireland would be formed from these fragments. It merged the independent civil-rights MPs, the Nationalist MPs, Paddy Devlin from the NILP, and Gerry Fitt from Republican Labour; and absorbed the active supporters of the Nationalist, National Democratic, and Republican Labour parties. The SDLP presented itself as a left-of-center party, which favored civil rights for all, a just distribution of wealth, and pledged itself to work for Irish unity by consent.[118] The NILP vote shrank dramatically in the February 1969 election; though it drew support from both Protestant and Catholic districts, it did best in the predominantly Catholic Falls, where Paddy Devlin won his seat. Further civil-rights demonstrations and the bombing of the Silent Valley reservoir, which was blamed on the IRA but later found to be the work of the UVF, prompted O'Neill's resignation on April 28, 1969. The UUP's MPs replaced him by his distant cousin Sir James Chichester-Clark (1923–2002): he defeated Faulkner by one vote, O'Neill's. As he later recalled, he voted for the man who had recently brought him down rather than the one who had been trying to bring him down for years.[119]

Ten days before O'Neill's resignation, a by-election for the Westminster parliament was held in mid-Ulster. Bernadette Devlin, aged 21, was returned as a Unity candidate, then the youngest woman ever elected to that august body.[j] All nationalists and civil-rights groups withdrew in her favor. The previous February, as a People's Democracy candidate, the young student had lost to the new prime minister in the safe unionist seat of South Londonderry. The contrast between the newly elected female radical and the new elderly prime minister could not have been greater. The Unionist major had served and been wounded in the Second World War, and was a direct descendant of Arthur Chichester, the founding settler colonialist, and of the Churchill and Peel families—as well as generations of Irish MPs and Lords. Bernadette Devlin, a working-class baby-boomer and grammar-school girl, was a final year undergraduate in Psychology at Queen's Belfast, who described her entry into Westminster as "the arrival of a peasant in the halls of the great." In an electrifying maiden speech, she foresaw the abolition of Stormont; Stratton Mills, a Unionist MP, sourly called her a mini-skirted Castro.[120]

Polarization was proceeding apace, and the leadership transition within the UUP did not stop the expression of minority discontent or loyalist attacks on civil-rights marches. During the summer of 1969, the RUC's protection of Orange marches sharply contrasted with the regime's earlier willingness to ban civil-rights marches. Escalating tensions culminated in Derry on August 12–14, with violent clashes between Catholics and the police, both the RUC and B Specials. The violence in Derry was replicated in Belfast, after activists in Derry—including

---

[118] For accounts of the party, see McAllister (1977); Gerard Murray (1998); Farren (2010).

[119] According to David Bleakley, William Morrison May ("Morris May") had been the UUP MP most likely to succeed Brookeborough; it was his early death in 1962 that triggered the rivalry between O'Neill and Faulkner, Bleakley 1974 63ff.

[120] Her autobiography is among the best of the 1968 student generation (Devlin 1969). Her memoirs, if she composes any, will be important. In 1981, along with her husband, she was the victim of a UFF assassination attempt.

Bernadette Devlin—called for Belfast to rise in support. Efforts to do just that were effectively pre-empted when loyalist mobs (and the police) attacked Catholic areas of Belfast. The police and the Specials killed six people on August 14. The British Army was deployed to both cities. The key instruments of Unionist control, the local security forces, had been thoroughly discredited in the British and international media. The RUC and the B Specials had been shown to permit—and indeed to participate in—attacks against civil-rights demonstrations. Some leaders of the civil-rights, nationalist, and Catholic organizations had risked these developments consciously—they sought to expose the "violence in the system," and the system had not disappointed. Reformers did so to encourage the British government to dismantle the UUP's control, revolutionaries to precipitate a more thoroughgoing crisis for either republican or socialist purposes, or both. No leaders however, proved able to control the consequences of the breakdown of control.

2.6

British Intervention

The Politics of Embarrassment, 1969–1972

The introduction of the Payment for Debt Act in 1971, ostensibly to break the rent and rates strike which followed the introduction of internment without trial, allowed the state to withdraw every single penny to which these people were entitled. When I complained that this was hitting women very severely I was told (by another faceless man) that I could advise them "to withdraw their conjugal rights from their husbands."

Inez McCormack, 1988[1]

When democracy is found wanting, it must be challenged, so at that point I got up and replied that the Home Secretary was "lying through his teeth." This caused uproar...

Bernadette Devlin, 1988[2]

Why did Westminster, Whitehall, and the parties of government in London listen to the civil-rights protests that emerged in 1967–8, and eventually intervene, between 1968 and 1972? After all, they had turned a blind eye in the 1920s, 1930s, the late 1940s, and the mid-1950s, when Catholic discontent or nationalist mobilization was effectively crushed, either when pogroms occurred, or when civil-service memoranda reported extensive discrimination and institutionalized bigotry. In his almost instant memoir, James Callaghan recalled: "The advice that came to me from all sides was on no account to get sucked into the Irish bog."[3] Roland Moyle, later minister of state at the Northern Ireland Office (1974–6), had accompanied Callaghan during the British intervention of 1969. He remembered

Up until then, the official doctrine, that's still in being today, was that Ireland's a pretty ghastly place for any British politician to be involved in and that because of Lloyd George's settlement in the 1920s it had been got out of British politics at Westminster

---

[1] McCormack (1988: 30). McCormack (1943–2013) was a feminist and trade-unionist activist, sponsor of the MacBride principles, and a Protestant social worker in West Belfast between 1970 and 1975. She championed the equality provisions in the Good Friday Agreement.

[2] Devlin (1988: 85).

[3] Callaghan (1973: 14). Callaghan held all four major UK offices that affect Northern Ireland: Chancellor (1964–7), Home Secretary (1967–70), Foreign Secretary (1974–6), and Prime Minister (1976–9).

and the more it stayed that way the happier everybody would be . . . that's paraphrasing, but it's not inaccurate.[4]

So, what had changed? Westminster and Whitehall were being explicitly addressed, as Ultach and Desmond Greaves had originally but separately suggested. Until the 1960s, the Catholic minority had articulated its grievances either through (but mostly at) the Irish government, or, to a lesser extent, at the Irish diaspora in Great Britain or America. They had expected or hoped that change would come from outside Northern Ireland rather than within the UK. The decision to address the metropolitan center in the 1960s implied some willingness to work within the Union, and accordingly made it more difficult for them to be ignored. In particular, the Labour cabinets of the 1960s reacted positively to being told that backwoods Ulster Protestants were the problem not the British government.

Contingent developments had forced open Westminster's ears and eyes. Complacency was no longer possible, because, as in the Deep South of the USA, national and global television made the brutal exercise of control over a local minority embarrassingly visible. Regimes whose international self-presentation in the cold war suggested that they were the homesteads of Western liberalism and human rights were visually confronted with their own squalid backyards. The British–Irish *rapprochement* that had occurred during Lemass's premiership made it difficult to ignore the appeal of the Republic that something be done to protect the minority. Jack Lynch, the Republic's new Taoiseach since Lemass's retirement,[a] made a crucial speech on August 13, 1969, in which he was heard to say that "we would not stand idly by." He had in fact said that "the Irish government can *no* longer stand by and see innocent people injured." Chichester-Clark attacked him for his "inflammatory" broadcast, though Lynch's immediate prime concern had been to provide reassurances to northern nationalists, and to manage the divisions within his own party (interventionists versus more cautiously inclined ministers). He had not been deliberately trying to inflame passions—that was not in his nature. Lynch called for the eventual ending of the partition of Ireland (the standard position of his party since its foundation and that of Ireland's constitution), announced the movement of troops and field hospitals to the border, and asked the British government to request that a UN peacekeeping force be sent to Northern Ireland. British troops went into Derry's Bogside the following day.

THE OPENING OF BRITISH MINDS

The British authorities had few alternatives to direct intervention. The UUP's instruments could no longer maintain stability. The RUC's 3,000 full-time officers were exhausted by the August riots (some said from strenuous participation). Fully calling out the Specials seemed a recipe for a chaotic bloodbath. Looking back, the Scarman Report of 1972 maintained that,

[4] Interview with the author, January 3, 1991.

when sectarian disturbances erupted in [August] 1969, the only effective instrument of control available to the Northern Ireland government was the RUC. If they called out the USC [the Specials], they ran the risk of deepening the conflict: if they called for the aid of the Army, they had to submit to the operational control of Whitehall. We are satisfied that these difficulties were present in the minds of the Minister for Home Affairs (NI) and his police advisers and influenced their decisions in July and August.[5]

Unlike the Deep South of the USA, there were no federal or metropolitan institutions within Northern Ireland, aside from army garrisons, that could be used to bypass local intransigence. Northern Ireland did not have a bill of rights policed by UK courts, and Catholics therefore had no possibility of pursuing a "march and litigation strategy."[6] The powers through which Great Britain could legislate for Northern Ireland were not publicly considered. Nevertheless, the decision to send troops was taken reluctantly.[7]

Pressure had been put on O'Neill's government to make reforms precisely to prevent this step. His successors had been informed that they should exhaust their own resources before calling on the British government, a decision that gave the local Ministry of Home Affairs a *carte blanche* to authorize the use of CS gas and to deploy the B Specials, with the explosive consequences that followed in the street battles of August 1969 in Derry and Belfast. Chichester-Clark requested that British troops be sent to Derry after Lynch's speech. Having foreseen this request, Wilson and James Callaghan, the UK Home Secretary, obliged. Unionists interpreted Lynch's speech as an invasion threat; Chichester-Clark called for troops to be sent to Northern Ireland's potentially most vulnerable invasion point. Among other reasons, London agreed to the request to pre-empt any possible Irish incursion, and to avoid the internationalization of the subject.

THE PRECIPITANTS OF INTERVENTION

The immediate sequence of events that precipitated the intervention of British troops flowed from the decision of Robert Porter, the Northern Ireland Minister of Home Affairs, to permit a traditional Apprentice Boys parade to go ahead in Derry on August 12, despite extensive warnings that trouble would ensue (Callaghan too was culpable: he had brushed off requests by Westminster MPs to intervene to stop the march). In the afternoon of the 12th the 15,000 strong parade was subjected to stoning attacks by Derry Catholic youth. Unsuccessful efforts were made to restore tranquility by Eddie McAteer, John Hume MP, Robin Chichester-Clark MP (brother of James), and Ivan Cooper MP—the latter was knocked unconscious by a brick. A barricade was then erected by the Catholic crowd. The police eventually baton-charged the crowd, and entered the Bogside, where they were attacked by petrol bombs and stones. At midnight, the minister authorized using CS gas to disperse the rioters, which led to the spectacle of the RUC making its way into the Bogside followed by a Protestant crowd stoning

---

[5] Scarman (1972: 1.11).   [6] Wright (1987: 97); Richard Rose (1976).
[7] Harold Wilson (1971: 871–2).

Catholic homes, and throwing missiles at the Bogsiders over the heads of the police. The following day the minister announced a ban on all parades, and troops were moved to the naval base in Derry—as a precautionary measure. Hume managed to broker a temporary truce—CS gas attacks would halt, and barricades would be left alone if the rioters withdrew—but by the evening the rioting had resumed. Riots and inter-communal attacks were occurring in many urban centers in the North—Belfast, Dungannon, Dungiven, Lurgan, and Newry. Prime Minister Chichester-Clark broadcast the immediate recall of Stormont, and announced: "We will also use the Special Constabulary to the full, not for riot or crowd control but to relieve the regular police." How that would be accomplished remained uncertain—and it sounded like a threat. Later the same evening, Lynch made his famous speech, which Chichester-Clark immediately condemned. The following day at Stormont Chichester-Clark declared: "We must, and we will treat the Government which seeks to wound us in our darkest hour as an unfriendly and implacable government, determined to overthrow by any means the state which enjoys the support of a majority of our electorate."

Meanwhile, in Derry, Bernadette Devlin had been seen breaking up stones for the use of those who wanted them, hoisting the Starry Plough, the flag of the Connolly Association, on the roof of flats overlooking riotous scenes, and heard demanding that Harold Wilson convene a constitutional conference finally to settle the Irish question. Some 8,500 Specials were called out as the RUC appeared exhausted in Derry and Belfast. These were the circumstances in which the request was issued for British troops (perhaps the request was sought). On August 15, the UK's junior foreign office minister, Lord Chalfont, told the Irish foreign minister, Dr Patrick Hillery, that neither a UN force nor a joint British–Irish force would be used to restore and maintain order. Within a week of the deployment of British troops, a seven-point Downing Street Declaration was issued by Wilson and Chichester-Clark. Its first point declared that "the border is not an issue," and that Northern Ireland affairs were exclusively the UK's jurisdiction—a blunt riposte to Lynch's government, intended to calm unionists, but probably delivered from some conviction on Callaghan's part, if not Wilson's. The declaration renewed pledges of reform, and committed both premiers to "full equality of treatment for all citizens," and in Northern Ireland "to the same equality of treatment and freedom from discrimination as obtains in the rest of the United Kingdom irrespective of political view or religion."[8] The troop deployment was to be temporary.

After August 1969, Callaghan was determined to keep British involvement to a minimum, and to withdraw quickly, an approach that ruled out the strategic option of abolishing Stormont, demanded by many nationalists, or fully integrating Northern Ireland into the rest of the UK—which would have caused difficulties with Ireland, with many Catholics, and annoyed pro-nationalists inside the Labour Party. More fundamentally, integration would have involved permanent embroilment, a commitment British officials had studiously resisted since 1921. The UK Home Office counseled Callaghan that taking over the government of Northern Ireland should be the "last thing" he should want.[9] The Labour

---

[8] Joint Declaration, Downing Street, August 19, 1969.   [9] Callaghan (1973: 22).

government was even unwilling to establish a Whitehall ministry to monitor Stormont.[10] Given the problems involved in foisting a united Ireland on the union- ists, and that Wilson's communiqué had declared that "the border is not an issue,"[11] London's options were narrowed to working for reform and promoting accommo- dation. British policymakers still judged that the UUP could be cajoled into making enough concessions to conciliate the minority while retaining its political base. "As no alternative instrument of government existed, it seemed to me better to win the agreement of the Ulster Unionists to what was necessary than to use the power of parliament to dismiss them."[12] The dramatic failure of this policy first publicly articulated by Callaghan led to the imposition of direct rule in 1972.

WAS NORTHERN IRELAND REFORMABLE?

Reforms were passed between August 1969 and June 1971. They apparently conceded the merits of the entire package of demands of the civil-rights move- ment. Professional public administration was to replace clientelism in local government. The local-government system would be reformed: its franchise would be based on "one person one vote."[b] Commissions of inquiry reported unfavorably on Stormont rule.[13] The most important prospective reforms in- cluded the disarming of the RUC,[14] the disbanding of the B Specials, and their replacement by a locally recruited force, the Ulster Defence Regiment, under the command of the British Army's GOC (NI), the creation of an independent Police Authority, and the establishment of a housing executive in late 1969—to take over the housing functions of the local authorities—and a Commissioner for Complaints in November 1969—to deal with complaints of discrimination by local authorities— the local counterpart of the Parliamentary Ombudsman, created in June. Reforms to the public prosecutions system took longer but were implemented by 1972, with the appointment of a Director of Public Prosecutions independent of the police force. Legislation making incitement to religious hatred a criminal offense was passed in July 1970, and a Ministry of Community Relations was created along with a Community Relations Commission. Local-government reforms accepted in December 1970 included not just full universal suffrage, but the creation of an independent commissioner to draw up electoral boundaries. Lastly, in June 1971, Faulkner, after he had succeeded Chichester-Clark, announced the establishment of three parliamentary committees, to be appointed proportionally from all parties represented in Stormont, to review government policy in social, environ- mental, and industrial services.

British intervention and the force-feeding of reforms sent shock waves through the UUP while failing to satisfy Catholics. Traditional distrust of English perfidy,

---

[10] Callaghan (1973: 66).   [11] Harold Wilson (1971: 875).   [12] Callaghan (1973: 24).
[13] Cameron (1969); Hunt (1969).
[14] One unsourced story, perhaps apocryphal, from McGuffin (1973: 84) reports that English police asked the RUC for files on all the terrorists in September 1970. Having been handed the records, mostly out of date, on the IRA, they asked "What about the UVF?" The reply was it did not exist, and they did not have records on loyalists.

which had persuaded unionists to regard devolution as a bulwark of the Union, was exacerbated by the known sympathies of Wilson for a united Ireland. The disbanding of the B Specials announced in the Hunt Report enraged working-class loyalist Protestants, provoking serious riots on the Shankill Road in October 1969.[c] On the 2nd of that month Paisley presented a petition to Chichester-Clark, signed by nearly 100,000 loyalists, expressing total opposition to the prospective disarming of the Specials. On the 10th, Chichester Clark announced the resignation and replacement of the head of the RUC, and on the same day the Hunt Report was published, and accepted. It proposed the replacement of the Specials by a smaller part-time force under the army, and a separate police reserve. On the following day, as the partial disarming of the RUC began, a massive confrontation occurred between loyalist crowds and the army and the police on the Shankill. During the evening riot an RUC constable Arbuckle was killed by a gun used by a UVF man, among other loyalist snipers operating that night. The army returned fire under orders, and two Protestant civilians were killed, George Dickie and Herbert Hawe, who were cousins: the first was judged to have been intoxicated at an inquest; the army's and civilian witness accounts gave conflicting accounts of the second man's actions before he was shot. The army's search of the Shankill on the following morning took away guns, petrol bombs, and offensive weapons. Crowds waved Union Jacks at the soldiers, and told Englishmen to go home. Over thirty people had been injured by gunshots, including fourteen soldiers, three police, and twenty civilians.[15] The crowds had shouted for the return of their Specials, and protests reverberated across the region.

The following week Thomas McDowell, 45, from Kilkeel, Co. Down, a member of Paisley's Free Presbyterian Church and a quarry foreman with ten children, was found badly injured from a bomb he had attempted to place at a power station in Ballyshannon, across the border in Co. Donegal. He died the following day.[16] He was a member of both the UVF and the Ulster Protestant Volunteers, and had been among those responsible for the UVF's infrastructural bombings that had ended O'Neill's premiership—because they were blamed on the IRA.[17] In the same month, Craig had declared that "Ulster stands at the brink of civil war," and had followed that warning by suggesting the federalization of the UK.[18] The Labour Secretary of State for Defence, Denis Healey, agreed with the first of Craig's statements; announcing the need to rotate troops to the BBC, he declared: "We are preventing a civil war."[19]

Loyalist rage and insecurity were intensely reinforced by the subsequent formation of the Provisional IRA and its ability to go on the offensive after the summer of 1970. The likelihood of unionist moderates being outflanked and displaced by hardliners also became apparent with electoral victories by loyalists in two Stormont by-elections in April 1970, and in the June 1970 Westminster general elections. In the latter contests, for the first time since the formation of Northern Ireland, the UUP won just eight of the twelve seats. Paisley won North Antrim, Devlin and Frank Maguire (Unity) won mid-Ulster and Fermanagh and South Tyrone respectively, and Fitt (Republican Labour) won West Belfast.

---

[15] The preceding account relies on Deutsch and Magowan (1973: 46–8) and McKittrick et al. (2004: 42–3).

[16] Boulton (1973: 94 ff.).   [17] McKittrick et al. (2004: 43–4).

[18] Deutsch and Magowan (1973: 49, 50).   [19] Deutsch and Magowan (1973: 50).

After Paisley's 1970 by-election victory, Chichester-Clark was replaced as vice-chairman of his own UUP branch at Castledawson by a local bus driver. Having helped depose the captain, Paisley demanded that the major should go. Pressured from the right, and deprived of some of its moderates when the bi-confessional Alliance Party of Northern Ireland (APNI) was formed in 1970, the UUP government called for spectacular security measures to control violence emanating from republicans and others. Much of Chichester-Clark's remaining premiership was spent trying to eliminate "no-go" areas, and pressurizing the army to implement security policies over which he had now lost control.

For many Catholics, the promised institutional reforms had little immediate effect upon their daily experience or life chances, and consequently did not arouse their enthusiasm. They were seen as "too little, too late." The replacement of the B Specials by another locally recruited force with the partisan title of the Ulster Defence Regiment seemed cosmetic—and unionist politicians proved adept in enabling ex-B men to pass into the UDR.[d] The disarming of the RUC did not last a year, and its rearmament was justified by the strength of IRA action. From a Protestant perspective, everything was changing on the security front, for the worse, but, from a Catholic perspective everything was staying the same—or getting worse. The proposed democratization of local government was rendered superfluous by the radical restructuring that transferred most of its powers to appointed boards and to Stormont, where the UUP still enjoyed a monopoly of power. Unemployment remained high, while the prospects for improvement in housing allocations were seriously set back by the need to rehouse the families forced out of their neighborhoods in the summer of 1969—a process that continued until 1971.[20] Simply put, what may have satisfied Catholics in 1967–8, or earlier, was no longer enough. Their expectations had been raised by British intervention; moderates wanted an end to the majority's exclusive control of the Stormont system; while republican radicals, including the militants of the Provisional IRA, wanted a united Ireland, and many saw the abolition of Stormont as the first step on that path.

THE RETURN OF THE TORIES AND OF INTERNMENT

In June 1970, a Conservative government was elected in London after Wilson had called a snap general election that he had been expected to win. Unionists celebrated the return of their traditional allies.[21] The new prime minister, Edward Heath, chose to support centrists in the UUP, opting to balance reform with repression. The Conservatives initially confirmed nationalist stereotypes.[22] The

---

[20] The Scarman Report identified more than 1,500 Catholic families and over 300 Protestant families whose houses were burned or who were intimidated into leaving their homes between July and September 1969 (Scarman 1972: 9–11).

[21] *Sunday Times* Insight Team (1972: 205 ff.).

[22] Key Conservative leaders were, however, embarrassed by their UUP cousins (Jeremy Smith 2006). In August 1972 Heath wrote to the chairman of his party that "I do not believe that we can continue to maintain an alliance with a sectarian party based on and largely controlled by the Orange lodges" (Patterson 2008: 495).

long record of Tory sympathy with the UUP, and the surviving formal links between the two parties, were not forgotten. A British Army curfew throughout the Falls Road in June 1970 is widely seen as a turning point in relations between the army and Catholics, persuading nationalists that the army had returned to its traditional partiality.[e] Four men died during the curfew, three shot by soldiers' bullets, one a freelance journalist from London, of Polish extraction, and one knocked over by a military vehicle, deliberately according to the Central Citizens' Defence Committee.[23] The curfew was followed by further hardline measures, including new emergency legislation, and a threat in early 1971 that the army would shoot petrol-bombers. Home Secretary Reginald Maudling declared in July 1971 what republicans were already insisting was true: the British Army's function was to "maintain the constitution of Northern Ireland."[24] That constitution currently meant Northern Ireland's place in the Union, and upholding its parliament. He also carelessly suggested his ambitions were confined to producing an "acceptable" level of violence. Former British ministers who had served in the Northern Ireland Office whom I interviewed in 1990-1 were united in indicting Maudling's tenure of office as disastrous.[25] "At the end of [1971] . . . Maudling, as he wrote in his *Memoirs*, was profoundly pessimistic," wrote William Whitelaw in his memoirs. With un-selfconscious racism Whitelaw added: "Of course, with his clear and logical brain, Reggie Maudling found the Irish mentality almost impossible to understand."[26]

Faced with the Provisionals' campaign to bring down Stormont and terminate the British state's presence in Ireland, Faulkner demanded that London let him use the tried and trusted mode of repression, internment without trial. He promised his Conservative counterpart that reforms would continue provided republican insurrection was repressed, arguing that without internment he could not command sufficient support to continue.[f] Heath granted this request, which was implemented on August 9, 1971, while he went yacht-racing.[g] Internment proved a political and security catastrophe.[27] It unified most Catholics in opposition, prompted civil and armed disobedience, brought what the counterinsurgency specialists would call international propaganda gains for the Provisional IRA, or extensive international embarrassment for the British. In sum, it proved the catalyst for a quantum leap in the scale of violence, as acknowledged at the time.[28] Among the reasons internment backfired were that the army had (unintentionally) signaled its intentions; the wrong people were arrested—suggesting poor intelligence;[29] only alleged republicans were arrested, and no loyalists;[h] and some internees were tortured—or experienced excessive ill-treatment, as some

---

[23] The accidental entrapment of an Italian film crew revealed the character of the curfew.

[24] Cited in de Paor (1971: p. xvii).

[25] Merlyn Rees referred to Maudling's tenure as "the moldering years" (interview with the author, December 18, 1990).

[26] Whitelaw (1989: 78).

[27] See my disagreement with Paul Wilkinson's *Terrorism and the Liberal State* (1977) on this subject; Wilkinson changed his mind in his second edition (1986), without saying why (Brendan O'Leary 1988).

[28] For a contemporary analysis, see Boyd (1972: 92), and also see Vol. 1, Ch. 1, pp. 75-83.

[29] McGuffin (1973: 87) estimated that no more than half of the 160 men held in the Crumlin Road jail had anything to do with the IRA; the rest were political opponents of the Unionists, from the

jurists managed to describe matters.[30] This torture was more extensive and widespread than any that had occurred in previous internment episodes, 1922–4, 1938–45, and 1956–61.[31]

In the month before internment began the newly formed SDLP had left the Stormont parliament, withdrawing its consent from the institutions of government—because Heath's and Faulkner's governments severally refused to hold an inquiry into two men who had been shot dead during riots in Derry. When the inquiry was refused by Faulkner, Hume declared that the SDLP would withdraw and set up the "Assembly of the Northern Irish People"—what became known as the "Dungiven Parliament." After internment had begun, the SDLP sponsored a civil-disobedience campaign, and in response Catholics withheld rents in public housing estates and the payment of rates to public-sector bodies on a massive scale. All IRA memoirs tell how internment led to a surge in volunteers.[32] Catholic radicalization preceded internment, but had been dramatically enhanced by it. A British rethink began. The UK Cabinet Secretary, Burke Trend, counseled Heath in September that "we should be warned—by Vietnam and Rhodesia, if we have forgotten our own earlier experience in dealing with recalcitrant colonies—against allowing ourselves to be drawn deeper in a situation from where there is no escape other than capitulation at the eleventh hour."[33] No rethinking was immediately evident among unionists. Rather than recognizing the strategic error of repressive counterinsurgency, unionists and loyalists claimed vindication of their fears: unfolding events proved that (all or most) Catholics had been disloyal republicans all along. On October 30, 1971, the *Republican News* reported that the Provisionals' Army Council had announced that the third phase in its operations had begun—namely, all-out resistance against British forces. The Provisionals' campaign would prove robust. Hegemonic control was over. Revolt had become thinkable, internationally public, and in the regime's face. It remained to be seen whether revolt would win, and what winning would look like.

Faulkner had proposed major reform before he took the disastrous step of introducing internment, including a new system of government based on cross-party committees, which envisaged a role for opposition MPs as chairs. He made these proposals at Stormont on the fiftieth anniversary of the opening of Northern Ireland's first parliament. His speech was well received by Fitt, Currie, and Paddy Devlin, and by Vivien Simpson of the NILP. His biographer described it as Faulkner's "finest moment" in the House of Commons.[34] Perhaps because this moment had gone so well, he decided to take the risk of introducing internment. Even though he had spoiled the reception of his plans, and so quickly, Faulkner did not abandon reform. A consultative paper, *The Future Development of the Parliament and Government of Northern Ireland*, was

People's Democracy, the NICRA, old retired ex-internees, trade unionists, public speakers, and "in some cases, people held on mistaken identity."

[30] Sir Edmund Compton (1971).   [31] McGuffin (1973: 21).

[32] See, e.g., Mac Stíofáin (1975: 192); Collins (1998: 41); Feeney (2009: 71–86); and see the interview with Tommy McKearney (Peter Taylor 1997: 100ff.). See also references at Vol 3. Ch. 7, pp. 139–42.

[33] Ó Beacháin (2014: 325).   [34] Bleakley (1974: 91).

published in October 1971. It conceded that critics of permanent majority rule had a point, but required a complex loyalty test—namely, *unreserved* acceptance of *overriding* principles: Northern Ireland's status as an integral part of the UK, in accordance with the Ireland Act of 1949. That left unclear whether a principled nationalist could join a future Belfast government. Did the inelegantly drafted legalese oblige the nationalist to become a unionist, or merely to accept a mechanism through which Irish unity could take place (one dependent upon the aforementioned permanent majority rule)? An independent Catholic, G. B. Newe, not a nationalist, was invited by Faulkner to join the cabinet for the first time. Further proposals were being worked on by Faulkner to consider a bill of rights and intergovernmental relations across the island but were unpublished when he resigned in March 1972. The entire sequencing suggests that Faulkner believed that he needed to offer enhanced minority participation first, then crush militant republicanism to assure his base, before then proceeding to incorporate non-violent Catholics. If that was his strategy, it did not work. Cardinal Conway became the first Catholic bishop in the twentieth century openly and unequivocally to condemn internment without trial.[35] The introduction of internment led Jack Lynch to call for the abolition of Stormont.[i] "The administration of Northern Ireland is now, and has been since it was created, directed at the suppression of the civil and human rights of more than a third of the population ... The Stormont regime, which has consistently repressed the non-Unionist population and bears responsibility for recurring violence, must be brought to an end."[36] He was not alone. The SDLP, the Nationalist Party, and the Republican Labour Party embarked upon civil disobedience to achieve immediate suspension of Northern Ireland's system of government.

The much-demanded magic weapon of internment failed to destroy the Provisionals, and led to a violent escalation that at least doubled most countable indicators of conflict, including death tolls, expulsions, and flight. In consequence, the disintegration of the UUP's cohesion continued. The establishment of no-go areas for the army and the police outraged the party's ultras. Loyalists organized around Paisley and Craig, who embraced radically different last-ditch proposals. Paisley argued that the "only solution to our problems is to have total and full integration with the United Kingdom."[37] His Democratic Unionist Party (DUP) was formed in September 1971. Craig's Vanguard Unionist Progressive Party was not officially formed until March 1973, but his Vanguard movement had begun earlier, and held increasingly large and quasi-militarized rallies throughout the region. Craig openly speculated about the federalization of the UK, leaving Northern Ireland in charge of its own security; dominion status for Northern Ireland; or a unilateral declaration of independence (UDI). Paisley's and Craig's extreme options were tailored solely to appeal to Protestants. Protestant men had joined paramilitary organizations in great numbers during 1970–2 and were engaged in murders of Catholic civilians on a major scale.[38]

---

[35] McGuffin (1973: 179, n. 8).   [36] *Irish Times*, August 13, 1971.
[37] May 5, 1972, at QUB (VanVoris 1975: 45).   [38] See Vol. 1, Ch. 1.

BLOODY SUNDAY AND THE END
OF THE UUP'S ONE-PARTY RULE

The fracturing of the UUP, and unionist opposition to its leaders' reluctant reform policies, the radicalization of the minority, and deteriorating security, increased perplexed uncertainty among British officials. Intense debates took place within the senior ranks of the military and police over the right security policy—hardline, as commended in Belfast by Brigadier Kitson, or softline, as commended by Frank Lagan of the RUC in Derry.[39] Uncertainty and embarrassment became public shame on January 30, 1972, when British paratroopers shot dead thirteen unarmed civilian civil-rights demonstrators who had been marching in Derry in protest against internment—another civilian who had been shot on the same day died later. The demonstration had been banned by the Unionist government, as had most recent marches, but the paratroopers and their military commanders were responsible for what became known as "Bloody Sunday."[40] Patrick Hillery, Ireland's foreign minister, told a press conference in New York that the British were "practicing the arts of war on our people. They have had internment without trial and torture in these camps. And now we are faced with the death sentence for those that protest."[41] Journalist Peter Taylor reported to the second Bloody Sunday inquiry that RUC officers had cheered the paratroopers. The first inquiry, the quickly generated Widgery Report, published in April 1972, accepted the false testimony of soldiers and their officers that they had been fired on by the IRA, and that some of the victims were riotous. This report was correctly regarded by nationalists (and moderate external observers) as an insult to the dead and injured; it remains an exemplary instance of injustice delivered from the highest rank of the British judiciary, in collusion with the executive. Lord Chief Justice Widgery heard his evidence in Coleraine. He refused to sit in Derry for the convenience of the local witnesses. Eddie McAteer memorably observed that "I suppose we are lucky he didn't also find that the thirteen committed suicide."[42]

It would be 1998 before the second Bloody Sunday inquiry was instituted, and, after long, expensive, but careful proceedings, its findings were published in June 2010. After hearing and cross-examining the testimony of some 900 people, and evaluating other documentary sources, Lord Saville and his colleagues pronounced that the dead and the injured were all innocent, and that the soldiers and one of their commanding officers, Colonel Derek Wilford OBE, who had disobeyed orders, were responsible for their deaths (see Box 2.6.1).[43] Soldiers had lied in court. None of the soldiers had fired in response to attacks by petrol-bombers or stone throwers, and none of the dead and injured was posing a threat to the soldiers nominally mandated to secure large numbers of arrests. Nearly forty years after the episode a different Conservative prime minister, David

---

[39] See Ó Dochartaigh (2004).
[40] See, *inter alia*, Government of Ireland (1997); Dermot P. J. Walsh (2000); Ziff (2000); Mullan and Scally (2002); Ó Dochartaigh (2004).
[41] *Irish Times*, February 2, 1972.   [42] *Irish Times*, April 20, 1972.
[43] Nine months after Bloody Sunday, Colonel Wilford had been awarded the OBE (McGuffin 1973: 171, n. 11).

Box 2.6.1. Excerpts from the conclusions to the Bloody Sunday Inquiry

---

The immediate responsibility for the deaths and injuries lies with those members of Support Company whose unjustifiable firing was the cause of those deaths and injuries. [4.1] . . . We have concluded that the explanation for such firing by Support Company soldiers after they had gone into the Bogside was in most cases probably the mistaken belief among them that republican paramilitaries were responding in force to their arrival in the Bogside. This belief was initiated by the first shots fired by Lieutenant N and reinforced by the further shots that followed soon after. In this belief soldiers reacted by losing their self-control and firing themselves, forgetting or ignoring their instructions and training and failing to satisfy themselves that they had identified targets posing a threat of causing death or serious injury. In the case of those soldiers who fired in either the knowledge or belief that no-one in the areas into which they fired was posing a threat of causing death or serious injury, or not caring whether or not anyone there was posing such a threat, it is at least possible that they did so in the indefensible belief that all the civilians they fired at were probably either members of the Provisional or Official IRA or were supporters of one or other of these paramilitary organisations; and so deserved to be shot notwithstanding that they were not armed or posing any threat of causing death or serious injury. Our overall conclusion is that there was a serious and widespread loss of fire discipline among the soldiers of Support Company. The question remains, however, as to whether others also bear direct or indirect responsibility for what happened. [5.4.] [In] our view [Lieutenant] Colonel Wilford should not have sent soldiers of Support Company into the Bogside for the following reasons:

- because in doing so he disobeyed the orders given by Brigadier MacLellan;
- because his soldiers, whose job was to arrest rioters, would have no or virtually no means of identifying those who had been rioting from those who had simply been taking part in the civil rights march; and
- because he should not have sent his soldiers into an unfamiliar area which he and they regarded as a dangerous area, where the soldiers might come under attack from republican paramilitaries, in circumstances where the soldiers' response would run a significant risk that people other than those engaging the soldiers with lethal force would be killed or injured by Army gunfire. [4.24]

There remains the suggestion that Colonel Wilford's soldiers should have been instructed that in order to minimise the risk to innocent people, if on going into the Bogside they came under attack from paramilitaries, or believed that this had happened, they should disengage and withdraw rather than return fire. In our view this is a hypothetical question, since for the first two of the reasons we have given above Colonel Wilford should not have sent soldiers into the Bogside, with or without special instructions [4.25]. In our view the organisers of the civil rights march bear no responsibility for the deaths and injuries on Bloody Sunday. [4.33]

Source: Report of the Bloody Sunday Inquiry (2010), vol. 1, ch, 5, <webarchive.nationalarchives.gov.uk// 20101103103930/http://report.bloody-sunday-inquiry.org/> (accessed August 2012).

Cameron, unequivocally apologized to the victims in the Westminster House of Commons, declaring that it was impossible to defend the indefensible. His words were broadcast in Derry, where a woman standing at its old Guildhall shredded a copy of the Widgery Report, which had covered up the soldiers' initial lies (or reported those that had been designed for them). The Lord Chief Justice of

England's report, written at the behest of Edward Heath, was a shameful cover-up. The ten volumes of the Saville inquiry will convince any skeptical but patient reader that the 1st Battalion of the Parachute Regiment had shot without due cause. Victims were shot in the back, or while crawling away. Martin McGuinness and others in the IRA, while armed that day, engaged in no activity that explained or excused the conduct of the paratroopers.

Bloody Sunday had followed a Civil Rights Association protest a week earlier, which had been mobilized against the then secret internment camp at Magilligan Strand, not far from Derry. The NICRA had demonstrated there, despite the Unionist government's region-wide ban on such marches. The demonstrators had been beaten up by a company of paratroopers on the beach. Rubber bullets had been fired at protestors' heads and bodies, and dozens badly injured, events witnessed by the *Guardian*'s Simon Winchester. Plainly it was deliberately reckless, or policy, to deploy the paratroopers in Derry so soon after this episode. The decision, however, signaled an unresolved debate among senior military and police over how to calm violent and peaceful protest. Winchester was also in attendance on Bloody Sunday. He saw paratroopers firing into the fleeing crowd, and toward him, and he filed his report that night.[44] His shocked contemporaneous—and subsequently vindicated—account stands in stark contrast to the title given to it by the editor or subeditor, "13 Killed as Paratroopers Break Riot," and to the editorial opinion filed in the same issue by John Cole, the paper's deputy editor and subsequently the BBC's chief political correspondent—an Ulster Protestant, unionist, and the former press secretary to Terence O'Neill.[j] Winchester was excluded from the press conference of the Widgery Report, reserved for accredited defense correspondents.[45]

Bloody Sunday detonated the most politically explosive eight weeks in Northern Irish history, punctuated by killings by all agents in the conflict.[46] Political rhetoric was heated on all sides. The day after, the usually temperate John Hume declared on the BBC that the "settlement to problems was a united Ireland or nothing," while Bernadette Devlin physically attacked Maudling in Westminster's House of Commons. Taoiseach Lynch announced a national day of mourning on February 2, and withdrew Ireland's ambassador from London. Harold Wilson, the Leader of the Labour Opposition, declared in the House of Commons that there could be no political solution without a united Ireland—with safeguards for Ulster Protestants—and subsequently went to meet Provisional Sinn Féin and IRA members in Dublin. Interviewed on Ireland's RTÉ, he called for all-party talks with no restricted agenda, and for a radical decision on internment. At Stormont Faulkner warned against hysterical unreason but hysterically insisted that Unionists would not tolerate a united Ireland. Craig floated the idea that the Bogside and the Creggan in Derry should be ceded to the Republic. A very large and peaceful crowd assembled for the funerals of the victims of Bloody Sunday in Derry's Bogside on the 2nd, but a larger crowd gathered in Dublin, and some within its ranks proceeded to burn the British Embassy. The Irish authorities decided not to

---

[44] "13 Killed as Paratroopers Break Riot," *Guardian*, January 31, 1972.
[45] See Winchester (1975).
[46] The following paragraphs build upon Deutsch and Magowan (1974: 152–67).

intervene, and the embassy was burned to the ground. The NICRA demanded an immediate end to internment, the withdrawal of the army from the North, the repeal of the Special Powers Act, an extension of the Race Relations Act, and announced a march in Newry on the 6th, which passed off peacefully. The chairman of the recently established Community Relations Commission, Dr Maurice Hayes, resigned. The Official IRA bombed the Officers' Mess of the Parachute Brigade at Aldershot in England—it killed seven people, five female caterers, a gardener, and one regimental officer, a Catholic priest. Three days later, the Officials attempted to assassinate the junior home affairs minister at Stormont, John Taylor. Six bullets were pumped into him by a submachine gun in Armagh—though one went through his head, he survived. On March 4, the Abercorn restaurant in Belfast, crowded with women and children, was blown up after a completely inadequate warning. Two women died, many more suffered horrendous and permanent injuries, including losses of limbs and eyes, which were the subject of intense moral horror: reliable authorities attribute the bombing to the IRA.[47] On March 10, the Provisionals announced a seventy-two-hour truce, and specified three conditions for its continuation: the withdrawal of British forces; amnesty of all political prisoners; and the abolition of Stormont. The NICRA declared it had collected more than 100,000 signatures on a petition calling for the release of detainees.

Legal turmoil had issued from the High Court on February 23, when Justices Lowry, O'Donnell, and Gibson overturned the convictions of John Hume and Ivan Cooper under the Special Powers Act. The Government of Ireland Act was at last properly applied. It did not allow the Northern government to direct the armed forces of the Crown. The British government at Westminster had to introduce retrospective emergency legislation to render the direction of the army lawful. Subsequently, in Dáil Éireann, Ritchie Ryan, a future Fine Gael Minister of Finance, asked the Taoiseach whether HMS *Maidstone*, the prison ship holding internees, was within Ireland's territorial waters, suggesting that the matter be brought before the International Court of Justice at the Hague. In response, Lynch accepted that it was possible that the ship was within Ireland's jurisdiction, because territorial waters had not been addressed in the Government of Ireland Act, but he argued that attention should be focused on the human-rights torture cases that the Dublin government had placed before the European Commission on Human Rights. Earlier he had argued at his party's annual conference that he would like to see power-sharing in the North before Irish unification, and in a further bid to calm the waters had said that the Irish police had instructions to carry out their duties against the IRA. The Irish government had welcomed the offer of the good offices of the UN Secretary General on February 7, before it was turned down the following day by the British government. The international ramifications of Bloody Sunday were further demonstrated when the Foreign Affairs Committee of the US House of Representatives held hearings on Northern Ireland for three days at the end of the month.

Meanwhile, the Orange Order gathered over 330,000 signatures for a new covenant that pledged to maintain the Union, while Northern (invariably

---

[47] McKittrick et al. (2004: 161 ff.).

Protestant) rugby teams refused to travel south because a one-minute silence was scheduled to be held before the games to honor the dead of Bloody Sunday. Bill Craig addressed increasingly large Vanguard rallies on successive weekends in Lisburn, Coleraine, Ballymena, and Portadown, culminating in a huge event in Belfast. He regularly used blood-curdling language, infamously declaring that "we must build up dossiers of the men and the women who are the enemies of this country because if and when the politicians fail us, it may be our job to liquidate the enemy,"[48] and that "God help those who get in our way, for we mean business." These remarks were taken as cues by loyalist militias that needed little encouragement. Craig subsequently declared that he had the names, photographs, and descriptions of more than 500 IRA men.[49]

Heath's government responded actively to developments, even though it was preoccupied with the passage of what became the European Communities Act. It quietly fixed the Widgery inquiry to exonerate the Parachute Regiment, but accepted the minority verdict of Lord Gardiner in the inquiry led by Justice Parker that had been established to evaluate the techniques used to interrogate detainees. Gardiner, unlike his judicial peers Parker and Boyd-Carpenter, had deemed the methods morally unjustifiable in peace or war: hooding, prolonged forced standing against a wall, deprivation of food and sleep, and subjection to intense noise.[50] Heath declared these methods—long used in Britain's colonial repression of insurgencies—would no longer be used, a decision welcomed by Wilson.[51] Having met the leadership of the new Alliance Party, Heath and his colleagues engaged in intense talks with Faulkner and the senior UUP leadership. Unionist backbenchers spelled out their party's redlines. They would reject any initiative by Heath's government that involved any move toward a united Ireland; any element of direct rule or reduction in the powers of the Northern government or parliament; and "any proposals for community government, government by commission, or proportional representation in the cabinet." In short, "No Surrender" in institutional language. By then, Heath was making it publicly clear that, while the status of Northern Ireland could be changed only by consent, there would have to be meaningful participation by the minority in local decision-making, while his colleague Maudling was reflecting in the Commons on the financial burden that Northern Ireland occasioned to the rest of the UK, a less subtle form of pressure. In mid-March the London cabinet put three proposals to its Belfast counterpart: to hold periodic plebiscites on the border to confirm the principle of consent; to start phasing out internment; and to accept the transfer of security policy and powers to London. The last proposal

---

[48] This quotation is from Boyd (1972: 100); other authors and reporters provide slight variants of Craig's words, delivered at a rally on March 18, 1972.

[49] O'Doherty (2007: 119).

[50] Gardiner's judgments were an indictment of Faulkner, the prime minister who had simultaneously held the portfolio of Home Secretary.

[51] The following week Amnesty International reported that the initial detainees had been subjected to ill-treatment that amounted to brutality, and that the UK authorities had thereby violated the Universal Declaration of Human Rights and the European Convention on Human Rights and Fundamental Freedoms.

was unacceptable to Faulkner's cabinet, which indicated it would resign. Confronted by this defiance, the Conservative leadership of Heath, Maudling, Lord Carrington, and William Whitelaw chose a previously excluded option. The suspension of Stormont and its replacement by direct rule were announced in March 1972.[52] The Westminster government had discovered its inability to influence the Belfast government at sufficient pace and responsiveness without directly invoking section 75 of the Government of Ireland Act, a step British officials had referred to as their "hydrogen bomb."[53]

Back-room efforts at arbitration had failed. Reforms, made under British pressure, had been unconvincingly presented as originating from Stormont in the hope that the 1920–5 settlements could be rescued without fundamental constitutional restructuring. These attempts had failed. Unionists were used to fifty years of autonomy, and loath to cooperate in ending or reforming their own hegemony. Faulkner tellingly protested from the balcony of Stormont to an enormous (and illegal) crowd rallied by Craig's Vanguard movement against the suspension of Northern Ireland's government: Northern Ireland was not, he declared, "a coconut colony."[54] The racism of the remark perhaps needs to be underlined. Coconut colonies in the Pacific warranted Crown colony government, whereas colonies of settlers of British stock did not.[k] Had he been questioned, however, Faulkner would have rejected the idea that Northern Ireland was a colony of any kind—and consequently should never have been subject to any form of colonial government. The cabinet of what was once known as the imperial parliament remained unmoved by these protests.[l] Direct rule was to begin, or, rather, to begin again. This era of government by the descendants of settlers was over, though that was not yet evident to all; whether their dominance was to end was another matter.

CONCLUSION

The evolution and timing of the outbreak of the conflict that can be dated from 1966 or 1969 are underexplained by the internal-conflict paradigm that once dominated research on the subject.[55] Partisan histories by unionists, nationalists, and Marxists are of little help.[56] Fresh efforts are still being made—sometimes by politicians in Ireland hostile to Sinn Féin, sometimes by unionist historians and commentators—to put the entire onus on the IRA for initiating and sustaining the recent violent conflict.[57] Yet plainly both loyalist and police killing in 1966

---

[52] On April 6, 1971, Harold Wilson told the Westminster Commons that his cabinet had drafted a bill to apply direct rule, and it was available to the Heath government. He had previously told his cabinet colleagues that such a bill had been prepared as early as March 1969 (Castle 1984: 708).

[53] Richard Rose (1971: 143).

[54] *Irish Times*, March 28, 1972; see Faulkner and Houston (1978: 157).

[55] Whyte (1983, 1988, 1990).   [56] McGarry and O'Leary (1995: chs 1–4).

[57] English (2003) is an exception in his account of the IRA.

and in 1969 preceded organized republican killing in the latest round of conflict. The formation of the Provisionals occurred after the civil-rights movement had been repressed, not before. The UUP's British-authorized repression, especially internment, evidently triggered more violence than it prevented. Unlike in the 1950s, the Irish government was not prepared to match the Unionists in applying internment—de Valera's successors, like their citizens, did not initially blame Northern nationalists or the civil-rights movement for the return to violence, and some among them supplied the Citizens Defence Committee and Northern republicans with cash and arms.

The conflict was not just internally rooted. Hegemonic control had owed much to outside pressures and incentives, and responses to those pressures and incentives. The contestation and then the collapse of control in the decade 1963–72 flowed from post-1945 developments in the British and Irish states that had reshaped Northern Ireland. British imperialism and Irish governmental irredentism, the respective "national character traits" of the London and Dublin governments, were still present, but had been diminishing before 1968. O'Neill's reformist dispositions were timely. His capacity and will to implement them proved radically insufficient: unionists had built a system of ethnic privilege that they could not easily dissolve without causing disarray among their own ranks. O'Neill lacked a strong internal constituency for reforming unionism.

The Stormont regime had survived so long because it was supported by specific patterns of British and Irish state development. It could not survive the conjunction of Irish governments genuinely intent on détente, British governments no longer willing to preside over overtly unequal citizenship, and a civil-rights movement modeled on the US demand for equality of all citizens. The crisis of the late 1960s starkly revealed that the limits to hegemonic control lay outside Northern Ireland. The behavior of local political agents, especially that of northern Catholics, was undoubtedly influenced by the world outside. What had seemed to most external observers a very insular place had always been externally influenced, but this time the outside mattered in unexpected ways. Some were inspired by the American civil-rights movement or Gandhi's non-violent disobedience, others by the wave of ultra-leftism that swept Europe and North America in response to the Vietnam war: 1968 was the year of student revolutionaries; of Paris, Prague, and Chicago; of protest against the Soviet and American imperiums; of the revival and transformation of ideological conflict throughout western Europe.[m] Northern Ireland's currents were moved by these wider tides of turmoil. Those who had proclaimed the era of good feelings and the end of ideology proved premature. The border became an issue; it could scarcely have been otherwise, given the history of its making, and its institutional repercussions. The national question had never gone away; rooted in the colonial past, it had been reawakened, with many intent on revolution or repression, others intent on revenge. While many were filled with resentment, rage, and fear, too few were filled with remorse or restraint. There were many policy errors made by individual and collective agents in the reignition of conflict, but it was not a tragedy of errors. The patterning of the emotions of antagonism was rooted in the colonial past and its unresolved ethnic repercussions.

APPENDIX 2.6.1. IRELAND'S POLICY TOWARD
NORTHERN IRELAND, 1969–1970

The policy of the Fianna Fáil government toward the North under Lemass in the 1960s has been called "technocratic anti-partitionism" by Tom Lyne, and "functional co-operation" by Donnacha Ó Beacháin.[58] The policy entailed tacit recognition of the Northern government, ending the focus on Great Britain as the root cause of partition, and thereby changing the perceived appropriate target of policy. Encouraging Northern nationalists to work within the Stormont system was part of this paradigm shift, as discussed in the previous two chapters. Under Lemass's successor, Lynch, this policy could not survive the crises of the later O'Neill years, especially the impact of the civil-rights movement, and its attempted repression by official and unofficial loyalists. It almost unavoidably led to criticism of the Northern government, thereby jeopardizing the recent hard-won detente. The crisis also led to emergency contingency planning that ended in a severe crisis in the Dublin cabinet.

Lynch had to manage a cabinet with three rivals who saw themselves as his potential successor, George Colley, Charles Haughey, and Neil Blaney. The last was an unreconstructed republican from Donegal; the first was not known to have strong republican sentiments. Haughey's became evident to his colleagues in the unfolding crisis. As the civil-rights movement began to be met with police and loyalist violence, especially from October 1968 onward, the Irish government reviewed its options. Lynch moved back toward traditional postures, under the pressure of public and party opinion, and at least three of his cabinet members, Haughey, Blaney, and Kevin Boland, sought a more advanced policy. Haughey's position is usually taken to have been opportunistic, which it may have been, but that is to forget that he was the son of Northerners, and of an IRA father, like Blaney and Boland, and doubtless he was affected by the intense atmosphere of the time. Boland's father, however, had dealt harshly with the IRA as one of de Valera's ministers, and so had Haughey as a justice minister, so their conduct can hardly be reduced to their family formations.

Under pressure, and perhaps as a distraction, the Irish government sought to reinternationalize the Northern question, by taking it to the United Nations, a move the aged Aiken regarded as unwise, though he appeased his colleagues by talking with the UN General Secretary. Later a more ambitious plan to take matters before the General Assembly, led by Foreign Minister Hillery, ended without impact—the UK, after all, was a member of the Security Council, and during the cold war the USA and France were the UK's reliable allies in that council. The Irish government ordered its army to the border in August 1969—as we have seen, that probably speeded up the British government's decision to send in its troops. That same month, elected Stormont MPs from Catholic constituencies lobbied publicly and privately for arms in Dublin to defend their communities, horrified and terrified by the burnings, and assaults by the police, the Specials, and loyalist mobs.

The Irish government also ordered its army, under-supplied and under-resourced, to provide plans for possible incursions into Northern Ireland. No fantasy of a full-scale conquest was envisaged. What was considered was bringing Great Britain to the conference table through crossing the border, and creating an incident, or incidents, that might have brought in the UN. The army worked up scenarios, most of which envisaged the incursions taking place if Northern nationalists were endangered by mass burnings, or killings on the model of the pogroms of the 1920s, or those of August 1969. The government also authorized military training for Northerners, seeking to avoid aiding those regarded as Marxists in the IRA; such aid was quickly cut back when it was exposed, and eventually terminated.

---

[58] Lyne (1990); Ó Beacháin (2014).

A government subcommittee, with Haughey in the lead as the Minister of Finance, was put in charge of contingency planning for aid for the North; both relief aid and arms provision were envisaged. Between February and April 1970, Irish military intelligence sought to import a significant fresh consignment of arms, advised by channels known to Minister Blaney. Captain James Kelly was in charge of the project to import arms. The purpose was to supply Northern citizens' defense committees—some of whose members became members of the Provisional IRA—to help them defend themselves in doomsday scenarios, if the government deemed that appropriate. Kelly reported to the Director of Army Military Intelligence, Michael Heffernon, who reported to the Minister of Defence, Jim Gibbons. Haughey gave general clearance at customs. The plan became known to the senior civil servant at Justice, Peter Berry, a longstanding hardline opponent of the IRA. He sought to block the imports, on Clifford's account thereby improperly overruling his own minister, and perhaps jeopardizing his own position. Berry claimed that the arms were for the IRA, and went, irregularly, to the aged President de Valera, and then to Lynch. Separately, Berry, and perhaps others linked to British intelligence, briefed the opposition leader, Liam Cosgrave of Fine Gael, who went to see Lynch. Lynch responded by firing Blaney and Haughey. Subsequently, criminal conspiracy charges were launched against Haughey, Captain Kelly, John Kelly (widely agreed to be a key figure in the formation of the Provisional IRA), and a Belgian businessman, Albert Luykx, an acquaintance of Blaney who had been part of the thwarted import scheme. Blaney was also charged, but released when the district court found he had no case to answer. To cut a long story short, one trial was declared a mistrial, and the second led to the acquittal of all the defendants by the jury.[59] Their defense had been that the operation was authorized, and conducted covertly to avoid British knowledge. The jury plainly believed them. Gibbons, who had been summonsed for the Prosecution, proved a wholly inept and incredible witness who could not explain multiple obvious authorizations that formed part of the same pattern.

Lynch's government, in conjunction with the principal parliamentary opposition, refused to accept the verdict of the court, though it could not alter the defendants' status as free men. Allegations were made that the jury had been tampered with—subsequently denied by the foreman of the jury, interviewed thirty years later. The suggestion was made that the jury was emotionally sympathetic to the defendants—in short, biased. But reading the record of the court proceedings—carefully recovered and represented by Clifford[60] 2009—will persuade reasonable persons that the jurors were right to acquit the defendants. Among multiple curiosities, they were charged for an authorized operation that was in fact called off. Captain Kelly wrote two powerful memoirs to clear his name; they had to be self-published,[61] and the release of some subsequent cabinet documentation has vindicated his claim that he was acting under orders.[62] On Clifford's account, Berry was the moving force in insisting upon a trial, and rigged matters to try to secure a successful prosecution. She makes a good case, but not all will be persuaded.

It had in fact been Irish government policy at least until April 1970 that Catholics in the North should have some means of self-defense to prevent what had happened in the 1920s, what happened in August 1969, and what appeared to be in danger of happening again.

[59] The details are in Clifford's 700-page tome (2009a), which is far easier to read than trying to piece together press reports and the parliamentary record, which she also examines. The first trial started on September 22, 1970; the jury was discharged one week later. The second trial started on October 6; the defendants were acquitted on October 23.
[60] Clifford (2009a).
[61] The UK's Foreign and Commonwealth Office appears to have successfully induced the publisher Collins to withdraw from publishing Kelly's book—a proof of the text may have been supplied to both governments (Ó Beacháin 2014: 311).
[62] Kelly (1971, 1999).

It was not policy to create a united Ireland through conquest; rather, there was contingency planning, not enacted, to consider incursions to internationalize the conflict. It is not surprising that such plans were never implemented. The reconstruction of Lynch's cabinet, purged of harder-line republicans, signaled a shift toward a less risky Irish policy, both in words and in contingency planning. The internal unity of the party was deeply ruptured. At the Fianna Fáil conference of 1971, delegates came close to blows, with one faction shouting "We want Jack," while the other responded with "Union Jack." Minister Gibbons was openly called a perjurer by party delegates, which is what the trials had suggested, and the archives confirm.

The sources for this bald summary are in the accompanying footnote.[63] The best general treatment is in Ó Beacháin (2014); the detail is in Clifford (2006a, b, 2009a, b), who has performed a public service, even for those who do not share her distinct worldview. Dillon (1991) cannot be relied upon, because he has some basic facts wrong—notably, Peter Berry was the senior civil servant at the head of ministry of Justice, not the head of the Guards, even if he treated Special Branch as his own bailiwick. Dillon writes without documentation and reports abundant anonymous information, too much of which appears to make British intelligence better informed and judging better than seems plausible—unless Berry was an agent, for which there is no compelling evidence. This summary should make it clear that it is hard to be persuaded by heroic characterizations of Lynch, or by the orthodox demonization of Haughey as the man who armed the IRA. Though he was later found demonstrably corrupt, and possibly corrupt throughout his public life, Haughey's corruption has no bearing on whether he acted in 1969–70 outside government policy. He had helped shape policy with Lynch's delegated authority and knowledge. Too much of the literature is toxically aligned for or against Haughey and Lynch, and their proxies, and rarely shows evidence of engagement with the court proceedings, or the shameful efforts to manipulate them. The reader of Clifford's documentation will conclude that, after the exposure of his government's policy by Peter Berry's maneuvers, Lynch found himself between a rock and a hard place. One part of the state had been kept from the knowledge of what another part had authorized. The choice was to admit government policy, for which Lynch had had little enthusiasm, and face up to the domestic and international embarrassment, or to fire two of his two party rivals for allegedly unauthorized conduct, and, as its corollary, to send another minister to lie in court against yet another. The jury's verdict has greater integrity than do many of the fulsome portraits of "honest Jack" who saved his state. Clifford rightly identifies a key puzzle. If Haughey was so dangerous, so out of control, why did Lynch subsequently restore him to the cabinet? And why did other Fianna Fáil stalwarts work with him?

---

[63] Clifford (2006a, b, 2009a, b) and Ó Beacháin (2014); for an orthodox defense of Lynch, Berry, and the author, see O'Malley (2014), and see also Justin O'Brien (2000); the latter, despite its title, does not have much about the trial itself.

Acknowledgments

Lori Salem, my wife and a specialist in writing among other crafts, has improved my 'Merican English. John McGarry of the Queen's University Canada, my friend since high school, my regular co-author for over twenty-five years, and from whom I regularly learn, is owed thanks beyond measure. He has made many useful corrections and suggestions and initiated significant parts of earlier versions of Volume 2, Chapter 5. My other co-authors on Irish matters over the years, including John Coakley, Geoffrey Evans, John Garry, Jorgen Elklit, Bernie Grofman, Tom Lyne, Chris McCrudden, Paul Mitchell, John Peterson, and Alex Schwartz, should recognize their imprints if they have time to spare. Dominic Byatt deserves immense thanks for patiently awaiting a text he may have believed would never arrive. Olivia Wells and her colleagues brought order to the submitted typescript; Hilary Walford copy-edited all three volumes with dignified skill; and Gillian Northcott Liles produced the indexes with superb attention to detail. Thanks also to Clement Raj and his co-workers. Oxford's independent referees were very kind with particular chapters while assiduously correcting errors. I must single out for special thanks Nicholas Canny, John A. Hall, Joe Lee, Breandán Mac Suibhne, Ian McBride, Kerby Miller, and Éamonn Ó Ciardha. Among political scientists I owe much to John Coakley, Don Horowitz, Arend Lijphart, Ian S. Lustick, Nicholas Sambanis, Cahal McCall, Peter McLoughlin, Niall Ó Dochartaigh, and especially Jennifer Todd, mostly through reading their works, but also through numerous conversations, and ructions at conferences. I regret that I was unable to give a copy of this book to Ernest Gellner, who examined my doctorate, or to Walker Connor, who examined my life. I regret that Pat Conway of Belfast will be able to find errors here.

This book has been in the making for over twelve years, and builds upon reading, research, interviews, and writing over thirty-five years. I owe my freedom to travel regularly to the UK and Ireland to Leonard Lauder's endowment of my chair at the University of Pennsylvania—where numerous research assistants were exceptionally helpful in double-checking data, and in the composition of maps and graphics, especially Meghan Hussey, Blake Harden, Kyle Pickett, Joseph Benedick, Alec Ward, Anna Garson, and Mike Coyne. At various junctures I have benefited from research funding from the Nuffield Foundation (UK), the Atlantic Foundation (Ireland), the United States Institute of Peace, a Sawyer–Mellon seminar grant, and the Rockefeller Foundation (Bellagio). Some of the fruits of all that assistance is evident here. Chuck Feeney, founder of the Atlantic Foundation, and a genuinely unique philanthropist who has managed to spend down his endowment, has been a friend since the early 1990s, and introduced me to the USA, little knowing I would make my way there a decade later. Other Irish Americans whom I encountered then, and who were consistently helpful to me later, include Niall O'Dowd, publisher, the late Bill Flynn, philanthropist, Joe Jamieson, trade unionist, former lawyer, and Congressman Bruce Morrison, Trina Vargo now of the Mitchell Fellowship program, and Sharon Waxman now the President of the Free Labour Association (they worked in the office of the late Senator Edward Kennedy when I first met them). I have also benefited immensely from a visiting professorship at Queen's Belfast since 2012, conjointly held with an international fellowship at the Senator George J. Mitchell Institute for Global Peace, Security and Justice, established at Queen's Belfast; for these kind hostings I am indebted to Shane O'Neill, Hastings Donnan, David Phinnemore, Yvonne Galligan, John Garry, and Alister Miskimmon. I am also grateful for a Moore Institute fellowship at the National University of Ireland–Galway in 2014, where my hosts were Professor Dan Carey, and its founding director, Nicholas Canny. At Penn, I have been aided by all of my colleagues in Political Science, and a few in History, notably Jonathan Steinberg, and by a succession of chairs of the Political Science department, who believed I would finish this project: Jack Nagel, Rogers Smith, Avery Goldstein, Ed Mansfield, and Anne Norton. For help at key junctures I wish warmly to acknowledge the help of Deans Sam Preston and Steve Fluharty. Among my former Ph.D. students at LSE and Penn, I am especially indebted to Professors Katharine Adeney, Michael Kerr, Bill Kissane, David Bateman, Stephan Stohler, and Etain Tannam, and to Drs Brighid Brooks-Kelly, Kathleen Cavanaugh, Alex Channer, Shelley Deane, Abby Innes, Tristan Mabry, Michael McGrath, and Brendan O'Duffy. Former LSE colleagues Tim Besley, Patrick Dunleavy, Jim Hughes, and Gwen Sasse were helpful in ways that they may have forgotten, as were the late Alan Beattie and George Jones. Numerous interviewees cannot be thanked in person, mostly British and Irish officials, but I can thank Ambassadors Anne Anderson, Edward Barrington, Niall Burgess, Joe Hayes, Eugene Hutchinson, Barbara Jones, Philip MacDonagh, Adrian O'Neill and Seán Ó hUiginn of Irish distinction, and John Chilcott, Jonathan Phillips, Quentin Thomas, and the late Tony Brennan of British eminence. Lastly, I want to thank the following who at various junctures informed, fed, housed, or otherwise assisted me, in ways they may not even recognize, all of which went into the work that finished these volumes: the Abdul-Rahmans of Duhok, Erbil, and London, Alex Anderson, Harriet Arnold and Ali Willmore, Brian Barrington, the late Brian Barry, Christine Bell, Paul Bew, Anna-Mária Bíró, Matthijs Bogaards, the late Kevin Boyle, Sumantra Bose, Kieran Bradley, Sharon L. Burke, Bill Burke-White, Francis Campbell, Anne Cadwallader, Deirdre and Patrick Close, Martin Collins, Paul Collier, Richard Conley, the late Mary and Walker Connor and their son Dan, Cathie Connor, Daniele Conversi, Karl Cordell, Peggy S. Czyzak-Dannenbaum and Karl Dannenbaum, Christian Davenport, Seamus and Ciaran Deane, Deaglán de Bréadùn Elizabeth Doering, Rowan Duffin-Jones, Mark Durkan, Clare and David Edgerton, David and the late Brian Farrell, Brian Feeney, Helga Feeney, Bill Finan, Craig Fowlie, Peter W. Galbraith, Garret and the late Kate FitzGerald, the late Ernest Gellner and his son David, Steve Greer, Adrian Guelke, Jeroen Gunning, Tom Hadden, John Healy, Michael and Zsuzsanna Ignatieff, Joy Ann James, Stuart J. Kaufman, Tina Kempin, Julie Kipp, Gunnar Helgi Kristinsson, Brighid Laffan, Jena Laske, Michael Laver, Dominic Lieven, Neo Loizides, David Lynch Siobhán Lyons, Dianne and Tom Lyne, Carol, Paul, and Andrew McAllister, the McCambridge and McLoughlin families of Cushendall, Iain McLean, the late Kevin McNamara and his son Brendan, Carolyn Marvin, Joanne McEvoy, Kieran McEvoy, Alan McGuckian, the late Martin McGuinness, David McKittrick, Molly McNulty, Monica McWilliams, Nicola Meyrick, Frank Millar, Dan Miodownik, Margaret Moore, Michael Moran, Tanni Mukhopadhyay, Paul Muldoon, Jack and Barbara Nagel, Tom Nairn, Fionnuala Ní Áolain, Diarmuid Ó Mathúna, Bernard and Mary O'Mahony, Margaret O'Callaghan, Brian O'Connell, John O'Dowd, Ian O'Flynn, the O'Learys of London, Cork, Oxford, and Doncaster, the O'Mahonys of Cork, Dublin, and Kinsale, Kevin O'Rourke, Chris Pluta, Chris Pomery, Mads (Matt) Qvortrup, Erik Ringmar, Richard Rose, Bob Rowthorn, Khaled Salih, Patricia and Michael Scullin, Nancy and the late Al Stepan, Jane-Marie and Damian Treanor, and Karin von Hippel. Innumerable librarians were helpful in Belfast, London, and Philadelphia.

Sections of this book resemble a palimpsest or a recension. *The Politics of Antagonism: Understanding Northern Ireland*, by Brendan O'Leary and John McGarry, published by the Athlone Press in 1993 and in 1996 (2nd edition), and reissued by Bloomsbury in 2016, provided base materials for some of Volume 2. This, however, is a mostly fresh set of volumes, reflecting improvements in my knowledge, and modifications and improvements of earlier judgments. This book differs in the minor matters of American spelling and style, but also in substantive matters, of content, conceptualization, mood, and expectation. American English is used to demonstrate that this citizen of Ireland and the United States has no fundamental objection to voluntary integration and can happily embrace dual identifications. British, Irish, or Ulster English are preserved in official statements, official titles, and nomenclature. Volume 1, Chapter 1, has fresh data compared with *The Politics of*

Antagonism, and uses the deservedly highly regarded *Lost Lives* study,[1] and other official and independent sources. These results do not significantly alter the analysis of the conflict first drawn in *The Politics of Antagonism* for the period 1969–89, which reworked research with Brendan O'Duffy. This more precise evidence has not required me, fortunately, to alter significantly the general account of responsibilities for violence, or of the proportional degrees and scale of human suffering, or the trajectories of violence. The pioneering analyses of Michael McKeown and of the Irish Information Partnership, notably Tom Lyne and Marian Laragy, with which I was associated (on its advisory board), have been broadly confirmed, though rendered more granular. They are appropriately emended through the astonishingly commendable work of David McKittrick, Brian Feeney, Chris Thornton, Seamus Kelters, and David McVea, and that of the independent researcher Malcolm Sutton.

Each section of the history is preceded by a conceptual 'conspectus'—on respectively colonialism, control, and consociation. Disagreement with efforts to deny or dilute the colonial framing, and the facts it captures, are rendered, I hope, without too much rancor or sarcasm.[2] As Thomas Paine might have said, there is too much pity for past plumage: in this case, that which passes under the description of the Irish Kingdom. Why British political elites failed to find a federal or autonomy solution for the status of Ireland before 1912 is considered anew. Partition is extensively treated, including in comparative perspective. My understanding of twentieth-century Ireland has been revised to reflect the work of my peers, especially but not only younger scholars who have examined freshly released public archives and private papers. Throughout I have focused especially on the memoirs of major figures, fully conscious of the need to check them against contemporaneous sources. The merits of reading Northern Ireland's history between 1921 and 1969 through the concept of control is nevertheless affirmed, and extended. Volume 3 expands, integrates, and refashions work published elsewhere, but includes entirely novel material, and is run together as a single narrative.

The Politics of Antagonism, drafted in 1990–1, published in 1993, concluded on a somber note, noticed by some reviewers, especially its penultimate sentence, namely: "The widespread despair that the cruel conflict will continue with no end in sight, has solid empirical foundations." The last sentence was not similarly noticed, namely: "Two centuries after the United Irishmen promised to 'abolish the memory of all past dissension' the statecraft required to break the manacles of the past has not yet materialized." Such statecraft was hoped for, and with many others I made modest contributions toward that possibility, in my case as an adviser to the British Labour Party front-bench parliamentary team (led by Kevin McNamara and subsequently by Dr Marjorie (Mo) Mowlam), further advisory work with the Irish-American Morrison delegation, and through numerous contacts with Irish officials and politicians, including in the UUP, DUP, Alliance, the SDLP, and Sinn Féin. Whether in drafting or co-drafting proposals for institutional, electoral, or police reform I was promoting statecraft influenced by consociational thought.

Such statecraft materialized in the making of the Agreement of 1998, even though its implementation was slow and sometimes painful, and remains uncertain. The initiating and transformative roles played by the leaders of Northern Irish and Irish political parties

---

[1] The 2004 edition of this book is used, updated where necessary until 2010 by other sources and my own monitoring. For a review of the first edition, see Brendan O'Leary, "3,636 so far, and Counting (Review of David McKittrick et al., *Lost Lives: The Stories of the Men, Women and Children who Died as a Result of the Northern Ireland Troubles*)," *Times Higher Education Supplement*, March 3, 2000.

[2] Academic disputes, some of which may matter, are mostly conducted in the endnotes. Having once been described by the late Keith Jeffery as part of a team of academic carnivores, perhaps I need to declare that scholars are not fit for consumption, raw or cooked, though they often make for good reading.

and paramilitary organizations deserve and receive full recognition here, as do those of British and Irish politicians, and their officials. The peace process was not, however, some drama of orchestral maneuvering in the light. Though there were many maneuvers, there was no conductor, and at times the process was quasi-anarchic, even for the minor players privileged to observe some action behind the front stage. The authors of *The Politics of Antagonism* feared indifference. Today my concerns are different. One is a mild but falling fear of complacency. Belfast's power-sharing government has not and could not escape the storm-blown crises from the bursting of the long bubbles in Ireland and the UK. Preoccupied with the latest great depression created by predatory financial capitalism, and the invention of the Euro without sufficient fiscal foresight or backing, public officials in London and Dublin had already begun to act prematurely as if their missions in Northern Ireland were accomplished before 2016. They might yet fail to do what is required to protect the Agreements of 1998 and 2006, matters addressed in the final two chapters of the third volume. Local unionist and nationalist politicians may take unnecessary risks with what has been painfully constructed, and a UK Prime Minister and Secretary of State may yet behave with insufficient intelligence or prudence; and, as I write, the USA appears intent on withdrawing its special envoy without any evidence of mission accomplished.

No author can expect to silence wishful thinking or terminate sour grapes. All authors earn criticisms of their own and are absurd if they hope they will have the last word. I expect to be corrected and revised in due course—or ignored. But it is impossible not to observe with irritation the revival or creation of glib or accusatory writings or rewritings of history—for example, claims that British intelligence defeated the IRA; that the IRA alone caused the Troubles; that internment worked; that the civil-rights movement was predominantly hijacked by neo-Trotskyists; that the Stormont regime was a "normal" British local government; that the conflict was overwhelmingly sectarian rather than national or ethnic in character; that integration could have worked, at any time, but for papist resistance; that the southern Irish were never interested in reunification; that unionists were always willing to accept power-sharing—they just did not want any role for the Irish government; that the Good Friday Agreement was "Sunningdale for slow learners;" that 9/11 led the IRA to decommission; that the RUC did not need to be reformed out of existence; that loyalist violence was simply reactive rather than proactive; that British policy has always been consistent, since 1921, 1925, 1949, 1968, 1972, 1973, 1979, 1985 or 1998—that is, depending on the proponent's selective illusion. This book provides correctives to such claims, sometimes quietly. Yet its author is old enough to know that facts and good arguments do not finish the life of bad ideas. No truly bad political idea dies out, not least because some attention-seeking or counter-suggestive historian (or politician) will be keen to resuscitate it. Being older and less confident of the eventual victory of truth over its rivals, I have sought to restrain a counter-glibness. The executioner's tone sometimes adopted by historians is controlled. Combat mostly takes place in footnotes and endnotes from which general readers may avert their gaze. Barbs remain, but rest assured that many more were eliminated.

Many think that oblivion is the appropriate destination for Northern Ireland's history. Unfortunately for them Northern Ireland is now squarely in the way of the political traffic jam being created by the UK's intended secession from the EU. Many wanted to conclude that this was an old quarrel, a time-lag from Europe's religious past, of no pertinence for the rest of the world, an event that like some painful relationships is best forgotten. It is not because I have devoted much of the short span of a life to this subject that I think it is too early to consign knowledge of its trajectories to oblivion or to the antiquarian. Even if the conflict may now be managed entirely peacefully—occasionally disturbed by the marcher or the bomber or the politician who has learned nothing and forgotten everything of importance—discussion of the conflict's causation and resolution remains instructive. There are "lessons-to-be-learned" from Northern Ireland for conflicts elsewhere. These should, however, focus on the institutions and policies that can trigger or manage ethno-national conflicts, and on the merits of power-sharing arrangements for deeply divided places. The easy ideas of inclusive or unconditional peace processes, or of funding civil society, NGOs, and first- and second-track diplomacy, or emphasizing the roles of third-party mediators, should, by contrast, be treated with appropriate caution. Success has many parents, but not all claims to parenthood are compelling. Conflict analysis must certainly avoid three perils: primitive primordialism, hyper-constructivism, and handing interpretive authority to the sociologists of religion.

When composing and editing what is published here, I took breaks by walking beside the Schuykill river in Philadelphia or by walking or hiking in the Glens of Antrim, in both cases with folk music playing in my headphones. Many Irish folk songs lament lost lives. The Irish, North and South, the British in Ireland, North and South, the Northern Irish, and the Irish abroad, in North America, the Antipodes, and elsewhere, have good reasons to be far more cheerful than many of the mournful wailings from the island of my birth would allow. In keeping with that perspective, I conclude by trying to temper the entirely rational gloom that has followed the referendum held on the UK's membership of the European Union in June 2016, and the treatment of Northern Ireland as collateral damage. The future cannot be known, but some futures are more likely than others and I hope readers will find some that I sketch in these pages to be of current value. Whether they will retain pertinence will be decided by others.

Brendan O'Leary

Philadelphia and Cushendall
December 31, 2017

Notes

2.1. CONCEPTUAL CONSPECTUS

a. In the French system, the power of presidents waxes and wanes depending on their levels of parliamentary support (Elgie 2005; Skach 2005). Robert Elgie is the comparative specialist on this model (Elgie 1993, 1999, 2001, 2011; Elgie and Moestrup 2007, 2008; Elgie et al. 2016). In the German system, the constructive vote of confidence obliges the popular chamber to vote in an alternative government if it is about to oust the existing one; see, e.g., Gordon R. Smith (1989); Skach (2005). For general discussions of presidentialism and parliamentarism, see, among others, Dunleavy et al. (1990); Horowitz (1991); Lijphart (1992); Linz (1993); Rhodes and Dunleavy (1995); Riggs (1997); Stepan and Skach (2001); Cheibub (2002); McGarry (2012).

b. In slightly different ways, both Alan Ward and Alvin Jackson interpret Northern Ireland's experience between 1920 and 1972 as an indictment of the feasibility of Gladstonian home rule (Alan J. Ward 1994; Jackson 2003). They are right to indict its unworkable financial provisions, but neglect detailed thought on the minority-rights provisions: the workability of the relevant "securities," depended upon British oversight. We will never know whether a British government would have been as passive toward a discriminatory Dublin government presiding over a united Ireland as it was toward the Belfast government. For a sophisticated discussion of "securities" such as juries, assemblies, and elections, see Elster (2013).

c. Memmi (1990). His relentless analysis of the antagonistic pair in his book's title bears comparison with key passages in Hegel's *Phenomenology of Mind*—the master–slave dialectic. In the German philosopher's account, the master seeks recognition of the rightness of his domination, while the slave seeks recognition of his humanity; neither, however, can satisfy the other. A similar paradox is found in the dialogue between Simonides, the poet, and the tyrant, Hiero; see Strauss et al. (1991).

d. The civil servant Kenneth Bloomfield, former speech-writer to Terence O'Neill, and later advisor to successive Northern Irish prime ministers and British secretaries of state, fully acknowledges injustice and discrimination under the UUP, but holds "the Catholic and nationalist minority" "partly" to blame for unionist misconduct because they failed to play "a constructive and responsible part in the organs of the new jurisdiction" (Bloomfield 2007: 151). Here the blame for disloyalty is expressed *sotto voce*.

e. The relevant party can be nominally of one people, but in fact represent a subsection of that people. The Ba'ath Party in Saddam Hussein's Iraq described itself as pan-Arabist; it thereby excluded non-Arab peoples—e.g., Kurds—from its goals, though they were not formally excluded from membership (especially if they were willing to be Arabized). Within the party, in the course of its evolution, especially under Saddam Hussein, a shift took place within its top ranks, so that the party expressed the dominance of Sunni Arabs while incorporating some Shiite Arabs (and "Arabized" Kurds); see, e.g., Sassoon (2012) and Makiya (1998/1989).

2.2. NOT AN INCH

a. The subsequent Viscount Craigavon (1871–1940) was the son of a wealthy distiller. He began his adult life as a stockbroker, served for the Empire in the Boer War, and was elected to Westminster in 1906. He emerged alongside Carson as a major unionist figure in the 1910–18 parliament, and as a gun-runner. He held office in Lloyd

George-led coalition governments after 1916, before becoming the premier of North-ern Ireland. He was made a baronet in 1918 (a hereditary title, which wins the title Sir), and in 1927 a viscount, a lordship in the fourth rank of the British peerage system, below an earl but above a baron. The third Viscount, his grandson, sits in the House of Lords, as one of the "elected" hereditary peers.

b. For British public opinion throughout 1918–22, see the unsurpassed study by Boyce (1972). Carson's first public threat to mobilize the UVF, made on the previous July 12, had been widely condemned in the British press, and prompted the Conservative MP Lt-Col. Aubrey Herbert to apologize for supporting Ulster's resistance in 1914, and to condemn the "loyalty" of Carson as but the "loyalty of Shylock" (Boyce 1972: 107).

c. Eunan O'Halpin (2009) is kinder to Greenwood in the Cambridge *Dictionary of Irish Biography*, arguing that he "neither originated nor administered coercive policy," but "became identified with it as its most conspicuous spokesman." Greenwood has found a magnanimous biographer who instructs us that his wife Margo was one of Lloyd George's lovers, and a separate interlocutor with the prime minister in 1920–2, who was probably more influential than her husband in influencing the prime minister both to be stubborn and in his policy shifts on Ireland (MacLaren 2015). In cabinet Greenwood favored "dominion home rule" rather than "Gladstonian home rule" long before the prime minister.

d. For contemporaneous and subsequent republican accounts, see Kenna (1922) and McDermott (2001) respectively; for accounts of "the burnings" outside Belfast based on newspaper, court, and public records, see Lawlor (2009); and see the same author's account of border skirmishes in Lawlor (2011). For a unionist account of the period, see Follis (1995). For balanced appraisals empathetic to nationalists and unionists respect-ively, see Phoenix (1994) and Parkinson (2004)—the latter does not agree there was a pogrom. Máire and Conor Cruise O'Brien referred matter-of-factly to Protestant pogroms against Catholics in 1922, including in the third and revised edition of their concise history of Ireland (O'Brien and O'Brien 1985: 150).

e. Horowitz's framework could be profitably applied to Sean Farrell's discussion (2009) of riots and rituals in Ulster, to Andrew Boyd's history (1969) of riots in Belfast (which rewrites the Victorian commissioners' accounts), and to A. C. Hepburn's accounts (1990, 1996) of urban riots in Belfast. In this grim history, threat perceptions, rumors, parading precipitants, targeting to create local homogeneity, attacking the target where it is spatially weakest, the leaderless character of riots, forced displacement being more evident that outright plans to kill, and the inability or unwillingness of police to perform their functions, all, in turn play their patterned roles over two centuries.

f. See Boyd (1969); Budge and O'Leary (1973); Hepburn (2003). The Belfast Town Police were disbanded in 1865 after an investigation by a royal commission—they were found to be partisan, sectarian, and incompetent. The RIC that replaced them in the policing of Belfast until 1921 were more competent, and had a high Catholic composition, sometimes a majority of the regular officers in the city.

g. In his apologia for the B Specials, Sir Arthur Hezlet (1973: 13–14) wrote: "There was serious rioting at Banbridge, Dromore and Hillsborough and later on a smaller scale at Bangor and Newtownards and, in these predominantly Protestant towns, local Sinn Féin property suffered severely." He does not explain how the rioters knew whether the property was owned by Sinn Féiners. He also refers to "allegations" of reprisals by the Black and Tans and Auxiliaries, and suggests there "was not a shred of evidence" to implicate the RIC in the killing of the Lord Mayor of Cork, thereby diminishing his objectivity (pp. 17, 18).

h. In their investigation of the Northern Ireland cabinet papers, Paul Bew, Peter Gibbon, and Henry Patterson detected a division between populist ministers, notably exempli-fied by Craig, who focused on clientelist politics for Protestants, and anti-populists, or traditional Conservatives, who opposed such populism either on principle, or because they feared it would bring on unwelcome British intervention (Bew et al. 1979). In a memorable notice, published in *Political Studies*, Iain McLean commended the authors' valuable work in the archives, including their differentiation between populists and anti-populists, but complained their evidence was "violently forced into a framework [Althusserian Marxism] it just does not fit. The overall effect is as if St Thomas Aquinas had written a history of the National Bus Company."

i. In Eoin MacNeill's unpublished and unfinished memoirs there is a fascinating account of advice he gave to Devlin in 1934—namely: "to concentrate all attention on the British government," and to focus on the League of Nations, "Great Britain posed before the League as a model country, and nothing was more likely to shake her position than shifting the controversy outside Ulster" (Hand 1973: 273).

j. For example, the Home Minister Dawson Bates wrote to Craig in 1934 noting that he had been advised that early action to manipulate the wards in Omagh could prompt legal action which the Government would lose, and thereby open the cabinet to the charge of "indecent gerrymandering" (PRONI Cab. 9B/13/2). In the same private letter, however, Bates went on to describe to his prime minister his preliminary plans to organize gerrymandering in Derry (his expression); these proposals presumably conformed to norms of decent gerrymandering.

k. Lord Fitzalan wrote to Craig on July 5 that the Local Government Bill had been given at too short notice, noting in the same letter that he had been given a long list of recommendations for magistrates, of whom not one was Catholic. "I can quite imagine this is all right, and that very likely no Catholic eligible for the appointment can be found who will consent to serve. But it seems . . . to be a large order and likely to cause . . . a legitimate criticism if so many are now appointed without one of them being a Catholic" (PRONI Cab. 9B/40/1). Fitzalan was the first Catholic Lord Lieutenant appointed since James II, and that may have been a factor in his delay. Cardinal Logue had perhaps been unfair when asked for his comment on Fitzalan's appointment: he said he received it in the same manner as he would the appointment of a Catholic hangman (Rafferty 1994: 209).

l. Merlyn Rees, secretary of state 1974–6, similarly recalled: "The stories one heard about the RUC inspectors. When one visited Fermanagh, to see the Prime Minister Brooke, he had to go through the side door like a servant" (interview with author, Westminster, December 18, 1990).

m. Fitzpatrick (1988: 35, 108, 139), for example, believes that the Irish treaty negotiators and legislators succumbed to "the vague hope that Northern Ireland would eventually be dismembered" by the Commission; maintains that there was "no sound reason to expect that the casting vote of a British-appointed chairman would support any but the most minor alterations;" describes the commission's terms of reference as the "judicious deployment of waffle," and its eventual proceedings as "fatuous deliberation." Foster similarly describes the Commission as ending "in fiasco," and as unlikely "to have produced any major change." He correctly describes the impact on Northern nationalists, who were "now, more than ever, a marooned minority," under the impression of "a corrupt sell-out" (Foster 1988: 527).

n. One of the principal secretaries to the Irish delegation, John Chartres, maintained that the limiting words were introduced "in case the Boundary Commission should feel itself obliged to transfer small, distant, non-contiguous districts, such as the Glens of Antrim," an example explicitly used by Lloyd George to persuade the Irish delegation during the negotiations. This claim is verified by Lloyd George's defense of the treaty before the House of Commons (Matthews 2004: 53–4, 59; Hansard, HC, 5th ser., vol. 149, cols 38–42 (December 21, 1921)). But, as so often with Lloyd George, he subsequently gave a different emphasis: no deal had been struck on Fermanagh and

Tyrone, and the economic and geographic constraints would limit the Commission's reach. His positions at the two different stages in the debate are not strictly speaking inconsistent, but whether he had made a deal with Collins on Fermanagh and Tyrone depends on the meaning of a deal.

o. "Without one word of warning to Ulster, without one single communication to the Prime Minister or Government of Ulster—which, after all, you cannot altogether despise, as you are the parents of it . . . without one word of warning there is sprung upon them this: 'We have arranged with the Sinn Feiners that there is to be a Parliament for the whole of Ireland, that the six counties are to go in, and if you go in here is good news for you, because you are not to pay a 6s. Income Tax, but probably only a 1s.6d. one, and now how happy you ought to be.' Ulster is not for sale. Her loyalty does not depend upon taxes. Ulster values her heritage as citizens of the United Kingdom, and neither you nor the Press, nor your friends in the south of Ireland, need try to terrorise her by the bogey of her having to pay more. At the same time, I make this observation in passing, that it does seem an extraordinary idea of British justice that because Ulster will not join the enemies of this country, and will not go under the murder gang in Dublin, therefore she must pay higher taxation." The falsehoods in Carson's statement were mixed with some truth. The treaty's provisions would mean no subsidies for "Ulster." The full speech is at Hansard, HL, 5th ser, vol. 48, cols 36–53 (December 14, 1921). The outraged speaker also revealed he had a letter from Lloyd George from the 1916 negotiations committing the government to the integrity of the six counties.

p. "The triennial Local Government elections in Northern Ireland, which have now been completed, leave the Unionist party in the majority in every county and district council in the Six Counties, with the exception of Ballycastle Rural District Council, which was always Nationalist, and Newry No. 2 District Council" (Joseph Devlin, citing the *Evening Telegraph*, Hansard (NI), HC, vol. 10, cols 515–16 (1929). When boycotting was abandoned, nationalists usually won control of ten or eleven councils out of seventy-three, still well short of one-third.

q. Hansard (NI), HC, vol. 29, cols 1798–9 (1946). In the words of one of the opposition, Major Curran's speech "at least was devoid of all hypocritical trappings of the other Government speakers. He told us in a few trenchant words what exactly was the real meaning of this Bill . . . without any hypocrisy . . . He told us that this Bill was devised for the one reason of gerrymandering, and to keep those people who were in any way opposed to the Government completely and for ever in subjection" (Hansard (NI), HC, vol. 29, cols 1814–15 (1946)).

r. Barritt and Carter (1962: 100–4). When the more obvious mechanisms (segmented labor markets with residential patronage networks) were later identified, there was a mistaken tendency to neglect their historical origins. Hepburn's urban histories of Belfast show the key role played by rioting in establishing and reinforcing residential and workplace segregation—and thereby institutionally underpinning indirect discrimination (Hepburn, 1996: *passim*).

s. Londonderry originally had a good press as a liberal aristocrat—he had advocated cooperation with nationalists at the Convention of 1917–18, and his failed attempt to create a non-denominational primary-school system consolidated this impression. But his role as an appeaser of Nazi Germany—his regular guest Ribbentrop became known as the "Londonderry Herr"—has destroyed his reputation, not least because of his collusion in upper-class anti-Semitism. As the Munich conference unfolded, his cousin, Churchill, wrote to him that his policy was being applied. For a brief account by his biographer, see Fleming (2005).

t. Conor Cruise O'Brien (1991: 30) argued that the IRA was "attempting to enforce" the claim in Articles 2 and 3: "They have no democratic mandate, but they derive a certain credibility—and durability—from the fact that their objective, a united Ireland, is also the professed objective of all the democratic political parties whose members are drawn from the nationalist population."

2.3. DIGESTING DECOLONIZATION

a. The Church of Ireland, unprompted it seems, replaced its prayers for the monarch in the South when Ireland left the Commonwealth. By 2004 its prayer book was fully partitioned—addressed to the rulers of the European Union and to Ireland as a whole in the South, but addressing the rulers of the European Union and (if I have read correctly) Elizabeth II in the North. "Some Prayers and Thanksgivings," <https://www.ireland.anglican.org/prayer-worship/book-of-common-prayer/2004-texts> (accessed June 2016).

b. From a UK legal perspective, the debate in Dáil Éireann that started in December 1921 was not a formal ratification proceeding, but a debate to approve the treaty, which was not ratified until the Parliament of Southern Ireland was convened to do so: in British eyes that was the body authorized to ratify. From an Irish republican perspective, whether pro- or anti-, the debate was a true ratification debate, which centered on whether to accept the legal consequences of the British perspective on the treaty.

c. Austin Stack (1880–1929), from Kerry, was a winning all-Ireland GAA football captain, who had joined the IRB, an income-tax inspector and founder of the Volunteers in Kerry, where he was commandant during the 1916 Rising, and criticized for not attempting to liberate Roger Casement. He was arrested and sentenced to penal servitude for life after the Easter Rising. He achieved prominence in the Volunteers' struggle to achieve status as political prisoners, and became honorary secretary of Sinn Féin. He was a Sinn Féin TD in the first three Dáils, and, as Minister of Home Affairs in De Valera's cabinet, oversaw the novel republican courts; he supported the anti-treaty IRA in the civil war, and was Minister for Finance in the "Republican government." After he had been captured, he led a hunger strike that left him seriously impaired and contributed to his early death. He did not join Fianna Fáil.

d. Born in England, raised in Wexford, Liam Mellows (1892–1922) was recruited young into Na Fianna Éireann and the IRB. An early Volunteer, he was influenced by Connolly, and organized the Volunteers in Galway, for which he was deported to England. Smuggled to the USA after the Rising, he was De Valera's agent in the USA, and later the IRA's director of purchases during the war of independence. Vigorously anti-treaty, he was a member of the Republican garrison in the Four Courts at the start of the civil war, after which he was arrested. He was executed by the Provisional Government of the IFS in retaliation for the assassination of Seán Hales TD—see Greaves (1971).

e. Séamus Robinson (1988–1961) was born in Belfast, and joined Na Fianna Éireann under Bulmer Hobson in his early teens, before entering a seminary in Scotland. He abandoned monkdom to join the Volunteers in 1913, and fought impressively in the 1916 Rising in Dublin. Elected commanding officer of the 3rd Tipperary Brigade of the IRA, he led an ambush to capture gelignite at Soloheadbeg on the day the first Dáil convened. Two RIC men died—on what is now seen as the first day of the War of Independence; Robinson saw it as a continuation of organization since the Rising. By April 1921, he was the second in command of the IRA 2nd Southern Division. Elected a TD for Waterford–Tipperary East in the second Dáil, he opposed the treaty, and at the outbreak of the civil war was appointed O/C of the IRA Southern Division. Critical of Liam Lynch and others, he later joined Fianna Fáil, and served as Senator (1928–35). He was a founding member of the Bureau of Military History, so not surprisingly his statement and its attached appendices are among the most interesting in its archive,

<http://www.bureauofmilitaryhistory.ie/reels/bmh/BMH.WS1721.pdf#page=113> (accessed June 2016). He insisted, albeit with mordant humor, that the "insurgent Separatists of Ireland were the normal, natural, (common)—sensible people in Ireland."

f. Usually known as Seán Mac Eoin (1893–73), he was later a Chief of Staff of Ireland's army, a deputy for Cumann na nGaedheal and Fine Gael, Minister for Justice (1948–51), and Minister for Defence (1951, 1954–7). He twice ran for the presidency of Ireland, in 1945 and 1959.

g. Robert Erskine Childers (1870–1922) was the exceptionally talented son of an English Orientalist and an Irish mother from the Barton family of Glendalough. Educated at Cambridge, as an adult he moved successively from being an imperialist and unionist to a home ruler and then a dominion home ruler, and ended as an ardent republican. He acquired deep constitutional expertise as a parliamentary clerk in the House of Commons, and was networked within major Liberal circles, including the Runcimans. He married an American republican from Boston, Molly Osgood, with whom he shared a passion for sailing—a skill employed in the Howth gun-running of 1914— and served with British forces in both the Boer and the First World wars, winning a Distinguished Service Cross. At war's end, he joined Sinn Féin, partly under the influence of Robert and Dulcibella Barton; Robert was his cousin, with whom he had been brought up. Childers wrote both the *Riddle of the Sands* (1903), a famous spy novel, and *The Framework of Home Rule* (1911). His legal expertise led to his appointment as secretary to the treaty delegation. Childers earned the distinction of being utterly condemned both by Churchill (as a traitor) and by Griffith (as a damned Englishman). He is deservedly the subject of multiple biographies, though none is very satisfactory—see Cox (1975) and Boyle (1977).

h. O'Higgins (1892–1927), a nephew of Parnell's lieutenant Tim Healy, became one of the staunchest defenders of the treaty. As the Minister for Home Affairs (later renamed Justice), he held a key portfolio during the defeat of the anti-treatyites, 1922–7. He served as Cosgrave's deputy as the vice-president of the Executive Council after the death of Griffith and Collins, and was widely regarded as his most likely successor. He had just become the Minister for External Affairs when he was assassinated. O'Higgins's father was killed in a republican raid during the civil war. Perhaps the most important Irish state-builder after Collins and de Valera, O'Higgins told the Dáil in March 1923 that "we were the most conservative-minded revolutionaries that ever put through a successful revolution." The one biography of note is that by Terence de Vere White (1948).

i. Eamonn Duggan (1874–1936), participant in the 1916 Rising, lawyer, and former Director of Intelligence in the IRA who helped negotiate the truce in 1921, was the son of an RIC officer from Co. Armagh. Subsequently a Sinn Féin, Cumann na nGaedheal, and Fine Gael TD, in the IFS he served as Minister for Home Affairs, Minister without Portfolio, parliamentary secretary to the Minister for Defence and to the Executive Council, and as a Senator.

j. The only major ethnic abuse that sullied the debate was precipitated by the *Freeman's Journal*, whose leader writer maintained that de Valera did not have the "instinct of an Irishman in his blood," and that he was listening too much to an English renegade— namely, Erskine Childers (*Freeman's Journal*, January 5, 1922). The Dáil denounced the abuse. After the debate, discourse became more fractious. On January 10, 1922, admittedly after several days of baiting by anti-treaty TDs, in both public and private sessions, the newly elected president of Dáil Éireann Arthur Griffith spoiled the tenor of his office. Childers, after a lengthy preface, had asked: "Will the Provisional Government function under the statutory powers conferred by the [Government of Ireland] Partition Act?," suggesting Griffith had failed to answer in a previous reply. After interruptions, Griffith said: "I want to say that President de Valera made a statement—a generous statement—and I replied. Now [striking the table] I will not reply to any Englishman in this Dáil [applause]." There followed this exchange: "MR P. O'KEEFE: It is nearly time we had that. PRESIDENT A. GRIFFITH: It is about time. MR ERSKINE CHILDERS: My nationality is a matter for myself and for the constituents that sent me here. PRESIDENT A. GRIFFITH: Your constituents did not know what your nationality was. MR ERSKINE CHILDERS: They have known me from my boyhood days—since I was about half a dozen years of age. PRESIDENT A. GRIFFITH: I will not reply to any damned Englishman in this Assembly." For the record, Childers's mother was Irish; his father was not; no one had questioned his appropriateness as secretary to the delegation on the grounds of his nationality or competence, or forgotten his role in the Howth gun-running for the Volunteers. Griffith may have been relying on (or irritated by) the irony of hearing the chief intellectual republican positions articulated in an English accent, but his rudeness was inexcusable, <http://oireachtasdebates.oireachtas.ie/Debates%20Authoring/DebatesWebPack.nsf/takes/dail1922011000005?opendocument> (accessed July 12, 2014).

k. For an excellent survey of the problems posed by Collins to biographers, see Lee (1998)—his arguments did not deter Hart (2005) among others. For a sparkling collection on Collins's significance for the Irish state, see Doherty and Keogh (1998). Lee (1989: 63–5) provides an eloquent assessment of the significance of his loss for the Irish state. Enthusiasts for speculation can choose, among other options, whether Collins would have become a democratic consolidationist, as de Valera eventually proved to be; a social democrat committed to a strong state-led development program; or an Irish Ataturk (who would have tried to conquer Northern Ireland, and set up an authoritarian all-island regime). Collins has perhaps been too consistently presented as a moderate and a democratic peacemaker to differentiate him from the supposedly uniformly dictatorial anti-treatyites. John M. Regan (2013) argues that in the summer of 1922 Collins essentially took and exercised power as a dictator: the president of the IRB and Chairman of the Provisional Government took control of both the Free State Army and the cabinet at the outbreak of the civil war, and did not consult his cabinet colleagues, or the recently elected third Dáil, over the assault on the Four Courts. In Collins's defense, he had little time (given Churchill's ultimatum over the Four Courts); he had been chosen by his colleagues, a majority of the second Dáil, to chair the Provisional Government; and his actions over the Four Courts and at the outset of the civil war were hardly exceptional uses of executive emergency powers, common to both transitional and permanent governments—in many republics the commander-in-chief of the armed forces is also the chief executive. His decision to resist convening the third Dáil is the most important issue raised by Regan; Cosgrave did convene parliament to ratify his succession to Collins.

l. Frank Aiken (1898–1983), Armagh-born and Armagh-buried farmer, inventor, politician, and IRA commander of the 4th Northern Division during the War of Independence and the civil war. After he had been accused of at least one sectarian atrocity by unionist critics, his home and properties, and those of close relatives, were burned by B Specials. He was a member of Sinn Féin 1917–25, a founding member of Fianna Fáil, elected to Dáil Éireann continuously for fifty years, 1923–73, and served successively as Minister for Defence under various titles (1932–45), Finance (1945–8), and External Affairs (1951–4, 1957–69), and as Tanaiste (deputy PM) (1965–9). He refused to stand for the presidency at the end of de Valera's term, and was strongly opposed to the rehabilitation of Charles Haughey in 1972–3. He tried to remain neutral during the civil war because of his focus on the North, but eventually took the anti-treaty side—though he intermittently called for an early end. He succeeded Liam Lynch as Chief of Staff of the IRA, and issued the commands that ended the civil war in May 1923. He excelled as Ireland's foreign minister, promoting an independent policy—neutral, pro-decolonization, favoring nuclear disarmament during the cold war, and critical of apartheid, defending the rights of small nations, such as Hungary and Tibet, and seeking to mediate between Israel and the Arab states. His is the first signature on the Non-Proliferation of Nuclear Arms Treaty, and his remarkable career is finally receiving the attention it merits (Evans and Kelly 2014).

Bryce Evans, one of the editors of this biographical collection on Aiken, describes the sectarian atrocity of which he was accused as follows: "Responding to the gang rape of a heavily pregnant local Catholic woman by a group of Ulster Special Constables, Aiken's men carried out a notorious reprisal massacre in the town of Altnaveigh, which lies on the Down/Armagh border, on June 17, 1922. Several innocent members of a small Presbyterian community were shot dead in cold blood." The chapter by Robert Lynch, in the same collection, counts six dead in the atrocity. He references the rape of a Mrs McGuill, the wife of a friend of Aiken, after recounting the atrocity, but uses the term "alleged" regarding the rape (and regarding another assault on one of McGuill's female servants); and describes the evidence that Aiken was responsible for the reprisal as "circumstantial" but nevertheless "compelling'—he does not say allegedly compelling. Irish historians, once again, rarely agree on facts—allegedly. Aiken's references to the reprisal, made in Dáil Éireann, describe taking action against Specials for attempted rape, not civilians (Dáil Éireann Debates, vol. 32, col. 173 (October 23, 1929), <http:// oireachtasdebates.oireachtas.ie/debates%20authoring/debateswebpack.nsf/takes/ dail1929102300032?opendocument>). Aiken never took responsibility for the atrocity at Altnaveigh, and the circumstantial allegations remain circumstantial.

m. The best treatment of the third Sinn Féin is found in Feeney (2002). The best single-volume long-run historical treatment of Fianna Fáil's republicanism and its policy toward the IRA and the North may be found in Ó Beacháin (2014); a lively account of the party in the Haughey years was written by the *Irish Times* journalist Dick Walsh (1986). O'Donnell (2007) covers the party's evolution from Lynch to Ahern.

n. Lyons, a Protestant, became Provost of Trinity College, Dublin; the O'Briens were agnostics of Catholic origin—CCO'B, a graduate of Trinity, had been left wing and republican but became conservative and anti-republican, and formally a unionist; Foster, a graduate of Trinity and professor at Oxford, is of southern Protestant origin. His treatment of the subject is measured, and accurate, noting, for example, that in 1926 Protestants accounted for 28 percent of farmers with over 200 acres, and 18 percent of the entire professional class, when they comprised just over 8 percent of the population of the IFS; by "1936 the Protestant proportion of Irish employers and business executives was 20–5 per cent; bank officials, 53 per cent; commercial representatives, 39 per cent; lawyers, 38 per cent. A modest, unofficial form of 'Ascendancy' lingered on" (Foster 1988: 534).

o. The doctoral thesis was awarded at Trinity College Dublin in 1993, externally examined by Charles Townshend and internally supervised by David Fitzpatrick. The revised version was published as *The IRA & its Enemies: Violence and Community in Cork 1916–1923* (1998), to widespread acclaim by diverse reviewers, including Tom Garvin, Roy Foster, Anthony McIntyre, Eunan O'Halpin, and Colm Tóibín. *The IRA at War 1916–23* followed in 2003, a collection of Hart's most significant articles in professional journals. A lively biography of *Mick: The Real Michael Collins* (2005), and some other essays were published before his premature death.

p. It is irrelevant to a defense of Hart's methods whether this evaluation referenced information given to the British forces by local Protestants in 1921 or 1922—because, as Regan points out, deciding this matter was impossible until the relevant documents were declassified in 2001—i.e., after Hart had published his confident and unambiguous conclusions, and when he had ignored this *Record*, <http://www.drb.ie/reviews/west-cork-and-the-writing-of-history> (accessed July 2016).

q. As John M. Regan has made clear, what is methodologically important is not whether this alternative explanation is true, but that Hart, aware of this alternative, chose to ignore it in pursuit of his preferred explanation. Subsequent defenses of Hart, which try to show the alternative explanation is false, may be empirically correct, but are beside the point: the flaw is "elision," and it seems that some of Hart's defenders fail to understand this point. Rather than refuting a plausible and known alternative explanation, he simply ignored it.

r. Remarkably he did not formally object to or obstruct the Coronation oath—of no legal significance, the jurists assure us. It included not only a pledge to the Protestant Reformed Religion but had the king swearing "to govern the peoples of Great Britain, Ireland, Canada . . ." Through official channels, an oral message was communicated: "Mr MacDonald should know that the attitude of the Government of Saorstát Éireann towards the Coronation . . . can only be one of detachment and protest, so long as our country is partitioned and the religious service implies discrimination (to put it mildly) against the faith of the majority of the people of this country" (No. 14 NAI 2006/39, Documents on Irish Foreign Policy, <http://www.difp.ie/docs/1937/Coronation-oath/ 2160.htm> (accessed June 2016).)

s. Treasury officials referred to these as bribes. "Blackmail and bluff (oddly enough called 'loyalty') have for many years been the accepted methods of Northern Ireland. It is high time these parochial die-hards were made to face up to a touch of reality." The UUP regime showed critical weaknesses in 1938; it did not participate in the negotiations, and, when it was consulted, the evidence suggests to those who wish to be uncharitable, its key ministers consistently sought to wreck them. When Hoare, a diehard, sought gestures of goodwill toward the South, Andrews, the future prime minister, blamed uncooperative northern nationalists, and declared it was "suicidal for the Northern Government to help the people who wished to destroy them." Chamberlain made the side payments in a separate deal with Craig. The latter's volte-face came to the knowledge of the two men who would succeed him, Andrews and Brooke, only in a joint meeting with British ministers, which Craig had ordered them to attend without their officials (McMahon 1984: 279, 272, 278).

2.4. THE UNEXPECTED STABILIZATION OF CONTROL

a. Hansard (NI), HC, vol. 2,. pp. 633–4 (May 22, 1922). The citation is from the first budget speech by Hugh MacDowell Pollock (1852–1937), the first Minister of Finance (1921–37). Director of a flour merchant's, ropeworks, and insurance company, previously Belfast Harbour Commissioner from 1900, and president of Belfast Chamber of Commerce from 1917 to 1918, Pollock argued that imperial sentiment rather than cold finance should apply to the Specials. He helped make it so.

b. Hansard, HC, vol. 371 cols 1390–1 (May 20, 1941); vol. 371, col. 17189 (May 27, 1941). Churchill admitted that "it would be more trouble than it is worth to enforce such a policy." On the day Churchill reopened the subject, the Secretary of State for War was asked the percentage of men of military age serving in His Majesty's Forces [from] Northern Ireland, and the comparable figure for Great Britain, but could not provide accurate information, because many people went from the South to enlist in the North, and men from Northern Ireland sometimes enlisted in Great Britain: Hansard, HC, vol. 371, cols 1369–70 (May 20, 1941).

c. Midgley had won a seat for the NILP in 1933 in Belfast's Dock constituency, with Catholic support. He had remained silent during the riots of 1935—for differing interpretations of his conduct, see Hepburn (1996: 200, n. 91), and Walker (1985: 77–8). His republican stance on the Spanish civil war, unlike his anti-republican stance in the North, earned him the hostility of pro-Franco Catholics, who helped him lose his seat in 1938. For Midgley's and his micro-party's journey from labor unionist to a more right-wing and indeed Orange unionist position, see Walker (1984, 1985).

d. Lee (1989: 257) describes Brooke as "more fundamentally sectarian than Craig." This evaluation resembles having to decide whether Enoch Powell was more fundamentally racist than Jean-Marie Le Pen, but for once I must disagree with Lee. Brookeborough was a tough realist, who maintained the control system that Craig had built through improvisation; he believed it had to be maintained by rigorous exclusion, not because of his religious convictions but because of his (national) loyalty to the British connection; stability had to come before justice—his interview with VanVoris (1975: 3–11) is good evidence for this position.

e. In correspondence, Prof. Brian Girvin has indicated that there is a case to be made that approximately 80,000 from the South and the same number from the North volunteered between 1939 and 1945 (totals that include those with home addresses in the North or South who were already in the British forces in 1939) (email exchanges, July 2016).

f. My father interrupted his chemistry degree at University College Cork to serve in the RAF between 1944 and 1947; he was no enthusiast for de Valera, but thought neutrality was the right policy for Ireland.

g. For usefully contrasting appraisals of de Valera's relations with the IRA after the formation of Fianna Fáil, see Fanning (1983b) and Ó Beacháin (2014); the former displays and respects the integrity of de Valera's commitment to order and majority-rule; the latter writes from a civil libertarian perspective.

h. The immediate impetus for these events was the IRA's assassination in 1936 of retired Vice-Admiral Henry Boyle Townshend Somerville, a Protestant of Cromwellian extraction—for the offense of advising Irishmen intent on joining the British armed forces—and its execution of an alleged informant the following month. On the former event, the memoir of Joseph O'Neill (focused on the parallel lives of his Ottoman and Irish grandfathers) is a fascinating and indispensable work of literature, which names those culpable for the admiral's killing, though the author wrote before parts of Peter Hart's history of west Cork came into question (Joseph O'Neill 2001). Somerville's older sister, Edith, was a distinguished novelist.

i. Southern gerrymandering was different from the Northern variety. It was not organized to unify an ethnic or religious majority against a minority. It was, however, organized in the interests of the dominant party. It was more constrained and restrained. STV was proportional in its outcomes, especially when the district magnitude was four or more. Lee (1989: 296) mockingly describes MacEntee's redistricting, especially its claim to allow for the return of migrants from Great Britain, "as one of the most delicious pieces of fiction ever designed by even a harassed electoral cartographer to frustrate the will of the people" (see also pp. 294–8).

j. Cahir Healy MP was interned as a security risk in Brixton Prison in London in July 1941: an alleged letter to a priest, intercepted by the British wartime censor, according to a secret memorandum in the Irish Department of Foreign Affairs files, was said to have declared that in "the event of a negotiated peace the Germans should be left in no doubt as to the wishes of himself and his politician friends as to the help they could give to Germany" (cited in Staunton 2001: 146). Different and firmer documentary evidence, but reliant on Irish police files from August 1940, suggests that some Northern nationalists proposed to "place the Catholic minority in the north under the protection of the Axis powers," and their meetings were chaired by Senator Thomas McLaughlin, a close contact of Cardinal McRory (Staunton 2001: 144–5).

k. In introducing Martin Dillon's *The Dirty War* (1991) Conor Cruise O'Brien in his foreword managed to conjure up General Order No. 8 as a part of a "new policy" in which the Provisional IRA received support for the Dublin government in 1969–70 for concentrating its operations "inside Northern Ireland." There were interactions between the Dublin government and the emergent Provisionals in 1969–70 (see Vol. 2, Ch. 6, appendix), but General Order No. 8 dated back to 1954 (see Bell 1997: 266, and previous editions of his work; see also Robert W. White 2006: 49). A unionist historian, and an admirer of O'Brien, not commenting on this foreword, has separately observed that the order had been first drafted in 1948 (English 2003: 71). O'Brien's foreword was therefore itself a specimen of the dirty war—i.e., disinformation. He had been a propagandist for Irish unity in the 1950s; he gradually became an anti-IRA propagandist from *c.*1972, ending as a wholly subscribed partisan unionist.

2.5. LOSING CONTROL, 1958–1972

a. Cameron (1969); Arthur (1974: 23); Farrell, Michael (1976); Buckland (1981); Purdie (1990). An oblique and not entirely persuasive contra-argument is advanced in Bew et al. (1996: 149–53). They target the Cameron Commission's explanation that a less deferential and "much larger middle class" lay behind the civil-rights movement, (Cameron 1969: 15). Bew et al. concede to the Commission that the size of Catholic professionals and managerial class more than doubled in the North between 1911 and 1971, so their objection is not to the size argument, but to its timing. Their claim is that the growth of this class had already occurred before 1961—and imply that could not be directly related to the education changes of 1947. But this counterargument has no purchase against the cohort of 1960s students or young activists identified in the text (see Vol. 2, Ch. 5, pp. 160–1), who were undoubtedly beneficiaries of expanded educational provision—those who were 22 in 1968 had started grammar school in 1958. Where Bew et al. innovate is in pointing to a larger more disadvantaged working and unemployed class developing in the five decades after 1911.

b. Edwards (2008) regards the party as having been retrospectively vindicated, suggesting that mass mobilization inevitably led to violence, a judgment that appears to leave the regime's security forces off the hook; he also endorses his supervisor Graham Walker's view that, had the British Labour Party responded to the NILP earlier, then the necessary pressure might have been successfully applied to O'Neill earlier, and thereby have achieved more timely reform. Edwards successfully protests that the NILP had managed its internal differences tolerably well, but the quotation he provides from one of its leader's memoirs is telling: "If we shouted too little [about civil rights], we should forfeit the support of those moderate and constructive Catholics who were now willing to join the party despite its commitment to partition . . . If we shouted too loud, we should arouse Protestant fears, which had been half-dormant, and precipitate a speedy return to the politics of violence" (Brett 1978: 133). Charles Brett was reflecting back on a speech he had made in 1963.

c. He made efforts to intensify Scots–Irish ethnic ties in the USA as part of the promotion of inward investment. He had high hopes. In a private letter to the editor of the *Belfast Telegraph* of June 24, 1965, O'Neill reported that a Scotch–Irish tycoon had said to him in Philadelphia: "You know what . . . the Scotch–Irish own America and the Southern Irish run it" (Gailey 1995: 96–7).

d. Faulkner and Houston (1978: 40). Arthur Brian Deane Faulkner (1921–77) became prime minister March 1971–March 1972 and was Chief Executive of Northern Ireland January–May 1974. Faulkner had boarded at a Protestant school in Dublin. His college education at QUB was disturbed by the Second World War, in which he did not serve, working in the family shirt-making business. Elected as Stormont's youngest MP ever in 1949, he achieved early prominence as a hardline supporter of Orange Order marching "rights." Having married Lucy Forsythe, a TCD graduate and former journalist who had been Brooke's secretary, he became Chief Whip for the UUP (1956–9).

As Minister of Home Affairs (1959–63), he oversaw the complete defeat of the IRA's "border campaign." Under O'Neill, he was an able Minister of Commerce (1963–9) and successfully attracted inward investment. He resigned from the cabinet in January 1969. As Minister of Development 1969–71, he implemented reforms of local government. Having started as a hardliner, he became a genuine advocate of power-sharing within Northern Ireland and across the island, though he never lost his reputation for Machiavellian opportunism. For a generous treatment of his life up until 1974, which credits him with reforming his own outlook, see the biography by the NILP's David Bleakley (1974). For a contrasting indictment of Faulkner as "foremost among the guilty men," whose "whole political career had shown him to be nothing but a purveyor of hatred," see Andrew Boyd (1972: 132); it was published after Faulkner's first premiership. Faulkner died after falling from his horse, shortly after having been elevated to the Lords.

e. Harry West (1917–2004) was the leader of the Ulster Unionist Party 1974–9, despite having been dismissed by O'Neill for exploiting insider knowledge to purchase land that he knew was about to be developed as a small airport—West's action was euphemistically described as a result of his having been "ill-advised" (Faulkner and Houston 1978: 80). The episode confirmed nationalists in their conviction that Ulster Unionists tolerate corruption more than they tolerate moderation in their leaders. Brookeborough defended West, and so did many UUP MPs, convinced that O'Neill was punishing West for attempting to undermine him (Bleakley 1974: 73).

f. Greaves (1913–88) joined the Communist Party in 1934 and remained a member until his death. He was the founder of the Connolly Association, and highly active in Great Britain in anti-partitionist mobilization. The biographies of Connelly and Mellows are still read, and are more readable than most subsequent efforts to treat their subjects (Greaves 1961, 1971).

g. In his memoir Austin Currie (2004: 9–10) asks himself whether he would have initiated this protest had he known it would initiate a process that would lead to the loss of nearly 4,000 lives, and answers in the negative. His candid self-questioning prompts the question of whether there would not have been some other civil disobedience protest movement.

h. Greaves supported a bill of rights to constrain Stormont, and divide unionists between progressives and reactionaries, but did not seek its abolition because he thought direct rule would make Irish reunification more difficult (Coughlan 1990: 10–11). This position later became influential among some within the Official IRA, and later the Workers' Party.

i. The best considered account of the outbreak of conflict in Derry is the doctoral thesis published by Ó Dochartaigh (1997); it will age much better than the more immediately written memoir of a central protagonist (McCann 1974). See also Frank Curran (1986).

j. No Unionist female MPs were elected to Westminster until 2001, when Sylvia Hermon (1955–) (née Paisley), a former law lecturer, and Iris Robinson (née Collins) were elected for North Down and Strangford respectively. Unlike Devlin, they had locally famous husbands at the time of their election: Mr Hermon had been the Chief Constable of the RUC, and Mr Robinson was the deputy leader of the DUP and future first minister. In the same election, Michelle Gildernew (1970–) was elected for Sinn Féin, with a different heritage—she hailed from a family active in the Caledon housing dispute of 1968 that galvanized the Civil Rights Association.

2.6. BRITISH INTERVENTION

a. Cork-born Jack Lynch (1917–99), previously the Minister of Finance, and of Commerce, was the first Irish party leader and prime minister not to have fought in the 1916 rebellion: John Costello (prime minister 1948–51, 1954–7) of Fine Gael had not been his party's leader. A Gaelic sports star (in hurling and football) and a barrister, Lynch was prime minister from 1966 until 1973, and again from 1977 until 1979. He had clearly defeated his rival George Colley, though he was regarded as a compromise candidate by two rivals who withdrew from the race, Charles Haughey and Neil Blaney. Lynch is regarded as one of the greatest ever dual GAA stars; the unkind suggested he was equally skilled at playing two games in politics.

b. Writing contemporaneously, the cautious Cornelius O'Leary (1969: 308), no relation, judged that "the grievances were mainly, though not entirely, in the field of local government. The exclusion of nearly one-third of the adult population from the local government register ... would not have been so important if it has not been associated in the Catholic mind with rigging of electoral boundaries and the judicious allocation of local authority housing to preserve Unionist hegemony in marginal areas." While casting a cold-eye on unionist and nationalist illusions, the article reveals its time: there is no mention of the IRA, nor of loyalist paramilitaries.

c. Denis Healey, defense minister in the Labour government, had warned his cabinet colleagues in August 1969 that standing down the Specials "might arouse intense feeling," and in September told them that British troops were being increasingly vilified by the "poor white" Protestants (Castle 1984: 701, 708). Though Healey was of Irish (Catholic) origin, he had avoided all Irish questions in his career—his thinking then reflected the comparative framing of Northern Ireland as analogous to the southern states of the USA.

d. This policy probably stopped a full-scale settler revolt against the metropole. The policy was publicly anticipated by Brookeborough's son, Captain John Brooke MP. Shortly after the Hunt Report had been announced, he urged the Specials to stick to their guns, and looked forward to seeing them in the new defense force (Deutsch and Magowan 1973: 49).

e. This was the contemporary assessment (*Sunday Times* Insight Team 1972), widely agreed by subsequent commentators. The army's General Freeland appears to have believed that a show of force was necessary to control the IRA's growth in the Falls (Dewar 1985). The curfew caused hardship as the army conducted door-to-door searches, which resembled domicide, and was broken by women and children bringing food in as relief (for the idea of domicide, see Porteous and Smith 2001). The army reported many wounded. The Falls residents accused the soldiers of wanton destruction, looting, and harassment.

f. He was facilitated in his ambitions by what may have been a panicked decision of the Lynch government, under its new Justice minister, Desmond O'Malley, appointed during the "Arms crisis" (see Vol. 2, Ch. 6, pp. appendix 2.6.1). In December 1970, the Irish government notified the Council of Europe of its intention to derogate from the European Convention on Human Rights, a preliminary step before the introduction of internment. O'Malley's target was Saor Éire, a minuscule organization, that O'Malley subsequently claimed was planning to kidnap government ministers. The government was accused of succumbing to British pressure by republicans and nationalists, north and south of the border, who believed it had given Faulkner the green light. Despite relentless pressure, the Irish government avoided internment, however, though it did pass emergency legislation, and began intensive control of public broadcasters, including censorship (Ó Beacháin 2014: 309–11).

g. Faulkner's memoir (Faulkner and Houston 1978: 106) represented himself as more reluctant and wiser than he seemed at the time. Official British state papers released in January 2002 revealed that Heath had failed to heed GOC General Harry Tuzo's warnings against internment. Before this truth was confirmed, Lee (1989: 437) had sardonically observed: "If the reported reluctance among both political and military decision-makers is ... true, the decision to [intern] must count as a particularly bizarre case."

h. Only one Protestant was initially interned, the lecturer, libertarian anarchist, and co-founder of the People's Democracy, and therefore the highly atypical John McGuffin

(1942–2002). He went on to produce two books based on this experience, both very sprightly, fluent, and compelling criticisms of the torture and ill-treatment suffered by detainees, and the history of internment in general (McGuffin 1973, 1974). Both books are reliable. These experiences reshaped McGuffin's politics. He wrote for the republican press before he left for San Francisco, where he trained as a lawyer, and, according to Eamonn McCann, advertised his services as a defense attorney as follows: "Sean McGuffin, Attorney at Law, Irish-friendly—No crime too big, no crime too small." He returned to Northern Ireland in 1998.

i. There were rumors in 1971 that, if Faulkner agreed to intern both loyalists and republicans, then Lynch would have reciprocated with internment in the South (McGuffin 1973: 61), but I have been unable to find evidence that such an exchange was contemplated. Lynch counseled the British Ambassador against the policy. Subsequent to the introduction of internment in the North, some Irish officials did fly kites in which internment would be introduced in the South in return for an Irish say in the future of the North and power-sharing in the North.

j. Patrick Anderson, in forthcoming work, has pointed out that editorials in the *Guardian* newspaper in 1969 argued that Catholics should have voted for O'Neill. They displayed "short-sightedness," instead of voting for the UUP landowner, Orange Lodge master, and British captain. Editorials in the same newspaper, many probably written by John Cole, had subsequent recommendations for Catholics: they "should respond to Protestant reforms" rather than provoking Protestants through rioting and "insisting on educational apartheid;" they should join the RUC instead of attacking the police with "a hatred they took in with their mothers' milk;" they should get the IRA to stop instead of helping them; and they should recognize Northern Ireland, rather than "abjure any Catholic who does; and should not push self-determination too far or they would face the wrath of loyalist paramilitaries." Indeed, "sensible Catholics would prefer the army," "shelve the issue of Partition," and, not least, "discipline their children." Among other matters, Anderson's work is a blistering and well-documented indictment of editorializing in the *Guardian* and the *Observer* in the years 1968–74.

k. Retiring as Belfast's Lord Mayor in May 1972, Alderman Sir John Cairns declared that Britain's policies had relegated Ulster to "the status of a Fuzzy Wuzzy colony" (Deutsch and Magowan 1974: 181). Such casually racist language was then widespread. An antirepublican journalist reports a Derry comedian assessing that the shock of Bloody Sunday was that "we had imagined that the Brits . . . would recognize that we were not fuzzy wuzzies but were just the same as themselves . . . that they would behave better here than they had in Aden. But we were just mad Paddies to the Paras" (O'Doherty 2007: 98).

l. Henry Patterson argues that "Republicanism grew more from British weakness than the iron fist." Drawing upon archival reports of UK representatives sent to monitor the UUP's government in 1969–71, he concludes that it was because these officials diagnosed the unionist community as supremacist, and because they wanted to avoid Catholic alienation, that they allowed the Provisionals to "develop their capacities largely unimpeded by the state" (Patterson 2008: 509, 508). That appeasement allowed the IRA to grow is an argument more typically associated with reactionaries, but Patterson's point seems to be that it was impossible for the UUP governments to reform while its supporters' anxieties were heightened by loss of control over the B Specials and the police. It would seem to follow, however, that he must either think that direct rule should have happened earlier, or that a more astute combination of reform and repression of the IRA should have been the policy formula—presumably repression of the Official as well as the Provisional IRA. On this curious account, while Great Britain's relationship to Northern Ireland was not colonial, its key officials' mentalities were driven by colonial misunderstandings.

m. Simon Prince's account (2007) of Northern Ireland's '68 places the civil-rights movements and the far left in People's Democracy in the international context of student movements. Those who have not read the works of Arthur, McCann, Devlin, or Farrell may be surprised by Prince's rediscoveries, but he goes seriously awry when he argues that Northern Ireland should be compared with France and Germany in these years, rather than with other cases of colonialism or control. No French or German regime had excluded Protestants or Catholics in the twentieth century. Northern Ireland was distinctive in democratic western Europe in the systematic exclusion of a locally large minority differentiated by nationality, ethnicity, and religion. Prince thereby unintentionally absolves the British state, the UUP, the RUC, and the B Specials of their culpability, and by implication suggests that Northern Ireland's local leftists, on their own, brought the house down. It was not so.

Bibliography

Abercrombie, Nicholas, Stephen Hill, and Bryan Turner (1980). *The Dominant Ideology Thesis*. London: Allen & Unwin.

Adam, Heribert (1971). *Modernizing Racial Domination: The Dynamics of South African Politics*. Berkeley and Los Angeles: University of California Press.

Addison, Paul (1994). *The Road to 1945: British Politics and the Second World War*. 2nd edn. London: Pimlico.

Akenson, Donald H. (1975). *A Mirror to Kathleen's Face: Education in Independent Ireland, 1922–1960*. Montreal: McGill-Queen's University Press.

Akenson, Donald H. (1992). *God's Peoples: Covenant and Land in South Africa, Israel, and Ulster*. Ithaca, NY: Cornell University Press.

Akenson, Donald H., and J. F. Fallin (1970). "The Irish Civil War and the Drafting of the Irish Free State Constitution," *Eire-Ireland*, 1: 10–26.

Ali, Taisier Mohamed Ahmed, and Robert O. Matthews (1999) (eds). *Civil Wars in Africa: Roots and Resolution*. Montreal: McGill-Queen's University Press.

Anderson, Perry (1976). "The Antinomies of Antonio Gramsci," *New Left Review*, 100: 5–78.

Anderson, Perry (2009). *The New Old World*. London: Verso.

Anderson, Perry (2017). *The Antinomies of Antonio Gramsci, with a New Preface*. London: Verso.

Aristotle (1962). *The Politics*, trans. T. Sinclair. Harmondsworth: Penguin.

Arthur, Paul (1974). *The People's Democracy, 1968–1973*. Belfast: Blackstaff.

Arthur, Paul (1977). "Devolution as Administrative Convenience: A Case Study of Northern Ireland," *Parliamentary Affairs*, 30: 97–106.

Arthur, Paul (1984). *Government and Politics of Northern Ireland*. 2nd edn. London: Longman.

Arthur, Paul (2000a). "Home Rule and Devolution in Ulster," in H. T. Dickinson and Michael Lynch (eds), *The Challenge to Westminster: Sovereignty, Devolution and Independence*. East Linton: Tuckwell Press, 143–53.

Arthur, Paul (2000b). *Special Relationships: Britain, Ireland and the Northern Ireland Problem*. Belfast: Blackstaff.

Aughey, Arthur (1989). *Under Siege: Ulster Unionism and the Anglo-Irish Agreement*. London: Hurst.

Augusteijn, Joost (1996). *From Public Defiance to Guerrilla Warfare: The Experience of Ordinary Volunteers in the Irish War of Independence, 1916–1921*. Dublin: Irish Academic Press.

Augusteijn, Joost (2002). *The Irish Revolution, 1913–1923*. Basingstoke: Palgrave.

Aunger, Edmund A. (1975). "Religion and Occupational Class in Northern Ireland," *Economic and Social Review*, 7/1: 1–17.

Aunger, Edmund A. (1981). *In Search of Political Stability: A Comparative Study of New Brunswick and Northern Ireland*. Montreal: McGill-Queens University Press.

Baram, Amatzia (1991). *Culture and Ideology in the Formation of Ba'athist Iraq, 1968–1989*. New York: St Martin's Press.

Bardon, Jonathan (1992). *A History of Ulster*. Belfast: Blackstaff.

Barker, Ernest (1911). "Empire," in *Encyclopaedia Britannica*, Cambridge: Cambridge University Press, ix. 347–56.

Barrington, T. J. (1972). "Council of Ireland in the Constitutional Context," *Administration*, 20: 28–49.

Barritt, Denis P., and Charles F. Carter (1962). *The Northern Ireland Problem: A Study in Group Relations*. 1st edn. London: Oxford University Press.

Barritt, Denis P., and Charles F. Carter (1972/1962). *The Northern Ireland Problem: A Study in Group Relations*. 2nd edn. London: Oxford University Press.

Barton, Brian (1988). *Brookeborough: The Making of a Prime Minister*. Belfast: Institute of Irish Studies, The Queen's University of Belfast.

Barton, Brian (1989). *The Blitz: Belfast in the War Years*. Belfast: Blackstaff.

Barton, Brian (1992). "Relations between Westminster and Stormont during the Attlee Premiership," *Irish Political Studies*, 7: 1–20.

Barton, Brian (1996). "The Impact of World War II on Northern Ireland and on Belfast-London Relations," in Peter Catterall and Sean McDougall (eds), *The Northern Ireland Question in British Politics*. Basingstoke: Macmillan, 47–70.

Bell, G. (1976). *The Protestants of Ulster*. London: Pluto Press.

Bell, J. Bowyer (1979). *The Secret Army: The IRA 1916–1979*. 3rd edn. Dublin: Academy Press.

Bell, J. Bowyer (1997). *The Secret Army: The IRA 1916–1979*. Rev. 3rd edn. London: Routledge.

Bergmann, Werner (2003). "Pogroms," in Wilhelm Heitmeyer and John Hagan (eds), *International Handbook of Violence Research*. Dordrecht: Klewer, 351–67.

Bew, Paul (2007). *Ireland: The Politics of Enmity 1789–2006*. Oxford: Oxford University Press.

Bew, Paul, and Henry Patterson (1982). *Seán Lemass and the Making of Modern Ireland, 1945–66*. Dublin: Gill & Macmillan.

Bew, Paul, Peter Gibbon, and Henry Patterson (1979). *The State in Northern Ireland, 1921–72: Political Forces and Social Classes*. Manchester: Manchester University Press.

Bew, Paul, Peter Gibbon, and Henry Patterson (1996). *The State in Northern Ireland 1921–1972: Political Forces and Social Classes*. Rev. and updated edn. Manchester: Manchester University Press.

Bielenberg, Andy, John Borgonovo, and James S. Donnelly Jr (2014). "'Something of the Nature of a Massacre': The Bandon Valley Killings Revisited," *Éire-Ireland*, 49/3: 7–59.

Bleakley, David (1974). *Faulkner: Conflict and Consent in Irish Politics*. Oxford: Mobrays: Alden Press.

Bloomfield, Kenneth (2007). *A Tragedy of Errors: The Government and Misgovernment of Northern Ireland*. Liverpool: Liverpool University Press.

Bogaards, Matthijs (2008). "Comparative Strategies of Political Party Regulation," in Benjamin Reilly and Per Nordlund (eds), *Political Parties in Conflict-Prone Societies: Regulation, Engineering and Democratic Development*. Tokyo: United Nations University Press, 48–66.

Boulton, David (1973). *The UVF, 1966–73: An Anatomy of Loyalist Rebellion*. Torc Books. Dublin: Gill & Macmillan.

Bowen, Elizabeth, Brendan Clifford, and Jack Lane (2009). *Notes on Eire: Espionage Reports to Winston Churchill, 1940–42*. 3rd edn. Millstreet, Co. Cork: Aubane Historical Society.

Bowen, Kurt Derek (1983). *Protestants in a Catholic State: Ireland's Privileged Minority*. Montreal and Dublin: McGill-Queen's University Press and Gill & Macmillan.

Bowman, John (1982). *De Valera and the Ulster Question, 1917–73*. Oxford: Oxford University Press.

Boyce, D. George. (1972). *Englishmen and Irish Troubles: British Public Opinion and the Making of Irish Policy, 1918–1922*. London: Jonathan Cape.

Boyd, Andrew (1969). *Holy War in Belfast*. 1st edn. Travlee: Anvil Books.

Boyd, Andrew (1972). *Brian Faulkner and the Crisis of Ulster Unionism*. Tralee: Anvil Books.

Boyd, Andrew (2005). *Holy War in Belfast*. 4th edn. Belfast: Donaldson Archives.

Boyle, Andrew (1977). *The Riddle of Erskine Childers*. London: Hutchinson.

Brass, Paul R. (1996) (ed.). *Riots and Pogroms*. New York: New York University Press.

Brennan, Robert (2002). *Ireland Standing Firm and Eamon de Valera: A Memoir.* ed. Richard H. Rupp, Dublin: University College Dublin Press.

Brett, Charles E. B. (1978). *Long Shadows Cast Before: Nine Lives in Ulster, 1625–1977.* Edinburgh: John Bartholemew.

Brewer, John, Adrian Guelke, Ian Hume, Edward Moxon-Browne, and Richard A. Wilford (1988). *The Police, Public Order and the State: Policing in Great Britain, Northern Ireland, the Irish Republic, the USA, Israel, South Africa and China.* New York: St Martin's Press.

Bromage, Arthur W. (1937a). "Constitutional Developments in Saorstát Eireann and the Constitution of Éire: I, External Affairs," *American Political Science Review,* 31/5 (October), 842–61.

Bromage, Arthur W. (1937b). "Constitutional Developments in Saorstát Eireann and the Constitution of Éire: II, Internal Affairs," *American Political Science Review,* 31/6: 1050–70.

Bromage, Arthur W, and Mary C. Bromage (1940). "The Irish Constitution: A Discussion of Its Theoretical Aspects," *Review of Politics,* 2/2: 145–66.

Brown, R. (1986). *Social Psychology.* 2nd edn. New York: Free Press.

Brubaker, Rogers (1996). *Nationalism Reframed: Nationhood and the National Question in the New Europe.* Cambridge: Cambridge University Press.

Bruce, Steve (1986). *God Save Ulster! The Religion and Politics of Paisleyism.* Oxford: Oxford University Press.

Bryan, Dominic (2000). *Orange Parades: The Politics of Ritual, Tradition and Control.* Anthropology, Culture & Society. London: Pluto Press.

Buckland, Patrick (1973). *Irish Unionism 1885–1923: A Documentary History.* 1st edn. Belfast: Her Majesty's Stationery Office.

Buckland, Patrick (1979). *The Factory of Grievances: Devolved Government in Northern Ireland, 1921–39.* Dublin: Gill & Macmillan.

Buckland, Patrick (1980). *James Craig, Lord Craigavon.* Dublin: Gill & Macmillan.

Buckland, Patrick (1981). *A History of Northern Ireland.* Dublin: Gill & Macmillan.

Budge, Ian, and Cornelius O'Leary (1973). *Belfast: Approach to Crisis: A Study of Belfast Politics, 1613–1970.* London: Macmillan.

Callaghan, James (1973). *A House Divided: The Dilemma of Northern Ireland.* London: Collins.

Calvert, Harry (1968). *Constitutional Law in Northern Ireland; A Study in Regional Government.* London: Stevens & Sons.

Cameron, Lord (1969). "Disturbances in Northern Ireland: Report of the Commission Appointed by the Governor of Northern Ireland." Belfast. HMSO, <http://cain.ulst.ac.uk/hmso/cameron.htm> (accessed May 2012).

Campaign for Social Justice (1969). "Northern Ireland: The Plain Truth." 2nd edn. Dungannon: CSJ.

Campaign for Social Justice (1989/1964). "Northern Ireland. Why Justice Cannot Be Done: The Douglas Home Correspondence," in Conn McCluskey (ed.), *Up off their Knees: A Commentary on the Civil Rights Movement in Northern Ireland.* Galway: Conn McCluskey and Associates, app. II.

Canning, Paul (1985). *British Policy towards Ireland, 1921–41.* Oxford: Clarendon Press.

Carty, R. Kenneth (1983). *Electoral Politics in Ireland: Party and Parish Pump.* Dingle: Brandon Book Publishers.

Castle, Barbara (1984). *The Castle Diaries 1964–70.* London: Weidenfeld & Nicolson.

Cathcart, Rex (1984). *The Most Contrary Region: The BBC in Northern Ireland, 1924–1984.* Belfast: Blackstaff.

Chambers, Anne (2014). *T. K. Whitaker: Portrait of a Patriot.* Dublin: Transworld Ireland.

Cheibub, Jose Antonio (2002). "Presidentialism and Democratic Performance," in Andrew Reynolds (ed.), *The Architecture of Democracy: Constitutional Design, Conflict Management and Democracy.* Oxford: Oxford University Press, 104–40.

Clayton, Pamela (1996). *Enemies and Passing Friends: Settler Ideologies in Twentieth Century Ulster*. London: Pluto Press.

Clements, Ben, and Nick Spencer (2014). "Voting and Values in Britain: Does Religion Count?" *Theos*, <www.theos.com> (accessed summer 2014).

Clifford, Angela (2006a). *August 1969, Ireland's Only Appeal to the United Nations: A Cautionary Tale of Humiliation and Moral Collapse*. Arms Crisis Series No. 1, A Belgast Magazine No. 26. Belfast: A Belfast Magazine (Athol Books).

Clifford, Angela (2006b). *Military Aspects of Ireland's Arms Crisis*. Arms Crisis Series No. 2, A Belfast Magazine No. 29. Belfast: A Belfast Magazine (Athol Books).

Clifford, Angela (2009a). *The Arms Conspiracy Trial. Ireland 1970: The Prosecution of Charles Haughey, Captain Kelly and others*. Arms Crisis Series No. 3, A Belfast magazine No. 33. The Northern Ireland Question in British Politics. Belfast: A Belfast Magazine (Athol Books).

Clifford, Angela (2009b). *The Arms Crisis: What Was it All About?* Arms Crisis Series No. 4, A Belfast Magazine No. 34. 2nd edn. Belfast: A Belfast Magazine (Athol Books).

Clifford, Brendan (2011). *Northern Ireland: What Is It?* Belfast: Athol Books.

Coakley, John (1980). "The Significance of Names: The Evolution of Irish Party Labels," *Études Irelandaises*, 5: 171–81.

Coakley, John, and Michael Gallagher (1993) (eds). *Politics in the Republic of Ireland*. 2nd edn. Galway: PSAI Press.

Collier, David, and Steven Levitsky (1997). "Research Note. Democracy with Adjectives: Conceptual Innovation in Comparative Research," *World Politics*, 49 (April), 430–51.

Collins, Eamon (1998). *Killing Rage*. London: Granta Books.

Compton, Paul A. (1985). "An Evaluation of the Changing Religious Composition of the Population of Northern Ireland." Mimeo.

Compton, Sir Edmund (1971). *Report of the Inquiry into Allegations against the Security Forces of Physical Brutality in Northern Ireland Arising out of Events on 9th August 1971*. London. HMSO, <http://cain.ulst.ac.uk/hmso/compton.htm> (accessed May 2012).

Coogan, Tim Pat (1990). *Michael Collins*. London: Arrow Books.

Coogan, Tim Pat (1993). *De Valera*. London: Hutchinson.

Coogan, Tim Pat (2002). *The IRA*. Fully rev. and updated. 1st Palgrave edn. New York: Palgrave.

Coughlan, Anthony (1990). *C. Desmond Greaves, 1913–1988: An Obituary Essay*. Studies in Irish Labour History 1. Dublin: Irish Labour History Society.

Cox, Thomas J. (1975). *Damned Englishman: A Study of Erskine Childers (1870–1922)*. Hicksville, NY: Exposition Press.

Crawford, Robert G. (1987). *Loyal to King Billy: A Portrait of the Ulster Protestants*. London: C. Hurst & Co.

Cronin, Sean (1972). *The McGarrity Papers: Revelations of the Irish Revolutionary Movement in Ireland and America, 1900–1940*. Tralee: Anvil Books.

Cronin, Sean (1983). *Irish Nationalism: A History of its Roots and Ideology*. London: Pluto Press.

Cronin, Sean (1985). "The Making of NATO and the Partition of Ireland," *Eire-Ireland*, 20/2: 6–18.

Cronin, Sean (1987). *Washington's Irish Policy, 1916–1986: Independence, Partition, Neutrality*. Dublin: Anvil Books.

Cronin, Sean, and Richard Roche (1973) (eds). *Freedom the Wolfe Tone Way*. Tralee: Anvil Books.

Curl, James S. (1986). *The Londonderry Plantation, 1609–1914: The History, Architecture, and Planning of the Estates of the City of London and its Livery Companies in Ulster*. Chichester: Phillimore.

Curl, James S. (2000). *The Honourable the Irish Society and the Plantation of Ulster, 1608–2000: The City of London and the Colonisation of County Londonderry in the Province of Ulster in Ireland: A History and Critique*. Chichester: Phillimore.

Curran, Frank (1986). *Derry: Countdown to Disaster*. Dublin: Gill & Macmillan.

Curran, Joseph M. (1980). *The Birth of the Irish Free State, 1921–1923*. Tuscaloosa: University of Alabama Press.

Currie, Austin (2004). *All Hell Will Break Loose*. Dublin: O'Brien Press.

Dahl, Robert A. (1989). *Democracy and its Critics*. New Haven: Yale University Press.

Darby, John (1976). *Conflict in Northern Ireland: The Development of a Polarised Community*. Dublin: Gill & Macmillan.

Davies, Norman (1999). *The Isles: A History*. Basingstoke: Macmillan.

de Paor, Liam (1971). *Divided Ulster*. 2nd edn. Harmondsworth: Penguin Books.

Delaney, Enda (2000). *Demography, State and Society: Irish Migration to Britain, 1921–1971*. Liverpool: Liverpool University Press.

Deutsch, Richard, and Vivien Magowan (1973) (eds). *Northern Ireland 1968–73: Chronology of Events. Volume 1. 1968–71*. Belfast: Blackstaff.

Deutsch, Richard, and Vivien Magowan (1974) (eds). *Northern Ireland 1968–73. Chronology of Events. Volume 2. 1972–73*. Belfast: Blackstaff.

Deutsch, Richard, and Vivien Magowan (1975) (eds). *Northern Ireland 1968–73. Chronology of Events. Volume 3. 1974*. Belfast: Blackstaff.

Devlin, Bernadette (1969). *The Price of My Soul*. London: Pan Books in association with André Deutsch.

Devlin, Bernadette (1988). "A Peasant in the Halls of the Great," in Michael Farrel (ed.), *Twenty Years On*. Dingle: Brandon Books, 75–88.

Dewar, Michael (1985). *The British Army in Northern Ireland*. London: Arms & Armour.

Dillon, Myles (1960). Comment, *University Review* 2/2 (Summer), 22–27.

Dillon, Martin (1991). *The Dirty War*. London: Hutchinson.

Ditch, John (1988). *Social Policy in Northern Ireland between 1939–1950*. Aldershot: Averbury Gower.

Doherty, Gabriel, and Dermot Keogh (1998) (eds). *Michael Collins and the Making of the Irish State*. Cork: Mercier Press.

Dolan, Anne (2003). *Commemorating the Irish Civil War: History and Memory, 1923–2000*. Cambridge: Cambridge University Press.

Dolan, Jay P. (2008). *The Irish Americans: A History*. New York: Bloomsbury Press.

Donnelly, James S., Jr (2012). "Big House Burnings in County Cork during the Irish Revolution, 1920–21," *Eire-Ireland*, 47/3–4: 141–97.

Dooley, Brian (1998). *Black and Green: The Fight for Civil Rights in Northern Ireland and Black America*. London: Pluto Press.

Doyle, John (1994). "Workers and Outlaws: Unionism and Fair Employment in Northern Ireland," *Irish Political Studies*, 9: 41–60.

Dudley Edwards, Owen (1987). *Éamon de Valera*, ed. Kenneth O. Morgan. Political Portraits. Cardiff: GPC Books.

Dunleavy, Patrick (1991). *Democracy, Bureaucracy and Public Choice: Economic Explanations in Political Science*. Brighton: Harvester.

Dunleavy, Patrick, George W. Jones, and Brendan O'Leary (1990). "British Prime Ministers and Parliament," *Public Administration*, 68/1: 123–40.

Dwyer, T. R. (1977). *Irish Neutrality and the USA, 1939–45*. Dublin: Gill & Macmillan.

Dwyer, T. Ryle (1983). "Eamon de Valera and the Partition Question," in John P. O'Carroll and John A. Murphy (eds), *De Valera and his Times*. Cork: Cork University Press, 74–91.

Edwards, Aaron (2008). "'Unionist Derry is Ulster's Panama': The Northern Ireland Labour Party and the Civil Rights Issue. *Irish Political Studies*, 23/3: 387–410.

Elgie, Robert (1993). *The Role of the Prime Minister in France, 1981–91*. Basingstoke: Macmillan Press.

Elgie, Robert (1999). *Semi-Presidentialism in Europe*. Comparative European Politics. Oxford: Oxford University Press.

Elgie, Robert (2001). *Divided Government in Comparative Perspective.* Comparative Politics. Oxford: Oxford University Press.

Elgie, Robert (2005). "From Linz to Tsebelis: Three Waves of Presidential/Parliamentary Studies?," *Democratization*, 12/1: 106–22.

Elgie, Robert (2011). *Semi-Presidentialism: Sub-Types and Democratic Performance.* Oxford: Oxford University Press.

Elgie, Robert, and Sophia Moestrup (2007). *Semi-Presidentialism outside Europe: A Comparative Study.* London: Routledge.

Elgie Robert, and Sophia Moestrup (2008). *Semi-Presidentialism in Central and Eastern Europe.* Manchester: Manchester University Press.

Elgie, Robert, Emiliano Grossman, and Amy Mazur (2016). *The Oxford Handbook of French Politics.* Oxford: Oxford University Press.

Elliott, Sidney (1973). *Northern Ireland Parliamentary Election Results, 1921–72.* Chichester: Political Reference Publications.

Elster, Jon (2013). *Securities against Misrule: Juries, Assemblies, Elections.* Cambridge: Cambridge University Press.

English, Richard (2003). *Armed Struggle: The History of the IRA.* London: Macmillan.

Esman, Milton J. (1973). "The Management of Communal Conflict," *Public Policy*, 21/1: 49–78.

Evans, Bryce (2011). *Seán Lemass: Democratic Dictator.* Cork: Collins Press.

Evans, Bryce, and Stephen Kelly (2014) (eds). *Frank Aiken: Nationalist and Internationalist.* Dublin: Irish Academic Press.

Fanning, Ronan (1977). "Leadership and the Transition from the Politics of Revolution to the Politics of Party: The Example of Ireland 1914–1939," in *XIV International Congress of Historical Sciences, 1975, San Francisco.* New York: Arno Press, 1741–68.

Fanning, Ronan (1978). *The Irish Department of Finance, 1922–58.* Dublin: Institute of Public Administration.

Fanning, Ronan (1979). "The United States and Irish Participation in NATO: The Debate of 1950," *Irish Studies in International Affairs*, 1: 1.

Fanning, Ronan (1983a). *Independent Ireland.* Dublin: Helicon.

Fanning, Ronan (1983b). "'The Rule of Order': Eamon de Valera and the IRA, 1925–1940," in John P. O'Carroll and John A. Murphy (eds), *De Valera and his Times.* Cork: Cork University Press. 160–73.

Farrell, Brian (1970a). "The Drafting of the Irish Free State Constitution: I," *Irish Jurist*, 5/1: 115–40.

Farrell, Brian (1970b). "The Drafting of the Irish Free State Constitution II," *Irish Jurist*, 5/2: 343–56.

Farrell, Brian (1971a). "The Drafting of the Irish Free State Constitution III," *Irish Jurist*, 6/1 (Summer), 111–35.

Farrell, Brian (1971b). "The Drafting of the Irish Free State Constitution IV," *Irish Jurist*, 6/2 (Winter), 345–59.

Farrell, Brian (1985). "The Unlikely Marriage: De Valera, Lemass and the Shaping of Modern Ireland," *Études Irelandaises*, 10 (December), 215–22.

Farrell, Brian (1988) (ed.). *De Valéra's Constitution and Ours.* Dublin: Gill & Macmillan.

Farrell, Michael (1976). *Northern Ireland: The Orange State.* 1st edn. London: Pluto Press.

Farrell, Michael (1980). *Northern Ireland: The Orange State.* 2nd edn. London: Pluto Press.

Farrell, Michael (1983). *Arming the Protestants: The Formation of the Ulster Special Constabulary and the Royal Ulster Constabulary, 1920–7.* London: Pluto Press.

Farrell, Sean (2009). *Riots and Rituals. Sectarian Violence and Political Culture in Ulster.* The University Press of Kentucky.

Farren, Seán (2010). *The SDLP. The Struggle for Agreement in Northern Ireland, 1970–2000.* Dublin: Four Courts Press.

Faulkner, Brian, and John Houston (1978). *Memoirs of a Statesman*. London: Weidenfeld & Nicolson.

Feeney, Brian (2002). *Sinn Féin: A Hundred Turbulent Years*. Dublin: O'Brien Press.

Feeney, Brian (2009). *Insider: Gerry Bradley's Life in the IRA*. Dublin: O'Brien Press.

Fisk, Robert (1985). *In Time of War: Ireland, Ulster and the Price of Neutrality, 1939–45*. London: Paladin Books.

Fitzpatrick, David (1998). *The Two Irelands, 1912–1939*. Oxford: Oxford University Press.

Fitzpatrick, David (2014). *Descendancy: Irish Protestant Histories since 1795*. Cambridge: Cambridge University Press.

Flackes, William D., and Elliot, Sydney (1989). *Northern Ireland: A Political Directory, 1968–88*. Rev. and updated edn. Belfast: Blackstaff.

Flackes, William D., and Elliot, Sydney (1994). *Northern Ireland: A Political Directory*. Belfast: Blackstaff.

Fleming, Neil (2005). "'The Londonderry Herr': Lord Londonderry and the Appeasement of Nazi Germany," *History Ireland*, 13: 1.

Follis, Bryan A. (1995). *A State under Siege. The Establishment of Northern Ireland, 1920–1925*. Oxford: Oxford University Press.

Foner, Eric (2005). *Reconstruction: America's Unfinished Revolution, 1863–1877, with a New Introduction by the Author*. The New American Nation Series. 2nd edn. New York: Francis Parkman Prize Edition History Book Club.

Foster, Roy F. (1988). *Modern Ireland, 1600–1972*. London: Allen Lane.

Gailey, Andrew (1995). *Crying in the Wilderness. Jack Sayers: A Liberal Editor in Ulster, 1939–69*. Belfast: Institute of Irish Studies, The Queen's University of Belfast.

Gallagher, Frank (1957). *The Indivisible Island: The Story of the Partition of Ireland*. London: Gollancz.

Gallagher, Michael (1979). "The Pact General Election of 1922," *Irish Historical Studies*, 21/84: 404–21.

Gallagher, Michael (1993). *Irish Elections 1922–44. Results and Analysis*. Sources for the Study of Irish Politics. Limerick: PSAI Press.

Garson, Anna (2017). "'Please Give Justice': The Cushendall Incident, Sectarian Violence, and Anglo-Irish Relations, 1920–22." BA Honors thesis, University of Pennsylvania.

Garvin, Tom (1981). "The Origins of the Party System in Independent Ireland," in *The Evolution of Irish Nationalist Politics*. Dublin: Gill & Macmillan, 135–77.

Garvin, Tom (1987). *Nationalist Revolutionaries in Ireland, 1858–1928*. Oxford: Oxford University Press.

Garvin, Tom (1996). *1922: The Birth of Irish Democracy*. Dublin: Gill & Macmillan.

Garvin, Tom (2005). *Preventing the Future: Why Was Ireland So Poor for So Long?* Dublin: Gill & Macmillan.

Garvin, Tom (2009). *Judging Lemass: The Measure of the Man*. Dublin: Royal Irish Academy.

Garvin, Tom (2011). *News from a New Republic: Ireland in the 1950s*. Dublin: Gill & Macmillan.

Gellner, Ernest (1983). *Nations and Nationalism*. Oxford: Basil Blackwell.

Girvin, Brian (2006). *The Emergency: Neutral Ireland 1939–45*. London: Macmillan.

Girvin, Brian, and Geoffrey Roberts (1998). "The Forgotten Volunteers," *History•Ireland* (March), 46–51.

Girvin, Brian, and Geoffrey Roberts (2000) (eds). *Ireland and the Second World War: Politics, Society and Remembrance*. Dublin: Four Courts Press.

Government of Ireland (1997). *Bloody Sunday and the Report of the Widgery Tribunal: The Irish Government's Assessment of the New Material*. Dublin: Stationery Office.

Greaves, C. Desmond (1961). *The Life and Times of James Connolly*. London: Lawrence & Wishart.

Greaves, C. Desmond (1971). *Liam Mellows and the Irish Revolution*. London: Lawrence & Wishart.

Haddick-Flynn, Kevin (1999). *Orangeism: The Making of a Tradition*. Dublin: Wolfhound Press.

Hand, Geoffrey J. (1973). "MacNeill and the Boundary Commission," in F. X. Martin and F. J. Byrne (eds), *The Scholar Revolutionary: Eoin MacNeill, 1867–1945, and the Making of the New Ireland*. Shannon: Irish University Press, 201–75.

Hanley, Brian (2002). *The IRA, 1926–1936*. Dublin: Four Courts Press.

Harbinson, John Fitzsimons (1973). *The Ulster Unionist Party, 1882–1973: Its Development and Organization*. Belfast: Blackstaff.

Hardiman, Niamh (1989). *Pay, Politics, and Economic Performance in Ireland 1970–1987*. Oxford: Oxford University Press.

Harkness, David W. (1969). *The Restless Dominion: The Irish Free State and the British Commonwealth of Nations 1921–31*. 1st edn. Basingstoke: Macmillan.

Harkness, David (1977). "The Difficulties of Devolution: The Post-War Debate at Stormont," *Irish Jurist*, 12: 176–86.

Harkness, David (1983). *Northern Ireland since 1920*. Dublin: Helicon.

Harkness, D. W. (1988). "The Constitutions of Ireland and the Development of National Identity, 1919–1984," *Journal of Commonwealth and Comparative Politics*, 26/2: 135–46.

Harkness, David W. (1996). *Ireland in the Twentieth Century: Divided Island*. New York: St Martin's Press.

Harris, Mary (1993). *The Catholic Church and the Foundation of the Northern Ireland State*. Cork: Cork University Press.

Harris, Mary (2003). "Religious Divisions, Discrimination and the Struggle for Dominance in Northern Ireland," in Guðmundur Hálfdanarson (ed.), *Racial Discrimination and Ethnicity in European History, Clio's Workshop II*. Pisa: Pisa University Press, 205–35.

Hart, Peter (1998). *The IRA and Its Enemies: Violence and Community in Cork, 1916–1923*. Oxford: Oxford University Press.

Hart, Peter (2003). *The IRA at War, 1916–1923*. Oxford: Oxford University Press.

Hart, Peter (2005a). "Hart to Heart," *History Ireland*, 13/2 (March–April), 48–51.

Hart, Peter (2005b). *Mick: The Real Michael Collins*. London: Macmillan.

Hay, Denys (1955–6). "The Use of the Term 'Great Britain' in the Middle Ages," *Proceedings of the Society of Antiquaries of Scotland*, 89, 55–66.

Hepburn, Anthony C. (1990). "The Belfast Riots of 1935," *Social History*, 15/1: 75–96.

Hepburn, Anthony C. (1996). *A Past Apart: Studies in the History of Catholic Belfast*. Belfast: Ulster Historical Foundation.

Hepburn, Anthony C. (2003). "The Failure of Chronic Violence: Belfast," in *Contested Cities in the Modern World*. Basingstoke: Palgrave Macmillan, 158–88.

Hepburn, Anthony C. (2008). *Catholic Belfast and Nationalist Ireland in the Era of Joe Devlin, 1871–1934*. Oxford: Oxford University Press.

Hewitt, Christopher (1981). "Catholic Grievances, Catholic Nationalism and Violence in Northern Ireland during the Civil Rights Period: A Reconsideration," *British Journal of Sociology*, 32/3: 362–80.

Hezlet, Arthur Richard, Sir (1973). *The "B" Specials: A History of the Ulster Special Constabulary*. London: Pan Books.

Hogan, Gerard W., and Clive Walker (1989). *Political Violence and the Law in Ireland*. Manchester: Manchester University Press.

Hopkinson, Michael (1988). *Green against Green: The Irish Civil War*. Dublin: Gill & Macmillan.

Hopkinson, Michael (1990). "The Craig–Collins Pacts of 1922: Two Attempted Reforms of the Northern Ireland Government," *Irish Historical Studies*, 27/106: 145–58.

Horgan, John (1997). *Seán Lemass: The Enigmatic Patriot*. Dublin: Gill & Macmillan.

Horowitz, Donald L. (1973). "Direct, Displaced and Cumulative Ethnic Aggression," *Comparative Politics*, 6 (October), 1–16.

Horowitz, Donald L. (1991). "The Constructive Uses of Presidentialism," in *A Democratic South Africa? Constitutional Engineering in a Divided Society*. Berkeley and Los Angeles: University of California Press, 205–14.

Horowitz, Donald L. (2001). *The Deadly Ethnic Riot*. Berkeley and Los Angeles: University of California Press.

Horowitz, Donald L. (2006). "Constitutional Courts: A Primer for Decision Makers," *Journal of Democracy*, 17/4: 125–37.

Howard, Michael C., and King, John E. (1989). *A History of Marxian Economics, 1883–1929. Volume I*. Princeton: Princeton University Press.

Hunt, Baron (1969). "Report of the Advisory Committee on Police in Northern Ireland." Belfast: HMSO, October, <http://cain.ulst.ac.uk/hmso/hunt.htm> (accessed May 2012).

Inglis, Tom (1987). *Moral Monopoly: The Catholic Church in Modern Irish Society*. Dublin: Gill & Macmillan.

Jackson, Alvin (2003). *Home Rule: An Irish History, 1800–2000*. Oxford: Oxford University Press.

Jeffery, Keith (2006). *Field Marshal Sir Henry Wilson: A Political Soldier*. Oxford: Oxford University Press.

Johnson, D. S. (1980)."Northern Ireland as a Problem in the Economic War 1932–38," *Irish Historical Studies*, 22/86: 144–61.

Jordan, Anthony (2006). *W. T. Cosgrave 1880–1965: Founder of Modern Ireland*. Dublin: Westport Books.

Katzenstein, Peter J. (1985). *Small States in World Markets: Industrial Policy in Europe*. Ithaca, NY: Cornell University Press.

Kaufmann, Eric P. (2007). *The Orange Order: A Contemporary Northern Irish History*. New York: Oxford University Press.

Keane, Barry (2012). "Ethnic Cleansing? Protestant Decline in West Cork Between 1911 and 1926." *History•Ireland*, 20: 2.

Keane, Barry (2014). *Massacre in West Cork: The Dunmanway and Ballygroman Killings*. Cork: Mercier Press.

Kearney, Richard (1997). *Postnationalist Ireland: Politics, Culture, and Philosophy*. London: Routledge.

Keatinge, Patrick (1984). *A Singular Stance: Irish Neutrality in the 1980s*. Dublin: Institute of Public Administration.

Kedourie, Elie (1960). *Nationalism*. London: Hutchinson.

Kelly, James (1971). *Orders for the Captain?* Dublin: James Kelley.

Kelly, James (1999). *The Thimble Riggers: The Dublin Arms Trials of 1970*. Dublin: James Kelly.

Kelly, J. M. (1980). *The Irish Constitution*. Dublin: Jurist Publishing Co.

Kelly, J. M, G. W Hogan, and G. Whyte (1987). *Supplement to the Irish Constitution*. Dublin: Jurist Publishing Co.

Kenna, G. B. (1922). *Facts & Figures of the Belfast Pogrom*. Dublin: O'Connell Publishing Co.

Kennedy, Denis (1988). *The Widening Gulf: Northern Attitudes to the Independent Irish State, 1919–1949*. Belfast: Blackstaff.

Kennedy, Kieran A., Thomas Giblin, and Deirdre McHugh (1988). *The Economic Development of Ireland in the Twentieth Century*. London: Routledge.

Kent, Brad (2016) (ed.). *The Selected Essays of Sean O'Faolain*. Montreal: McGill-Queen's University Press.

Keogh, Dermot (1988). "The Irish Constitutional Revolution: An Analysis of the Making of the Irish Constitution," in Frank Litton (ed.), *The Constitution of Ireland 1937–1987*. Dublin: Institute of Public Administration, 4–84.

Keogh, Dermot (2000). "Irish Neutrality and the First Application for Membership of the EEC, 1961–3," in Michael Kennedy and Joseph Morrison Skelly (eds), *Irish Foreign Policy, 1919–66: From Independence to Internationalism*. Dublin: Four Courts Press, 265–85.

Keogh, Dermot, and Andrew McCarthy (2007). *The Making of the Irish Constitution 1937: Bunreacht na hEireann*. Cork: Mercier Press.

Keown, Gerard (2016). *First of the Small Nations: The Beginnings of Irish Foreign Policy in the Interwar Years, 1919–1932*. Oxford: Oxford University Press.

King, Gary, Robert O. Keohane, and Sidney Verba (1994). *Designing Social Inquiry: Scientific Inference in Qualitative Research*. Princeton: Princeton University Press.

Kissane, Bill (2002). *Explaining Irish Democracy*. Dublin: University College Dublin Press.

Kissane, Bill (2005). *The Politics of the Irish Civil War*. Oxford: Oxford University Press.

Kissane, Bill (2007). "Éamon de Valera and the Survival of Democracy in Interwar Ireland," *Journal of Contemporary History*, 42/ 2: 211–24.

Kitson, Frank (1971). *Low Intensity Operations: Subversion, Insurgency and Peace-Keeping*. London: Faber & Faber.

Kleinrichert, Denise (2001). *Republican Internment and the Prison Ship Argenta 1922*. Dublin: Irish Academic Press.

Kohn, Leo (1932). *The Constitution of the Irish Free State*. London: George Allen & Unwin.

Kuper, Leo, and M. G. Smith (1969) (eds). *Pluralism in Africa*. Berkeley and Los Angeles: University of California Press.

Laffan, Michael (1983). *The Partition of Ireland, 1911–25*. Dundalk: Dundalgan Press.

Laffan, Michael (1999). *The Resurrection of Ireland: The Sinn Féin Party, 1916–1923*. Cambridge: Cambridge University Press.

Lawlor, Pearse (2009). *The Burnings 1920*. Cork: Mercier Press.

Lawlor, Pearse (2011). *The Outrages 1920–1922. The IRA and the Ulster Special Constabulary in the Border Campaign*. Cork: Mercier Press.

Lawrence, Reginald James (1965). *The Government of Northern Ireland; Public Finance and Public Services, 1921–1964*. Oxford: Clarendon Press.

Lee, J. Joseph (1989). *Ireland, 1912–1985: Politics and Society*. Cambridge: Cambridge University Press.

Lee, J. Joseph (1998). "The Challenge of a Collins Biography," in Gabriel Doherty and Dermot Keogh (eds), *Michael Collins and the Making of the Irish State*. Cork: Mercier Press, 19–38.

Lee, J. Joseph (2001). "De Valera's Use of Words: Three Case-Studies," *Radharc*, 2 (November), 75–100.

Lemarchand, René (1970). *Rwanda and Burundi*. New York: Praeger.

Lijphart, Arend (1992) (ed.). *Parliamentary versus Presidential Government*. Oxford Readings in Politics and Government. Oxford: Oxford University Press.

Lindberg, Leon, and Stuart A. Scheingold (1970). *Europe's Would-Be Polity: Patterns of Change in the European Community*. Englewood Cliffs, NJ: Prentice Hall.

Lindblom, Charles E. (1959). "The Science of 'Muddling Through,'" *Public Administration Review*, 19: 79–88.

Linz, Juan J. (1993). "Statebuilding and Nationbuilding," *European Review*, 1/4: 355–69.

Longford, Lord, and Thomas P. O'Neill (1970). *Eamon de Valera*. Dublin: Gill & Macmillan.

Lustick, Ian S. (1980). *Arabs in the Jewish State: Israel's Control of a National Minority*. Modern Middle East Series, 6. Austin: University of Texas Press.

Lynch, Robert John (2006). *The Northern IRA and the Early Years of Partition, 1920–1922*. Dublin: Irish Academic Press.

Lyne, Thomas (1990). "Ireland, Northern Ireland and 1992: The Barriers to Technocratic Anti-Partitionism," *Public Administration*, 68/4: 417–33.

Lynn, Brendan (1997). *Holding the Ground: The Nationalist Party in Northern Ireland, 1945–1972*. Aldershot: Ashgate Publishing.

Lyons, Francis Stuart Leland (1967). "The Minority Problem in the 26 Counties," in Frank McManus (ed.), *The Years of the Great Test*. Cork: Mercier Press, 92–103.

Lyons, Francis Stuart Leland (1973a). "From War to Civil War in Ireland: Three Essays on the Treaty Debate," in Brian Farrell (ed.), *The Irish Parliamentary Tradition*. Dublin: Gill & Macmillan.

Lyons, Francis Stuart Leland (1973b). *Ireland since the Famine*. 2nd rev. edn. London: Fontana.

Mabry, Tristan, John McGarry, Margaret Moore, and Brendan O'Leary (2013) (eds), *Divided Nations and European Integration*. Philadelphia: University of Pennsylvania Press.

McAllister, Ian (1975). "Political Opposition in Northern Ireland: The National Democratic Party," *Economic and Social Review*, 6/3: 353–66.

McAllister, Ian (1977). *The Northern Ireland Social Democratic and Labour Party: Political Opposition in a Divided Society*. London: Macmillan.

Macardle, Dorothy (1965). *The Irish Republic: A Documented Chronicle of the Anglo-Irish Conflict and the Partitioning of Ireland, with a Detailed Account of the Period 1916–1923*. New York: Farrar, Straus and Giroux.

McCann, Eamonn (1974). *War and an Irish Town*. Harmondsworth: Penguin Books.

McCauley, Clark (2001). "Review of Donald L. Horowitz's "The Deadly Ethnic Riot,"" *Conflict, Security and Development*, 1/3: 164–8.

McCluskey, Conn (1989). *Up off their Knees: A Commentary on the Civil Rights Movement in Northern Ireland*. Galway: Conn McCluskey and Associates.

McColgan, John (1977). "Implementing the 1921 Treaty: Lionel Curtis and Constitutional Procedure," *Irish Historical Studies*, 20/79: 312–33.

McCormack, Inez (1988). "Faceless Men: Civil Rights and After," in Michael Farrel (ed.), *Twenty Years On*. Dingle: Brandon Books, 25–38.

McCullagh, David (1998). *A Makeshift Majority: The First Inter-Party Government, 1948–51*. Dublin: Institute of Public Administration.

McDermott, Jim (2001). *Northern Divisions: The Old IRA and the Belfast Pogroms, 1920–22*. Belfast: Beyond the Pale.

MacDonald, Michael (1986). *Children of Wrath: Political Violence in Northern Ireland*. Cambridge: Polity.

McGarry, Fearghal (2002). *Frank Ryan*. Dundalk: Dundalgan Press.

McGarry, John (2001). "Globalization, European Integration and the Northern Ireland Conflict," in Michael Keating and John McGarry (eds), *Minority Nationalism and the Changing International Order*. Oxford: Oxford University Press, 295–324.

McGarry, John (2012). "Is Presidentialism Necessarily Non-Collegial?," *Ethnopolitics*, ahead-of-print: 1–4.

McGarry, John, and Brendan O'Leary (1995). *Explaining Northern Ireland: Broken Images*. Oxford: Blackwell Publishers.

McGrath, Michael P. M. (2000). *The Catholic Church and Catholic Schools in Northern Ireland: The Price of Faith*. Dublin: Irish Academic Press.

McGuffin, John (1973). *Internment*. Tralee: Anvil Books.

McGuffin, John (1974). *The Guineapigs*. Harmondsworth: Penguin Books.

MacIntyre, Tom (1971). *Through the Bridewell Gate: A Diary of the Dublin Arms Trial*. London: Faber & Faber.

McKay, Susan (2000). *Northern Protestants: An Unsettled People*. Belfast: Blackstaff.

McKeown, Ciaran (1984). *The Passion of Peace*. Belfast: Blackstaff.

McKeown, Michael (1986). *The Greening of a Nationalist*. Lucan, Co. Dublin: Murlough Press.

McKittrick, David, Seamus Kelters, Brian Feeney, and Chris Thornton (2004). *Lost Lives: The Stories of the Men, Women and Children who Died as a Result of the Northern Ireland Troubles*. 2nd rev. edn. Edinburgh: Mainstream Publishing.

MacLaren, Roy (2015). *Empire and Ireland: The Transatlantic Career of the Canadian Imperialist Hamar Greenwood 1870–1948*. Montreal: McGill-Queen's University Press.

McLean, Iain (1981). "Review of Paul Bew, Peter Gibbon and Henry Patterson, *The State in Northern Ireland*," *Political Studies*, 29/2 (June), 301.

McLoughlin, P. J. (2010). *John Hume and the Revision of Irish Nationalism*. Manchester: Manchester University Press.

McMahon, Deirdre (1984). *Republicans and Imperialists: Anglo-Irish Relations in the 1930s*. New Haven: Yale University Press.

McNeill, Ronald J. (1922). *Ulster's Stand for Union*. London: John Murray.

MacQueen, Norman (1983). "Ireland's Entry to the United Nations," in Tom Gallagher and James O'Connell (eds), *Contemporary Irish Studies*. Manchester: Manchester University Press, 65–79.

Macstiofain, Sean (1975). *Memoirs of a Revolutionary*. Farnborough: Gordon Cremonesi.

Maguire, Martin (1993). "A Socio-Economic Analysis of the Dublin Protestant Working Class," *Irish Economic and Social History*, 20: 35–61.

Maguire, Martin (2008). *The Civil Service and the Revolution in Ireland, 1912–38: Shaking the Blood-Stained Hand of Mr Collins*. Manchester: Manchester University Press.

Mair, Peter (1978). "The Break-Up of the United Kingdom: The Irish Experience of Regime Change, 1918–1949," *Journal of Commonwealth and Comparative Studies*, 16/3: 288–302.

Mair, Peter (1987). *The Changing Irish Party System: Organisation, Ideology and Electoral Competition*. London: Pinter Publishers.

Mair, Peter (1992). "Explaining the Absence of Class Politics in Ireland," in J. H. Goldthorpe and C. T. Whelan (eds), *The Development of Industrial Society in Ireland*. Oxford: Oxford University Press, 383–410.

Makiya, Kanan (1998/1989). *Republic of Fear: The Politics of Modern Iraq*. Berkeley and Los Angeles: University of California Press.

Mansergh, Nicholas (1936). *The Government of Northern Ireland: A Study in Devolution*. London: G. Allen & Unwin.

Mansergh, Nicholas (1966). "Ireland and the British Commonwealth of Nations: The Dominion Settlement," in T. D. Williams (ed.), *The Irish Struggle, 1916–26*. London: Routledge.

Mansergh, Nicholas (1991). *The Unresolved Question: The Anglo-Irish Settlement and Its Undoing, 1912–72*. New Haven: Yale University Press.

Mansion House Anti-Partition Conference (1950a). "Discrimination: A Study in Injustice." Dublin: All-Party Anti-Partition Conference.

Mansion House Anti-Partition Conference (1950b). "Ireland's Right to Unity." Dublin: All-Party Anti-Partition Conference.

Mansion House Anti-Partition Conference (1950c). "One Vote Equals Two." Dublin: All-Party Anti-Partition Conference.

Matthews, Kevin (2004). *Fatal Influence: The Impact of Ireland on British Politics, 1920–1925*. Dublin: University College Dublin Press.

Mazower, Mark (2012). *Governing the World: The History of an Idea, 1815 to the Present*. New York: Penguin.

Meehan, Elizabeth M. (2000). "Britain's Irish Question: Britain's European Question? British–Irish Relations in the Context of European Union and the Belfast Agreement," *Review of International Studies*, 26/1: 83–97.

Meehan, Niall (2014). "Examining Peter Hart," *Field Day Review*, 10/1: 103–47.

Memmi, Albert (1990). *The Colonizer and the Colonized*, trans. Howard Greenfeld. London: Earthscan Publications.

Milward, Alan (2005). *Politics and Economics in the History of the European Union*. London: Routledge.

Milward, Alan, George Brennan, and Federico Romero (1992). *The European Rescue of the Nation State*. London: Routledge.

Mitchell, Arthur, and Padraig Ó Snodaigh (1985). *Irish Political Documents 1916-1949*. Blackrock: Irish Academic Press.

Moloney, Ed, and Andy Pollak (1986). *Paisley*. Swords, Co. Dublin: Poolbeg Press.

Montesquieu, Charles de Secondat, Baron de (1989/1748). *The Spirit of the Laws*, trans. Anne Cohler, Basia Miller, and Harold Stone. Cambridge Texts in the History of Political Thought. Cambridge: Cambridge University Press.

Montgomery, Bernard (1958). *Memories of Field Marshal the Viscount Montgomery of Alamein*. London: Collins.

Moran, David P. (1905/2006). *The Philosophy of Irish Ireland*. Dublin: University College Dublin Press.

Morgan, David Gwynn (1990). *Constitutional Law of Ireland: The Law of the Executive, Legislature and Judicature*. Dublin: Round Hall Press.

Moynihan, Maurice (1980). *Speeches and Statements by Eamon de Valera, 1917–73* [includes some speeches in Irish]. Dublin: Gill & Macmillan.

Mulholland, Marc (2004). "Why Did Unionists Discriminate?," in Sabine Wichert (ed.), *From the United Irishmen to Twentieth-Century Unionism: Essays in Honour of A. T. Q. Stewart*. Dublin: Four Courts Press, 187–206.

Mulholland, Marc (2013). *Terence O'Neill*. Historical Association of Ireland. Life and Times New Series. Dublin: University College Dublin Press.

Mullan, Don, and John Scally (2002). *Eyewitness Bloody Sunday*. 4th edn. Dublin: Merlin Publishing.

Murphy, Brian P., and Niall Meehan (2008). *Troubled History: A 10th Anniversary Critique of Peter Hart's The IRA and its Enemies*, introduction by Ruan O'Donnell, <www.academia.edu> (accessed June 2012).

Murphy, Gerard (2010). *The Year of Disappearances: Political Killings in Cork, 1921–1922*. Dublin: Gill & Macmillan.

Murray, Gerard (1998). *John Hume and the SDLP: Impact and Survival in Northern Ireland*. Dublin: Irish Academic Press.

Murray, Patrick (2000). *Oracles of God: The Roman Catholic Church and Irish Politics, 1922–37*. Dublin: University College Dublin Press.

Murray, Russell C. (2006). "Belfast: The Killing Fields," in Frederick Wilgar Boal, Stephen A. Royle, and Maura E. Pringle (eds), *Enduring City: Belfast in the Twentieth Century*. Belfast: Blackstaff Press and Royal Irish Academy, 221–37.

Nelson, Sarah (1984). *Ulster's Uncertain Defenders: Protestant Political, Paramilitary, and Community Groups and the Northern Ireland Conflict*. Modern Irish Society. Belfast: Appletree Press.

Northern Ireland Office (1974). *Northern Ireland: Finance and the Economy, Discussion Paper I*. London: Northern Ireland Office.

Norton, Christopher (2014). *The Politics of Constitutional Nationalism in Northern Ireland: Between Grievance and Reconciliation*. Manchester: Manchester University Press.

Ó Beacháin, Donnacha (2014). *Destiny of the Soldiers—Fianna Fáil, Irish Republicanism and the IRA, 1926–1973: The History of Ireland's Largest and Most Successful Political Party*. Dublin: Gill & Macmillan.

Ó Broin, Leon (1991). *Michael Collins*. Dublin: Gill & Macmillan.

Ó Dochartaigh, Niall (1997). *From Civil Rights to Armalites: Derry and the Birth of the Irish Troubles*. Cork: Cork University Press.

Ó Dochartaigh, Niall (2004). "Bloody Sunday: It could All have Turned out Differently," *Irish Times*, November 20, 13.

O'Brien, Conor Cruise (1974). *States of Ireland*. 2nd edn. St Albans: Panther Books.

O'Brien, Conor Cruise (1991). "Nationalists and Democrats," *New York Review of Books*, 29–31.

O'Brien, Conor Cruise (1998). *Memoir: My Life and Themes*. London: Profile Books.

O'Brien, Justin (2000). *The Arms Trial*. Dublin: Gill & MacMillan.

O'Brien, Máire, and Conor Cruise O'Brien (1985). *A Concise History of Ireland*. 3rd rev. edn. London: Thames and Hudson.

O'Doherty, Malachi (2007). *The Telling Year: Belfast 1972*. Dublin: Gill & Macmillan.

O'Donnell, Catherine (2007). *Fianna Fáil, Irish Republicanism and the Northern Ireland Troubles 1968-2005*. Dublin: Irish Academic Press.

O'Dowd, Liam (1990). "Introduction," trans. in *The Colonizer and the Colonized*. London: Earthscan Publications.

O'Dowd, Liam, Bill Rolston, and Mike Tomlinson (1980). *Northern Ireland: Between Civil Rights and Civil War*. London: CSE Books.

O'Halloran, Clare (1987). *Partition and the Limits of Irish Nationalism: An Ideology under Stress*. Dublin: Gill & Macmillan.

O'Halpin, Eunan (2012). "Counting Terror: Bloody Sunday and *The Dead of the Irish Revolution*," in David Fitzpatrick (ed.), *Terror in Ireland, 1916-1923*. Dublin: Lilliput Press. 141-57.

O'Hanlon, Paddy (2011). *End of Term Report*. Northern Ireland,: Paddy O'Hanlon Publishing.

O'Leary, Brendan (1988). "Review Article on Terrorism," *British Journal of Criminology*, 28/1: 97-107.

O'Leary, Brendan (1989). "Guiltless Passions of a Unionist Liberal: Review of Tom Wilson's *Ulster: Conflict and Consensus*," *Irish Times*, October 7.

O'Leary, Brendan (1997)."On the Nature of Nationalism: A Critical Appraisal of Ernest Gellner's Writings on Nationalism," *British Journal of Political Science*, 27/2: 191-222.

O'Leary, Brendan (2001). "The Elements of Right-Sizing and Right-Peopling the State," in Brendan O'Leary, Ian S. Lustick, and Tom Callaghy (eds), *Right-Sizing the State: The Politics of Moving Borders*. Oxford: Oxford University Press, 15-73.

O'Leary, Brendan (2002). "In Praise of Empires Past: Myths and Method of Kedourie's *Nationalism*," *New Left Review*, 2nd ser, 18: 106-30.

O'Leary, Brendan (2007). "Analyzing Partition: Definition, Classification and Explanation," *Political Geography*, 26/8: 886-908.

O'Leary, Brendan (2010). "Electoral Systems and the Lund Recommendations," in Marc Weller and Katharine Nobbs (eds), *Political Participation of Minorities: A Commentary on International Standards and Practice*. Oxford: Oxford University Press, ch. 12, pp. 363-400.

O'Leary, Brendan (2011). "Debating Partition: Evaluating the Standard Justifications," in Kurt Cordell and Stefan Wolff (eds), *The Routledge Handbook of Ethnic Conflict*. London: Routledge, 140-57.

O'Leary, Brendan, and John McGarry (2012). "The Politics of Accommodation and Integration in Democratic States," in Adrian Guelke and Jean Tournon (eds), *The Study of Politics and Ethnicity: Recent Analytical Developments*. The World of Political Science: The Development of the Discipline Book Series. Leverkusen, Opladen: Barbara Budrich, 79-116.

O'Leary, Brendan, and John Tirman (2007). "Introduction: Thinking about Durable Political Violence," in Marianne Heiberg, Brendan O'Leary, and John Tirman (eds), *Terror, Insurgency and the State*. Philadelphia: University of Pennsylvania Press, 1-17.

O'Leary, Cornelius (1969)."Northern Ireland: The Politics of Illusion," *Political Quarterly*, 40/3: 307-15.

O'Leary, Cornelius (1990). "Professor Lee's Ireland: Paper Presented to the Annual Meeting of the Irish Political Studies Association of Ireland." Cork, October.

O'Leary, Cornelius, and Patrick Maume (2004). *Controversial Issues in Anglo-Irish Relations 1910-1921*. Dublin: Four Courts Press.

O'Leary, Richard (1999). "Change in the Rate and Pattern of Religious Intermarriage in the Republic of Ireland," *Economic and Social Review*, 30/2: 119-32.

O'Malley, Desmond (2014). *Conduct Unbecoming—A Memoir*. Dublin: Gill & Macmillan.

O'Neill, Joseph (2001). *Blood-Dark Track: A Family History*. London: Granta.

O'Neill, T. P. (1972) (ed.). *Dáil Éireann, Private Sessions of the Second Dáil*. Dublin: Stationery Office.

O'Rourke, Kevin (1991). "Burn Everything British but their Coal: The Anglo-Irish Economic War of the 1930s," *Journal of Economic History*, 51/2: 357–66.

O'Sullivan, Michael (1994). *Seán Lemass: A Biography*. Dublin: Blackwater Press.

Oakeshott, Michael (1939). *The Social and Political Doctrines of Contemporary Europe*. Cambridge: Cambridge University Press.

Osborne, Robert D. (1979). "The Northern Ireland Parliamentary Electoral System: The 1929 Reapportionment," *Irish Geography*, 12: 42–56.

Pakenham, Frank (1967). *Peace by Ordeal: An Account, from First-Hand Sources, of the Negotiation and Signature of the Anglo-Irish Treaty, 1921*. 4th edn. London: New English Library.

Palley, Claire (1966). *The Constitutional History and Law of Southern Rhodesia 1888–1965, with Special Reference to Imperial Control*. Oxford: Clarendon Press.

Palley, Claire (1972). "The Evolution, Disintegration and Possible Reconstruction of the Northern Ireland Constitution," *Anglo-American Law Review*, 1: 368–476.

Parkin, Frank (1979). *Marxism and Class Theory: A Bourgeois Critique*. London: Tavistock Press.

Parkinson, Alan F. (2004). *Belfast's Unholy War: The Troubles of the 1920s*. Dublin: Four Courts Press.

Patterson, Henry (2006). *Ireland since 1939: The Persistence of Conflict*. Dublin: Penguin Ireland.

Patterson, Henry (2008). "The British State and the Rise of the IRA, 1969–71: The View from the Conway Hotel," *Irish Political Studies*, 23/4: 491–21.

Phoenix, Eamon (1994). *Northern Nationalism: Nationalist Politics, Partition and the Catholic Minority in Northern Ireland 1890–1940*. Belfast: Ulster Historical Foundation.

Phoenix, Éamon (1998). "Michael Collins—the Northern Question 1916–1922," in Gabriel Doherty and Dermot Keogh (eds), *Michael Collins and the Making of the Irish State*. Cork: Mercier Press, 92–116.

Pocock, J. G. A. (1980). *Three British Revolutions: 1641, 1688, 1776*. Princeton: Guildford: Princeton University Press.

Pocock, J. G. A. (1982), "The Limits and Divisions of British History: In Search of an Unknown Subject," *American Historical Review*, 87/2 (April), 311–36.

Pocock, J. G. A. (1985). *Virtue, Commerce, and History: Essays on Political Thought and History, Chiefly in the Eighteenth Century*. Cambridge: Cambridge University Press.

Pocock, J. G. A. (1987). *The Ancient Constitution and the Feudal Law: A Study of English Historical Thought in the Seventeenth Century*. 2nd edn. Cambridge: Cambridge University Press.

Pocock, J. G. A. (1989a). *Politics, Language and Time: Essays on Political Thought and History*. 2nd edn. Chicago: University of Chicago Press.

Pocock, J. G. A. (1989b). "Machiavelli, Harrington and English Political Ideologies in the Eighteenth Century," in *Politics, Language and Time: Essays on Political Thought and History*. Chicago: University of Chicago Press, 104–47.

Pocock, J. G. A. (1999). "The New British History in Atlantic Perspective: An Antipodean Commentary," *American Historical Review*, 104/2: 490–500.

Pocock, J. G. A. (2003). *The Machiavellian Moment: Florentine Political Thought and the Atlantic Republican Tradition*. 2nd edn. Princeton: Princeton University Press.

Pocock, J. G. A. (2005). *The Discovery of Islands: Essays in British History*. Cambridge: Cambridge University Press.

Pocock, J. G. A. (2009). *Political Thought and History: Essays on Theory and Method*. Cambridge: Cambridge University Press.

Pocock, J. G. A., Gordon J. Schochet, and Lois G. Schwoerer (1993). *The Varieties of British Political Thought, 1500–1800*. Cambridge: Cambridge University Press.

Polybius (1979). *The Rise of the Roman Empire*, trans. Ian Scott-Kilvert. Penguin Classics. Harmondsworth: Penguin.

Porteous, J. Douglas, and Sandra E. Smith (2001). *Domicide: The Global Destruction of Home*. Montreal and Kingston: McGill-Queen's University Press.

Porter, Norman (1996). *Rethinking Unionism: An Alternative Vision for Northern Ireland*. Belfast: Blackstaff.

Prager, Jeffrey (1986). *Building Democracy in Ireland: Political Order and Cultural Integration in a Newly Independent Nation*. Cambridge: Cambridge University Press.

Prince, Simon (2007). *Northern Ireland's '68: Civil Rights, Global Revolt and the Origins of the Troubles*. Dublin: Irish Academic Press.

Pringle, Derek G. (1980). "Electoral Systems and Political Manipulation: A Case Study of Northern Ireland in the 1920s," *Economic and Social Review*, 11/3: 187–205.

Purdie, Bob (1983). "The Friends of Ireland: British Labour and Irish Nationalism, 1945–49," in Tom Gallagher and James O'Connell (eds), *Contemporary Irish Studies*. Manchester: Manchester University Press, 81–94.

Purdie, Bob (1986). "The Irish Anti-Partition League, South Armagh and the Abstentionist Tactic 1945–58," *Irish Political Studies*, 1: 67–77.

Purdie, Bob (1988). "Was the Civil Rights Movement a Republican/Communist Conspiracy?," *Irish Political Studies*, 3: 33–41.

Purdie, Bob (1990). *Politics in the Streets: The Origins of the Civil Rights Movement in Northern Ireland*. Belfast: Blackstaff.

Rabushka, Alvin, and Kenneth A. Shepsle (2009/1972). *Politics in Plural Societies: A Theory of Democratic Instability*. New York: Pearson Longman.

Rafferty, Oliver P. (1994). *Catholicism in Ulster, 1603–1983: An Interpretative History*. London: C. Hurst & Co.

Regan, John M. (1998). "Michael Collins–The Legacy and the Intestacy," in Gabriel Doherty and Dermot Keogh (eds), *Michael Collins and the Making of the Irish State*. Cork: Mercier Press, 117–26.

Regan, John M. (1999). *The Irish Counter-Revolution, 1921–36*. Dublin: Gill & Macmillan.

Regan, John M. (2013). *Myth and the Irish State*. Sallins: Irish Academic Press.

Rhodes, R. A. W., and Patrick Dunleavy (1995) (eds). *Prime Minister, Cabinet and Core Executive*. Basingstoke: Macmillan.

Riggs, F. W. (1997). "Presidentialism versus Parliamentarism: Implications for Representativeness and Legitimacy," *International Political Science Review*, 18/3: 253–78.

Ron, James (2003). *Frontiers and Ghettos: State Violence in Serbia and Israel*. Berkeley and Los Angeles: University of California Press.

Rose, Paul (2001). *How the Troubles Came to Northern Ireland*. Basingstoke: Palgrave.

Rose, Richard (1971). *Governing without Consensus: An Irish Perspective*. London: Faber & Faber.

Rose, Richard (1976). "On the Priorities of Citizenship in the Deep South and Northern Ireland," *Journal of Politics*, 38/2: 247–91.

Rowthorn, Bob, and Naomi Wayne (1988). *Northern Ireland: The Political Economy of Conflict*. Cambridge: Polity Press.

Rumpf, Erhard, and Anthony C. Hepburn (1977). *Nationalism and Socialism in Twentieth Century Ireland*. Liverpool: Liverpool University Press.

Ryan, Meda (1986). *Liam Lynch: The Real Chief*. Cork: Mercier.

Sanger, Clyde (1995). *Malcolm MacDonald: Bringing an End to Empire*. Montreal, Toronto, and Liverpool: McGill-Queens and Liverpool University Press.

Sassoon, Joseph (2012). *Saddam Hussein's Ba'ath Party: Inside an Authoritarian Regime*. Cambridge: Cambridge University Press.

Scarman, Justice (1972). "Violence and Civil Disturbances in Northern Ireland in 1969, Report of Tribunal of Inquiry, Presented to Parliament by Command of His Excellency the Governor of Northern Ireland (Cmnd 566). Belfast. Her Majesty's Stationery Office, <http://cain.ulst.ac.uk/hmso/scarman.htm> (accessed May 2012).

Shaw, Bernard (1930). *The Collected Works of Bernard Shaw. Plays. XI. John Bull's Other Island, How He Lied to Her Husband, Major Barbara.* Ayot St Lawrence Edition. New York: Wm H. Wise & Co.

Simpson, John (1983). "Economic Development: Cause or Effect in the Northern Ireland Conflict," in John Darby (ed.), *Northern Ireland: The Background to the Conflict.* Belfast: Appletree Press.

Skach, Cindy (2005). *Borrowing Constitutional Designs: Constitutional Law in Weimar Germany and the French Fifth Republic.* Princeton: Princeton University Press.

Smith, Anthony D. (1992). "Nationalism and the Historians," *International Journal of Comparative Sociology*, 33/1–2: 58–80.

Smith, David, and Gerald Chambers (1987). *Equality and Inequality in Northern Ireland, Part I: Employment and Unemployment.* London: Policy Studies Institute.

Smith, Gordon R. (1989). *Politics in Western Europe: A Comparative Analysis.* Aldershot: Gower.

Smith, Jeremy (2006). "Ever Reliable Friends? The Conservative Party and the Ulster Unionists," *English Historical Review*, 121/490: 70–103.

Smith, M. G. (1965). *The Plural Society in British West Indies.* Berkeley and Los Angeles: University of California Press.

Smith, Murray (1995). "The Title *An Taoiseach* in the 1937 Constitution," *Irish Political Studies*, 10: 179–84.

Smooha, Sammy (1980). "Control of Minorities in Israel and Northern Ireland," *Comparative Studies in Society and History*, 22/2: 256–80.

Staunton, Enda (1997). "Reassessing Michael Collins's Northern Policy," *Irish Studies Review*, 5/20: 9–11.

Staunton, Enda (2001). *The Nationalists of Northern Ireland 1918–1973.* Dublin: Columba Press.

Stepan, Alfred, and Cindy Skach (2001). "*Constitutional Frameworks and Democratic Consolidation: Parliamentarism versus Presidentialism*," in *Arguing Comparative Politics.* Oxford: Oxford University Press, 257–75.

Stepan, Alfred, Juan J. Linz, and Yogendra Yadav (2011). Crafting State-Nations: India and Other Multinational Democracies. Baltimore: Johns Hopkins University Press.

Stewart, Anthony Terence Quincey (1986). *The Narrow Ground: Patterns of Ulster History.* Belfast: Pretani Press.

Strauss, E. (1957). *Irish Nationalism and British Democracy.* London.

Strauss, Leo, Alexandre Kojeve, Victor Gourevitch, and Michael S. Roth (1991). *On Tyranny.* New York: Macmillan.

Sunday Times Insight Team (1972). *Ulster.* Harmondsworth: Penguin.

Szporluk, Roman (1991). *Communism and Nationalism: Karl Marx versus Friedrich List.* New York: Oxford University Press.

Taagepera, Rein, and Matthew Soberg Shugart (1989). *Seats and Votes: The Effects and Determinants of Electoral Systems.* New Haven, CT: Yale University Press.

Tannam, Etain (1999). *Cross-Border Cooperation in the Republic of Ireland and Northern Ireland.* Basingstoke: Macmillan Press.

Taylor, Charles (1993). *Reconciling the Solitudes: Essays in Canadian Federalism and Nationalism.* Montreal: McGill-Queen's University Press.

Taylor, Peter (1997). *Provos: The IRA and Sinn Féin.* London: Bloomsbury Publishing.

Todd, Jennifer (1990). "Northern Irish Nationalist Political Culture," *Irish Political Studies*, 5: 31–44.

Townshend, Charles (2014). *The Republic: The Fight for Irish Independence 1918–1923.* London: Penguin.

Tully, James (1995). *Strange Multiplicity: Constitutionalism in an Age of Diversity.* Cambridge: Cambridge University Press.

Ultach (1940). "The Persecution of Catholics in Northern Ireland," *Capuchin Annual* pp. 161–167, 170–175.

Ultach et al (1943) "The Real Case Against Partition," Capuchin Annual (1943), pp. 283–361 [published separately as a pamphlet under the title Orange Terror]

Utley, Thomas Edwin (1975). *Lessons of Ulster.* London: J. M. Dent & Sons.

van Dam, Nikolaos (2011). *The Struggle for Power in Syria: Politics and Society under the Asad and the Baʿath Party.* London: I. B. Tauris.

Van den Berghe, Pierre (1969). "Pluralism and the Polity: A Theoretical Explanation," in Leo Kuper and M. G. Smith (eds), *Pluralism in Africa.* Berkeley and Los Angeles: University of California Press, 67–81.

van Parijs, Philippe (2011). *Linguistic Justice for Europe and for the World.* Oxford: Oxford University Press.

VanVoris, W. H. (1975). *Violence in Ulster: An Oral Documentary.* Amherst, MA: University of Massachusetts Press.

Walker, Graham S. (1984). "The Commonwealth Labour Party in Northern Ireland, 1942–7," *Irish Historical Studies,* 24/93 (May), 69–91.

Walker, Graham S. (1985). *The Politics of Frustration: Harry Midgley and the Failure of Labour in Northern Ireland.* Manchester: Manchester University Press.

Wall, Maureen (1966). "Partition: The Ulster Question (1916–1926)," in T. Desmond Williams (ed.), *The Irish Struggle, 1916–1926.* London: Routledge and Kegan Paul, 79–93.

Walsh, Dermot P. J. (2000). *Bloody Sunday and the Rule of Law in Northern Ireland.* Dublin: Gill & Macmillan.

Walsh, Dick (1986). *The Party: Inside Fianna Fáil.* Dublin: Gill & Macmillan.

Ward, Alan J. (1969). *Ireland and Anglo-American Relations, 1899–1921.* London: Weidenfeld & Nicolson.

Ward, Alan J. (1994). *Irish Constitutional Tradition: Responsible Government and Modern Ireland, 1782–1992.* Dublin: Catholic University of America Press.

Ward, Alec (2017). "Orange, Green, and Blue: Police Reform and Sectarian Politics in Northern Ireland, 1922–2001." BA Honors Thesis, University of Pennsylvania.

Weber, Max (1977/1918). "Politics as a Vocation," in Hans H. Gerth and C Wright Mills (eds), *From Max Weber: Essays in Sociology.* London: Routledge, 77–128.

Weitzer, Ronald J. (1990). *Transforming Settler States: Communal Conflict and Internal Security in Northern Ireland and Zimbabwe.* Berkeley and Los Angeles: University of California Press.

Weitzer, Ronald J. (1995). *Policing under Fire: Ethnic Conflict and Police–Community Relations in Northern Ireland.* Albany, NY: New York University Press.

Whelan, Bernadette (2000a). "Integration or Isolation? Ireland and the Invitation to Join the Marshall Plan," in Michael Kennedy and Joseph Morrison Skelly (eds), *Irish Foreign Policy, 1919–66: From Independence to Internationalism.* Dublin: Four Courts Press, 203–21.

Whelan, Bernadette (2000b). *Ireland and the Marshall Plan, 1947–57.* Dublin: Four Courts Press.

Whelan, Bernadette (2015). "Recognition of the Irish Free State, 1924: The Diplomatic Context to the Appointment of Timothy Smiddy as the First Minister to the US," *Irish Studies in International Affairs,* 26: 1–5.

White, Jack (1975). *Minority Report: The Protestant Community in the Irish Republic.* Dublin: Gill & Macmillan.

White, Robert W. (2006). *Ruairí Ó Brádaigh: The Life and Politics of an Irish Revolutionary*. Bloomington: Indiana University Press.

White, Terence de Vere (1948). *Kevin O'Higgins*. London: Methuen & Co.

Whitelaw, William (1989). *The Whitelaw Memoirs*. London: Arium Press.

Whyte, John H. (1979). *Church and State in Modern Ireland, 1923–1979*. 2nd edn. Dublin: Gill & Macmillan.

Whyte, John H. (1983). "How Much Discrimination Was there under the Unionist Regime, 1921–68?," in Tom Gallagher and James O'Connell (eds), *Contemporary Irish Studies*. Manchester: Manchester University Press.

Whyte, John H. (1988). "Interpretations of the Northern Ireland Problem," in Charles Townshend (ed.), *Consensus in Ireland: Approaches and Recessions*. Oxford: Oxford University Press, 24–46.

Whyte, John H. (1990). *Interpreting Northern Ireland*. Oxford: Oxford University Press.

Wilkinson, Paul (1977/1986). *Terrorism and the Liberal State*. London: Macmillan.

Wilson, Harold (1971). *The Labour Government, 1964–1970: A Personal Record*. Harmondsworth: Penguin.

Wilson, Thomas (1955) (ed.). *Ulster under Home Rule*. Oxford: Oxford University Press.

Wilson, Tom (1989). *Ulster: Conflict and Consent*. Oxford: Basil Blackwell.

Winchester, Simon (1975). *Northern Ireland in Crisis: Reporting the Ulster Troubles*. New York: Holmes & Meier.

Wright, Frank (1973). "Protestant Ideology and Politics in Ulster." *European Journal of Sociology*, 14: 213–80.

Wright, Frank (1987). *Northern Ireland: A Comparative Analysis*. Dublin: Gill & Macmillan.

Younger, Calton (1972). *A State of Disunion: Arthur Griffith, Michael Collins, James Craig, Eamon de Valera*. London: Fontana/Collins.

Ziff, Trisha (2000) (ed.). *Hidden Truths: Bloody Sunday 1972*. Santa Monica, CA: Smart Art Press.

Index of Names

Note: Tables and boxes are indicated by an italic *t* and *b* following the page number. Footnotes are indicated by 'n' following the page number.

General Index

Note: Tables, figures, boxes, and maps are indicated by an italic *t*, *f*, *b*, and *m* following the page number. Footnotes are indicated by 'n' following the page number.